THE CENTRAL INTELLIGENCE AGENCY AND OVERHEAD RECONNAISSANCE

THE CENTRAL INTELLIGENCE AGENCY AND OVERHEAD RECONNAISSANCE

The U-2 and OXCART Programs, 1954-1974

GREGORY W. PEDLOW AND DONALD E. WELZENBACH

FOREWORD BY CHRIS POCOCK

Skyhorse Publishing

First Skyhorse Publishing edition 2016
Foreword and Preface Copyright © 2016 by Skyhorse Publishing

Skyhorse Publishing books may be purchased in bulk at special
discounts for sales promotion, corporate gifts, fund-raising, or
educational purposes. Special editions can also be created to
specifications. For details, contact the Special Sales Department,
Skyhorse Publishing, 307 West 36th Street, 11th Floor, New York,
NY 10018 or info@skyhorsepublishing.com.

Skyhorse® and Skyhorse Publishing® are registered trademarks of
Skyhorse Publishing, Inc.®, a Delaware corporation.

Visit our website at www.skyhorsepublishing.com.

10 9 8 7 6 5 4 3 2 1

Library of Congress Cataloging-in-Publication Data is available on file.

Cover design by Rain Saukas

Print ISBN: 978-1-63450-688-5
Ebook ISBN: 978-1-63450-851-3

Printed in the United States of America

Contents

Foreword (2016) by Chris Pocock...xi

Preface (2016) by Gregory W. Pedlow................................xv

Foreword (1992) xix

Preface (1992) xxiii

CHAPTER 1: SEARCHING FOR A SYSTEM.........................1
The Need for High-Altitude Reconnaissance.....................................1
    Early Postwar Aerial Reconnaissance 3
    New Approaches to Photoreconnaissance 5
    The Air Force Search for a
        New Reconnaissance Aircraft...9
    Lockheed CL-282 Supporters and the CIA...............................16
Scientists and Overhead Reconnaissance 21
    The BEACON HILL Report..21
    Concern about the Danger of a Soviet
        Surprise Attack 23
    The Air Force Intelligence Systems Panel...............................25
    British Overflight of Kapustin Yar...27
    The Intelligence Systems Panel and the CL-282....................29
    The Technological Capabilities Panel 32
    Project Three Support for the Lockheed CL-282 34
    A Meeting with the President 39
    CIA and Air Force Agreement on the CL-282 40

CHAPTER 2: DEVELOPING THE U-2 46
The Establishment of the U-2 Project......................................46
Funding Arrangements for Project AQUATONE..........................51

Major Design Features of the U-2...53
The Development of the Camera System 56
Preparations for Testing the U-2...62
Security for the U-2 Project...65
The CIA–Air Force Partnership...66
Technical Challenges to High-Attitude Flight............................68
Delivery of the First U-2 73
Initial Testing of the U-2...75
U-2s, UFOs, and Operation BLUE BOOK 78
Hiring U-2 Pilots...80
Pilot Training...82
Final Tests of the U-2..84
Three Fatal Crashes in 1956 87
Coordination of Collection Requirements...................................88
Preparations to Handle the Product of U-2 Missions...................90
The Impact of the Air Force Project GENETRIX Balloons............91
AQUATONE Briefings for Selected Members of Congress.............95
The U-2 Cover Story..96

**CHAPTER 3: U-2 OPERATIONS IN THE SOVIET
BLOC AND MIDDLE EAST, 1956-1958**....................................99
The Deployment of Detachment A to Lakenheath...................... 100
The Move to Wiesbaden.. 101
President Eisenhower's Attitude toward Overflights 103
First Overflights of Eastern Europe... 107
First U-2 Flights over the Soviet Union...................................... 109
Soviet Protest Note... 117
The End of the Bomber Gap... 119
Tactical Intelligence from U-2s during the Suez Crisis............ 121
Renewed Overflights of the Soviet Union................................. 129
Radar-Deceptive "Dirty Birds".. 138
The New Detachment C.. 141
Detachment B Flights from Pakistan 143
The Decline of Detachment A.. 147
Declining Overflight Activity... 149

Concerns about Soviet Countermeasures against the U-2 154
More Powerful Engines for the U-2 156
Intervention in Lebanon, 1958 157
British Participation in the U-2 Project 159
The U-2 Project at the Beginning of 1959 162

**CHAPTER 4: THE FINAL OVERFLIGHTS OF THE
SOVIET UNION, 1959-1960** 164
The U-2 and the "Missile-Gap" Debate 164
The Last Overflight: Operation GRAND SLAM 177
The Aftermath of the U-2 Downing 185
The Withdrawal of the Overseas Detachments 189
The Fate of Francis Gary Powers 191
Changes in Overflight Procedures after May 1960 196

CHAPTER 5: U-2 OPERATIONS AFTER MAY 1960 205
U-2 Operations in Latin America 208
   U-2 Support to the Bay of Pigs Invasion 208
   Aerial Refueling Capability for the U-2 210
   U-2 Coverage during the Cuban Missile Crisis 210
   U-2s over South America 223
U-2 Operations in Asia 223
   Detachment C and the Indonesian Revolt of 1958 223
   China Offshore Islands Dispute of 1958 228
   U-2 Support for DDP Operations in Tibet 229
   U-2Cs for Detachment C 230
   U-2 Crash in Thailand 231
   End of Detachment C Operations 231
   Detachment G Missions over Laos and
      North Vietnam 232
   New Detachment on Taiwan 234
   Use of Detachment H Aircraft by US Pilots 242
   U-2s in India 243
   Increasing Responsibilities, Inadequate
      Resources in Asia 245

Advanced ECM Equipment for Detachment H 250
The End of U-2 Overflights of Mainland China 252
Peripheral Missions by Detachment H 254
Operation SCOPE SHIELD over North Vietnam 256
Improvements in U-2 Technology 257
Modification of U-2s for Aircraft
    Carrier Deployment 257
Use of Carrier-Based U-2 to Film a French
    Nuclear Test Site 258
A New Version of the U-2 260
Replacement of the Original U-2s with U-2Rs 262
The Final Years of the U-2 263
Support to Other Agencies 263
Overseas Deployment Exercises and Missions 265
The Phaseout of the Office of Special Activities 267

CHAPTER 6: THE U-2'S INTENDED SUCCESSOR:
PROJECT OXCART, 1956-1968 268
The Evaluation of Designs for a Successor to the U-2 269
Competition between Lockheed and Convair 277
The Selection of the Lockheed Design 281
Efforts to Reduce the A-12's Radar Cross Section 285
The OXCART Contract 287
New Technologies Necessitated by OXCART's
    High Speed 288
Designing the OXCART's Cameras 290
Choosing Pilots for OXCART 292
Selection of a Testing Site for the OXCART 293
Delivery of the First OXCART 296
Changes in the Project Management 297
OXCART's First Flights 298
Speed-Related Problems 300
New Versions of the OXCART 301
The Question of Surfacing a Version of the OXCART 302
Additional Problems during Final Testing 306

Discussions on the OXCART's Future Employment.................308
First A-12 Deployment: Operation BLACK SHIELD...............316
The End of the OXCART Program.......................................320
Possible Successors to the OXCART..325
Summary of the OXCART Program 326

CHAPTER 7: CONCLUSION.......................................328
U-2 Overflights of the Soviet Union.....................................328
Participation of Allies in the U-2 Program......................333
U-2s as Collectors of Tactical Intelligence....................334
Advances in Technology..334
Cooperation with the Air Force...335
Impact of the Overhead Reconnaissance Program on the CIA...........336

Appendix A: Acronyms...338
Appendix B: Key Personnel.......................................340
Appendix C: Electronic Devices Carried by the U-2 348
Appendix D: U-2 Overflights of the Soviet Union,
       4 July 1954-1 May 1960......................................350
Appendix E: Unmanned Reconnaissance Projects...............352
Bibliography...355
Index..362

FOREWORD (2016)

The two fabulous spyplanes described in this book have fascinated me for most of my adult life. The history of the U-2 and the A-12 and SR-71 Blackbird series is a heady mix of audacity, bravery, secrecy, and technological prowess. Sixty years after its first flight, the U-2 is still serving as the world's premier high-altitude reconnaissance aircraft. More than forty years after its first flight, the Blackbird is still recognized as an aerodynamic masterpiece to match the current state-of-the-art.

Both aircraft were conceived and sponsored by the CIA and subsequently embraced by the US Air Force. This book therefore tells only part of their story. But what a story it is! The scientist whose vision and influence prompted extraordinary action by government. The aircraft designer who made good on his promise to "Be Quick, Be Quiet, Be on Time." The economics professor who mastered the management of complex high-tech projects. The President who understood the value—and the limitations—of covert action. The supporting cast of engineers, mission planners, pilots, photo interpreters, and intelligence analysts, whose diligence and determination made a success of it all.

But this book also tells a story of disappointment. When the U-2 began flying over the Soviet Union in 1956, the CIA expected that its high cruising altitude would prevent interception by Soviet fighters. The Agency further hoped that Soviet radars would not detect a relatively small aircraft at 70,000 feet. That hope was dashed, a protest followed from Moscow, and the President never again gave blanket permission for overflights.

Much the same happened with the A-12. It was designed with a low radar cross-section, but the Soviets deployed a new early-warning radar that could nevertheless detect it. After the shootdown of the U-2 on May Day 1960, and the subsequent political furore, the White House was never likely to grant permission for A-12 overflights of the Soviet Union. The CIA's OXCART program withered and eventually died.

How does this book treat the May Day incident? Over the intervening years, many observers have questioned the decision to launch this mission. The authors usefully describe the growing concern, from technical analysis, that the new Soviet SA-2 missile could reach the U-2. They also describe the pressure on the intelligence community in the preceding months to determine whether the Soviet Union really had achieved superiority in the deployment of ballistic missiles. The judgment of this book, namely that "the risks had increased substantially. (But) the lure of the prospective intelligence gain from each mission was too strong," accords with my own.

Contrary to popular belief, May Day 1960 did not mark the end of the U-2 program. The authors describe the aircraft's continued use throughout the 1960s over Cuba, China, Vietnam, and elsewhere. Chinese nationalist pilots from Taiwan braved SA-2 missiles over China in their U-2s, and five were shot down. But when American pilots were required to fly over territory defended by that missile—North Korea, North Vietnam—they did it in the less vulnerable A-12.

Some readers will be puzzled by the existence of parallel programs—CIA and US Air Force—for both these aircraft during the 1960s. The authors broach this subject in their coverage of the Cuban Missile Crisis, when "overt" military U-2 flights superseded "covert" civilian flights. In fact, the US government has always valued the option of deniability when staging reconnaissance flights. Today, the CIA and the US Air Force both operate MQ-1/9 Predator/Reaper UAVs. The CIA flies out of bases overseas that the host nation wishes to remain secret. In my book *50 Years of the U-2*, I describe the interplay between the two U-2 programs.

Parallel operations of the CIA's A-12 and the Air Force's SR-71 ended in 1968, a decision that was partly budget-driven. The CIA stopped flying the U-2 six years later, but not before it had sponsored the development of an enlarged and improved version.

In subsequent years, that sponsorship has paid off tremendously for the US. For while the Air Force finally retired its Blackbirds in 1998, the improved version of the U-2 has continued in service to this day. With its sophisticated digital sensor suite, networked communications, and protection from interception by an advanced defensive system, today's U-2 is a far cry from the one that took off on its maiden flight in 1955. But the concept is still the same—fly an aircraft high enough to collect intelligence on potential adversaries that cannot be obtained by any other means.

—Chris Pocock
Author, *50 Years of the U-2* and *Dragon Lady Today*

PREFACE (2016)
The CIA's Official History of the U-2 and OXCART Programs: A Look Back after 26 Years

When I left academia to join the CIA's History Staff in January 1986, I was soon asked to work on the official, classified history of the Agency's overhead reconnaissance programs. Donald E. Welzenbach, a member of the Directorate of Science and Technology on a rotational assignment with the History Staff, had already prepared a large manuscript that covered all of the Agency's overhead reconnaissance programs—both manned aircraft and the later satellite programs—and had conducted many interviews with key individuals inside and outside of the CIA. The Chief of the History Staff, J. Kenneth McDonald, wanted me to revise and edit this manuscript—which had focused primarily on technological aspects of the programs and internal CIA decision-making—and also add additional material that placed the Agency's activities and decisions within their historical context. After reviewing the draft manuscript I recommended splitting it into two volumes, one covering aircraft and the other covering satellites, because the levels of clearance required for the two subjects were very different. Thus Ken McDonald and I decided that the manned aircraft history could be published at the Secret level in order to enable wide distribution within the intelligence community, whereas the satellite volume would have to stay at the Top Secret Codeword level.

During the next 3¾ years I spent most of my time as a CIA Historian working on the manned aircraft volume. I conducted additional research in President Eisenhower's papers and other archives to learn more about the Eisenhower Administration's decision-making with regards to the U-2 program, in particular the decisions to authorize each of the overflights of the Soviet Union. I also looked at media coverage of the two big "gaps" of the 1950s, the so-called "bomber gap" and "missile gap" that had played such an important role in putting pressure on the Eisenhower Administration to learn more about the Soviet Union's actual capabilities in these areas. I supplemented this research in classified and unclassified records with additional interviews, including General (Retired) Andrew J. Goodpaster, who as a Colonel had served as the White House Staff Secretary for President Eisenhower and had been a key participant at meetings in which the President took decisions on overflights of the Soviet Union. When the subjects of the additional interviews were primarily technical, Don Welzenbach joined me for the interviews, in particular those conducted at Lockheed, where we visited the famous "Skunk Works" (I still use the Skunk Works coffee mug that I acquired during that visit). The final version of the text was mainly my work, but I could never have written it without having had the benefit of the extensive research and interviews that Don had done before I joined the History Staff.

Most of the information regarding the CIA's manned reconnaissance aircraft was no longer highly sensitive by the 1980s. After all, the existence of a CIA-led program of reconnaissance flights over the Soviet Union had been revealed in a spectacular fashion when Francis Gary Powers's U-2 was shot down over the Soviet Union in May 1960. Thus writing this history at the Secret level was generally not a problem, and the older, more highly classified documents cited in the history could be downgraded to the new level. But there was one subject that I could not mention at the Secret level in the 1980s: the National Reconnaissance Office

(NRO). Its name and the very fact of its existence were still classified at the Top Secret Codeword level, so I had to remove any references to the name NRO itself and keep my references to its role in the manned aircraft program very general. Thus in the preface to the manuscript that I completed in 1989 (and was published in 1992), I wrote, "Some aspects of the overhead reconnaissance program, particularly those involving satellites and related interagency agreements, have had to be described in very general terms." The existence of the National Reconnaissance Office was not declassified until September 1992, after the CIA's history of overhead reconnaissance had been published.

While conducting this additional research on the U-2 and OXCART programs, I read every book I could find on these aircraft, the CIA, and the Eisenhower Administration. A key source in understanding the US Air Force's search for a new, high-altitude reconnaissance aircraft in the early 1950s was Jay Miller's *Lockheed U-2*, published in 1983. This lavishly illustrated book became the source for some of the photographs used in the CIA's history of the U-2 because they illustrated important points for which I could not find similar photos within the Agency. Due to the classified nature of our publication at that time, I could not contact the publisher to ask permission to use these photos, but I did give credit in footnotes for the information found in Miller's very informative book.

Shortly before I finished the manuscript and left the Agency at the end of September 1989 to take up a new post with NATO (as the Chief of the Historical Office at the Supreme Headquarters Allied Powers Europe, a post I held until I retired in July 2015), a new book came out on the U-2: Chris Pocock's *Dragon Lady: The History of the U-2 Spyplane*. I quickly read it with great interest and was amazed by how much information he had been able to compile despite not having access to the official, classified records. In my Preface to the official history I wrote:

After the present study of the Agency's overhead reconnaissance projects was completed, a new book on the U-2 was published in the United Kingdom. Chris Pocock's *Dragon Lady: The History of the U-2 Spyplane* is by far the most accurate unclassified account of the U-2 program. Pocock has been able to compensate for his lack of access to classified documents by interviewing many former participants in the program, especially former pilots. Pocock is also quite familiar with aircraft itself, for he had worked with Jay Miller on the latter's excellent technical study of the U-2: *Lockheed U-2* (1983).

In the twenty-six years since I wrote those words, Chris has continued to find more and more information about the U-2 and its missions, and has published four more books on the subject: *The U-2 Spyplane: Toward the Unknown* (2000); *50 Years of the U-2* (2005); *The Black Bats—CIA spy Flights over China from Taiwan* (2010); and *Dragon Lady Today: The Continuing Story of the U-2 Spyplane* (2014). Thus anyone looking for information about the U-2 now should not just read the official history but should also consult Chris's very detailed and highly accurate U-2 books.

After the CIA released a heavily redacted version of the overhead reconnaissance history in 1998, a number of independent publishers created mediocre quality reprints of the book by taking the low resolution photocopies released by the Agency and putting their own covers on it. I am therefore glad that Skyhorse Publishing has prepared this new edition that includes the much more complete release of 2013 and has been professionally typeset for a more attractive and readable appearance.

—Gregory W. Pedlow

FOREWORD (1992)

This History Staff Monograph offers a comprehensive and authoritative history of the CIA's manned overhead reconnaissance program, which from 1954 to 1974 developed and operated two extraordinary aircraft, the U-2 and the A-12 OXCART. It describes not only the program's technological and bureaucratic aspects, but also its political and international context. The manned reconnaissance program, along with other overhead systems that emerged from it, changed the CIA's work and structure in ways that were both revolutionary and permanent. The formation of the Directorate of Science and Technology in the 1960s, principally to develop and direct reconnaissance programs, is the most obvious legacy of the events recounted in this study.

The authors tell an engrossing story. The struggle between the CIA and the US Air Force to control the U-2 and A-12 OXCART projects reveals how the manned reconnaissance program confronted problems that still beset successor programs today. The U-2 was an enormous technological success: its first flight over the USSR in July 1956 made it immediately the most important source of intelligence on the Soviet Union. Using it against the Soviet target it was designed for nevertheless produced a persistent tension between its program managers and the President. The program managers, eager for coverage, repeatedly urged the President to authorize frequent missions over the Soviet Union. President Eisenhower, from the outset doubtful of the prudence and propriety of invading Soviet airspace, only reluctantly allowed any overflights at all. After the Soviets shot down Francis

Gary Powers's U-2 on 1 May 1960, President Eisenhower forbade any further U-2 flights over the USSR. Since the Agency must always assess a covert operation's potential payoff against the diplomatic or military cost if it fails, this account of the U-2's employment over the Soviet Union offers insights that go beyond overhead reconnaissance programs.

Indeed, this study should be useful for a variety of purposes. It is the only history of this program based upon both full access to CIA records and extensive classified interviews of its participants. The authors have found records that were nearly irretrievably lost and have interviewed participants whose personal recollections gave information available nowhere else. Although the story of the manned reconnaissance program offers no tidy model for imitation, it does reveal how resourceful managers coped with unprecedented technological challenges and their implications for intelligence and national policy. For this reason, the program's history provides profitable reading for intelligence professionals and policymakers today.

Many people made important contributions to the production of this volume. In the History Staff's preparation of the manuscript, Gerald Haines did the final revision, [redacted] again demonstrated her high talent as a copy editor, and [redacted] provided staunch secretarial support throughout. As usual, we are indebted to more members than we can name from the Publications, Design, and Cartography Centers in the Office of Current Production and Analytic Support, whose lively interest in the publication went far beyond the call of duty. Their exceptional professional skill and the masterly work of the Printing and Photography Group combined to create this handsome volume.

Donald E. Welzenbach, who began this study, and Gregory W. Pedlow, who completed it, brought complementary strengths to this work. A veteran of CIA service since 1960, Mr. Welzenbach began research on this study in 1983, when he joined the DCI

History Staff on a rotational assignment from the Directorate of Science and Technology. After tireless documentary research and extensive interviewing, he finished a draft manuscript of the history before returning to his directorate. In early 1986, Gregory W. Pedlow, a new member of the DCI History Staff, was assigned to complete the study. A Johns Hopkins University Ph.D. who has served as an Army intelligence officer and University of Nebraska professor of history, Dr. Pedlow undertook important research in several new areas, and reorganized, edited, and revised the entire manuscript before leaving CIA to become NATO Historian in late 1989. The final work, which has greatly benefited from both authors' contributions, is the CIA's own history of the world's first great overhead reconnaissance program.

—J. Kenneth McDonald
Chief, CIA History Staff

PREFACE (1992)

When the Central Intelligence Agency came into existence in 1947, no one foresaw that, in less than a decade, it would undertake a major program of overhead reconnaissance, whose principal purpose would be to fly over the Soviet Union. Traditionally, the military services had been responsible for overhead reconnaissance, and flights deep into unfriendly territory only took place during wartime. By the early 1950s, however, the United States had an urgent and growing need for strategic intelligence on the Soviet Union and its satellite states. At great risk, US Air Force and Navy aircraft had been conducting peripheral reconnaissance and shallow-penetration overflights, but these missions were paying a high price in lives lost and increased international tension. Furthermore, many important areas of the Soviet Union lay beyond the range of existing reconnaissance aircraft. The Air Force had therefore begun to develop a high-altitude reconnaissance aircraft that would be able to conduct deep-penetration reconnaissance missions over the Soviet Union. President Dwight D. Eisenhower and his civilian scientific advisers feared that the loss of such an aircraft deep in Soviet territory could lead to war and therefore authorized the development of new nonmilitary aircraft, first the U-2 and later the A-12 OXCART, to be manned by civilians and operated only under cover and in the greatest secrecy. Primary responsibility for this new reconnaissance program was assigned to the Central Intelligence Agency, but the Air Force provided vital support.

The Agency's manned overhead reconnaissance program lasted 20 years. It began with President Eisenhower's authorization of the U-2 project in late 1954 and ended with the transfer of the remaining Agency U-2s to the Air Force in 1974. During this period the CIA developed a successor to the U-2, the A-12 OXCART, but this advanced aircraft saw little operational use and the program was canceled in 1968 after the Air Force deployed a fleet of similar aircraft, a military variant of the A-12 called the SR-71.

Neither of these aircraft remains secret today. A great deal of information about the U-2 and its overflight program became known to the public after 1 May 1960, when the Soviet Union shot down a CIA U-2 and publicly tried its pilot, Francis Gary Powers. Four years later, at press conferences in February and July 1964, President Lyndon B. Johnson revealed the existence of the OXCART-type of aircraft, although only in its military YF-12A (interceptor) and SR-71 (strategic reconnaissance) versions.

The two CIA reconnaissance aircraft have also been the subject of a number of books, beginning with David Wise's and Thomas B. Ross's *The U-2 Affair* in 1962 and then Francis Gary Powers's memoirs, *Operation Overflight,* in 1970. Two recent books give many more details about the U-2 and OXCART aircraft: Michael Beschloss's *Mayday: Eisenhower, Khrushchev and the U-2 Affair* (1986) and William Burrows's *Deep Black: Space Espionage and National Security* (1987). Although well written and generally accurate, these books suffer from their authors' lack of access to classified official documentation. By drawing upon the considerable amount of formerly classified data on the U-2 now available to the public, Beschloss has provided an accurate and insightful depiction of the U-2 program in the context of the Eisenhower administration's overall foreign policy, but his book does contain errors and omissions on some aspects of the U-2 program. Burrows's broader work suffers more from the lack of classified documentation, particularly in the OXCART/SR-71 section, which concentrates on the Air Force aircraft because little information about the Agency's aircraft has been officially declassified and released.

After the present study of the Agency's overhead reconnaissance projects was completed, a new book on the U-2 was published in the United Kingdom. Chris Pocock's *Dragon Lady: The History of the U-2 Spyplane* is by far the most accurate unclassified account of the U-2 program. Pocock has been able to compensate for his lack of access to classified documents by interviewing many former participants in the program, especially former pilots. Pocock is also quite familiar with aircraft itself, for he had worked with Jay Miller on the latter's excellent technical study of the U-2: *Lockheed U-2* (1983).

There has also been a classified official study of the U-2 and OXCART programs. In 1969 the Directorate of Science and Technology published a *History of the Office of Special Activities* by Helen Hill Kleyla and Robert D. O'Hern. This 16-volume Top Secret Codeword study of the Agency's reconnaissance aircraft provides a wealth of technical and operational information on the two projects but does not attempt to place them in their historical context. Without examining the international situation and bureaucratic pressures affecting the president and other key policymakers, however, it is impossible to understand the decisions that began, carried out, and ended the CIA's reconnaissance aircraft projects.

In preparing this study of CIA's overhead reconnaissance program, the authors drew on published sources, classified government documents, and interviews with key participants from the CIA, Air Force, contractors, scientific advisory committees, and the Eisenhower administration. The interviews were particularly important for piecing together the story of how the CIA became involved in overhead reconnaissance in the first place because Agency documentation on the prehistory of the U-2 project is very sketchy and there are no accurate published accounts.

Research on the period of actual reconnaissance operations included the records of the Director of Central Intelligence, the Office of Special Activities in the Directorate of Science and Technology, and the Intelligence Community Staff, along with documents from the Eisenhower Presidential Library in Abilene, Kansas, and additional interviews.

Both authors are grateful for the assistance they have received from many individuals who played important roles in the events they recount. Without their help a good deal of this story could never have become known. The assistance of Agency records management officers in the search for documents on the overhead reconnaissance program is also greatly appreciated.

To ensure that this study of the Agency's involvement in overhead reconnaissance reaches the widest possible audience, the authors have kept it at the Secret classification level. As a result, some aspects of the overhead reconnaissance program, particularly those involving satellites and related interagency agreements, have had to be described in very general terms. The omission of such information is not significant for this book, which focuses on the Agency's reconnaissance aircraft.

1

Searching for a System

THE NEED FOR HIGH-ALTITUDE RECONNAISSANCE
For centuries, soldiers in wartime have sought the highest ground
or structure in order to get a better view of the enemy. At first it
was tall trees, then church steeples and bell towers. By the time
of the American Civil War and the Franco-Prussian War of 1870-
71, observers were using hot-air balloons to get up in the sky for
a better view of the "other side of the hill." With the advent of dry
film, it became possible to carry cameras into the sky to record the
disposition of enemy troops and emplacements. Indeed, photoreconnaissance proved so valuable during World War I that in 1938
Gen. Werner von Fritsch, Commander in Chief of the German Army,
predicted: "The nation with the best aerial reconnaissance facilities
will win the next war."[1]

By World War II, lenses, films, and cameras had undergone
many improvements, as had the airplane, which could fly
higher and faster than the primitive craft of World War I. Now
it was possible to use photoreconnaissance to obtain information

---

[1] Roy M. Stanley II, *World War II Photo Intelligence* (New York: Scribners,
1981), p. 16.

1

about potential targets before a bombing raid and to assess the effectiveness of the bombing afterward.

Peacetime applications of high-altitude photography at first included only photomapping and surveying for transcontinental highways and mineral and oil exploration. There was little thought given to using photography for peacetime espionage until after World War II, when the Iron Curtain rang down and cut off most forms of communication between the Soviet Bloc of nations and the rest of the world.

By 1949 the Soviet Union and the states of Eastern Europe had been effectively curtained off from the outside world, and the Soviet military carried out its planning, production, and deployment activities with the utmost secrecy. All Soviet strategic capabilities—bomber forces, ballistic missiles, submarine forces, and nuclear weapons plants—were concealed from outside observation. The Soviet air defense system, a prime consideration in determining US retaliatory policies, was also largely an unknown factor.

Tight security along the Soviet Bloc borders severely curtailed the movement of human intelligence sources. In addition, the Soviet Union made its conventional means of communication—telephone, telegraph, and radio-telephone—more secure, thereby greatly reducing the intelligence available from these sources. The stringent security measures imposed by the Communist Bloc nations effectively blunted traditional methods for gathering intelligence: secret agents using covert means to communicate intelligence, travelers to and from target areas who could be asked to keep their eyes open and report their observations later, wiretaps and other eavesdropping methods, and postal intercepts. Indeed, the entire panoply of intelligence tradecraft seemed ineffective against the Soviet Bloc, and no other methods were available.

Early Postwar Aerial Reconnaissance

Although at the end of World War II the United States had captured large quantities of German photos and documents on the Soviet Union, this material was rapidly becoming outdated. The main source of current intelligence on the Soviet Union's military installations was interrogation of prisoners of war returning from Soviet captivity. To obtain information about Soviet scientific progress, the intelligence community established several programs to debrief German scientists who had been taken to the Soviet Union after the end of the war but were now being allowed to leave.[2]

Interrogation of returning Germans offered only fragmentary information, and this source could not be expected to last much longer. As a result, in the late 1940s, the US Air Force and Navy began trying to obtain aerial photography of the Soviet Union. The main Air Force effort involved Boeing RB-47 aircraft (the reconnaissance version of the B-47 jet-propelled medium bomber) equipped with cameras and electronic "ferret" equipment that enabled aircrews to detect tracking by Soviet radars. At that time the

---

[2] At the end of World War II, the British had established Project DRAGON to gain information from German scientists who had worked on the Peenemunde rocket project, and the term DRAGON later was used to refer to individuals possessing scientific or technical information. In 1948 the US Air Force set up Project WRINGER in Germany to gather intelligence on the Soviet Union from defectors and refugees; this project was later absorbed into the combined armed forces/CIA Defector Reception Center (DRC), which began operations in February 1951. In October 1951, a separate organization to exploit individuals with scientific or technical backgrounds, especially German scientists who had worked inside the Soviet Union, came into existence. This organization was known as the Returnee Exploitation Group (REG) and was located in Frankfurt. By 1958 the flow of scientists was so small that the REG merged with the DRC. [Redacted]. *The Defector Reception Center Germany, 1951 to 1967,* Clandestine Service Historical Series CSHP-41 (CIA: History Staff, 1972), pp 5-6, 29-30 (S).

Soviet Union had not yet completely ringed its borders with radars, and much of the interior also lacked radar coverage. Thus, when the RB-47s found a gap in the air-warning network, they would dart inland to take photographs of any accessible targets. These "penetration photography" flights (called SENSINT—sensitive intelligence—missions) occurred along the northern and Pacific coasts of Russia. One RB-47 aircraft even managed to fly 450 miles inland and photograph the city of Igarka in Siberia. Such intrusions brought protests from Moscow but no Soviet military response.[3]

In 1950 there was a major change in Soviet policy. Air defense units became very aggressive in defending their airspace, attacking all aircraft that came near the borders of the Soviet Union. On 8 April 1950, Soviet fighters shot down a US Navy Privateer patrol aircraft over the Baltic Sea. Following the outbreak of the Korean war in June 1950, the Soviet Union extended its "severe air defense policy" to the Far East. In the autumn of 1951, Soviet aircraft downed a twin-engine US Navy Neptune bomber near Vladivostok. An RB-29 lost in the Sea of Japan on 13 June 1952 was probably also a victim of Soviet fighters. The United States was not the only country affected by the new aggressive Soviet air defense policy; Britain and Turkey also reported attacks on their planes.[4]

---

[3] A. L. George, *Case Studies of Actual and Alleged Overflights, 1930-1953*, Rand Study RM-1349 (Santa Monica: Rand, 1955) (S). Arthur S. Lundahl and Dino Brugioni, interview by Donald E. Welzenbach, tape recording, Washington, DC, 14 December 1983 (TS Codeword). Recordings, transcripts, and notes for the interviews conducted for this study are on file at the DCI History Staff.

[4] Jeffrey Richelson states on page 121 of *American Espionage and the Soviet Target* (New York: Morrow, 1987) that "the first recorded attack by Soviet air defense forces, in this case fighters, occurred on October 22, 1949." In this incident, however, Soviet fighters did not attempt to hit the US aircraft; they merely fired warning shots. The real change in Soviet policy did not occur until the April 1950 downing of the US Navy Privateer. George, *Case Studies,* pp 1-2, 6, 9-16 (S).

The Soviet Union's air defense policy became even more aggressive in August 1952, when its reconnaissance aircraft began violating Japanese airspace over Hokkaido, the northernmost Japanese home island. Two months later, on 7 October 1952, Soviet fighter aircraft stalked and shot down a US RB-29 flying over Hokkaido. Aerial reconnaissance of the Soviet Union and surrounding areas had become a very dangerous business.

Despite the growing risks associated with aerial reconnaissance of the Soviet Bloc, senior US officials strongly believed that such missions were necessary. The lack of information about the Soviet Union, coupled with the perception that it was an aggressive nation determined to expand its borders—a perception that had been greatly strengthened by the Soviet-backed North Korean invasion of South Korea in June 1950—increased US determination to obtain information about Soviet intentions and capabilities and thus reduce the danger of being surprised by a Soviet attack.

New Approaches to Photoreconnaissance

While existing Navy and Air Force aircraft were flying their risky reconnaissance missions over the Soviet Union, the United States began planning for a more systematic and less dangerous approach using new technology. One of the leading advocates of the need for new, high-altitude reconnaissance aircraft was Richard S. Leghorn, a Massachusetts Institute of Technology graduate and employee of Eastman Kodak who had commanded the Army Air Forces' 67th Reconnaissance Group in Europe during World War II. After the war he returned to Kodak but maintained his interest in photoreconnaissance. Leghorn strongly believed in the need for what he called pre-D-day reconnaissance, that is, reconnaissance of a potential enemy before the outbreak of actual hostilities, in contrast to combat reconnaissance in wartime. In papers presented in 1946 and 1948, Leghorn argued that the United States needed to develop such a capability, which would require high-altitude aircraft and high-resolution cameras. The outbreak of the Korean war gave Leghorn an opportunity to put his ideas into effect. Recalled to active duty by the Air Force, Lieutenant Colonel Leghorn became the head of the Reconnaissance Systems Branch of the Wright Air Development Command at Dayton, Ohio, in April 1951.[5]

In Leghorn's view, altitude was the key to success for overhead reconnaissance. Since the best Soviet interceptor at that time, the MIG-17, had to struggle to reach 45,000 feet,[6] Leghorn reasoned that an aircraft that could exceed 60,000 feet would be safe from Soviet fighters. Recognizing that the fastest way to produce a high-altitude reconnaissance aircraft was to modify an existing aircraft, he began looking for the highest flying aircraft available in the Free World. This search soon led him to a British twin-engine medium bomber—the Canberra—built by the English Electric Company. The Canberra had made its first flight in May 1949. Its speed of 469 knots (870 kilometers per hour) and its service ceiling of 48,000 feet made the Canberra a natural choice for high-altitude reconnaissance work. The Royal Air Force quickly developed a reconnaissance version of the Canberra, the PR3 (the PR stood for photoreconnaissance), which began flying in March 1950.[7]

At Leghorn's insistence, the Wright Air Development Command invited English Electric representatives to Dayton in the summer of 1951 to help find ways to make the Canberra

---

[5] Richard S. Leghorn, interview by Donald E. Welzenbach, tape recording, Washington, DC, 19 August 1985 (S).

[6] 13,716 meters. To avoid giving a false impression of extremely precise measurements, original English measuring system figures in round numbers have not been converted to the metric system. To convert feet to meters, multiply by 0.3048. To convert airspeeds in knots (nautical miles per hour) to kilometers per hour, multiply by 1.85.

[7] Dick van der Aart, *Aerial Espionage, Secret Intelligence Flights by East and West* (Shrewsbury, England: Airlife Publishing, 1985), p. 18.

fly even higher. By this time the Air Force had already adopted the bomber version of the Canberra, which the Glenn L. Martin Aircraft Company was to produce under license as the B-57 medium bomber. Leghorn and his English Electric colleagues designed a new Canberra configuration with very long high-lift wings, new Rolls-Royce Avon-109 engines, a solitary pilot, and an airframe that was stressed to less than the standard military specifications. Leghorn calculated that a Canberra so equipped might reach 63,000 feet early in a long mission and as high as 67,000 feet as the declining fuel supply lightened the aircraft. He believed that such a modified Canberra could penetrate the Soviet Union and China for a radius of 800 miles from bases around their periphery and photograph up to 85 percent of the intelligence targets in those countries.

Leghorn persuaded his superiors to submit his suggestion to the Pentagon for funding. He had not, however, cleared his idea with the Air Research and Development Command, whose reconnaissance division in Baltimore, headed by Lt. Col. Joseph J. Pellegrini, had to approve all new reconnaissance aircraft designs. Pellegrini's unit reviewed Leghorn's design and ordered extensive modifications. According to Leghorn, Pellegrini was not interested in a special-purpose aircraft that was only suitable for covert peacetime reconnaissance missions, for he believed that all Air Force reconnaissance aircraft should be capable of operating under wartime conditions. Pellegrini therefore insisted that Leghorn's design meet the specifications for combat aircraft, which required heavily stressed airframes, armor plate, and other apparatus that made an aircraft too heavy to reach the higher altitudes necessary for safe overflights of the Soviet Bloc. The final result of Leghorn's concept after its alteration by Pellegrini's staff was the RB-57D in 1955, whose maximum altitude was only 64,000 feet. Meanwhile Leghorn, frustrated by the rejection of his original concept, had transferred to the Pentagon in early 1952 to work for Col. Bernard A. Schriever, Assistant for Development Planning to the Air Force's Deputy Chief of Staff for Development.[8]

In his new position Leghorn became responsible for planning the Air Force's reconnaissance needs for the next decade. He worked closely with Charles F. (Bud) Wienberg—a colleague who had followed him from Wright Field—and Eugene P. Kiefer, a Notre Dame-educated aeronautical engineer who had designed reconnaissance aircraft at the Wright Air Development Center during World War II. All three of these reconnaissance experts believed that the Air Force should emphasize high-altitude photoreconnaissance.

Underlying their advocacy of high-altitude photoreconnaissance was the belief that Soviet radars would not be able to track aircraft flying above 65,000 feet. This assumption was based on the fact that the Soviet Union used American-built radar sets that had been supplied under Lend-Lease during World War II. Although the SCR-584 (Signal Corps Radio) target-tracking radar could track targets up to 90,000 feet, its high power consumption burned out a key component quickly, so this radar was normally not turned on until an early warning radar had detected a target. The SCR-270 early warning radar could be left on for much longer periods and had a greater horizontal range (approximately 120 miles) but was limited by the curvature of the earth to a maximum altitude of 40,000 feet. As a result, Leghorn, Kiefer, and Wienberg believed that an aircraft that could ascend to 65,000 feet before entering an area being swept by the early warning radar would go undetected, because the target-tracking radars would not be activated.[9]

The problem with this assumption was that the Soviet Union, unlike Britain and the United States, had continued to improve radar

---

[8] Leghorn interview (S).
[9] Ivan A. Getting, interview by Donald E. Welzenbach, Los Angeles, 28 August 1988 (U).

technology after the end of World War II. Even after evidence of improved Soviet radar capabilities became available, however, many advocates of high-altitude overflight continued to believe that aircraft flying above 65,000 feet were safe from detection by Soviet radars.

The Air Force Search for a New Reconnaissance Aircraft

With interest in high-altitude reconnaissance growing, several Air Force agencies began to develop an aircraft to conduct such missions. In September 1952, the Air Research and Development Command gave the Martin Aircraft Company a contract to examine the high-altitude potential of the B-57 by modifying a single aircraft to give it long, high-lift wings and the American version of the new Rolls-Royce Avon-109 engine. These were the modifications that Richard Leghorn had suggested during the previous year.[10]

At about the same time, another Air Force office, the Wright Air Development Command (WADC) in Dayton, Ohio, was also examining ways to achieve sustained flight at high altitudes. Working with two German aeronautical experts—Woldemar Voigt and Richard Vogt—who had come to the United States after World War II, Air Force Maj. John Seaberg advocated the development of a new aircraft that would combine the high-altitude performance of the latest turbojet engines with high-efficiency wings in order to reach ultrahigh altitudes. Seaberg, an aeronautical engineer for the Chance Vought Corporation until his recall to active duty during the Korean war, was serving as assistant chief of the New Developments Office of WADC's Bombardment Branch.

By March 1953, Seaberg had expanded his ideas for a high-altitude aircraft into a complete request for proposal for "an aircraft weapon system having an operational radius of 1,500 nm [nautical miles] and capable of conducting pre- and post-

---

[10] Philip G. Strong, Chief, Operations Staff, OSI, Memorandum for the Record, "Reconnaissance Capabilities," 21 August 1953, OSI records (S).

strike reconnaissance missions during daylight, good visibility conditions." The requirement stated that such an aircraft must have an optimum subsonic cruise speed at altitudes of 70,000 feet or higher over the target, carry a payload of 100 to 700 pounds of reconnaissance equipment, and have a crew of one.[11]

The Wright Air Development Command decided not to seek proposals from major airframe manufacturers on the grounds that a smaller company would give the new project a higher priority and produce a better aircraft more quickly. In July 1953, the Bell Aircraft Corporation of Buffalo, New York, and the Fairchild Engine and Airplane Corporation of Hagerstown, Maryland, received study contracts to develop an entirely new high-altitude reconnaissance aircraft. In addition, the Glenn L. Martin Company of Baltimore was asked to examine the possibility of improving the already exceptional high-altitude performance of the B-57 Canberra. By January 1954 all three firms had submitted their proposals. Fairchild's entry was a single-engine plane known as M-195, which had a maximum altitude potential of 67,200 feet; Bell's was a twin-engine craft called the Model 67 (later the X-16), which had a maximum altitude of 69,500 feet; and Martin's design was a big-wing version of the B-57 called the Model 294, which was to cruise at 64,000 feet. In March 1954, Seaberg and other engineers at Wright Field, having evaluated the three contending designs, recommended the adoption of both the Martin and Bell proposals. They considered Martin's version of the B-57 an interim project that could be completed and deployed rapidly while the more advanced concept from Bell was still being developed.[12]

---

[11] Jay Miller, *Lockheed U-2,* Aerograph 3 (Austin, Texas: Aerofax, 1983), p. 10.

[12] The request for proposal, known as "Design Study Requirements, Identification No. 53WC-16507," has been reprinted in Miller, *Lockheed U-2*, pp. 10-11.

Air Force headquarters soon approved Martin's proposal to modify the B-57 and was very much interested in the Bell design. But word of the competition for a new reconnaissance airplane had reached another aircraft manufacturer, the Lockheed Aircraft Corporation, which submitted an unsolicited design.

Lockheed had first become aware of the reconnaissance aircraft competition in the fall of 1953. John H. (Jack) Carter, who had recently retired from the Air Force to become the assistant director of Lockheed's Advanced Development Program, was in the Pentagon on business and dropped in to see Eugene P. Kiefer, an old friend and colleague from the Air Force's Office of Development Planning (more commonly known as AFDAP from its Air Force office symbol). Kiefer told Carter about the competition for a high-flying aircraft and expressed the opinion that the Air Force was going about the search in the wrong way by requiring the new aircraft to be suitable for both strategic and tactical reconnaissance.

Immediately after returning to California, Carter proposed to Lockheed Vice President L. Eugene Root (previously the top civilian official in the Air Force's Office of Development Planning) that Lockheed also submit a design. Carter noted that the proposed aircraft would have to reach altitudes of between 65,000 and 70,000 feet and correctly forecast, "If extreme altitude performance can be realized in a practical aircraft at speeds in the vicinity of Mach 0.8, it should be capable of avoiding virtually all Russian defenses until about 1960." Carter added, "To achieve these characteristics in an aircraft which will have a reasonably useful operational life during the period before 1960 will, of course, require very strenuous efforts and extraordinary procedures, as well as nonstandard design philosophy." Some of the "nonstandard" design characteristics suggested by Carter were the elimination of landing gear, the disregard of military specifications, and the use of very low load factors. Carter's memorandum closed with a warning that time was of the essence: "In order that this special aircraft can have a reasonably long and useful life, it is obvious that its development must be greatly accelerated beyond that considered normal."[13]

Lockheed's senior officials approved Carter's proposal, and early in 1954 the corporation's best aircraft designer—Clarence L. (Kelly) Johnson—began working on the project, then known as the CL-282 but later to become famous under its Air Force designator—the U-2. Already one of the world's leading aeronautical engineers, Kelly Johnson had many successful military and civilian designs to his credit, including the P-38, P-80, F-104, and Constellation. Johnson quickly came up with a radical design based upon the fuselage of the F-104 jet fighter but incorporating a high-aspect-ratio sailplane wing. To save weight and thereby increase the aircraft's altitude, Johnson decided to stress the airframe to only 2.5 units of gravity (g's) instead of the military specification strength of 5.33 g's. For the power plant he selected the General Electric J73/GE-3 nonafterburning turbojet engine with 9,300 pounds of thrust (this was the same engine he had chosen for the F-104, which had been the basis for the U-2 design).[14] Many of the CL-282's design features were adapted from gliders. Thus, the wings and tail were detachable. Instead of a conventional landing gear, Johnson proposed using two skis and a reinforced belly rib for landing—a common sailplane technique—and a jettisonable wheeled dolly for takeoff. Other features included an unpressurized cockpit and a 15-cubic-foot payload area that could accommodate 600 pounds of sensors. The CL-282's maximum altitude would be just over 70,000 feet with

---

[13] Miller, *Lockheed U-2,* p. 12.

[14] Lockheed Corporation, "Strategic Reconnaissance and Intelligence," Development Planning Note #1, 30 November 1953 (U).

a 2,000-mile range. Essentially, Kelly Johnson had designed a jet-propelled glider.[15]

Early in March 1954, Kelly Johnson submitted the CL-282 design to Brig. Gen. Bernard A. Schriever's Office of Development Planning. Eugene Kiefer and Bud Wienberg studied the design and recommended it to General Schriever, who then asked Lockheed to submit a specific proposal. In early April, Kelly Johnson presented a full description of the CL-282 and a proposal for the construction and maintenance of 30 aircraft to a group of senior Pentagon officials that included Schriever's superior, Lt. Gen. Donald L. Putt, Deputy Chief of Staff for Development, and Trevor N. Gardner, Special Assistant for Research and Development to the Secretary of the Air Force. Afterward Kelly Johnson noted that the civilian officials were very much interested in his design but the generals were not.[16]

The CL-282 design was also presented to the commander of the Strategic Air Command (SAC), Gen. Curtis E. LeMay, in early April by Eugene Kiefer, Bud Wienberg, and Burton Klein from the Office of Development Planning. According to Wienberg, General LeMay stood up halfway through the briefing, took his cigar out of his mouth, and told the briefers that, if he wanted high-altitude photographs, he would put cameras in his B-36 bombers and added that he was not interested in a plane that had

---

[15] Miller, *Lockheed U-2*, p. 12. For more details on Kelly Johnson's original proposal, see "Profile of CL-282 High Altitude Aircraft prepared by Lockheed Aircraft Corporation, 5 March 1954" in Helen H. Kleyla and Robert D. O'Hern, *History of the Office of Special Activities*, DS&T, Directorate of Science and Technology Historical Series OSA-1, 16 vols (CIA: DS&T, 1969), chap. 1, annex 2 (TS Codeword). The 16 volumes of this history contain 20 chapters, each paginated separately. Future references will be shortened to *OSA History*, followed by the relevant chapter and page numbers.

[16] Kelly Johnson Papers, "Log for Project X," April 1954, Lockheed Corporation, Advanced Development Projects Division, Burbank, California.

The Lockheed CL-282

no wheels or guns. The general then left the room, remarking that the whole business was a waste of his time.[17]

Meanwhile, the CL-282 design proceeded through the Air Force development channels and reached Major Seaberg at the Wright Air Development Command in mid-May. Seaberg and his colleagues carefully evaluated the Lockheed submission and finally rejected it in early June. One of their main reasons for doing so was Kelly Johnson's choice of the unproven General Electric J73 engine. The engineers at Wright Field considered the Pratt and Whitney J57 to be the most powerful engine available, and the designs from Fairchild, Martin, and Bell all incorporated this engine. The absence of conventional landing gear was also a perceived shortcoming of the Lockheed design.[18]

Another factor in the rejection of Kelly Johnson's submission was the Air Force preference for multiengine aircraft. Air Force reconnaissance experts had gained their practical experience during World War II in multiengine bombers. In addition, aerial photography experts in the late 1940s and early 1950s emphasized focal length as the primary factor in reconnaissance photography and, therefore, preferred large aircraft capable of accommodating long focal-length cameras. This preference reached an extreme in the early 1950s with the development of the cumbersome 240-inch Boston camera, a device so large that the YC-97 Boeing Stratocruiser that carried it had to be partially disassembled before the camera could be installed. Finally, there was the feeling shared by many Air Force officers that two engines are always better than one because, if one fails, there is a spare to get the aircraft back to base. In reality, however, aviation records show that single-engine aircraft have always been more reliable than multiengine planes.

---

[17] C. F. Wienberg, telephone conversation with Donald E. Welzenbach, 23 July 1988 (U).

[18] Miller, *Lockheed U-2,* p. 12.

Furthermore, a high-altitude reconnaissance aircraft deep in enemy territory would have little chance of returning if one of the engines failed, forcing the aircraft to descend.[19]

On 7 June 1954, Kelly Johnson received a letter from the Air Force rejecting the CL-282 proposal because it had only one engine and was too unusual and because the Air Force was already committed to the modification of the Martin B-57.[20] By this time, the Air Force had also selected the Bell X-16; the formal contract calling for aircraft was signed in September. Despite the Air Force's selection of the X-16, Lockheed continued to work on the CL-282 and began seeking new sources of support for the aircraft.

Lockheed CL-282 Supporters and the CIA

Although the Air Force's uniformed hierarchy had decided in favor of the Bell and Martin aircraft, some high-level civilian officials continued to favor the Lockheed design. The most prominent proponent of the Lockheed proposal was Trevor Gardner, Special Assistant for Research and Development to Air Force Secretary Harold E. Talbott. Gardner had many contacts in west coast aeronautical circles because before coming to Washington he had headed the Hycon Manufacturing Company, which made aerial cameras in Pasadena, California. He had been present at Kelly Johnson's presentation on the CL-282 at the Pentagon in early April 1954 and believed that this design showed the most promise for reconnaissance of the Soviet Union. This belief was shared by Gardner's special assistant, Frederick Ayer, Jr., and Garrison Norton, an adviser to Secretary Talbott.[21]

---

[19] Allen F. Donovan, interview by Donald E. Welzenbach, Corona del Mar, California, 20 May 1985 (S).

[20] Johnson, "Log for Project X," 7 June 1954.

[21] Garrison Norton, interview by Donald E. Welzenbach, tape recording, Washington, DC, 23 May 1983 (S); Michael R. Beschloss, *Mayday: Eisenhower, Khrushchev and the U-2 Affair* (New York: Harper & Row, 1986), p. 79.

According to Norton, Gardner tried to interest SAC commander LeMay in the Lockheed aircraft because Gardner envisioned it primarily as a collector of strategic, rather than tactical, intelligence. But General LeMay had already shown that he was not interested in an unarmed aircraft. Gardner, Ayer, and Norton then decided to seek CIA support for the high-flying aircraft. At that time the Agency's official involvement in overhead reconnaissance was limited to advising the Air Force on the problems of launching large camera-carrying balloons for reconnaissance flights over hostile territory (for the details of this program, see chapter 2). The Chief of the Operations Staff in the Office of Scientific Intelligence, Philip G. Strong, however, served on several Air Force advisory boards and kept himself well informed on developments in reconnaissance aircraft.[22]

Gardner, Norton, and Ayer met with Strong in the Pentagon on 12 May 1954, six days before the Wright Air Development Command began to evaluate the Lockheed proposal. Gardner described Kelly Johnson's proposal and showed the drawings to Strong. After this meeting. Strong summarized his impressions of the Air Force's search for a high-altitude reconnaissance aircraft:

> *Proposals for special reconnaissance aircraft have been received in the Air Staff from Lockheed, Fairchild, and Bell...The Lockheed proposal is considered to be the best. It has been given the type designation of CL-282 and in many respects is a jet-powered glider based essentially on the Lockheed Day Fighter XF-104. It is primarily subsonic but can attain transonic speeds*

---

[22] Strong was a colonel in the Marine Corps Reserve and often used that title even though he was not on active duty. He later advanced to the rank of brigadier general in the reserve. For Strong's contacts with senior Air Force officials concerning the CL-282, see the Norton interview (S).

*over the target with a consequent loss of range. With
an altitude of 73,000 feet over the target it has a combat radius of 1,400 nautical miles...The CL-282 can be
manufactured mainly with XF-104 jigs and designs...
The prototype of this plane can be produced within
a year from the date of order. Five planes could be
delivered for operations within two years.*

*The Bell proposal is a more conventional aircraft
having normal landing gear. As a result, its maximum
altitude over target is 69,500 feet and the speed and
range are not as good as the Lockheed CL-282.*[23]

Gardner's enthusiasm for the CL-282 had given Strong the false
impression that most Air Force officials supported the Lockheed
design. In reality, the Air Force's uniformed hierarchy was in the
process of choosing the modified version of the Martin B-57 and
the new Bell X-16 to meet future reconnaissance needs.

During their meeting with Strong, Trevor Gardner, Frederick
Ayer, and Garrison Norton explained that they favored the CL-282
because it gave promise of flying higher than the other designs and
because at maximum altitude its smaller radar cross section might
make it invisible to existing Soviet radars. The three officials asked
Strong if the CIA would be interested in such an aircraft. Strong
promised to talk to the Director of Central Intelligence's newly
hired Special Assistant for Planning and Coordination, Richard M.
Bissell, Jr., about possible Agency interest in the CL-282.[24]

---

[23] Philip G. Strong, Memorandum for the Record, "Special Aircraft for
Penetration Photo Reconnaissance," 12 May 1954, OSI records (now in
OSWR), job 80R-01424, box 1 (S).

[24] Karl H. Weber, *The Office of Scientific Intelligence. 1949-68,* Directorate of
Science and Technology Historical Series OSI-1 (CIA: DS&T, 1972), vol. 1,
tab A, pp. 16-17 (TS Codeword).

Richard Bissell had already had an active and varied career before he joined the CIA. A graduate of Groton and Yale, Bissell studied at the London School of Economics for a year and then completed a doctorate at Yale in 1939. He taught economics, first at Yale and then from 1942 at the Massachusetts Institute of Technology (MIT), where he became a full professor in 1948. During World War II, Bissell had managed American shipping as executive officer of the Combined Shipping Adjustment Board. After the war, he served as deputy director of the Marshall Plan from 1948 until the end of 1951, when he became a staff member of the Ford Foundation. His first association with the Agency came in late 1953, when he undertook a contract study of possible responses the United States might use against the Soviet Bloc in the event of another uprising such as the East Berlin riots of June 1953. Bissell quickly concluded that there was not much hope for clandestine operations against Bloc nations. As he remarked later: "I know I emerged from that exercise feeling that very little could be done." This belief would later make Bissell a leading advocate of technical rather than human means of intelligence collection.[25]

Bissell joined the Agency in late January 1954 and soon became involved in coordination for the operation aimed at overthrowing Guatemalan President Jacobo Arbenz. He was, therefore very preoccupied when Philip Strong approached him in mid-May 1954 with the concept of the proposed spyplane from Lockheed. Bissell said that the idea had merit and told Strong to get some topflight scientists to advise on the matter. Afterward he returned to the final planning for the Guatemalan operation and promptly forgot about the CL-282.[26]

---

[25] Thomas Powers, *The Man Who Kept the Secrets: Richard Helms and the CIA* (New York: Alfred A. Knopf, 1979), p. 79; Beschloss, *Mayday,* pp. 86-89.
[26] Memorandum for H. Marshall Chadwell, Assistant Director/Scientific Intelligence, from Chief, Support Staff, OSI, "Review of OSA Activities Concerned with Scientific and Technical Collection Techniques," 13 May 1955, p. 6, OSI (OSWR) records, job 80R-01424, box 1 (S); Richard M. Bissell, Jr., interview by Donald E. Welzenbach, tape recording, Farmington, Connecticut, 8 November 1984 (S).

Meanwhile, Strong went about drumming up support for high-altitude overflight. In May 1954 he persuaded DCI Allen W. Dulles to ask the Air Force to take the initiative in gaining approval for an overflight of the Soviet guided-missile test range at Kapustin Yar. Dulles's memorandum did not mention the CL-282 or any of the other proposed high-altitude aircraft. CIA and Air Force officials met on several occasions to explore the overflight proposal, which the Air Force finally turned down in October 1954.[27]

Although Allen Dulles was willing to support an Air Force overflight of the Soviet Union, he was not enthusiastic about the CIA undertaking such a project. Few details about Dulles's precise attitude toward the proposed Lockheed reconnaissance aircraft are available, but many who knew him believe that he did not want the CIA to become involved in projects that belonged to the military, and the Lockheed CL-282 had been designed for an Air Force requirement. Moreover, high-altitude reconnaissance of the Soviet Union did not fit well into Allen Dulles's perception of the proper role of an intelligence agency. He tended to favor the classical form of espionage, which relied on agents rather than technology.[28]

At this point, the summer of 1954, Lockheed's CL-282 proposal still lacked official support. Although the design had strong backers among some Air Force civilians and CIA officials, the key decision makers at both Air Force and CIA remained unconvinced. To make Kelly Johnson's revolutionary design a reality, one additional source of support was necessary: prominent scientists serving on government advisory boards.

---

[27] Memorandum for Richard M. Bissell, Special Assistant to the Director for Planning and Coordination, from Philip G. Strong, Chief, Operations Staff, OSI, "Overflight of Kapustin Yar," 15 October 1954, OSI (OSWR) records, job 80R-01424, box 1 (TS, downgraded to S).

[28] Powers, *Man Who Kept the Secrets*, pp. 103-104; Edwin H. Land, interview by Donald E. Welzenbach, tape recording, Cambridge, Massachusetts, 17 and 20 September 1984 (TS Codeword); Robert Amory, Jr., interview by Donald E. Welzenbach and Gregory W. Pedlow, Washington, DC, 22 April 1987 (S).

SCIENTISTS AND OVERHEAD RECONNAISSANCE

Scientists and engineers from universities and private industry had played a major role in advising the government on technical matters during World War II. At the end of the war, most of the scientific advisory boards were disbanded, but within a few years the growing tensions of the Cold War again led government agencies to seek scientific advice and assistance. In 1947 the Air Force established a Scientific Advisory Board, which met periodically to discuss topics of current interest and advise the Air Force on the potential usefulness of new technologies. The following year the Office of Defense Mobilization established the Scientific Advisory Committee, but the Truman administration made little use of this new advisory body.[29]

The BEACON HILL Report

In 1951 the Air Force sought even more assistance from scientists because the Strategic Air Command's requests for information about targets behind the Iron Curtain could not be filled. To look for new ways of conducting reconnaissance against the Soviet Bloc, the Air Force's Deputy Chief of Staff for Development, Maj. Gen. Gordon P. Saville, added 15 reconnaissance experts to an existing project on air defense known as Project LINCOLN, then under way at the Massachusetts Institute of Technology. By the end of the year, these experts had assembled in Boston to begin their research. Their headquarters was located over a secretarial school on Beacon Hill, which soon became the codename for the reconnaissance project. The consultants were called the BEACON HILL Study Group.

The study group's chairman was Kodak physicist Carl F. P. Overhage, and its members included James G. Baker and Edward M. Purcell from Harvard; Saville Davis from the *Christian*

---

[29] For more information on the Air Force's use of scientists see Thomas A. Sturm, *The USAF Scientific Advisory Board: Its First Twenty Years. 1944-1964* (Washington, DC: USAF Historical Office, 1967) (U).

Science Monitor; Allen F. Donovan from the Cornell Aeronautical Laboratory; Peter C. Goldmark from Columbia Broadcasting System Laboratories; Edwin H. Land, founder of the Polaroid Corporation; Stewart E. Miller of Bell Laboratories; Richard S. Perkin of the Perkin-Elmer Company; and Louis N. Ridenour of Ridenour Associates, Inc. The Wright Air Development Command sent Lt. Col. Richard Leghorn to serve as its liaison officer.[30]

During January and February 1952, the BEACON HILL Study Group traveled every weekend to various airbases, laboratories, and firms for briefings on the latest technology and projects. The panel members were particularly interested in new approaches to aerial reconnaissance, such as photography from high-flying aircraft and camera-carrying balloons. One of the more unusual (albeit unsuccessful) proposals examined by the panel was an "invisible" dirigible. This was to be a giant, almost flat-shaped airship with a blue-tinted, nonreflective coating; it would cruise at an altitude of 90,000 feet along the borders of the Soviet Union at very slow speeds while using a large lens to photograph targets of interest.[31]

After completing these briefings at the end of February 1952, the BEACON HILL Study Group returned to MIT, where the panel members spent the next three months writing a report detailing their recommendations for ways to improve the amount and quality of intelligence being gathered on the Soviet Bloc. Published as a classified document on 15 June 1952, the *BEACON HILL Report* advocated radical approaches to obtain the information

---

[30] USAF, Project LINCOLN, *BEACON HILL Report; Problems of Air Force Intelligence and Reconnaissance*, Massachusetts Institute of Technology, 15 June 1952, pp. v, xi; app. A (S, downgraded to C).

[31] Allen F. Donovan, telephone conversation with Donald E. Welzenbach, 21 June 1985 (U); James G. Baker, interview by Donald E. Welzenbach, tape recording, Washington, DC, 24 April 1985 (S).

needed for national intelligence estimates. Its 14 chapters covered radar, radio, and photographic surveillance; examined the use of passive infrared and microwave reconnaissance; and discussed the development of advanced reconnaissance vehicles. One of the report's key recommendations called for the development of high-altitude reconnaissance aircraft:

> *We have reached a period in history when our peacetime knowledge of the capabilities, activities and dispositions of a potentially hostile nation is such as to demand that we supplement it with the maximum amount of information obtainable through aerial reconnaissance. To avoid political involvements, such aerial reconnaissance must be conducted either from vehicles flying in friendly airspace, or—a decision on this point permitting—from vehicles whose performance is such that they can operate in Soviet airspace with greatly reduced chances of detection or interception.*[32]

Concern about the Danger of a Soviet Surprise Attack

The Air Force did not begin to implement the ideas of the *BEACON HILL Report* until the summer of 1953. By this time interest in reconnaissance had increased after Dwight D. Eisenhower became President in January 1953 and soon expressed his dissatisfaction with the quality of the intelligence estimates of Soviet strategic capabilities and the paucity of reconnaissance on the Soviet Bloc.[33]

To President Eisenhower and many other US political and military leaders, the Soviet Union was a dangerous opponent that appeared to be moving inexorably toward a position of military

---

[32] *BEACON HILL Report,* pp. 164, 167-168 (S). This section of the report was written by Allen Donovan and Louis Ridenour.

[33] Lundahl and Brugioni interview (TS Codeword).

parity with the United States. Particularly alarming was Soviet progress in the area of nuclear weapons. In the late summer of 1949, the Soviet Union had detonated an atomic bomb nearly three years sooner than US experts had predicted. Then in August 1953—a scant nine months after the first US test of a hydrogen bomb—the Soviet Union detonated a hydrogen bomb manufactured from lithium deuteride, a technology more advanced than the heavy water method used by US scientists. Thus, new and extremely powerful weapons were coming into the hands of a government whose actions greatly disturbed the leaders of the West. Only two months before the successful hydrogen bomb test, Soviet troops had crushed an uprising in East Berlin. And, at the United Nations, the Soviet Bloc seemed bent on causing dissension between Western Europe and the United States and between the developed and undeveloped nations. This aggressive Soviet foreign policy, combined with advances in nuclear weapons, led officials such as Secretary of State John Foster Dulles to see the Soviet Union as a menace to peace and world order.

The Soviet Union's growing military strength soon became a threat not just to US forces overseas but to the continental United States itself. In the spring of 1953, a top secret RAND study pointed out the vulnerability of the SAC's US bases to a surprise attack by Soviet long-range bombers.[34]

Concern about the danger of a Soviet attack on the continental United States grew after an American military attache sighted a new Soviet intercontinental bomber at Ramenskoye airfield, south of Moscow, in 1953. The new bomber was the Myasishchev-4, later designated Bison by NATO. Powered by jet engines

---

[34] RAND Corporation, Plans Analysis Section, "Vulnerability of U.S. Strategic Power to a Surprise Attack in 1956," RAND Special Memorandum No. 15, Santa Monica, California: the RAND Corporation, April 15, 1953 (TS, declassified May 1967).

rather than the turboprops of Russia's other long-range bombers, the Bison appeared to be the Soviet equivalent of the US B-52, which was only then going into production. Pictures of the Bison taken at the Moscow May Day air show in 1954 had an enormous impact on the US intelligence community. Unlike several other Soviet postwar aircraft, the Bison was not a derivative of US or British designs but represented a native Soviet design capability that surprised US intelligence experts. This new long-range jet bomber, along with the Soviet Union's large numbers of older propeller and turboprop bombers, seemed to pose a significant threat to the United States, and, in the summer of 1954, newspapers and magazines began publishing articles highlighting the growing airpower of the Soviet Union. Pictures of the Bison bomber featured prominently in such stories.[35]

The Air Force Intelligence Systems Panel

Even before the publication of photographs of the Bison raised fears that the Soviet bomber force might eventually surpass that of the United States, the Air Force had already established a new advisory body to look for ways to implement the main recommendation of the *BEACON HILL Report*—the construction of high-flying aircraft and high-acuity cameras. Created in July 1953, the Intelligence Systems Panel (ISP) included several experts from the BEACON HILL Study Group: Land, Overhage, Donovan, and Miller. At the request of the Air Force, the CIA also participated in the panel, represented by Edward L. Allen of the Office of Research

---

[35] "AF Cites Red Bomber Progress," *Aviation Week,* May 24, 1954, p. 14; "Is Russia Winning the Arms Race?" *US News and World Report,* June 18, 1954, pp. 28-29; "Russia Parades Airpower as *'Big Stick,'*" *Aviation Week*, June 28, 1954, p. 15; "Red Air Force: The World's Biggest," *Newsweek,* August 23, 1954, pp. 28-33.

and Reports (ORR) and Philip Strong of the Office of Scientific Intelligence (OSI).[36]

The chairman of the new panel was Dr. James G. Baker, a research associate at the Harvard College Observatory. Baker had been involved in aerial reconnaissance since 1940, when he first advised the Army Air Corps on ways to improve its lenses. He then established a full-scale optical laboratory at Harvard—the Harvard University Optical Research Laboratory—to produce high-quality lenses. Since the university did not wish to continue manufacturing cameras and lenses after the end of the war, the optical laboratory moved to Boston University, which agreed to sponsor the effort as long as the Air Force would fund it. Baker decided to remain at Harvard, so his assistant, Dr. Duncan E. Macdonald, became the new head of what was now called the Boston University Optical Research Laboratory (BUORL). Baker's association with the Air Force did not end with the transfer of the optical laboratory to Boston University, because he continued to design lenses to be used in photoreconnaissance.[37]

The ISP first met at Boston University on 3 August 1953. To provide background on the poor state of US knowledge of the Soviet Union, Philip Strong informed the other panel members that the best intelligence then available on the Soviet Union's interior was photography taken by the German Luftwaffe during World War II. Since the German photography covered only the Soviet Union west of the Urals, primarily west of the Volga River,

---

[36] Memorandum for Robert Amory, Jr., Deputy Director, Intelligence, from Edward L. Allen, Chief, Economic Research, ORR, and Philip G. Strong, Chief, Operations Staff, OSI, "Meeting of the Intelligence Systems Panel of the Scientific Advisory Board, USAF," 26 August 1953, OSI (OSWR) records, job 80R-01424, box 1 (S).
[37] Baker interview (S). In 1957, after the Air Force decided to cut back its funding of BUORL, Duncan Macdonald and Richard Leghorn (by then retired from the Air Force) formed their own corporation—Itek—and purchased the laboratory from Boston University (Leghorn interview [S]).

many vital regions were not included. The ISP would, therefore, have to look for ways to provide up-to-date photography of all of the Soviet Union. Several Air Force agencies then briefed the panel members on the latest developments and proposed future projects in the area of aerial reconnaissance, including new cameras, reconnaissance balloons, and even satellites. Among the Air Force reconnaissance projects discussed were multiple sensors for use in existing aircraft such as the RB-47, RB-52, and RB-58; Project FICON—an acronym for "fighter conversion"— for adapting a giant 10-engine B-36 bomber to enable it to launch and retrieve a Republic RF-84F Thunderflash reconnaissance aircraft; reconnaissance versions of the Navajo and Snark missiles; the high-altitude balloon program, which would be ready to go into operation by the summer of 1955; and the search for a new high-altitude reconnaissance aircraft.[38]

The wide variety of programs discussed at the conference were all products of the Air Force's all-out effort to find a way to collect intelligence on the Communist Bloc. Some of the schemes went beyond the existing level of technology; others, like the camera-carrying balloons, were technically feasible but involved dangerous political consequences.

British Overflight of Kapustin Yar

The British were also working on high-altitude reconnaissance aircraft. In 1952 the Royal Air Force (RAF) began Project

---

[38] Memorandum for Robert Amory, Jr., Deputy Director, Intelligence, from Edward L. Allen, Chief, Economic Research, ORR, and Philip G. Strong, Chief, Operations Staff, OSI, "Meeting of the Intelligence Systems Panel of the Scientific Advisory Board, USAF," 26 August 1953; Memorandum for H. Marshall Chadwell, Assistant Director/Scientific Intelligence, from Chief, Support Staff, OSI, "Review of OSA Activities Concerned with Scientific and Technical Collection Techniques," 13 May 1955, p. 6, OSI (OSWR) records, job 80R-01424, box 1 (S); Donovan interview, 22 May 1985 (S).

ROBIN, which was designed to modify the Canberra bomber for high-altitude reconnaissance. This project was probably inspired by Richard Leghorn's collaboration with English Electric Company designers in 1951, when they calculated ways to increase the altitude of the Canberra. The RAF equipped the new Canberra PR7 with Rolls-Royce Avon-109 engines and gave it long, fuel-filled wings. The range of this variant of the Canberra was now 4,300 miles, and, on 29 August 1955, it achieved an altitude of 65,880 feet.[39]

Sometime during the first half of 1953, the RAF employed a high-altitude Canberra on a daring overflight of the Soviet Union to photograph the missile test range at Kapustin Yar. Because of advanced warning from either radar or agents inside British intelligence, the overflight did not catch the Soviet Union by surprise. Soviet fighters damaged and nearly shot down the Canberra.[40] Rumors about this flight reached Washington during the summer of 1953, but official confirmation by the United Kingdom did not come until February 1954. While on a six-week tour of Europe to study aerial reconnaissance problems for the US Air Force's Scientific Advisory Board, James Baker was briefed by RAF intelligence officials on the Canberra overflight of the Soviet Union. On 22 and 23 March 1954, he reported on it to the full Scientific Advisory Board at Langley AFB, Virginia.

Baker also chaired the next meeting of the Air Force's Intelligence Systems Panel in late April 1954 but could not tell

---

[39] Van der Aart, *Aerial Espionage,* p. 18; Philip G. Strong, Chief, Operations Staff, OSI, Memorandum for the Record, "Meeting of Air Force Scientific Advisory Board, 18-21 October 1953," 26 October 1953, OSI (OSWR) records, job 80R-01424, box 1 (TS, downgraded to S).

[40] Stewart Alsop, *The Center* (New York: Popular Library, 1968), p. 194; Beschloss, *Mayday,* pp. 78-79. Both of these books state that the project included the CIA, but there is no evidence to support this assertion.

its members about the British overflight of Kapustin Yar because they were not cleared for this information. The panel did, however, discuss the modifications for high-altitude flight being made to the US Canberra, the B-57.[41]

The Intelligence Systems Panel and the CL-282

The next Intelligence Systems Panel meeting took place on 24 and 25 May at Boston University and the Polaroid Corporation. Panel member Allen F. Donovan from the Cornell Aeronautical Laboratory evaluated the changes being made to the B-57 by the Martin Aircraft Company. Even without Martin's specifications or drawings, Donovan had been able to estimate what could be done to the B-57 by lengthening the wings and lightening the fuselage. He had determined that alterations to the B-57 airframe would not solve the reconnaissance needs expressed in the *BEACON HILL Report*. Theoretically, he explained to the panel, any multiengine aircraft built according to military specifications, including the B-57, would be too heavy to fly above 65,000 feet and hence would be vulnerable to Soviet interception. To be safe, Donovan explained, penetrating aircraft would need to fly above 70,000 feet for the entire mission.[42]

Development of such an aircraft was already under way, Donovan continued, for Philip Strong of the CIA had told him that the Lockheed Aircraft Corporation had designed a light-weight, high-flying aircraft. ISP chairman Baker then urged Donovan to travel to southern California to evaluate the Lockheed design and gather ideas on high-altitude aircraft from other aircraft manufacturers.

When he was finally able to make this trip in late summer, Donovan found the plane that he and the other ISP members had been seeking. On the afternoon of 2 August 1954, Donovan met

---

[41] Baker interview (S).
[42] Donovan interview (S); Baker interview (S).

with L. Eugene Root, an old Air Force acquaintance who was now a Lockheed vice-president, and learned about the Air Force's competition for a high-altitude reconnaissance aircraft. Kelly Johnson then showed Donovan the plans for Lockheed's unsuccessful entry. A lifelong sailplane enthusiast, Donovan immediately recognized that the CL-282 design was essentially a jet-propelled glider capable of attaining the altitudes that he felt were necessary to carry out reconnaissance of the Soviet Union successfully.[43]

Upon his return east on 8 August, Donovan got in touch with James Baker and suggested an urgent meeting of the Intelligence Systems Panel. Because of other commitments by the members, however, the panel did not meet to hear Donovan's report until 24 September 1954 at the Cornell Aeronautical Laboratory. Several members, including Land and Strong, were absent. Those who did attend were upset to learn that the Air Force had funded a closed competition for a tactical reconnaissance plane without informing them. But once Donovan began describing Kelly Johnson's rejected design for a jet-powered glider, they quickly forgot their annoyance and listened intently.

Donovan began by stressing that high-altitude reconnaissance aircraft had to fly above 70,000 feet to be safe from interception. Next, he set out what he considered to be the three essential requirements for a high-altitude spyplane: a single engine, a sailplane wing, and low structural load factors. Donovan strongly favored single-engine aircraft because they are both lighter and more reliable than multiengine aircraft. Although a twin-engine aircraft could theoretically return to base on only one engine, Donovan explained, it could only do so at a much lower altitude, about 34,000 feet, where it was sure to be shot down.

The second of Donovan's essential factors, a sailplane wing (in technical terms a high-aspect-ratio, low-induced-drag wing),

---

[43] Donovan interview (S).

was needed to take maximum advantage of the reduced thrust of a jet engine operating in the rarefied atmosphere of extreme altitude. Because of the thinness of the atmosphere above 70,000 feet, engineers estimated that the power curve of a jet engine would fall off to about 6 percent of its sea-level thrust.

Finally, low structural load factors, like those used by transport aircraft, were necessary to reduce weight and thereby achieve maximum altitude. Donovan explained that strengthening wings and wingroot areas to withstand the high speeds and sharp turns mandated by the standard military airworthiness rules added too much weight to the airframe, thereby negating the efficiency of the sailplane wing.

In short, it was possible to achieve altitudes in excess of 70,000 feet, but only by making certain that all parts of the aeronautical equation were in balance: thrust, lift, and weight. The only plane meeting these requirements, Donovan insisted, was Kelly Johnson's CL-282 because it was essentially a sailplane. In Donovan's view, the CL-282 did not have to meet the specifications of a combat aircraft because it could fly safely above Soviet fighters.[44]

Donovan's arguments convinced the Intelligence Systems Panel of the merits of the CL-282 proposal, but this panel reported to the Air Force, which had already rejected the CL-282. Thus, even though the Lockheed CL-282 had several important sources of support by September 1954—the members of the Intelligence Systems Panel and high-ranking Air Force civilians such as Trevor Gardner—these backers were all connected with the Air Force. They could not offer funds to Lockheed to pursue the CL-282 concept because the Air Force was already committed to the Martin RB-57 and the Bell X-16. Additional support from outside the Air Force was needed to bring the CL-282 project to life, and this support would come from scientists serving on high-level advisory committees.

---

[44] Donovan interview (S); Baker interview (S).

The Technological Capabilities Panel

The Eisenhower administration was growing increasingly concerned over the capability of the Soviet Union to launch a surprise attack on the United States. Early in 1954, Trevor Gardner had become alarmed by a RAND Corporation study warning that a Soviet surprise attack might destroy 85 percent of the SAC bomber force. Gardner then met with Dr. Lee DuBridge, President of the California Institute of Technology and Chairman of the Office of Defense Mobilization's Science Advisory Committee, and criticized the committee for not dealing with such essential problems as the possibility of a surprise attack. This criticism led DuBridge to invite Gardner to speak at the Science Advisory Committee's next meeting. After listening to Gardner, the committee members decided to approach President Eisenhower on the matter. On 27 March 1954, the President told them about the discovery of the Soviet Bison bombers and his concern that these new aircraft might be used in a surprise attack on the United States. Stressing the high priority he gave to reducing the risk of military surprise, the President asked the committee to advise him on this problem.[45]

The President's request led Chairman DuBridge to ask one of the most prominent members, MIT President James R. Killian, Jr., to meet with other Science Advisory Committee members in the Boston area to discuss the feasibility of a comprehensive scientific assessment of the nation's defenses. At their meeting at MIT on 15 April 1954, the group called for the recruitment of such a task force if the President endorsed the concept.

On 26 July 1954, President Eisenhower authorized Killian to recruit and lead a panel of experts to study "the country's technological capabilities to meet some of its current problems." Killian

---

[45] Beschloss, *Mayday,* pp. 73-74; Technological Capabilities Panel of the Science Advisory Committee, *Meeting the Threat of Surprise Attack*, 14 February 1955, p. 185 (hereafter cited as *TCP Report*) (TS/Restricted Data, downgraded to S).

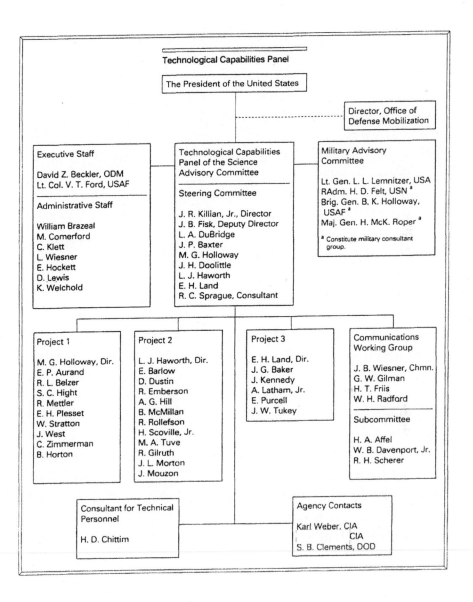

Technological Capabilities Panel

The President of the United States

Director, Office of Defense Mobilization

Executive Staff

David Z. Beckler, ODM
Lt. Col. V. T. Ford, USAF

Administrative Staff

William Brazeal
M. Comerford
C. Klett
L. Wiesner
E. Hockett
D. Lewis
K. Welchold

Technological Capabilities Panel of the Science Advisory Committee

Steering Committee

J. R. Killian, Jr., Director
J. B. Fisk, Deputy Director
L. A. DuBridge
J. P. Baxter
M. G. Holloway
J. H. Doolittle
L. J. Haworth
E. H. Land
R. C. Sprague, Consultant

Military Advisory Committee

Lt. Gen. L. L. Lemnitzer, USA
RAdm. H. D. Felt, USN [a]
Brig. Gen. B. K. Holloway, USAF [a]
Maj. Gen. H. McK. Roper [a]

[a] Constitute military consultant group.

Project 1

M. G. Holloway, Dir.
E. P. Aurand
R. L. Belzer
S. C. Hight
R. Mettler
E. H. Plesset
W. Stratton
J. West
C. Zimmerman
B. Horton

Project 2

L. J. Haworth, Dir.
E. Barlow
D. Dustin
R. Emberson
A. G. Hill
B. McMillan
R. Rollefson
H. Scoville, Jr.
M. A. Tuve
R. Gilruth
J. L. Morton
J. Mouzon

Project 3

E. H. Land, Dir.
J. G. Baker
J. Kennedy
A. Latham, Jr.
E. Purcell
J. W. Tukey

Communications Working Group

J. B. Wiesner, Chmn.
G. W. Gilman
H. T. Friis
W. H. Radford

Subcommittee

H. A. Affel
W. B. Davenport, Jr.
R. H. Scherer

Consultant for Technical Personnel

H. D. Chittim

Agency Contacts

Karl Weber, CIA
                     CIA
S. B. Clements, DOD

quickly set up shop in offices located in the Old Executive Office Building and organized 42 of the nation's leading scientists into three special project groups investigating US offensive, defensive, and intelligence capabilities, with an additional communications working group. The Technological Capabilities Panel (TCP) groups began meeting on 13 September 1954. For the next 20 weeks, the members of the various panels met on 307 separate occasions for briefings, field trips, conferences, and meetings with every major unit of the US defense and intelligence establishments. After receiving the most up-to-date information available on the nation's defense and intelligence programs, the panel members began drafting their report to the National Security Council.[46]

Project Three Support for the Lockheed CL-282

Even before the final Technological Capabilities Panel report was ready, one of the three working groups took actions that would have a major impact on the US reconnaissance program. Project Three had the task of investigating the nation's intelligence capabilities. Its chairman was Edwin H. (Din) Land, the inventor of the polarizing filter and the instant camera. When James Killian asked Land to head Project Three, Land had to make a major decision about his career. At the time, the 45-year-old millionaire was on a leave of absence from Polaroid and was living in Hollywood, advising Alfred Hitchcock on the technological aspects of making three-dimensional movies. Land decided to give up his interest in cinema's third dimension and return east to Polaroid and the panel appointment.[47]

---

[46] James R. Killian, Jr., *Sputnik, Scientists, and Eisenhower: A Memoir of the First Special Assistant to the President for Science and Technology* (Cambridge: MIT Press, 1977), p. 68: Beschloss, *Mayday*, p. 74; *TCP Report*, pp. 185-186 (S).

[47] James R. Killian, Jr., interview by Donald E. Welzenbach, tape recording, Cambridge, Massachusetts, 2 November 1984 (S); Land interview (TS Codeword).

Land's Project Three was the smallest of the three Technological Capabilities Panel projects, for he preferred what he called "taxicab committees"—committees small enough to fit into a single taxicab. The Project Three committee consisted of Land; James Baker and Edward Purcell of Harvard; chemist Joseph W. Kennedy of Washington University, St. Louis; mathematician John W. Tukey of Princeton University and Bell Telephone Laboratories; and Allen Latham, Jr., of Arthur D. Little, Inc., an engineer and former treasurer of the Polaroid Corporation.[48]

In mid-August 1954, Land and Baker went to Washington to arrange for the various intelligence organizations to brief the Project Three study group. As the briefings progressed, the panel members became more and more distressed at the poor state of the nation's intelligence resources. Land later noted, "We would go in and interview generals and admirals in charge of intelligence and come away worried. Here we were, five or six young men, asking questions that these high-ranking officers couldn't answer." Land added that the Project Three members were also not overly impressed with the Central Intelligence Agency.[49]

Land learned the details of Lockheed's proposed CL-282 aircraft soon after he arrived in Washington. Philip Strong showed him Kelly Johnson's conceptual drawing of the plane and told him that the Air Force had rejected it. Although Land had heard Allen Donovan briefly mention a Lockheed design for a high-flying aircraft at the 24-25 May meeting of Baker's Intelligence Systems Panel, he did not realize that that plane and the one in Strong's drawing were the same. As soon as Land saw Strong's copy of the CL-282 drawing, however, he telephoned Baker to say, "Jim, I think I have the plane you are after."[50]

---

[48] *TCP Report,* p. 188 (S).

[49] Land interview (TS Codeword).

[50] Baker interview (S).

A few days later, when Land showed Kelly Johnson's conceptual drawing to Baker and the other Project Three members, they all became enthusiastic about the aircraft's possibilities. Although Baker had heard Allen Donovan's brief mention of the Lockheed design in May, he had not yet seen a drawing of the aircraft because Donovan did not report to the ISP on his early-August trip to Lockheed until 24 September. After seeing the CL-282 drawing, Baker began designing a camera and lens system that would fit in the Lockheed craft.[51]

At the end of August, Land discussed the CL-282 with Allen Dulles's Special Assistant for Planning and Coordination, Richard Bissell, who came away from the meeting without any definite ideas as to what Land wanted to do with the aircraft. Overhead reconnaissance was not uppermost in Bissell's mind at the time, and it was unclear to him why he had even been contacted.[52] Bissell's outstanding academic credentials, his acquaintanceship with James Killian through his previous teaching experience at MIT, and his direct access to DCI Dulles may have led the Technological Capabilities Panel members to consider him the best CIA point of contact.

Although surprised that he had become involved in the CL-282 project, Bissell's interest was piqued, and he set out to learn what he could about reconnaissance systems. In early September 1954, Bissell had Douglas E. Ashford, a young Air Force officer on his staff, put together a general status report on air reconnaissance programs. Bissell forwarded the 16-page study to the Deputy Director of Central Intelligence (DDCI), Lt. Gen. Charles Pearre Cabell, USAF, on 24 September. In a covering memorandum, Bissell

---

[51] Ibid.
[52] Bissell interview (S).

called Cabell's attention to a section of the report about a "stripped or specialized aircraft" called the Lockheed CL-282.[53]

By September 1954, Land's Project Three study group had become very much interested in the Lockheed CL-282 design. Their interest grew even stronger when James Baker told them of Allen Donovan's strong case for the CL-282 at the 24-25 September meeting of the ISP. It is not possible to determine exactly when the Land committee decided to back the CL-282; in fact, there may never have been a formal decision as such. In view of Land's impulsive nature, he probably seized upon the CL-282 design as being a workable concept and immediately began developing it into a complete reconnaissance system.

During September and October the Project Three study group met frequently to discuss the Lockheed design and the reconnaissance equipment it would carry. Meetings were small, generally with fewer than 10 participants; Garrison Norton was often the only government official in attendance. At times outside experts joined in the proceedings. When the discussion turned to cameras and film, Land invited Dr. Henry Yutzy, Eastman Kodak's film expert, and Richard S. Perkin, President of the Perkin-Elmer Company, to participate. For discussions on the J57 engine, the panel members asked Perry W. Pratt, Pratt and Whitney's chief engineer, to attend. Kelly Johnson also met with the panel to review plans for the CL-282 system.[54]

By the end of October, the Project Three meetings had covered every aspect of the Lockheed design. The CL-282 was to be more than an airplane with a camera, it was to be an integrated intel-

---

[53] Memorandum for DDCI Charles Pearre Cabell from R.M Bissell, Special Assistant to the Director for Planning and Coordination, "Aerial Reconnaissance," 24 September 1954, DCI Records, job 80-B-1676R, box 25 (TS, downgraded to S).

[54] Killian, *Sputnik, Scientists, and Eisenhower,* p. 82.

ligence-collection system that the Project Three members were confident could find and photograph the Soviet Union's Bison bomber fleet and, thus, resolve the growing "bomber gap" controversy. It was not just the Lockheed aircraft that had captured the Land group's fancy; the plane was seen as the platform for a whole new generation of aerial cameras that several committee members had been discussing since the BEACON HILL and Intelligence Systems Panel meetings. James Baker was in the process of developing a revolutionary new camera with tremendously improved resolution and film capacity, and the Eastman Kodak company was working on new thin, lightweight film.[55]

By October 1954, the Project Three study group had drafted a complete program for an overhead reconnaissance effort based on the CL-282 aircraft. The one remaining question was who would conduct the overflights. The committee's members, particularly Land, were not in favor of the Air Force conducting such missions in peacetime. Firmly believing that military overflights in armed aircraft could provoke a war, they argued for civilian overflights in unarmed, unmarked aircraft. In their view, the organization most suited for this mission was the Central Intelligence Agency.[56]

In late October 1954, the Project Three panel discussed the CL-282 system concept with DCI Allen Dulles and the Secretary of the Air Force's Special Assistant for Research and Development, Trevor Gardner. Dulles was reluctant to have the CIA undertake the project. He did not like to involve the CIA with military projects, even ones that the military had rejected, like the CL-282. Furthermore, the DCI strongly believed that the Agency's mission lay in the use of human operatives and secret communications, the classic forms of intelligence gathering. Land came away from this meeting with the impression that Dulles somehow thought overflights were not fair

---

[55] Land interview (TS Codeword).
[56] Land interview (TS Codeword); Baker interview (S).

play. Project Three committee members were nevertheless convinced that technology, particularly in the form of the CL-282 and the new camera designs, would solve the nation's intelligence problems.[57]

A Meeting with the President
Allen Dulles's reluctance to involve the CIA in the CL-282 project did not stop the Project Three committee from pursuing its aims because it was able to go over Dulles's head and appeal directly to the President. Having participated in the BEACON HILL Study and the Intelligence Systems Panel, several Project Three members had definite ideas on how to improve intelligence collection, ideas that they were determined to present to the highest levels of government. They were able to do so because the Land committee was part of a panel commissioned by President Eisenhower to examine the nation's intelligence community and recommend changes. The committee thus had a direct line to the White House through James Killian's contacts there.

Early in November 1954, Land and Killian met with President Eisenhower to discuss high-altitude reconnaissance. Killian's memoirs contain an account of this crucial meeting:

Land described the [CL-282] system using an unarmed plane and recommended that its development be undertaken. After listening to our proposal and asking many hard questions, Eisenhower approved the development of the system, but he stipulated that it should be handled in an unconventional way so that it would not become entangled in the bureaucracy of the Defense Department or troubled by rivalries among the services.[58]

---

[57] Land interview (TS Codeword).

[58] Killian, *Sputnik, Scientists, and Eisenhower*, p. 82. The exact date of the meeting cannot be determined, but it occurred during the first half of November 1954.

The scientists from the advisory committees and the President were thus in agreement that the new reconnaissance program should be controlled by the CIA, not the military.

CIA and Air Force Agreement on the CL-282

Meanwhile Edwin Land and his Project Three colleagues were working to convince Allen Dulles that the CIA should run the proposed overflight program. On 5 November Land wrote to the DCI strongly urging that the CIA undertake the CL-282 project:

> *Here is the brief report from our panel telling why we think overflight is urgent and presently feasible. I [Land] am not sure that we have made it clear that we feel there are many reasons why this activity is appropriate for CIA, always with Air Force assistance. We told you that this seems to us the kind of action and technique that is right for the contemporary version of CIA: a modern and scientific way for an Agency that is always supposed to be looking, to do its looking. Quite strongly, we feel that you must always assert your first right to pioneer in scientific techniques for collecting intelligence—and choosing such partners to assist you as may be needed. This present opportunity for aerial photography seems to us a fine place to start.*[59]

The letter had two attachments: a two-page summary of a complete operational plan for organizing, building, and deploying the CL-282 within a period of 20 months at a cost of $22 million and a three-page memorandum, entitled "A Unique Opportunity for Comprehensive Intelligence."

---

[59] Letter, Project Three Panel to DCI Allen F. Dulles, 5 November 1954, in *OSA History*, chap. 1, annex 1 (TS Codeword).

Aware of Dulles's preference for classical intelligence work, the Project Three memorandum stressed the superiority of the CL-282 program over traditional espionage methods:

> *We believe that these planes can go where we need to have them go efficiently and safely, and that no amount of fragmentary and indirect intelligence can be pieced together to be equivalent to such positive information as can thus be provided.*[60]

The Land committee memorandum also stressed the need for the CIA to undertake such reconnaissance missions rather than the Air Force, noting that "For the present it seems rather dangerous for one of our military arms to engage directly in extensive overflight." The committee members also listed the advantages of using the CL-282 rather than an Air Force aircraft:

> *The Lockheed super glider will fly at 70,000 feet, well out of the reach of present Russian interceptors and high enough to have a good chance of avoiding detection. The plane itself is so light (15,000 pounds), so obviously unarmed and devoid of military usefulness, that it would minimize affront to the Russians even if through some remote mischance it were detected and identified.*[61]

One additional advantage of the Lockheed design over the Air Force's proposed high-altitude reconnaissance aircraft was a faster completion time. Kelly Johnson had promised the Land committee

---

[60] Memorandum for DCI Allen F.Dulles from Project Three Panel, "A Unique Opportunity for Comprehensive Intelligence," 5 November 1954, p.3 (TS, downgraded to S) in *OSA History*, chap.1, annex 1 (TS Codeword).
[61] Ibid.

that his aircraft would be flying by August 1955, just eight months after he proposed to start construction. The Bell X-16 prototype was not scheduled for completion before the spring of 1956.

The strong advocacy of Killian and the other scientists on the various advisory committees concerned with overhead reconnaissance, combined with President Eisenhower's support, finally won over DCI Dulles, but a project of this magnitude also required the support of the Air Force. Some Air Force officials, however, feared that a decision to build the CL-282 might jeopardize the Air Force's own RB-57 and X-16 projects. Just one month earlier, in October 1954, the Wright Air Development Command had appealed to the Air Force Deputy Chief of Staff for Development, Lt. Gen. Donald L. Putt, to oppose the adoption of the Lockheed design. The officials argued that the Bell X-16 was a better design because it was more airworthy than the CL-282 and could be used throughout the Air Force in different types of missions because it had two engines, wheels, and an armor-plated, pressurized pilot's compartment. If J57 engines were diverted to the CL-282, the appeal to General Putt warned, there would not be enough of these popular powerplants to meet the needs of the X-16 program.[62]

Having heard of the Wright Air Development Command attack on the CL-282, Allen Donovan of the Intelligence Systems Panel met with General Putt on 19 October to argue in favor of the Lockheed design. This discussion led General Putt to meet with 15 scientists from the Technological Capabilities Panel on 18 November 1954 to discuss the merits of the four proposed reconnaissance aircraft. Also present as a briefer was Maj. John Seaberg from the Wright Air Development Command, who later recalled:

What I did was present the results of my comparative analysis of all four designs. I showed the relative high

---

[62] Donovan interview (S).

> *altitude performance capabilities of all four. I pointed*
> *out that aerodynamically the Bell, Fairchild, and Lock-*
> *heed designs were close. Martin's B-57, being a mod-*
> *ification, was not quite as capable. I stated that, in my*
> *opinion, the J73 [General Electric engine] would not*
> *be good enough to do the job in Johnson's airplane.*
> *And further, I overlaid a curve showing that with the*
> *J57 [Pratt & Whitney engine] installed, it would then*
> *be competitive with the Bell and Fairchild designs.*[63]

This meeting—along with the knowledge that President Eisenhower also supported the CL-282—helped win over the Air Force. To be on the safe side, however, the Air Force did not abandon the X-16 program until the Lockheed aircraft had begun flying.

On 19 November, the day after Seaberg's briefing, the final decision on the CL-282 came at a luncheon hosted by Air Force Secretary Talbott. The participants—Dulles and Cabell from the CIA; Gardner, Ayer, and General Putt from the Air Force; Kelly Johnson; and Edwin Land—all agreed "that the special item of material described by Lockheed was practical and desirable and would be sought....It was agreed that the Project should be a joint Air Force–CIA one but that, regardless of the source of the funds, whether AF or CIA, CIA unvouchered channels would be needed to pass the funds."[64]

It is interesting to note that Lockheed, which had originally developed the CL-282 on its own and had devoted considerable effort to promoting it, had to be persuaded to undertake the project in November 1954 because the company had become heavily committed to several other civilian and military projects. When Kelly Johnson received a call from Trevor Gardner on 17

---

[63] Quoted in Miller, *Lockheed U-2*, p. 13.
[64] Charles Pearre Cabell, Memorandum for the Record, "Luncheon Meeting with the Secretary of the Air Force," 19 November 1954, in *OSA History,* chap. 2, annex 4 (TS Codeword).

November asking him to come to Washington for conversations on the project, his instructions from Lockheed's senior management were "to not commit to any program during the visit, but to get the information and return." When he returned to California, Johnson noted in his project log that "I was impressed with the secrecy aspect and was told by Gardner that I was essentially being drafted for the project. It seemed, in fact, that if I did not talk quietly, I might have to take a leave of absence from my job at Lockheed to do this special project."[65] Of course, Kelly Johnson did not need to be drafted or persuaded into undertaking such a bold step forward in aircraft design. He used Gardner's statement to convince Lockheed's senior management to approve the project, which they did after meeting with Johnson when he returned to California on the evening of 19 November.

Four days later, on 23 November, the Intelligence Advisory Committee (IAC) approved DCI Dulles's request to undertake the CL-282 project. The following day Dulles signed a three-page memorandum, drafted by DDCI Cabell, asking President Eisenhower to approve the overhead reconnaissance project. That same afternoon, at a meeting attended by the Secretaries of State and Defense and senior Air Force officials, Dulles and Cabell presented the document to the President and received verbal authorization to proceed. Eisenhower told Dulles that the project was to be managed by the Agency and that the Air Force was to provide any assistance needed to get it operational.[66]

---

[65] Johnson, "Log for Project X," 17 and 19 November 1954.

[66] Charles Pearre Cabell, Memorandum for the Record, "Meeting at the White House," 24 November 1954 in *OSA History,* chap. 2, annex 8 (TS Codeword); Beschloss, *Mayday,* pp. 82-83; Andrew J. Goodpaster, Memorandum of Conference with the President, 24 November 1954, White House Office of the Staff Secretary, Alpha Series, Dwight D. Eisenhower Library (hereafter cited as WHOSS, Alpha, DDEL) (TS, declassified).

Thus, it was that the CIA entered into the world of high technology primarily because of decisions and actions taken outside the Agency: the Air Force's refusal to build the CL-282 aircraft, President Eisenhower's desire to have a sensitive overflight project conducted by a civilian agency rather than the military, and, above all, the determination by a small group of prominent scientists that the Lockheed design represented the best possible overhead reconnaissance system.[67]

---

[67] Scientists remained active in advising the government on overhead reconnaissance. In February 1955, the Technological Capabilities Panel issued its final report, which strongly urged the use of technology to gather intelligence. President Eisenhower strongly backed the panel's findings and directed government agencies to respond to the recommendations by June. The CIA's most important reaction to the Technological Capabilities Panel report was to create its own Scientific Advisory Board composed of the members of the Project Three Study Group with the addition of James Killian and Jerome B. Wiesner, professor of electrical engineering at MIT. Edwin Land served as chairman of the CIA Scientific Advisory Board for the next 10 years, and it soon became known unofficially as the Land Panel. This panel provided important advice to the Agency, particularly in the field of overhead reconnaissance.

President Eisenhower also acted to increase the amount and quality of scientific advice he was receiving. In January 1956 he established the President's Board of Consultants on Foreign Intelligence Activities (renamed the President's Foreign Intelligence Advisory Board in 1961) to oversee the intelligence community and advise him on intelligence matters. The board's first chairman was James Killian. In 1957 the President reorganized and upgraded the Office of Defense Mobilization's Science Advisory Committee, which became the President's Science Advisory Committee. He also named James Killian to be the first Special Assistant to the President for Science and Technology. In this new position Killian served as the President's scientific advisor and the chairman of the President's Scientific Advisoty Committee (Killian stepped down as chairman of the President's Board of Consultants on Foreign Intelligence Activities but remained a member). These actions by the President brought scientists into the White House and gave them considerable influence.

2

Developing the U-2

THE ESTABLISHMENT OF THE U-2 PROJECT

On 26 November 1954, the day after Thanksgiving, Allen Dulles called his special assistant, Richard Bissell, into his office to tell him that President Eisenhower had just approved a very secret program and that Dulles wanted Bissell to take charge of it. Saying it was too secret for him to explain, Dulles gave Bissell a packet of documents and told him he could keep it for several days to acquaint himself with the project. Bissell had long known of the proposal to build a high-altitude reconnaissance aircraft, but only in the most general terms. Now he learned in detail about the project that proposed sending aircraft over the Soviet Union.

Late on the morning of 2 December 1954, Dulles told Bissell to go to the Pentagon on the following day to represent the Agency at an organizational meeting for the U-2[1] project. Before leaving, Bissell asked Dulles which agency was to run the project. The DCI replied that nothing had been clearly decided. Bissell then asked who was going to pay for the project. Dulles answered: "That wasn't even mentioned. You'll have to work that out."[2]

---

[1] Although the Lockheed CL-282 was not designated as the U-2 until July 1955, this study will use the more widely known designator to avoid confusion.
[2] Bissell interview (S); *OSA History,* chap. 3, p. 1 (TS Codeword).

Bissell was accompanied by Herbert I. Miller, chief of the Office of Scientific Intelligence's Nuclear Energy Division, who soon became the executive officer of the overflight project. When Bissell and Miller arrived at the Pentagon on the afternoon of 3 December, they sat down with a group of key Air Force officials that included Trevor Gardner and Lt. Gen. Donald L. Putt. The participants spent very little time delineating Air Force and Agency responsibilities in the project, taking for granted that the CIA would handle the security matters. Much of the discussion centered on methods for diverting Air Force materiel to the program, particularly the Pratt & Whitney J57 engines, because a separate contract for the engines might jeopardize the project's security. The Air Force promised to turn over a number of J57 engines, which were then being produced for B-52s, KC-135s, F-100s, and RB-57s. Eventually Bissell asked who was going to pay for the airframes to be built by Lockheed. His query was greeted with silence. Everyone present had their eyes on him because they all expected the Agency to come up with the funds. Bissell rose from his chair, said he would see what he could do, and the meeting adjourned.[3]

After the meeting, Bissell told Dulles that the CIA would have to use money from the Contingency Reserve Fund to get the project going. The DCI used this fund to pay for covert activities, following approval by the President and the Director of the Budget. Dulles told Bissell to draft a memorandum for the President on funding the overflight program and to start putting together a staff for Project AQUATONE, the project's new codename.

At first the new "Project Staff" (renamed the Development Projects Staff in April 1958) consisted of Bissell, Miller, and the small existing staff in Bissell's Office of the Special Assistant to

---

[3] *OSA History,* chap. 3, p. 2 (TS Codeword); Bissell interview, 8 November 1984 (S); Beschloss, *Mayday,* p. 89.

Project AQUATONE Personnel

Special Assistant to the DCI for Planning and Coordination

Headquarters
CIA   18
USAF   7
       25

US Field Test Base
CIA   26
       26

Foreign Field Base A
CIA   16
USAF   34
Contract 52
          102

Foreign Field Base B
CIA   16
USAF   34
Contract 52
          102

Foreign Field Base C
CIA   16
USAF   34
Contract 52
          102

Total employees: CIA   92
                  USAF   109
                  Contract 156
                            357

the DCI. During the months that followed the establishment of the project, its administrative workload increased rapidly, and in May 1955 the project staff added an administrative officer, James A. Cunningham, Jr., a former Marine Corps pilot then working in the Directorate of Support. Cunningham stayed with the U-2 project for the next 10 years. Two other key project officials who began their duties early in 1955 were [redacted] the finance officer, and [redacted] the contracting officer.[4]

During the first half of 1955, the project staff grew slowly; many of the individuals working on overhead reconnaissance remained on the rolls of other Agency components. To achieve maximum security, Bissell made the project staff self-sufficient. Project AQUATONE had its own contract management, administrative, financial, logistic, communications, and security personnel, and, thus, did not need to turn to the Agency directorates for assistance. Funding for Project AQUATONE was also kept separate from other Agency components; its personnel and operating costs were not paid out of regular Agency accounts. As approving officer for the project, Richard Bissell could obligate funds in amounts up to $100,000; larger sums required the DCI's approval.[5]

At the end of April 1955, Bissell's staff developed, and the Deputy Director for Support approved, the first table of organization for Project AQUATONE. Once operational, the project would have a total of 357 personnel divided among project headquarters, a US testing facility, and three foreign field bases. CIA employees represented only one-fourth (92) of the total. The Air Force personnel commitment was larger, with 109 positions on the 1955 table of organization (this total does not include many

---

[4] *OSA History,* chap. 3, pp. 6-7, chap. 4, pp. 1-2, chap. 5, pp. 27-29 (TS Codeword); *Chronology of the Office of Special Activities, 1954-1968,* (CIA: DS&T, 1969), p. 2-4 (TS Codeword) (hereafter cited as *OSA Chronology*).
[5] *OSA History,* chap. 3, pp. 5-7 (TS Codeword).

other Air Force personnel, such as SAC meteorologists, who supported the U-2 project in addition to their other duties). The largest Project AQUATONE category was contract employees, with 156 positions in 1955. This category included maintenance and support personnel from Lockheed (five per aircraft), the pilots, and support personnel from other contractors for items such as photographic equipment.[6]

The first project headquarters was in CIA's Administration (East) Building at 2430 E Street, NW. Continued growth caused the AQUATONE staff to move several times during its first two years. On 1 May 1955, the project staff moved to the third floor of a small red brick building (the Briggs School) at 2210 E Street, NW. Then on 3 October, the staff moved to Wings A and C of Quarters Eye, a World War II "temporary" building on Ohio Drive, NW, in the West Potomac Park area of Washington. On 25 February 1956, the project staff moved again, this time to the fifth floor of the Matomic Building at 1717 H Street, NW. Here the staff remained for the next six years until it moved into the new CIA Headquarters building at Langley in March 1962. The final move came in January 1968, when the project staff (by that time known as the Office of Special Activities) moved to the [redacted].[7]

Bissell reported directly to the DCI, although in reality the DDCI, Gen. Charles Pearre Cabell, was much more closely involved in the day-to-day affairs of the overhead reconnaissance project. Cabell's extensive background in Air Force intelligence, particularly in overhead reconnaissance, made him ideally qualified to oversee the U-2 project. Cabell frequently attended White House meetings on the U-2 for the DCI.

---

[6] Project AQUATONE, Table of Organization, 28 April 1955 in *OSA History,* chap. 3, annex 15 (TS Codeword).

[7] *OSA History,* chap. 18, pp. 7-8 (TS Codeword); *OSA Chronology,* pp. 4, 7, 10, 45 (TS Codeword).

FUNDING ARRANGEMENTS FOR PROJECT AQUATONE
Although Allen Dulles had approved the concept of covert funding for the reconnaissance project, many financial details remained to be settled, including the contract with Lockheed. Nevertheless, work on the U-2 began as soon as the project was authorized. Between 29 November and 3 December 1954, Kelly Johnson pulled together a team of 25 engineers, which was not easy because he had to take them off other Lockheed projects without being able to explain why to their former supervisors. The engineers immediately began to work 45 hours a week on the project. The project staff gradually expanded to a total of 81 personnel, and the workweek soon increased to 65 hours.[8]

Kelly Johnson's willingness to begin work on the aircraft without a contract illustrates one of the most important aspects of this program: the use of unvouchered funds for covert procurement. Lockheed was well acquainted with the covert procurement process, having previously modified several aircraft for covert use by the CIA.

Covert funding for sensitive projects simplifies both procurement and security procedures because the funds are not attributable to the Federal Government and there is no public accountability for their use. Public Law 110, approved by the 81st Congress on 20 June 1949, designates the Director of Central Intelligence as the only government employee who can obligate Federal money without the use of vouchers. By using unvouchered funds, it is possible to eliminate competitive bidding and thereby limit the number of parties who know about a given project. The use of unvouchered funds also speeds up the Federal procurement cycle. A general contractor such as Lockheed can purchase much, if not all, of the supplies needed for a project without resorting at each

---

[8] Johnson, "Log for Project X," 29 November-3 December 1954 (U).

step to the mandated procurement procedures involving public, competitive bidding. [Redacted].

In mid-December 1954, President Eisenhower authorized DCI Dulles to use $35 million from the Agency's Contingency Reserve Fund to finance the U-2 project. Then on 22 December 1954, the Agency signed a letter contract with Lockheed, using the codename Project OARFISH. The Agency had proposed to give Lockheed "performance specifications" rather than the standard Air Force "technical specifications," which were more rigid and demanding, and Kelly Johnson agreed that such a move would save a lot of money. Lockheed's original proposal to the Air Force in May 1954 had been $28 million for 20 U-2s equipped with GE J73 engines. During negotiations with CIA General Counsel Lawrence R. Houston, Lockheed changed its proposal to $26 million for 20 airframes plus a two-seat trainer model and spares; the Air Force was to furnish the engines. Houston insisted that the Agency could only budget $22.5 million for the airframes because it needed the balance of the available $35 million for cameras and life-support gear. The two sides finally agreed on a fixed-price contract with a provision for a review three-fourths of the way through to determine if the costs were going to exceed the $22.5 million figure. The formal contract, No. SP-1913, was signed on 2 March 1955 and called for the delivery of the first U-2 in July 1955 and the last in November 1956. Meanwhile, to keep work moving at Lockheed, Richard Bissell wrote a check for $1,256,000 [redacted] and mailed it to Kelly Johnson's home on 21 February 1955.[9]

---

[9] John S. Warner, Office of the General Counsel, interview by Donald E. Welzenbach, Washington, DC, tape recording, 5 Aug 1983 (S); *OSA History*, chap. 5, pp. 1-2 and annex 42 (TS Codeword); Johnson, "Log for Project X," 21 February 1955.

As it turned out, no review of the contract was necessary at the three-fourths point. Lockheed delivered the aircraft not only on time but under budget. During the final contract negotiations in the spring of 1958, Lockheed and the US Government agreed on a price for the original 20 aircraft of $17,025,542 plus a profit of $1,952,055 for a total of $18,977,597—less than $1 million for each aircraft. Because its design was based on Lockheed's F-104, the U-2 was relatively inexpensive even though only a small number of aircraft had been ordered. Only the wings and tail were unique; Lockheed manufactured the other portions of the aircraft using the F-104's jigs and dies.

MAJOR DESIGN FEATURES OF THE U-2

Aware of the great need for secrecy in the new project, Kelly Johnson placed it in Lockheed's Advanced Development facility at Burbank, California, known as the Skunk Works.[10] Lockheed had established this highly secure area in 1945 to develop the nation's first jet aircraft, the P-80 Shooting Star. The small Skunk Works staff began making the detailed drawings for the U-2, which was nicknamed the "Angel" because it was to fly so high.

Kelly Johnson's approach to prototype development was to have his engineers and draftsmen located not more than 50 feet from the aircraft assembly line. Difficulties in construction were immediately brought to the attention of the engineers, who gathered the mechanics around the drafting tables to discuss ways to overcome the difficulties. As a result, engineers were generally able to fix problems in the design in a matter of hours, not days or weeks. There was no emphasis placed on producing neatly typed memorandums; engineers simply made pencil

---

[10] The Lockheed "Skunk Works" was named after the Kickapoo Joy Juice factory known as the "Skonk Works" in Al Capp's comic strip *Li'l Abner.*

notations on the engineering drawings in order to keep the project moving quickly.[11]

. A little more than a week after he had been authorized to begin the project, Kelly Johnson wrote a 23-page report detailing his most recent ideas on the U-2 proposal. The aircraft, he explained, would be designed to meet load factors of only 2.5 g's, which was the limit for transport aircraft rather than combat planes. The U-2 would have a speed of Mach 0.8 or 460 knots at altitude. Its initial maximum altitude would be 70,600 feet and the ultimate maximum altitude would be 73,100 feet. According to these early December 1954 specifications, the new plane would take off at 90 knots, land at 76 knots, and be able to glide 244 nautical miles from an altitude of 70,000 feet. After discussing the reconnaissance bay with James Baker, Johnson had worked out various equipment combinations that would not exceed the weight limit of 450 pounds. Johnson ended his report by promising the first test flight by 2 August 1955 and the completion of four aircraft by 1 December 1955. [12]

In designing the U-2 aircraft, Kelly Johnson was confronted with two major problems—fuel capacity and weight. To achieve intercontinental range, the aircraft had to carry a large supply of fuel, yet, it also had to be light enough to attain the ultrahigh altitudes needed to be safe from interception. Although the final product resembled a typical jet aircraft, its construction was unlike any other US military aircraft. One unusual design feature was the tail assembly, which—to save weight—was attached to the main body with just three tension bolts. This feature had been adapted from sailplane designs.

---

[11] Ben A. Rich (current head of the "Skunk Works"), interview by Donald E. Welzenbach and Gregory W. Pedlow, Burbank, California, 26 August 1988.
[12] Kelly Johnson, "A High-Altitude Reconnaissance Aircraft," 9 December 1954, Lockheed Contract Files, OSA Records (S).

The wings were also unique. Unlike conventional aircraft, whose main wing spar passes through the fuselage to give the wings continuity and strength, the U-2 had two separate wing panels, which were attached to the fuselage sides with tension bolts (again, just as in sailplanes). Because the wing spar did not pass through the fuselage, Johnson was able to locate the camera behind the pilot and ahead of the engine, thereby improving the aircraft's center of gravity and reducing its weight.

The wings were the most challenging design feature of the entire airplane. Their combination of high-aspect ratio and low-drag ratio (in other words, the wings were long, narrow, and thin) made them unique in jet aircraft design. The wings were actually integral fuel tanks that carried almost all of the U-2's fuel supply.

The fragility of the wings and tail section, which were only bolted to the fuselage, forced Kelly Johnson to look for a way to protect the aircraft from gusts of wind at altitudes below 35,000 feet, which otherwise might cause the aircraft to disintegrate. Johnson again borrowed from sailplane designs to devise a "gust control" mechanism that set the ailerons and horizontal stabilizers into a position that kept the aircraft in a slightly nose-up attitude, thereby avoiding sudden stresses caused by wind gusts. Nevertheless, the U-2 remained a very fragile aircraft that required great skill and concentration from its pilots.

The final major design feature was the lightweight, bicycle-type landing gear. The entire structure—a single oleostrut with two lightweight wheels toward the front of the aircraft and two small, solid-mount wheels under the tail—weighed only 208 pounds yet could withstand the force of touchdown for this 7-ton aircraft. Because both sets of wheels were located underneath the fuselage, the U-2 was also equipped with detachable pogos (long, curved sticks with two small wheels on them) on each wing to keep the wings level during takeoff. The pilot would drop the pogos immediately after takeoff so that they could be recovered and reused. The aircraft landed on its front and back landing gear and then gradually tilted over onto one of the wingtips, which were equipped with landing skids.[13]

THE DEVELOPMENT OF THE CAMERA SYSTEM

By December 1954, Kelly Johnson was at work on drawings for the U-2's airframe and Pratt & Whitney was already building the J57 jet engine, but no firm plans existed for the all-important cameras. Existing cameras were too bulky and lacked sufficient resolution to be used in high-altitude reconnaissance.

The workhorses of World War II aerial photography had been the Fairchild K-19 and K-21 framing cameras with lenses of varying focal lengths from 24 to 40 inches. Late in the war, the trimetrogon K-17 mapping-camera system came into use. This system consisted of three separate cameras which made three photographs simultaneously: a vertical, an oblique to the left, and an oblique to the right. The major shortcomings of the trimetrogon system were the large amount of film required and the system's lack of sharp definition on the obliques.

The standard aerial cameras available in the early 1950s could achieve resolutions of about 20 to 25 feet (7 to 8 meters) on a side when used at an altitude of 33,000 feet (10,000 meters), or about 25 lines per millimeter in current terms of reference. Such resolution was considered adequate because aerial photography was then used primarily to choose targets for strategic bombing, to assess bomb damage after air raids, and to make maps and charts. Unfortunately, a camera with a resolution of only 20 to 25 feet at a height of 33,000 feet was too crude to be used at twice that altitude. Indeed, for intelligence purposes a resolution of less

---

[13] For the design features of the U-2 in early 1955, see R. F. Boehme, *Summary Report: Reconnaissance Aircraft,* Lockheed Aircraft Corporation Report 10420, 28 January 1955, pp. 7-9, OSA Records, Job 74-B-645, box 1 (S).

than 10 feet was necessary to discern smaller targets in greater detail. This meant that any camera carried to altitudes above 68,000 feet had to be almost four times as good as existing aerial cameras in order to achieve a resolution of less than 10 feet. As a result, some scientists doubted that useful photography could be obtained from altitudes higher than 40,000 feet.[14]

The first success in designing very-high-acuity lenses came in the mid-1940s, when James G. Baker of Harvard and Richard S. Perkin of the Perkin-Elmer (P-E) Company of Norwalk, Connecticut, collaborated on a design for an experimental camera for the Army Air Force. They developed a 48-inch focal-length scanning camera that was mounted in a modified B-36 bomber. When tested over Fort Worth, Texas, at 34,000 feet, the new camera produced photographs in which two golf balls on a putting green could be distinguished (in reality, however, the "golf balls" were 3 inches in diameter). These photographs demonstrated the high acuity of Baker's lens, but the camera weighed more than a ton and was much too large to be carried aloft in an aircraft as small as the U-2.

Realizing that size and weight were the major restraining factors in developing a camera for the U-2, James Baker began working on a radically new system in October 1954, even before the CIA adopted the Lockheed proposal. Baker quickly recognized, however, that he would need almost a year to produce a working model of such a complex camera. Since Kelly Johnson had promised to have a U-2 in the air within eight months, Baker needed to find an existing camera that could be used until the new camera was ready. After consulting with his friend and colleague Richard Perkin, Baker decided to adapt for the U-2 an Air Force camera known as the K-38, a 24-inch aerial framing camera built by the Hycon Manufacturing Company of Pasadena, California.

---

[14] Baker interview (S).

Perkin suggested modifying several standard K-38 cameras in order to reduce their weight to the U-2's 450-pound payload limit. At the same time, Baker would make critical adjustments to existing K-38 lenses to improve their acuity. Baker was able to do this in a few weeks, so several modified K-38s, now known as A-1 cameras, were ready when the first "Angel" aircraft took to the air in mid-1955.[15]

CIA awarded Hycon a contract for the modified K-38 cameras, and Hycon, in turn, subcontracted to Perkin-Elmer to provide new lenses and to make other modifications to the cameras in order to make them less bulky. In its turn, Perkin-Elmer subcontracted to Baker to rework the existing K-38 lenses and later design an improved lens system. To keep his lens-designing efforts separate from his research associate duties at Harvard and his service on government advisory bodies, Baker established a small firm known as Spica, Incorporated, on 31 January 1955.

The A-1 camera system consisted of two 24-inch K-38 framing cameras. One was mounted vertically and photographed a 17.2° swath beneath the aircraft onto a roll of 9.5-inch film. The second K-38 was placed in a rocking mount so that it alternately photographed the left oblique and right oblique out to 36.5° onto separate rolls of 9.5-inch film. The film supplies unwound in opposite directions in order to minimize their effect on the balance of the aircraft. Both cameras used standard Air Force 24-inch focal-length lenses adjusted for maximum acuity by Baker. The development of the special rocking mount by Perkin-Elmer's Dr. Roderic M. Scott was a major factor in reducing the size and weight of the A-1 system, because the mount provided broad transverse coverage with a single lens, ending the need for two separate cameras.[16]

---

[15] Ibid.

[16] *OSA History*, chap. 1, annex 3, pp. 1-3 (TS Codeword).

U-2s equipped with the A-1 camera system also carried a Perkin-Elmer tracking camera using 2.75-inch film and a 3-inch lens. This device made continuous horizon-to-horizon photographs of the terrain passing beneath the aircraft. Because the A-1 system was new, it also included a backup camera system, a K-17 6-inch three-camera trimetrogon unit using 9-inch film.

While the A-1 system was still being developed, James Baker was already working on the next generation of lenses for high-altitude reconnaissance. Baker was a pioneer in using computers to synthesize optical systems. His software algorithms made it possible to model lens designs and determine in advance the effects that variations in lens curvatures, glass compounds, and lens spacings would have on rays of light passing through a lens. These "ray-tracing" programs required extensive computations, and for this he turned to the most modern computer available, an IBM CPC (card-programmed calculator) installation at nearby Boston University.[17]

Baker's new lenses were used in a camera system known as the A-2, which returned to a trimetrogon arrangement because of problems with the A-1 system's rocking mount. The A-2 consisted of three separate K-38 framing cameras and 9.5-inch film magazines. One K-38 filmed the right oblique, another the vertical, and a third the left oblique. The A-2 system also included a 3-inch tracking camera. All A-2 cameras were equipped with the new 24-inch f/8.0 Baker-designed lenses. These were the first relatively large photographic objective lenses to employ several aspheric surfaces. James Baker personally ground these surfaces and made the final bench tests on each lens before releasing it to the Agency. These lenses were able to resolve 60 lines per millimeter, a 240-percent improvement over existing lenses.[18]

---

[17] Ibid., chap. 1, pp. 7-8 (TS Codeword).

[18] "Basic Configuration and Camera Data," 24 January 1956, OSA Records (TS Codeword); *OSA History,* chap. 5, annex 44 (TS Codeword).

Once Baker and Scott had redesigned the 24-inch lens for the K-38 devices, they turned their attention to Baker's new camera design, known as the B model. It was a totally new concept, a high-resolution panoramic-type framing camera with a much longer 36-inch f/10.0 aspheric lens. The B camera was a very complex device that used a single lens to obtain photography from one horizon to the other, thereby reducing weight by having two fewer lenses and shutter assemblies than the standard trimetrogon configuration. Because its lens was longer than those used in the A cameras, the B camera achieved even higher resolution—100 lines per millimeter.

The B camera used an 18- by 18-inch format, which was achieved by focusing the image onto two counterrotating but overlapping 9.5-inch wide strips of film. Baker designed this camera so that one film supply was located forward, the other aft. Thus, as the film supplies unwound, they counterbalanced each other and did not disturb the aircraft's center of gravity.

The B camera had two modes of operation. In mode I, the camera used a single lens to make seven unique exposures from 73.5° on the far right and far left obliques to vertical photos beneath the aircraft, effectively covering from horizon to horizon. Mode II narrowed the lateral coverage to 21.5° on either side of vertical. This increased the available number of exposures and almost doubled the camera's operating time. Three of the seven B-camera frames provided stereo coverage. The complex B cameras were engineered by Hycon's chief designer, William McFadden.[19]

James Baker's idea for the ultimate high-altitude camera was the C model that would have a 240-inch focal length. In December 1954, he made preliminary designs for folding the optical path using three mirrors, a prism, and an f/20.0 lens system. Before working out the details of this design, however, Baker flew to

---

[19] Ibid.; Baker interview (S).

California in early January 1955 to consult with Kelly Johnson about the weight and space limitations of the U-2's payload compartment. Despite every effort to reduce the physical dimensions of the C camera, Baker needed an additional six inches of payload space to accommodate the bigger lens. When he broached this subject to Johnson, the latter replied, "Six more inches? I'd sell my grandmother for six more inches!"[20]

Realizing that the 240-inch lens was both too large and too heavy for the camera bay, Baker scaled the lens down to a 200-inch f/16.0 system. This was still too big. Further reductions followed, resulting by July 1955 in a 120-inch f/10.9 lens that met both the weight and space limitations. Later in the year, Baker decided to make the mirrors for the system out of a new, lightweight foamed silica material developed by Pittsburgh-Corning Glass Company. This reduced the weight significantly, and he was able to scale up the lens to a 180-inch f/13.85 reflective system for a 13- by 13-inch format. In the past, the calculations for such a complex camera lens would have taken years to complete, but thanks to Baker's ray-tracing computer program, he was able to accomplish the task in just 16 days.

When a C camera built by Hycon was flight-tested on 31 January 1957, project engineers discovered that its 180-inch focal length, which was five times longer than that of the B camera, made the camera very sensitive to aircraft vibration and led to great difficulty in aiming the C camera from altitudes above 68,000 feet. The engineers, therefore, decided to shelve the camera. More than five years later, a redesigned C camera was employed during the Cuban Missile Crisis in October 1962, but the results were not very satisfactory.

The failure of the C camera design was not a serious setback to the high-altitude reconnaissance program, because the B

---

[20] Baker interview (S).

camera proved highly successful. Once initial difficulties with the film-transport system were overcome, the B camera became the workhorse of high-altitude photography. An improved version known as the B-2 is still in use. Both of the earlier A-model cameras were phased out after September 1958.

During the period when he was designing lenses for the CIA's overhead reconnaissance program, James Baker was also working on classified lens designs for the Air Force and unclassified designs for the Smithsonian Institution. To protect the security of Baker's work for the Agency, Herbert Miller of the Development Projects Staff told Baker to work on lenses for the U-2 in the open and not make any effort to classify the documents connected with the project. Miller believed that by not calling attention to the effort through the use of special security measures, the project could be completed faster and still not be compromised. This "hiding in the open" strategy proved very successful.[21]

In addition to the camera systems, the U-2 carried one other important item of optical equipment, a periscope. Designed by James Baker and built by Walter Baird of Baird Associates, the optical periscope helped pilots recognize targets beneath the aircraft and also proved to be a valuable navigational aid.[22]

PREPARATIONS FOR TESTING THE U-2

As work progressed in California on the airframe, in Connecticut on the engines, and in Boston on the camera system, the top officials of the Development Projects Staff flew to California and Nevada to search for a site where the aircraft could be tested safely and secretly. On 12 April 1955 Richard Bissell and Col. Osmund Ritland (the senior Air Force officer on the project staff) flew over

---

[21] Ibid.

[22] Information supplied by James Baker to Donald E. Welzenbach, 12 May 1986 (U).

Nevada with Kelly Johnson in a small Beechcraft plane piloted by Lockheed's chief test pilot, Tony LeVier. They spotted what appeared to be an airstrip by a salt flat known as Groom Lake, near the northeast corner of the Atomic Energy Commission's (AEC) Nevada Proving Ground. After debating about landing on the old airstrip, LeVier set the plane down on the lakebed, and all four walked over to examine the strip. The facility had been used during World War II as an aerial gunnery range for Army Air Corps pilots. From the air the strip appeared to be paved, but on closer inspection it turned out to have originally been fashioned from compacted earth that had turned into ankle-deep dust after more than a decade of disuse. If LeVier had attempted to land on the airstrip, the plane would probably have nosed over when the wheels sank into the loose soil, killing or injuring all of the key figures in the U-2 project.[23]

Bissell and his colleagues all agreed that Groom Lake would make an ideal site for testing the U-2 and training its pilots. Upon returning to Washington, Bissell discovered that Groom Lake was not part of the AEC proving ground. After consulting with Dulles, Bissell and Miller asked the Atomic Energy Commission to add the Groom Lake area to its real estate holdings in Nevada. AEC Chairman Adm. Lewis Strauss readily agreed, and President Eisenhower also approved the addition of this strip of wasteland, known by its map designation as Area 51, to the Nevada Test Site. The outlines of Area 51 are shown on current unclassified maps as a small rectangular area adjoining the northeast corner of the much larger Nevada Test Site. To make the new facility in the middle of nowhere sound more attractive to his workers, Kelly

---

[23] *OSA History,* chap. 8, pp. 1-2 (TS Codeword); Miller, *Lockheed U-2,* pp. 19-20.

Johnson called it the Paradise Ranch, which was soon shortened to the Ranch.[24]

Although the dry lakebed could have served as a landing strip, project managers decided that a paved runway was needed so that testing could also take place during the times when rain-water runoff from nearby mountains filled the lake (at such times the base acquired yet another unofficial name, Watertown Strip). By July 1955 the base was ready, and Agency, Air Force, and Lockheed personnel began moving in.

SECURITY FOR THE U-2 PROJECT

On 29 April 1955, Richard Bissell signed an agreement with the Air Force and the Navy (which at that time was also interested in the U-2) in which the services agreed that the CIA "assumed primary responsibility for all security" for the overhead recon-naissance project (AQUATONE). From this time on, the CIA has been responsible for the security of overhead programs. This responsibility has placed a heavy burden on the Office of Security for establishing procedures to keep large numbers of contracts untraceable to the Central Intelligence Agency. The Office of Security has also had to determine which contractor employees require security clearances and has had to devise physical secu-rity measures for the various manufacturing facilities. Keeping the U-2 and subsequent overhead systems secret has been a time-consuming and costly undertaking.[25]

The most important aspect of the security program for the U-2 project was the creation of an entire new compartmented sys-

---

[24] *OSA History,* chap. 8, pp. 2-6 (TS Codeword); Johnson, "Log for Proj-ect X," 25-29 April 1955; Clarence L. "Kelly" Johnson with Maggie Smith, *Kelly: More Than My Share of It All* (Washington, DC: Smithsonian Institute Press, 1985), p. 123.

[25] *OSA History*, chap. 7, pp. 4-6 (TS Codeword).

tem for the product of U-2 missions. Access to the photographs taken by the U-2 would be strictly controlled, which often limited the ability of CIA analysts to use the products of U-2 missions.

The terminology used to describe U-2 aircraft and pilots also played a part in maintaining the security of the overhead reconnaissance program. To reduce the chances of a security breach, the Agency always referred to its high-altitude aircraft as "articles," with each aircraft having its own "article number." Similarly, the pilots were always called "drivers." In cable traffic the aircraft were known as KWEXTRA-00 (the two-digit number identified the precise aircraft; these numbers were not related to the three-digit article numbers assigned by the factory). The pilots were referred to as KWGLITTER-00 (the two-digit number identified the precise pilot). Thus, even if a message or document about overflight activities fell into unfriendly hands, the contents would simply refer to codewords or at worst to "articles" and "drivers," giving no indication of the nature of the program.[26]

Even the aircraft's onboard equipment required the involvement of CIA security planners. Thus, when Kelly Johnson ordered altimeters from the Kollman Instrument Company, he specified that the devices had to be calibrated to 80,000 feet. This immediately raised eyebrows at Kollman because its instruments only went to 45,000 feet. Agency security personnel quickly briefed several Kollman officials and produced a cover story that the altimeters were to be used on experimental rocket planes.[27]

THE CIA–AIR FORCE PARTNERSHIP

At the initial interagency meetings to establish the U-2 program in December 1954, the participants did not work out a clear delineation of responsibilities between the CIA and the Air Force. They

---

[26] Information supplied by James Cunningham to Donald E Welzenbach (S).
[27] Ibid.

agreed only that the Air Force would supply the engines and the Agency would pay for the airframes and cameras. With a myriad of details still unsettled, CIA and Air Force representatives began to work on an interagency agreement that would assign specific responsibilities for the program. These negotiations proved difficult. Discussions on this subject between DCI Allen Dulles and Air Force Chief of Staff Nathan Twining began in March 1955. Twining wanted SAC, headed by Gen. Curtis E. LeMay, to run the project once the planes and pilots were ready to fly, but Dulles opposed such an arrangement. The CIA–USAF talks dragged on for several months, with Twining determined that SAC should have full control once the aircraft was deployed. Eventually President Eisenhower settled the dispute. "I want this whole thing to be a civilian operation," the President wrote. "If uniformed personnel of the armed services of the United States fly over Russia, it is an act of war—legally—and I don't want any part of it."[28]

With the issue of control over the program settled, the two agencies soon worked out the remaining details. On 3 August 1955, Dulles and Twining met at SAC headquarters in Omaha to sign the basic agreement, titled "Organization and Delineation of Responsibilities— Project OILSTONE" (OILSTONE was the Air Force codename for the project). This pact gave the Air Force responsibility for pilot selection and training, weather information, mission plotting, and operational support. The Agency was responsible for cameras, security, contracting, film processing, and arrangements for foreign bases, and it also had a voice in the selection of pilots. All aeronautical aspects of the project—the construction and testing of the aircraft—remained the exclusive province of Lockheed.[29]

As a result of this agreement, CIA remained in control of the program, but the Air Force played a very important role as

---

[28] *OSA History,* chap. 3, pp. 8-15 (TS Codeword); Beschloss, *Mayday,* pp. 105-107.
[29] *OSA History,* chap. 3, p. 15 and annex 14 (TS Codeword).

well. As Richard Bissell later remarked about the U-2 project, "The Air Force wasn't just in on this as a supporting element, and to a major degree it wasn't in on it just supplying about half the government personnel; but the Air Force held, if you want to be precise, 49 percent of the common stock."[30]

One of the first Air Force officers assigned to Project OIL-STONE was Col. Osmund J. Ritland. He began coordinating Air Force activities in the U-2 program with Richard Bissell in December 1954. On 27 June 1955, Ritland became Bissell's deputy, although Air Force Chief of Staff Twining did not officially approve this assignment until 4 August, the day after the signing of the CIA–Air Force agreement. In March 1956, Colonel Ritland returned to the Air Force and was followed as deputy project director by Col. Jack A. Gibbs.

Another Air Force officer, Lt. Col. Leo P. Geary, joined the program in June 1955 and remained with it until August 1966, longer than any of the other project managers. Using the Air Force Inspector General's office as cover with the title of Project Officer, AFCIG-5, Geary served as the focal point for all Defense Department support to the U-2 and OXCART programs. His 11 years with the overhead reconnaissance projects provided a high degree of Air Force continuity.[31]

TECHNICAL CHALLENGES TO HIGH-ALTITUDE FLIGHT

To get the U-2 aircraft ready to fly, Lockheed engineers had to solve problems never before encountered. Among these problems was the need for a fuel that would not boil off and evaporate

---

[30] Speech given by Richard Bissell at CIA Headquarters, 12 October 1965 (TS Codeword).

[31] Brig. Gen. Leo A. Geary (USAF-Ret.), interview by Donald E. Welzenbach, tape recording, 3 April 1986 (S); *OSA History,* chap. 3, p. 3 (TS Codeword).

at the very high altitudes for which the aircraft was designed. Gen. James H. Doolittle (USAF, Ret.), a vice president of the Shell Oil Company who had long been involved in overhead reconnaissance (most recently as a member of the Technological Capabilities Panel), arranged for Shell to develop a special low-volatility, low-vapor-pressure kerosene fuel for the craft. The result was a dense mixture, known as LF-1A, JP-TS (thermally stable), or JP-7, with a boiling point of 300°F at sea level. Manufacturing this special fuel required petroleum byproducts that Shell normally used to make its "Flit" fly and bug spray. In order to produce several hundred thousand gallons of LF-1A for the U-2 project in the spring and summer of 1955, Shell had to limit the production of Flit, causing a nationwide shortage. Because of the new fuel's density, it required special tanks and modifications to the aircraft's fuel-control and ignition systems.[32]

Even more important than the problem of boiling fuel was the problem of boiling blood, namely the pilot's. At altitudes above 65,000 feet, fluids in the human body will vaporize unless the body can be kept under pressure. Furthermore, the reduced atmospheric pressure placed considerable stress on the pilot's cardiovascular system and did not provide adequate oxygenation of the blood. Keeping the pilot alive at the extreme altitudes required for overflights therefore called for a totally different approach to environmental equipment; it required a system that could maintain pressure over much of the pilot's body. The technology that enabled U-2 pilots to operate for extended periods in reduced atmospheric pressure would later play a major role in the manned space program.

---

[32] Land interview (TS Codeword); Bissell interview (S); James A. Cunningham, Jr., interview by Donald E. Welzenbach, Washington, DC, tape recording, 4 October 1983 (TS Codeword).

Advising the Agency on high-altitude survival were two highly experienced Air Force doctors, Col. Donald D. Flickinger and Col. W. Randolph Lovelace, II. Dr. Lovelace had begun his research on high-altitude flight before World War II and was a coinventor of the standard Air Force oxygen mask. In the early 1950s, he and Flickinger made daring parachute jumps from B-47 bombers to test pilot-survival gear under extreme conditions. Flickinger served as the medical adviser to Project AQUATONE for almost a decade.[33]

Flickinger and Lovelace suggested that the Agency ask the David Clark Company of Worcester, Massachusetts, manufacturer of environmental suits for Air Force pilots, to submit designs for more advanced gear for the U-2 pilots. David Clark expert Joseph Ruseckas then developed a complex life-support system, which was the first partially pressurized "spacesuit" for keeping humans alive for lengthy periods at ultrahigh altitudes. The effort to provide a safe environment for pilots at high altitudes also involved the Firewel Company of Buffalo, New York, which pressurized the U-2 cockpit to create an interior environment equivalent to the air pressure at an altitude of 28,000 feet. The system was designed so that, if the interior cockpit pressure fell below the 28,000-feet level, the pilot's suit would automatically inflate. In either case, he could obtain oxygen only through his helmet.[34]

The early models of these MC-2 and MC-3 partial-pressure suits were very uncomfortable for the pilots. To prevent loss of pressure, the heavy coverall had to fit tightly at the wrists and ankles (in the early models of these suits, the feet were not included in the pressurization scheme). The pilot had to wear gloves and a heavy helmet that tended to chafe his neck and shoulders and was prone to fogging. Problems with the pilot

---

[33] *OSA History*, chap 10, pp. 29-34 (TS Codeword).
[34] Ibid., chap. 5, p. 19 (TS Codeword).

life-support system were believed to have been the cause of several early crashes of the U-2.

Having gotten a pilot into this bulky suit and shoehorned him into his seat in the cockpit, the next problem was how to get him out in an emergency. The U-2 cockpit was very small, and the early models did not have an ejection seat. Even after an ejection seat was installed, pilots were reluctant to use it because they were afraid they would lose their legs below the knees when they were blown out of the cockpit. To save weight, the first pilot's seat was extremely simple with no height adjustment mechanism. Designed for pilots of above-average height, the seat could be adjusted for shorter pilots by inserting wooden blocks beneath the seat to raise it. In later versions of the aircraft, Kelly Johnson added a fully adjustable seat.[35]

The Air Force undertook bailout experiments at high altitudes from balloons in the autumn of 1955 to determine if the suit designed for the U-2 pilot would also protect him during his parachute descent once he was separated from the life-support mechanisms inside the aircraft. To avoid getting the "bends" during such descents or during the long flights, pilots had to don their pressure suits and begin breathing oxygen at least 90 minutes before takeoff so that their bodies would have time to dissipate nitrogen. This procedure was known as prebreathing. Once the pilots were in their suits, eating and drinking became a major problem, as did urination. The first model of the pressure suit, used by Lockheed test pilots, made no provision for urination. A subsequent model required the pilot to be catheterized before donning his flying suit. This method of permitting urination during flight proved very uncomfortable and, by the autumn of 1955, was replaced with an external bladder arrangement that

---

[35] Lecture by Maj. Gen. Patrick J. Halloran (former Air Force U-2 pilot) at the National Air & Space Museum, 24 April 1986 (U).

made the catheter unnecessary. To reduce elimination, pilots ate a low-bulk, high-protein diet on the day before and the morning of each mission.

To prevent pilots from becoming dessicated during the long missions—a condition aggravated by their having to breathe pure oxygen—provision was made for them to drink sweetened water. This was accomplished by providing a small self-sealing hole in the face mask through which the pilot could push a strawlike tube attached to the water supply. Project personnel also pioneered in the development of ready-to-eat foods in squeezable containers. These were primarily bacon- or cheese-flavored mixtures that the pilot could squeeze into his mouth using the self-sealing hole in the face mask. Despite all these precautions, U-2 pilots normally lost 3 to 6 pounds of body weight during an eight-hour mission.[36]

Food and water were not the only items provided to pilots on overflight missions; they also received a suicide pill. During the early 1950s, tales of Soviet secret police torture of captured foreign agents led Bissell and Cunningham to approach Dr. Alex Batlin of Technical Services Division in the Directorate of Plans[37] for ideas to help "captured" U-2 pilots avoid such suffering. Batlin suggested the method used by Nazi war criminal Hermann Goering, a thin glass ampule containing liquid potassium cyanide. He said a pilot had only to put the ampule in his mouth and bite down on the glass; death would follow in 10 to 15 seconds.

---

[36] Information supplied by James Cunningham and former U-2 pilots Carmine Vito, Hervey Stockman, Jacob Kratt, and Glendon Dunaway to Donald E. Welzenbach, May 1986.

[37] At the time this Directorate was known as the Deputy Directorate/Plans, with the slash interpreted to mean either "for" or "of." Terminology for the major subdivisions of the CIA and their directors has varied over the past four decades. For the sake of consistency, all titles of Directorates and Deputy Directors have been placed in the current Agency format: the organization is known as the "Directorate of X" and the head is known as the "Deputy Director for X."

Project AQUATONE ordered six of the poison ampules, called L-pills, and offered one to each pilot just before a mission. It was up to each pilot to decide if he wanted to take an L-pill with him. Some did; most did not.[38]

DELIVERY OF THE FIRST U-2

On 25 July, less than eight months after the go-ahead call from Trevor Gardner, Kelly Johnson was ready to deliver the first aircraft, known as article 341, to the "Paradise Ranch" site. With its long, slender wings and tail assembly removed, the aircraft was wrapped in tarpaulins, loaded aboard a C-124, and flown to Groom Lake, where Lockheed mechanics spent the next six days readying the craft for its maiden flight.

Before "Kelly's Angel" could actually take to the air, however, it needed an Air Force designator. Col. Allman T. Culbertson from the Air Force's Office of the Director of Research and Development pointed this out to Lieutenant Colonel Geary in July 1955, and the two officers then looked through the aircraft designator handbook to see what the options were. They decided that they could not call the project aircraft a bomber, fighter, or transport plane, and they did not want anyone to know that the new plane was for reconnaissance, so Geary and Culbertson decided that it should come under the utility aircraft category. At the time, there were only two utility aircraft on the books, a U-1 and a U-3. Geary told Culbertson that the Lockheed CL-282 was going to be known officially as the U-2.[39]

Johnson had designed the U-2 to use the Pratt & Whitney (P&W) J57/P-31 engine, which developed 13,000 pounds of thrust and weighed 3,820 pounds, giving it a power-to-weight ratio of

---

[38] Information supplied by James Cunningham to Donald E. Welzenbach; Sayre Stevens, Memorandum for the Record, "Discussion with Dr. Alex Batlin Re Project MKNAOMI," July 1975 (S).

[39] Geary interview (S).

3.4:1. When the U-2 first took to the air, however, these engines were not available because the entire production was needed to power specially configured Canberra RB-57Ds for the Air Force. The first U-2s therefore used P&W J57/P-37 engines, which were 276 pounds heavier and delivered only 10,200 pounds of thrust at sea level; the resulting power-to-weight ratio of 2.7:1 was almost 20 percent less efficient than the preferred P-31 version.[40]

To conduct lengthy missions over hostile territory, the U-2 needed to carry a large amount of fuel. Kelly Johnson used a "wet-wing" design for the U-2, which meant that fuel was not stored in separate fuel tanks but rather in the wing itself. Each wing was divided into two leak-proof compartments, and fuel was pumped into all the cavities within these areas; only the outer 6 feet of the wings were not used for fuel storage. The U-2 also had a 100-gallon reserve tank in its nose. Later, in 1957, Johnson increased the fuel capacity of the U-2 by adding 100-gallon "slipper" tanks under each wing, projecting slightly ahead of the leading edge.

One of the most important considerations in the U-2's fuel system was the need to maintain aircraft trim as the fuel was consumed. The aircraft therefore contained a complex system of feed lines and valves draining to a central sump, which made it impossible to provide the pilot with an empty/full type of fuel gauge. None of the first 50 U-2s had normal fuel gauges. Instead there were mechanical fuel totalizer/counters. Before the start of a mission, the ground crew set the counters to indicate the total amount of fuel in the wings, and then a flow meter subtracted the gallons of fuel actually consumed during the flight. The pilot kept a log of the fuel consumption shown by the counters and compared it with estimates made by mission planners for each leg of the flight. As a double check, U-2 pilots also kept track of their fuel consumption by monitoring airspeed and time in the air. Most pilots became

---

[40] *OSA History,* chap. 8, p. 13 (TS Codeword).

quite expert at this. Several who did not came up short of their home base during the 20 years these planes were flown.[41]

INITIAL TESTING OF THE U-2

Preliminary taxi trials began on 27 July 1955, when the first run down the newly completed runway took the plane to 50 knots. Lockheed's chief test pilot, Tony LeVier, was at the controls. A second taxi trial followed on 1 August. LeVier accelerated to 70 knots and began to try the ailerons. "It was at this point that I became aware of being airborne," LeVier noted afterward, "which left me with utter amazement, as I had no intentions whatsoever of flying. I immediately started back toward the ground, but had difficulty determining my height because the lakebed had no markings to judge distance or height. I made contact with the ground in a left bank of approximately 10 degrees." The U-2 bounced back into the air, but LeVier was able to bring it back down for a second landing. He then applied the brakes with little effect, and the aircraft rolled for a long distance before coming to a stop.[42]

Bissell, Cunningham, and Johnson saw the aircraft fall and bounce. Leaping into a jeep, they roared off toward the plane. They signaled to LeVier to climb out and then used fire extinguishers to put out a fire in the brakes. At a debriefing session that followed, LeVier complained about the poor performance of the brakes and the absence of markings on the runway. Damage to the prototype U-2 was very minor: blown tires, a leaking oleostrut on the undercarriage, and damaged brakes. This unplanned flight

---

[41] Information supplied by Norman Nelson, former director of Lockheed's Skunk Works, to Donald E. Welzenbach, 14 March 1986 (U); Miller, *Lockheed U-2*, pp. 77, 96.

[42] Transcripts of the test pilots' and observers' comments on the initial U-2 test flights have been published in "Secret First Flight of Article 001," *Spyplanes* vol. 2, 1988, pp. 64-71, 82-85.

was but a foretaste of the airworthiness of the U-2. New pilots all had difficulty in getting the U-2's wheels on the ground because at low speeds it would remain in ground effect and glide effortlessly above the runway for great distances.

Taxi trials continued for one more day and were followed by the first planned flight on 4 August 1955. LeVier was again at the controls and had been instructed by Kelly Johnson to land the U-2 by making initial contact with the main or forward landing gear and letting the plane settle back on the rear wheel. LeVier had disagreed with this approach, believing that the U-2 would bounce if he tried to touch down on the forward gear first. After flying the aircraft up to 8,000 feet, LeVier leveled off and began cycling the landing gear up and down: then he tested the flaps and the plane's stability and control systems. Finally, LeVier made his first landing approach. As the U-2 settled down, the forward landing gear touched the runway and the plane skipped and bounced into the air. LeVier made a second attempt to land front wheels first, and again the plane bounded into the air. With Kelly Johnson watching from a chase plane and giving a constant stream of instructions, LeVier made three more unsuccessful landing attempts. With the light fading and a thunderstorm fast approaching from the mountains to the west, LeVier made one last approach using the method he had advocated: letting the aircraft touch on its rear wheel first. This time the U-2 made a near-perfect landing, which came just in the nick of time. Ten minutes later, the thunderstorm began dumping an unheard-of 2 inches of rain, flooding the dry lakebed and making the airstrip unusable.[43]

Now that the first problems in flying and landing the U-2 had been worked out, Kelly Johnson scheduled the "official" first flight for 8 August 1955. This time outsiders were present, including Richard Bissell, Col. Osmond Ritland, Richard Horner, and

---

[43] Ibid., pp. 21-22; Johnson, "Log for Project X," 4 August 1955.

Garrison Norton. The U-2 flew to 32,000 feet and performed very well. Kelly Johnson had met his eight-month deadline.[44]

LeVier made an additional 19 flights in article 341 before moving on to other Lockheed flight test programs in early September. This first phase of U-2 testing explored the craft's stall envelope, took the aircraft to its maximum stress limit (2.5 g's), and explored its speed potential. LeVier soon flew the aircraft at its maximum speed of Mach 0.85. Flight tests continued, with the U-2 ascending to altitudes never before attained in sustained flight. On 16 August LeVier took the aircraft up to 52,000 feet. In preparation for this flight, the 42-year-old test pilot completed the Air Force partial-pressure suit training program, becoming the oldest pilot to do so. Testing at even higher altitudes continued, and on 8 September the U-2 reached its initial design altitude of 65,600 feet.[45]

On 22 September 1955, the U-2 experienced its first flameout at 64,000 feet—more than 12 miles up. After a brief restart, the J57/ P-37 engine again flamed out at 60,000 feet, and the aircraft descended to 35,000 feet before the engine could be relit. Engineers from Pratt & Whitney immediately set to work on this problem. The P-37 model engine had significantly poorer combustion characteristics than the preferred but unavailable P-31 version and therefore tended to flame out at high altitudes. Combustion problems usually became apparent as the U-2 began the final part of its climb from 57,000 to 65,000 feet, causing pilots to refer to this area as the "badlands" or the "chimney." Flameouts bedeviled the U-2 project until sufficient numbers of the more powerful P-31 engines became available in the spring of 1956.[46]

Meanwhile, with the airworthiness of the U-2 airframe proven, Lockheed set up a production line in the Skunk Works,

---

[44] Johnson, "Log for Project X," 8 August 1955.

[45] *OSA Chronology,* p. 7 (TS Codeword); Miller, *Lockheed U-2,* p. 22.

[46] *OSA History*, chap. 8, pp. 12-14 (TS Codeword).

but delivery of even the second-choice J57/P-37 engines became a major problem. Pratt & Whitney's full production capacity for these engines for the next year was contracted to the Air Force for use in F-100 fighters and KC-135 tankers. Colonel Geary, with the help of a colleague in the Air Force Materiel Command, managed to arrange the diversion of a number of these engines from a shipment destined for Boeing's KC-135 production line, making it possible to continue building the U-2s.[47]

As the deliveries of U-2 airframes to the testing site increased, a major logistic problem arose: how to transfer Lockheed employees from Burbank to Area 51 without arousing a great deal of curiosity. The project staff decided that the simplest approach would be to fly the essential personnel to the site on Monday morning and return them to Burbank on Friday evening. Frequent flights were also necessary to bring in supplies and visitors from contractors and headquarters. Therefore, a regularly scheduled Military Air Transport Service (MATS) flight using a USAF C-54 aircraft began on 3 October 1955. James Cunningham promptly dubbed this activity "Bissell's Narrow-Gauge Airline." Less than seven weeks after it started, a MATS aircraft bound for Area 51 crashed on 17 November, killing all 14 persons aboard the plane, including the Project Security Officer, CIA's William H. Marr, four members of his staff, and personnel from Lockheed and Hycon. This crash represented the greatest single loss of life in the entire U-2 program.[48]

U-2s, UFOs, AND OPERATION BLUE BOOK

High-altitude testing of the U-2 soon led to an unexpected side effect—a tremendous increase in reports of unidentified flying objects (UFOs). In the mid-1950s, most commercial airliners flew

---

[47] Geary interview (S).

[48] *OSA History*, chap. 7, pp. 17-19 (TS Codeword).

at altitudes between 10,000 and 20,000 feet and military aircraft like the B-47s and B-57s operated at altitudes below 40,000 feet. Consequently, once U-2s started flying at altitudes above 60,000 feet, air-traffic controllers began receiving increasing numbers of UFO reports.

Such reports were most prevalent in the early evening hours from pilots of airliners flying from east to west. When the sun dropped below the horizon of an airliner flying at 20,000 feet, the plane was in darkness. But, if a U-2 was airborne in the vicinity of the airliner at the same time, its horizon from an altitude of 60,000 feet was considerably more distant, and, being so high in the sky, its silver wings would catch and reflect the rays of the sun and appear to the airliner pilot, 40,000 feet below, to be fiery objects. Even during daylight hours, the silver bodies of the high-flying U-2s could catch the sun and cause reflections or glints that could be seen at lower altitudes and even on the ground. At this time, no one believed manned flight was possible above 60,000 feet, so no one expected to see an object so high in the sky.

Not only did the airline pilots report their sightings to air-traffic controllers, but they and ground-based observers also wrote letters to the Air Force unit at Wright Air Development Command in Dayton charged with investigating such phenomena. This, in turn, led to the Air Force's Operation BLUE BOOK. Based at Wright-Patterson, the operation collected all reports of UFO sightings. Air Force investigators then attempted to explain such sightings by linking them to natural phenomena. BLUE BOOK investigators regularly called on the Agency's Project Staff in Washington to check reported UFO sightings against U-2 flight logs. This enabled the investigators to eliminate the majority of the UFO reports, although they could not reveal to the letter writers the true cause of the UFO sightings. U-2 and later OXCART flights accounted for more than one-half of all UFO reports during the late 1950s and most of the 1960s.[49]

HIRING U-2 PILOTS

In authorizing the U-2 project, President Eisenhower told DCI Dulles that he wanted the pilots of these planes to be non-US citizens. It was his belief that, should a U-2 come down in hostile territory, it would be much easier for the United States to deny any responsibility for the activity if the pilot was not an American.

The initial effort to find U-2 pilots was assigned to the Directorate of Plans Air/Maritime Division (AMD). The DDP had excellent contacts [redacted] AMD operatives [redacted] asked that discreet inquiries be made to see if any [redacted] fliers were interested in a high-paying covert project. [Redacted] brought to the United States for training. Meanwhile, AMD hired an [redacted] flier residing in England, and he also came to the United States for training.

In theory the use of foreign pilots seemed quite logical; in practice it did not work out. The [redacted] and could only fly light aircraft. Language was also a barrier for the [redacted] although several were good fliers. Because Lieutenant Colonel Geary had taken a class of [redacted] through flying school at Randolph AFB in 1950, he got the job of training the [redacted] recruits in mid-1955. Geary arranged for an Air Force officer of [redacted] to stay with the group during a preliminary training program at Luke Air Force Base. The plan to use foreign pilots soon ran into trouble when only [redacted] pilots passed the school and reported to Area 51. They made only a few flights in the U-2, and by the autumn of 1955 they were out of the program.[50]

---

[49] Information supplied by James Cunningham to Donald E. Welzenbach (U).

[50] *OSA History*, chap. 10, pp. 1-10 (TS Codeword); Geary interview (S).

Even before the elimination of the [redacted] it was clear that there would not be enough trained foreign pilots available in time for deployment. Bissell therefore had to start the search for U-2 pilots all over again. Lt. Gen. Emmett (Rosy) O'Donnell, the Air Force's Deputy Chief of Staff for Personnel, authorized the use of Air Force pilots and provided considerable assistance in the search for pilots who met the high standards established by the Agency and the Air Force. The search included only SAC fighter pilots who held reserve commissions. The use of regular Air Force pilots was not considered because of the complexities involved in having them resign from the Air Force, a procedure that was necessary in order to hire them as civilians for the AQUATONE project.

SAC pilots interested in the U-2 project had to be willing to resign from the Air Force and assume civilian status—a process known as sheep-dipping—in order to conduct the overflights. Although Air Force pilots were attracted by the challenge of flying U-2s over hostile territory, they were reluctant to leave the service and give up their seniority. To overcome pilots' reluctance, the Agency offered handsome salaries, and the Air Force promised each pilot that, upon satisfactory conclusion of his employment with the Agency, he could return to his unit. In the meantime, he would be considered for promotion along with his contemporaries who had continued their Air Force careers.[51]

The selection process for Agency U-2 pilots was very rigorous. Because of the strain involved in flying at extreme altitudes for long periods of time, painstaking efforts were made to exclude all pilots who might be nervous or unstable in any way. The physical and psychological screening of potential U-2 pilots

---

[51] *OSA History*, chap. 10, pp. 5-6 (TS Codeword); Geary interview (S); Francis Gary Powers with Curt Gentry, *Operation Overflight* (New York: Holt, Rinehart, and Wilson, 1970), pp. 25-27.

was conducted by the Lovelace Foundation for Medical Education and Research in Albuquerque, New Mexico, under a contract signed with the CIA on 28 November 1955. The CIA's insistence on more stringent physical and mental examinations than those used by the Air Force to select pilots for its U-2 fleet resulted in a higher rejection rate of candidates. The Agency's selection criteria remained high throughout its manned overflight program and resulted in a much lower accident rate for CIA U-2 pilots than for their counterparts in the Air Force program.[52]

PILOT TRAINING

Even before the recruiting effort got under way, the Air Force and CIA began to develop a pilot training program. Under the terms of the OILSTONE agreement between the Agency and the Air Force, responsibility for pilot training lay with SAC. This essential activity was carried out under the supervision of Col. William F. Yancey, who was assigned to March AFB and flew to nearby Area 51 each day. Colonel Yancey was in charge of six SAC pilots who were to be trained by Lockheed test pilots to fly the U-2. Once they became qualified, these SAC pilots would become the trainers for the "sheep-dipped" former Reserve SAC pilots, who would fly U-2 missions for the CIA.

The original U-2 test pilot, Tony LeVier, trained several other Lockheed test pilots in the difficult art of flying the U-2. Eventually there were enough trained Lockheed pilots available to test the aircraft coming off the assembly line and also train the SAC pilots. Training was difficult because there was no two-seat model of the U-2. All instruction had to be given on the ground before takeoff and then over the radio once the craft was airborne. Almost 15 years elapsed before a two-seat U-2 was available for training new pilots. Despite the difficulties involved in training

---

[52] *OSA History*, chap. 10, pp. 5-6; chap. 5, p. 18 (TS Codeword).

U-2 pilots, Colonel Yancey had a cadre of six qualified Air Force U-2 pilots by September 1955. These six were now ready to train the Agency's pilots.[53]

Training pilots was not easy because the U-2 was a mixture of glider and jet. Although those chosen for the overflight program were all qualified fighter pilots, they now had to learn to fly the delicate U-2. Its large wings had tremendous lift but were also very fragile and could not survive the stresses of loops and barrel rolls. Moreover, the original U-2s were placarded, which meant that they could not be flown at sea level faster than 190 knots in smooth air or 150 knots in rough air. At operational altitude, where the air was much less dense, they could not exceed Mach 0.8 (394 knots). Speeds in excess of these limits could cause the wings or tail section to fall off.

Airspeed was a very critical factor for the U-2. At maximum altitude only 6 knots separated the speeds at which low-speed stall and high-speed buffet occurred. Pilots called this narrow range of acceptable airspeeds at maximum altitude the "coffin corner" because at this point the U-2 was always on the brink of falling out of the sky. If the aircraft slowed beyond the low-speed stall limit, it would lose lift and begin to fall, causing stresses that would tear the wings and tail off. A little too much speed would lead to buffeting, which would also cause the loss of the wings or tail. Flying conditions such as these required a U-2 pilot's full attention when he was not using the autopilot. Airspeed was such a critical factor that Kelly Johnson added a vernier adjustment to the throttle to allow the pilot to make minute alterations to the fuel supply.[54]

---

[53] *OSA History*, chap. 11, pp. 1-7 (TS Codeword).

[54] Cunningham interview (TS Codeword); John Parangosky, interview by Donald E. Welzenbach, tape recording, 6 March 1986 (S); information supplied by James Cherbonneaux to Donald E. Welzenbach (S).

Among the unique devices developed for the U-2 was a small sextant for making celestial "fixes" during the long overflights. Because cloud cover often prevented U-2 pilots from locating navigational points on the earth through the periscope, the sextant turned out to be the pilots' principal navigational instrument during the first three years of deployment. When clouds were not a factor, however, the periscope proved highly accurate for navigation. During the final tests before the aircraft became operational, U-2 pilots found they could navigate by dead reckoning with an error of less than 1 nautical mile over a 1,000-nm course.[55]

FINAL TESTS OF THE U-2

Flight-testing of the U-2 continued throughout the fall and winter of 1955-56 in order to test all the various systems. By mid-January 1956, SAC officials were so impressed that they also wanted to purchase a fleet of these planes. On 30 January, DCI Dulles agreed to have CIA act as executive agent for this transaction, which the Air Force called Project DRAGON LADY. To maintain secrecy, the Air Force transferred funds to the CIA, which then placed an order with Lockheed for 29 U-2s in configurations to be determined by the Air Force. The Air Force later bought two more U-2s, for a total of 31. The aircraft purchased for the Air Force were known as the Follow-On Group, which was soon shortened to FOG.[56]

Once enough pilots had been trained, Project AQUATONE managers concentrated on checking out the complete U-2 system: planes, pilots, navigation systems, life-support systems, and cameras. From 10 through 14 April 1956, U-2s equipped with A-2 cameras took off from Area 51 and made eight overflights of the United States in order to test the various flight and camera systems as part of the standard Air Force Operational Readiness

---

[55] Cunningham interview (TS Codeword).

[56] *OSA History,* chap. 5, pp. 25-26 (TS Codeword).

Inspection. Colonel Yancey and his detachment served as observers during this weeklong exercise.

Colonel Yancey's group carefully examined all aspects of the U-2 unit from flight crews to camera technicians and mission programmers. When the exercise was over, Yancey reported that the detachment was ready for deployment. He then briefed a high-level Pentagon panel that included the Secretary of the Air Force and the Chief of Air Staff. These officials concurred with Yancey's determination that the U-2 was ready for deployment.[57]

During these final tests in the spring of 1956, the U-2 once again demonstrated its unique airworthiness. On 14 April 1956, James Cunningham was sitting in his office in Washington when he received a call from Area 51 informing him that a westward-bound U-2 had experienced a flameout over the Mississippi River at the western border of Tennessee. After restarting his engine, the pilot reported a second flameout and engine vibrations so violent that he was unable to get the power plant to start again. Early in the program Bissell and Ritland had foreseen such an emergency and, with the cooperation of the Air Force, had arranged for sealed orders to be delivered to every airbase in the continental United States giving instructions about what to do if a U-2 needed to make an emergency landing.

Cunningham had the project office ask the pilot how far he could glide so they could determine which SAC base should be alerted. The pilot, who by this time was over Arkansas, radioed back that, given the prevailing winds and the U-2's 21:1 glide ratio, he thought he could reach Albuquerque, New Mexico. Within minutes Cunningham was on the phone to Colonel Geary in the Pentagon, who then had the Air Force's Assistant Director of Operations, Brig. Gen. Ralph E. Koon, call the commander of Kirtland AFB near Albuquerque. General Koon told the base

---

[57] Bissell interview (S); *OSA History*, chap. 11, pp. 15-16 (TS Codeword).

commander about the sealed orders and explained that an unusual aircraft would make a deadstick landing at Kirtland within the next half hour. The general then instructed the base commander to have air police keep everyone away from the craft and get it inside a hangar as quickly as possible.

After a half hour passed, the base commander called the Pentagon to ask where the crippled aircraft was. As he was speaking, the officer saw the U-2 touch down on the runway and remarked, "It's not a plane, it's a glider!" Even more surprised were the air police who surrounded the craft when it came to a halt. As the pilot climbed from the cockpit in his "space" suit, one air policeman remarked that the pilot looked like a man from Mars. The pilot, Jacob Kratt, later reported to Cunningham that, from the beginning of the first flameout until the landing at Albuquerque, the U-2 had covered over 900 miles, including more than 300 by gliding.[58]

Aside from this extraordinary gliding ability, however, the U-2 was a very difficult aircraft to fly. Its very light weight, which enabled it to achieve extreme altitude, also made it very fragile. The aircraft was also very sleek, and it sliced through the air with little drag. This feature was dangerous, however, because the U-2 was not built to withstand the G-forces of high speed. Pilots had to be extremely careful to keep the craft in a slightly nose-up attitude when flying at operational altitude. If the nose dropped only a degree or two into the nose-down position, the plane would gain speed at a dramatic rate, exceeding the placarded speed limit in less than a minute, at which point the aircraft would begin to come apart. Pilots, therefore, had to pay close attention to the aircraft's speed indicator because at 65,000 feet there was no

---

[58] Bissell interview (S); Cunningham interview (TS Codeword); Brig. Gen. Leo A. Geary, interview by Gregory W. Pedlow, Colorado Springs, Colorado, 12 October 1988 (S).

physical sensation of speed, without objects close at hand for the eye to use as a reference. [59]

THREE FATAL CRASHES IN 1956

The first fatality directly connected with flying the U-2 occurred on 15 May 1956, when test pilot Wilburn S. Rose, flying article 345A, had trouble dropping his pogos, the outrigger wheels that keep the wings parallel to the ground during takeoff. Once airborne, Rose made a low-level pass over the airstrip and shook loose the lefthand pogo. When he attempted to make a righthand turn to come back over the runway to shake loose the remaining pogo, Rose stalled the U-2 and it plunged to earth, disintegrating over a wide area. Three months later, on 31 August 1956, a second fatal crash occurred during a night-flying exercise. Frank G. Grace stalled article 354 at an altitude of about 50 feet when he tried to climb too steeply at takeoff. The craft fell, cartwheeled on its left wing, and struck a power pole near the runway. More experienced U-2 pilots always cut back abruptly on the throttle as soon as the pogo sticks fell away in order to avoid such stalls.

Before the year was out, two more U-2s were destroyed in crashes, one of them fatal. On 17 September 1956, article 346 lost part of its right wing while on its takeoff ascent from Lindsey Air Force Base in Wiesbaden, Germany. The aircraft disintegrated in midair, killing pilot Howard Carey. The loss of article 357 on 19 December 1956 resulted from pilot hypoxia. A small leak prematurely depleted the oxygen supply and impaired Robert J. Ericson's judgment as he flew over Arizona. Because of his inability to act quickly and keep track of his aircraft's speed, the U-2 exceeded the placarded speed of 190 knots and literally disintegrated when it reached 270 knots. Ericson managed to jettison

---

[59] James Cherbonneaux, Carmine Vito, and Hervey Stockman (former U-2 pilots), interview by Donald E. Welzenbach, Washington, DC, May 1986 (S).

the canopy and was sucked out of the aircraft at 28,000 feet. His chute opened automatically at 15,000 feet, and he landed without injury. The aircraft was a total loss.[60]

COORDINATION OF COLLECTION REQUIREMENTS

From the very beginning of the U-2 program, it was apparent that some sort of an interagency task force or office would be needed to develop and coordinate collection requirements for the covert overhead reconnaissance effort. In a three-page memorandum to DCI Dulles on 5 November 1954 setting forth the ideas of the Technological Capabilities Panel's Project 3 on this subject, Edwin Land wrote:

> *It is recommended that... a permanent task force, including Air Force supporting elements, be set up under suitable cover to provide guidance on procurement, to consolidate requirements and plan missions in view of priority and feasibility, to maintain the operation on a continuing basis, and to carry out the dissemination of the resulting information in a manner consistent with its special security requirements.[61]*

When the U-2's development and testing approached completion, Land's recommendation was put into effect. Following a meeting with Deputy Secretary of Defense Donald Quarles and Trevor Gardner (who had been promoted from his special assistant post to become Assistant Secretary of the Air Force for Research and Development), Richard Bissell established an Ad Hoc Requirements Committee (ARC) on 1 December 1955. He then named

---

[60] U-2 Accident Reports, folders 4, 10, and 14, OSA records, job 67-B-415, box 1 (S).

[61] *OSA History*, chap. 1, annex 1 (TS Codeword).

James Q. Reber to be Intelligence Requirements Officer for the U-2 project and chairman of the ARC. Reber was already experienced in coordination with other intelligence agencies, for he had headed the Directorate of Intelligence DI Office of Intelligence Coordination for four years. The first full-scale ARC meeting took place on 1 February 1956 with representatives from the Army, Navy, and Air Force present. Attending for the CIA were representatives from the Office of Research and Reports (ORR) and the Office of Scientific Intelligence (OSI). The CIA membership later expanded to include the Office of Current Intelligence (OCI) and a representative from the Directorate of Plans. In 1957 the National Security Agency (NSA) also began sending a representative. The State Department followed suit in 1960, although it had been receiving reports from the committee all along.[62]

ARC's main task was to draw up lists of collection requirements, primarily for the U-2, but also for other means of collection. These lists prioritized targets according to their ability to meet the three major national intelligence objectives concerning the Soviet Union in the mid-1950s: long-range bombers, guided missiles, and nuclear energy. The committee issued its list of targets for the use of the entire intelligence community using all available means of collection, not just for the CIA with the U-2.[63]

ARC gave the top priority target list to the Project Director, and the project staff's operations section then used the list to plan the flightpaths for U-2 missions. Although the requirements com-

---

[62] Minutes of the Ad Hoc Requirements Committee of 1 February 1956, Intelligence Community (IC) Staff records, COMIREX, job 33-B-121A, box 1, "ARC Minutes, 1956-1957"; Memorandum for the Joint Study Group from James Q. Reber, "Handling of Requirements for the U-2," 15 August 1960, IC Staff records, job 33-T-123A, box 10, "CHALICE (General)" (TS Codeword).
[63] Memorandum for the Joint Study Group from James Q. Reber, "Handling of Requirements for the U-2," 15 August 1960, IC Staff records, job 33-T-123A, box 10, "CHALICE (General)" (TS Codeword).

mittee was not responsible for developing flight plans, it assisted the planners with detailed target information as required. When a flight plan was ready for submission to the President for approval, the committee drew up a detailed justification for the selection of the targets. This paper accompanied the flight plan.[64]

In developing and prioritizing lists of targets, the committee members had to take into account the varying needs and interests of their parent organizations. Thus, the CIA representatives generally emphasized strategic intelligence: aircraft and munitions factories, power-generating complexes, nuclear establishments, roads, bridges, inland waterways. In contrast, the military services usually placed a heavier emphasis on order-of-battle data. The Air Force, in particular, had a strong interest in gathering intelligence on the location of Soviet and East European airfields and radars.

Although the committee members kept the interests of their services or agencies in mind, their awareness of the vital nature of their mission kept the level of cooperation high. The group always attempted to reach a consensus before issuing its recommendations, although occasionally this was not possible and one or more agencies would add a dissent to the recommendation of the committee as a whole.[65]

PREPARATIONS TO HANDLE THE PRODUCT OF U-2 MISSIONS

On 13 December 1954, DCI Allen Dulles and his assistant, Richard Bissell, briefed Arthur C. Lundahl, the chief of CIA's Photo-Intelligence Division (PID), on Project AQUATONE. At DCI Dulles's direction, Lundahl immediately set in motion within his division a compartmented effort, known as Project

---

[64] Ibid; James Q. Reber, interview by Donald E. Welzenbach and Gregory W. Pedlow, Washington, DC, 2 May 1987 (S).
[65] Reber interview (S).

EQUINE, to plan for the exploitation of overhead photography from the U-2 project. With only 13 members, the PID staff was too small to handle the expected flood of photographs that the U-2 would bring back, so in May 1955 the Directorate of Support (DS) authorized expanding PID to 44 persons. Soon afterward the division moved from its room in M Building to larger quarters in Que Building.

The Photo-Intelligence Division continued to expand in anticipation of large quantities of U-2 photography. Its authorized strength doubled in January 1956 when a new project known as HTAUTOMAT came into existence to exploit U-2 photography. All of the products from this project would be placed in the new control system. By the summer of 1956, the PID had moved to larger quarters in the Steuart Building at 5th Street and New York Avenue, NW. PID photointerpreters had already begun to work with U-2 photography following a series of missions in April 1956, when U-2s photographed a number of US installations that were considered analogous to high-priority Soviet installations. As a result of these preparations, PID was ready for the mass of photography that began coming when U-2 operations commenced in the summer of 1956.[66]

THE IMPACT OF THE AIR FORCE PROJECT GENETRIX BALLOONS

While the Agency was making its final preparations for U-2 overflights, the Air Force started a reconnaissance project that would cause considerable protest around the world and threaten the existence of the U-2 overflight program before it even began. Project GENETRIX involved the use of camera-carrying balloons

---

[66] For a more detailed history of photointerpretation in the CIA, see [redacted] *The National Photographic Interpretation Center,* vol. 1, *Antecedents and Early Years,* Directorate of Science and Technology Historical Series NPIC-2, December 1972, pp. 171-194 (S).

to obtain high-altitude photography of Eastern Europe, the Soviet Union, and the People's Republic of China. This project had its origins in a RAND Corporation study from 1951. By the end of 1955, the Air Force had overcome a number of technical problems in camera design and recovery techniques and had manufactured a large number of balloons for use in the project. President Eisenhower gave his approval on 27 December 1955, and two weeks later the launches from bases in Western Europe began. By the end of February 1956, the Air Force had launched a total of 516 balloons.[67]

Project GENETRIX was much less successful than its sponsors had hoped. Once launched, the balloons were at the mercy of the prevailing winds, and many tended to drift toward southern Europe and then across the Black Sea and the desert areas of China. These balloons therefore missed the prime target areas, which lay in the higher latitudes. Large numbers of balloons did not succeed in crossing the Soviet Union and China, some because they were shot down by hostile aircraft, others because they prematurely expended their ballast supplies and descended too soon. Only 46 payloads were eventually recovered (one more than a year later and the last not until 1958) from the 516 balloons that had been launched. In four of these payloads the camera had malfunctioned, and in another eight the photography was of no intelligence value. Thus, only 34 balloons succeeded in obtaining useful photographs.[68]

The low success rate of the Project GENETRIX balloons was not the only problem encountered; far more serious was the storm of protest and unfavorable publicity that the balloon

---

[67] P. G. Strong, Attachment to Memorandum for DCI Dulles, "Project GENETRIX Summary," 15 February 1956 (S).
[68] Final Report, Project 119L, 1st Air Division (Meteorological Survey) Strategic Air Command, 5 March 1956, D-582, General Summary (S, declassified 1979).

overflights provoked. Although the Air Force had issued a cover story that the balloons were being used for weather research connected with the International Geophysical Year, East European nations protested strongly to the United States and to international aviation authorities, claiming that the balloons endangered civilian aircraft. The Soviet Union sent strongly worded protest notes to the United States and the nations from which the balloons had been launched. The Soviets also collected numerous polyethelene gasbags, camera payloads, and transmitters from GENETRIX balloons and put them on display in Moscow for the world press.[69]

All of this publicity and protest led President Eisenhower to conclude that "the balloons gave more legitimate grounds for irritation than could be matched by the good obtained from them," and he ordered the project halted. On 7 February 1956 Secretary of State Dulles informed the Soviet Union that no more "weather research" balloons would be released, but he did not offer an apology for the overflights. [70]

Despite the furor caused by GENETRIX, Air Force Chief of Staff Twining proposed yet another balloon project only five weeks later, in mid-March 1956. This project would employ even higher flying balloons than GENETRIX and would be ready in 18 months. President Eisenhower informed the Air Force, however, that he was "not interested in any more balloons."[71]

---

[69] *New York Times*, 10 February 1956, p.1; *Omaha World Herald*, 11 February 1956, p. 1.

[70] Andrew J. Goodpaster, Memorandum for the Record, "10 February 1956 Conference of Joint Chiefs of Staff with the President," WHOSS, Alpha, DDEL (TS, declassified 1980); Stephen E. Ambrose, *Eisenhower: The President,* vol. 2 (New York: Simon and Schuster, 1984), p. 310.

[71] Quoted in Ambrose, *Eisenhower: The President*, p. 310.

Although the photo intelligence gained from Project GEN-ETRIX was limited in quantity, it was still some of the best and most complete photography obtained of the Soviet Union since World War II. It was referred to as "pioneer" photography because it provided a baseline for all future overhead photography. Even innocuous photos of such things as forests and streams proved valuable in later years when U-2 and satellite photography revealed construction activity.

Of still greater importance to the U-2 program, however, was the data that US and NATO radars obtained as they tracked the paths of the balloons—whose average altitude was 45,800 feet—over the Soviet Bloc. This data provided the most accurate record to date of high-altitude wind currents, knowledge that meteorologists were later able to put to use to determine optimum flightpaths for U-2 flights.

One completely fortuitous development from Project GENETRIX had nothing to do with the cameras but involved a steel bar. This bar served a dual purpose: the rigging of the huge polyethylene gasbag was secured to the top of the bar and the camera-payload and automatic-ballasting equipment was attached to the bottom. By sheer chance, the length of the bar—91 centimeters—corresponded to the wavelength of the radio frequency used by a Soviet radar known by its NATO designator as TOKEN. This was an S-band radar used by Soviet forces for early warning and ground-controlled intercept. The bar on the GENETRIX balloons resonated when struck by TOKEN radar pulses, making it possible for radar operators at US and NATO installations on the periphery of the Soviet Union to locate a number of previously unknown TOKEN radars.

These radar findings, coupled with other intercepts made during the balloon flights, provided extensive data on Warsaw Pact radar networks, radar sets, and ground-controlled interception techniques. Analysis of these intercepts revealed the altitude capabilities and tracking accuracy of radars, the methods used by Warsaw Pact nations to notify each other of the balloons' passage (handing off), and the altitudes at which Soviet aircraft could intercept the balloons. All of this information could be directly applied to future U-2 missions.[72]

These positive results from Project GENETRIX did not outweigh the political liabilities of the international protests. CIA officials became concerned that the ill will generated by balloon overflights could sour the Eisenhower administration on all overflights, including those by the U-2, which was just about ready for deployment. Therefore, DDCI Cabell wrote to Air Force Chief of Staff Twining in February 1956 to warn against further balloon flights because of the "additional political pressures being generated against all balloon operations and overflights, thus increasing the difficulties of policy decisions which would permit such operations in the future."[73]

In addition to its concern for the future of the U-2 program, the Agency feared that President Eisenhower's anger at balloon overflights might result in the curtailment of the balloon program that the Free Europe Committee—a covert Agency operation based in West Germany—used to release propaganda pamphlets over Eastern Europe.

AQUATONE BRIEFINGS FOR SELECTED MEMBERS OF CONGRESS

Although knowledge of the U-2 project was a closely guarded secret within both the Agency and the Eisenhower administration, DCI Dulles decided that a few key members of Congress should be told about the project. On 24 February 1956, Dulles

---

[72] Final Report, Project 119L, 1st Air Division (Meteorological Survey) Strategic Air Command, 5 March 1956, D-582, General Summary (TS, declassified 1979).
[73] Philip G. Strong, Attachment to Memorandum for DCI Dulles, "Project GENETRIX Summary," 15 February 1956, OSI records (S).

met with Senators Leverett Saltonstall and Richard B. Russell, the ranking members of the Senate Armed Services Committee and its subcommittee on the CIA. He shared with them the details of Project AQUATONE and then asked their opinion on whether some members of the House of Representatives should also be informed. As a result of the senators' recommendation that the senior members of the House Appropriations Committee should be briefed, Dulles later met with its ranking members, Representatives John Taber and Clarence Cannon. Official Congressional knowledge of the U-2 project remained confined to this small group for the next four years. The House Armed Services Committee and its CIA subcommittee did not receive a CIA briefing on the U-2 project until after the loss of Francis Gary Powers's U-2 over the Soviet Union in May 1960.[74]

THE U-2 COVER STORY

In February 1956, while the controversy over balloon flights was still raging and the U-2 was completing its final airworthiness tests, Richard Bissell and his staff began working on a cover story for overseas operations. It was important to have a plausible reason for deploying such an unusual looking plane, whose glider wings and odd landing gear were certain to arouse curiosity.

Bissell decided that the best cover for the deployment of the U-2 was an ostensible mission of high-altitude weather research by the National Advisory Committee on Aeronautics (NACA). Such a cover story, however, needed the approval of all concerned: Air Force intelligence, the Air Weather Service, the Third Air Force, the Seventh Air Division, the SAC U-2 project officer, the Air Force Headquarters project officer, and NACA's top offi-

---

[74] John S. Warner, Legislative Counsel, Memorandum for the Record, "AQUATONE Briefings," 18 November 1957, Office of Congressional Affairs records, job 61-357, box 2 (S); Warner interview (S).

cial, Dr. Hugh Dryden. Moreover, the CIA Scientific Advisory Committee was also consulted about the cover plan.

Senior CIA officials and the other agencies involved in providing cover for the U-2 approved the final version of the overall cover story at the end of March 1956. The project staff then began working on contingency plans for the loss of a U-2 over hostile territory. Bissell advised the project's cover officer to "produce a document which sets forth all actions to be taken...not only press releases and the public line to be taken, but also the suspension of operations and at least an indication of the diplomatic action... We should at least make the attempt in this case to be prepared for the worst in a really orderly fashion." The cover officer then prepared emergency procedures based on the overall weather research cover story, and Bissell approved these plans. There was one final high-level look at the cover story on 21 June 1956, the day after the first U-2 mission over Eastern Europe, when Bissell met with General Goodpaster, James Killian, and Edwin Land to discuss the pending overflights of the Soviet Union, including the proposed emergency procedures. Killian and Land disagreed with Bissell's concept and made a much bolder and more forthright proposal: in the event of the loss of a U-2 over hostile territory, the United States should not try to deny responsibility but should state that overflights were being conducted "to guard against surprise attack." This proposal was put aside for further thought (which it never received), and Bissell's weather research cover remained the basis for statements to be made after a loss. The project staff then went on to prepare a number of different statements to be used in various scenarios, including one in which the pilot was captured. Even in such a case, however, the proposed policy was for the United States to stick to the weather research cover story, a course of action that would prove disastrous in May 1960.[75]

---

[75] *OSA History*, chap. 8, pp. 30-35; chap. 11, annex 73 (TS Codeword).

3

U-2 Operations in the Soviet Bloc and Middle East, 1956-1968

By January 1956, everyone working on Project AQUATONE could see that the U-2 was nearing the time for operational deployment. During tests the aircraft had met all the criteria established in late 1954. Its range of 2,950 miles was sufficient to overfly continents, its altitude of 72,000 feet was beyond the reach of all known antiaircraft weapons and interceptor aircraft, and its camera lenses were the finest available.

Because the main targets for the U-2 lay behind the Iron Curtain, Bissell and his staff began looking for operational bases in Europe. The United Kingdom, America's closest ally, seemed the logical choice for U-2 bases, and, on 10 January 1956, Bissell flew to London to discuss the matter with Royal Air Force (RAF) and MI-6 officials. Their initial response was favorable, but they told Bissell that the proposal needed approval at a much higher level.

Bissell reported his findings to DCI Dulles, who promptly arranged to meet with Foreign Secretary Selwyn Lloyd in London to explore the possibility of winning the British Government's approval for the project. Dulles presented his case to Lloyd on 2 February, and, by early March, Prime Minister Anthony Eden approved the basing of U-2s in the United Kingdom. The U-2s were to use Lakenheath AFB, an RAF base also used by the USAF Strategic Air Command (SAC).[1]

THE DEPLOYMENT OF DETACHMENT A
TO LAKENHEATH

The first Agency U-2 detachment, consisting of four aircraft and pilots, was known publicly as the 1st Weather Reconnaissance Squadron, Provisional (WRSP-1). The "provisional" designation gave the U-2 detachments greater security because provisional Air Force units did not have to report to higher headquarters. WRSP-1, known within the Agency as Detachment A, began deploying to the United Kingdom on 29 April 1956. By 4 May, all of the detachment's personnel and equipment, including four aircraft, had arrived at Lakenheath.[2]

Shortly after deployment, on 7 May, the National Advisory Committee on Aeronautics (NACA) released an unclassified U-2 cover story stating that a Lockheed-developed aircraft would be flown by the USAF Air Weather Service to study such high-altitude phenomena as the jet stream, convective clouds, temperature and wind structures at jet-stream levels, and cosmic-ray effects up to 55,000 feet.[3]

Before overflights could begin from Lakenheath, however, several incidents occurred that dampened Prime Minister Eden's interest in having the U-2s on British territory. In mid-April 1956,

---

[1] *OSA History,* chap. 11, pp. 10-15 (TS Codeword).

[2] Ibid., pp. 17-18 (TS Codeword).

[3] Press Release of 7 May 1956 (U) in *OSA History,* chap. 7, annex 60 (TS Codeword).

a Soviet naval squadron brought Soviet leaders Nikita Khrushchev and Nikolai Bulganin on an official visit to the United Kingdom. Although the ships were docked in Portsmouth Harbor, a British counterintelligence operative and underwater expert, retired Royal Navy Commander Lionel Crabb, apparently undertook a mission to examine the hulls of these vessels but vanished in the process. His headless body was later found washed up on a beach. This so-called Frogman Incident caused an uproar in Parliament and a protest from Moscow that soured relations between the United Kingdom and the Soviet Union. To avoid further deterioration of Anglo-Soviet relations, the Prime Minister wrote to President Eisenhower on 16 May asking that overflights be postponed. Only two days later, a U-2 on a training flight from Lakenheath inadvertently penetrated the British radar network, causing RAF fighters to scramble. Afterward the Air Ministry made a public announcement that a special NACA aircraft was conducting high-altitude research in the United Kingdom. At about the same time, Richard Bissell learned that the State Department had told Prime Minister Eden that only one U-2 was based at Lakenheath, when in reality there were four.[4]

THE MOVE TO WIESBADEN

To avoid arousing further reaction in the United Kingdom and to begin the program of U-2 overflights beyond the Iron Curtain without further delay, Bissell moved Detachment A on 11 June 1956 to Wiesbaden, one of the busiest airfields in West Germany, without notifying West German authorities. The detachment commander, Col. Frederick McCoy, was disappointed in his hope that the redeployment of the U-2s could be accomplished without

---

[4] Christopher Andrew, *Her Majesty's Secret Service: The Making of the British Intelligence Community* (New York, 1986), pp. 495-496; Beschloss, *Mayday*, p. 116; *OSA History,* chap. 11, pp. 18-21 (TS Codeword).

drawing undue attention. The strange-looking planes, with bicycle-type wheels and wings so long they touched the ground after landing, aroused considerable interest. Wiesbaden was to be only a temporary home for Detachment A; the Air Force began preparing Giebelstadt near the East German border for use by the U-2s. Giebelstadt was an old World War II airbase that had been one of the launching sites for the GENETRIX balloons.[5]

Soon after the four U-2s arrived in Wiesbaden, they were refitted with the more powerful J57/P-31 engines. The new engines were better suited for operations behind the Iron Curtain because they were less likely to suffer flameouts than the earlier model. Once the new engines were installed, the aircraft received the designation U-2B.[6]

Bissell was anxious to get the overflights started by late June because SAC weather experts had predicted that the best weather for photographing the Soviet Union would be between 20 June and 10 July. Bissell, however, had not yet received final authorization from President Eisenhower to begin overflights of the Soviet Union. On 28 May 1956, when DCI Allen Dulles met with the President to discuss the U-2's readiness for operations, Eisenhower still made no decision on overflights. Three days later Dulles and Air Force Chief of Staff Nathan Twining prepared a paper for the President outlining "AQUATONE Operational Plans." In the meantime, President Eisenhower had entered Walter Reed Hospital for tests for an abdominal ailment that turned out to be ileitis, requiring an operation. During his recovery from surgery, Eisenhower would make his final decision on the overflight program.[7]

---

[5] *OSA History,* chap. 11, pp. 21-23 (TS Codeword).

[6] Ibid., pp. 23, 26 (TS Codeword).

[7] Ibid., pp. 23-25 and annex 73, "AQUATONE Operational Plans," 31 May 1956 (TS Codeword).

PRESIDENT EISENHOWER'S ATTITUDE TOWARD OVERFLIGHTS

The President had mixed feelings about overflights of the Soviet Union. Aware that they could provide extremely valuable intelligence about Soviet capabilities, he, nevertheless, remained deeply concerned that such flights brought with them the risk of starting a war. From the very beginning of the U-2 program, President Eisenhower had worked to minimize the possibility that overflights could lead to hostilities. He had always insisted that overflights by military aircraft were too provocative, and in 1954 he had therefore supported the Land committee's proposal for an unarmed civilian aircraft instead of the military reconnaissance planes favored by the Air Force. For the same reason, Eisenhower had resisted attempts by the Air Force to take the U-2 program away from the CIA in 1955.

In fact, the President's desire to avoid secret reconnaissance missions over the Soviet Union, with all their risks, led him to make his famous "Open Skies" proposal in the summer of 1955, when the U-2 was still under development but making good progress. At the Geneva summit conference on 21 July 1955, President Eisenhower offered to provide airfields and other facilities in the United States for the Soviet Union to conduct aerial photography of all US military installations if the Soviet Union would provide the United States with similar facilities in Russia. Not surprisingly, Soviet leader Nikita Khrushchev almost immediately rejected Eisenhower's offer. Although the President had hoped that the Soviet Union would accept his proposal, he was prepared for rejection. While Open Skies was still being considered, Eisenhower had stated, "I'll give it one shot. Then if they don't accept it, we'll fly the U-2."[8]

Even though President Eisenhower had approved every stage of the U-2's development, knowing full well that the aircraft was being built to fly over the Soviet Union, the actual decision to autho-

---

[8] Quoted in Beschloss, *Mayday*, p. 105.

rize such flights was very difficult for him. He remained concerned that overflights could poison relations with the Soviet Union and might even lead to hostilities. One argument that helped overcome the President's reluctance was the CIA's longstanding contention that U-2 flights might actually go undetected because Soviet radars would not be able to track aircraft at such high altitudes. This belief was based on a 1952 study of Soviet World War II-vintage radars and on 1955 tests using US radars, which—unknown to US officials—were not as effective as Soviet radars against high-altitude targets. Shortly before U-2 operations began, however, the CIA's Office of Scientific Intelligence (OSI) conducted a vulnerability study of the U-2 that was published on 28 May 1956. The study's conclusion was that "Maximum Soviet radar detection ranges against the Project aircraft at elevation in excess of 55,000 feet would vary from 20 to 150 miles...In our opinion, detection can therefore be assumed." The OSI study added, however, "It is doubtful that the Soviets can achieve consistent tracking of the Project vehicle."[9] Completed just three weeks before the initiation of overflights, this study seems to have had little impact on the thinking of the top project officials. They continued to believe that the Soviets would not be able to track the U-2 and might even fail to detect it, except for possible vague indications.[10]

Soviet radars were not President Eisenhower's only concern. Also fearing that a malfunction might cause a U-2 to crash inside the Soviet Union, he asked Allen Dulles what the consequences would be. The President's staff secretary, Col. Andrew J. Goodpaster, who was present at virtually all White House meetings on

---

[9] *OSA History,* chap. 11, p. 31 (TS Codeword). For the belief that the U-2 might go undetected see the Leghorn interview and Dwight D. Eisenhower, *Waging Peace, 1956-1961* (New York, 1965), p. 41.

[10] Richard M. Bissell, Jr., interview by Gregory W. Pedlow, tape recording, Farmington, Connecticut, 28 October 1988 (S).

the U-2 project and served as the President's intermediary to the CIA on this issue, later recalled:

> *Allen's approach was that we were unlikely to lose one. If we did lose one, the pilot would not survive... We were told—and it was part of our understanding of the situation—that it was almost certain that the plane would disintegrate and that we could take it as a certainty that no pilot would survive...and that although they would know where the plane came from, it would be difficult to prove it in any convincing way.*[11]

CIA assurances that the U-2 would probably not be detected, and that a crashed U-2 could not be traced back to the United States, helped overcome the President's worries about overflights. The most important reason why President Eisenhower decided to send reconnaissance aircraft over the Soviet Union, however, was the urgent need for accurate intelligence to confirm or disprove claims of Soviet advances in long-range bombers and missiles. The initial sighting of the new Soviet Bison bomber in the spring of 1954 had been followed by reported sightings of more than 30 of these bombers in the spring and summer of 1955 (in reality these were sightings of the same group of 10 aircraft that circled around out of sight and made several passes during a Soviet air show). Soon members of Congress were calling for investigations into the relative strength of the US and Soviet Air Forces.[12] Early in 1956, concern about a possible Soviet advantage in long-range bombers grew as Air Force Chief of Staff Twining informed the

---

[11] Quoted in Beschloss, *Mayday*, p. 118.

[12] Robert Hotz, "Russian Jet Airpower Gains Fast on US," *Aviation Week,* 23 May 1955, pp. 12-15; "Aviation Week Story Spurs Debate on US, Red Airpower Positions," *Aviation Week,* 30 May 1955, pp. 13-14.

Senate Armed Services Committee that the Soviet Union already had more Bisons than the United States had B-52s and that the Soviets would be able to "maintain this advantage for some time if they keep on the production curve we are now predicting."[13] By May 1956, reporting on the growing Soviet air strength was no longer confined to aviation journals; *U.S. News and World Report*, for example, featured articles headlined "Can Soviets Take the Air Lead?" and "Is U.S. Really Losing in the Air?"[14]

Alongside fear of possible Soviet superiority in long-range bombers came a new potential threat: Soviet progress in guided missile research. Trevor Gardner, Air Force Assistant Secretary for Research and Development, warned in September 1955 that "the most complex and baffling technological mystery today is not the Russian capability in aircraft and nuclear weapons but rather what the Soviet progress has been in the field of guided missiles."[15] On 30 January 1956, *Time* magazine made the guided missile its cover story. The article began by describing a hypothetical crisis set in 1962 in which the United States suffered a humiliating defeat because it had lagged behind the Soviet Union in guided missile development.[16] Just two weeks after this story appeared, the Soviets successfully tested a missile with a range of 900 miles, and President Eisenhower admitted at a press conference that the Soviet Union might be ahead of the United States in some areas of the missile field. Administration critic Senator Stuart Symington

---

[13] Claude Witze, "Russians Outpacing US in Air Quality, Twining Warns Congress," *Aviation Week,* 27 February 1956, pp. 26-28; Robert Hotz, "Russian Air Force Now Gaining in Quality," *Aviation Week,* 12 March 1956, p. 286.

[14] "Can Soviets Take the Air Lead? What LeMay, Wilson, Ike Say," *US News and World Report,* 11 May 1956, pp. 108-114; "Is U.S. Really Losing in the Air?" *US News and World Report,* 18 May 1956, pp. 25-27.

[15] William Coughlin, "Gardner Defends Greater R&D Spending," *Aviation Week,* 26 September 1955, p. 14.

[16] "Missiles Away," *Time*, 30 January 1956, pp. 52-55.

then claimed, "The facts are that our missile development may be ahead in the short-range area, but their missile development is ahead in the area that counts by far the most—the long-range area."[17] Fears of Soviet missile progress increased when Nikita Khrushchev stated on 23 April 1956, "I am quite sure that we shall have very soon a guided missile with a hydrogen-bomb warhead which could hit any point in the world."[18]

Faced with growing Congressional and public anxiety over Soviet offensive capabilities, President Eisenhower approved the proposed overflight program. Colonel Goodpaster relayed this decision to Bissell, Land, and Killian at a meeting on 21 June. The President nevertheless maintained tight control over the program and authorized only 10 days of overflights when operations over the Soviet Union were ready to start in early July 1956.[19]

FIRST OVERFLIGHTS OF EASTERN EUROPE

The CIA initiated U-2 flights over hostile territory even before the President granted final approval for overflights of the Soviet Union. After consulting with the Commander of US Air Force Europe, Richard Bissell used existing Presidential permission for Air Force overflights of the Soviet Union's East European satellites as his authority to plan a mission over Poland and East Germany. Bissell had informed the President of his intention to conduct such missions in the "AQUATONE Operational Plan" submitted on 31 May.

---

[17] Robert Hotz, "Firing of 900-Mile Russian Missile Spurs US Changes," *Aviation Week,* 20 February 1956, p. 27.

[18] "Is Russia Really Ahead in Missile Race?" *US News and World Report,* 4 May 1956, p. 34.

[19] *OSA History,* chap. 11, pp. 27-29 (TS Codeword); A. J. Goodpaster, Memorandum for the Record, 21 June 1956, WHOSS, Alpha, DDEL (TS).

The first operational use of a U-2 took place on Wednesday, 20 June 1956. Carl K. Overstreet flew a U-2 equipped with an A-2 camera over Poland and East Germany. At the end of the mission, Detachment A immediately rushed the exposed film to the United States for processing. The developed film arrived at the Photo-Intelligence Division (PID) on 22 June 1956. PID personnel considered the pictures obtained by mission 2003 to be of good quality.[20]

Following the success of this first mission, Bissell was eager to begin overflights of the Soviet Union. But even after the President granted his approval on 21 June, such missions could not yet take place for two reasons. First, President Eisenhower had agreed with a CIA and State Department recommendation that West German Chancellor Konrad Adenauer be informed in advance of US plans to overfly the Soviet Union from bases in Germany (in keeping with existing policies Adenauer was not informed about overflights of Eastern Europe). Second, Soviet party chief Nikita Khrushchev had invited representatives of the US Air Force to the Moscow Air Show, which opened on 23 June 1956. Led by Air Force Chief of Staff Nathan F. Twining, the delegation would be in the Soviet Union for a week, and General Twining requested that no overflights of the Soviet Union be staged until the Air Force delegation had left.[21]

Both of these restrictions on overflights of the Soviet Union were cleared up by the end of June. [redacted]

A few days later the Air Force delegation returned from Moscow, but now unfavorable weather prevented the start of operations against the Soviet Union.

---

[20] *OSA History,* chap. 11, p. 27 (TS Codeword); Mission folder 2003 (20 June 1956), OSA records, job 67-B-328, box 7 (TS Codeword).

[21] Nathan F. Twining, *Neither Liberty nor Safety* (New York: Holt, Rinehart & Winston, 1966), pp. 259-260; *OSA History,* chap. 11, p. 27 (TS Codeword).

While waiting for the clouds over the Soviet Union to clear, Detachment A carried out two more overflights of Eastern Europe on 2 July 1956: mission 2009 over Czechoslovakia, Hungary, and Bulgaria; and mission 2010 over East Germany, Poland, Hungary, and Romania. That afternoon Bissell and DDCI Cabell gave President Eisenhower a detailed briefing on the first U-2 overflight, which the President found "very interesting, very positive." Eisenhower was anxious to know, however, whether radars had tracked the aircraft. Bissell replied that, although East European radars had picked up the 20 June flight, radar operators had misread the altitude as only 42,000 feet. He added that the Agency was awaiting reports on that morning's flights to see if they, too, had been detected. Noting that the U-2 detachment had four aircraft working and could average up to two flights per day, Bissell told the President that the crews were "ready and eager to go in beyond the satellites" and overfly the center of the Soviet Union.[22]

Eisenhower replied that he thought it "urgent" to know whether the recent flights had been tracked by hostile radars. The President was obviously concerned that CIA estimates that the U-2 could fly virtually undetected were proving false. One of the reasons why he had approved the overflight program was the CIA's assurance that the Soviet Union would remain unaware of the flights or—at the very worst—receive only occasional, vague indications.

FIRST U-2 FLIGHTS OVER THE SOVIET UNION

The question of how well the Soviets could track U-2 flights had not yet been settled when the first overflights of the Soviet Union took place. On Wednesday, 4 July 1956, the U-2 known as Article 347 began the first flight over the Soviet Union. Final authorization

---

[22] Andrew J. Goodpaster's handwritten notes on 2 July 1956 meeting, WHOSS, Alpha, DDEL (TS).

First Overflights, 20 June - 5 July 1956

	Mission 2003	20 June
	Mission 2009	2 July
	Mission 2010	2 July

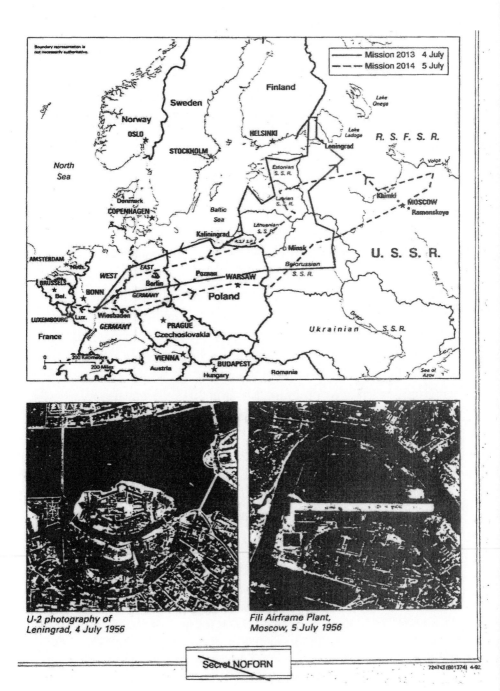

U-2 photography of
Leningrad, 4 July 1956

Fili Airframe Plant,
Moscow, 5 July 1956

724743 (B01374) 4-92

for mission 2013 had come shortly before takeoff. Late on the evening of 3 July, Bissell went to project headquarters in the Matomic Building to give the "Go" or "No go" decision. Although the President had approved the overflight, the final decision to start a mission depended on a number of factors, especially the weather over the target area and at the takeoff and landing sites. Bissell made the decision just before midnight Washington time, which was six o'clock in the morning in Wiesbaden. This pattern of last-minute approvals continued for the duration of the U-2 overflight program.[23]

When Wiesbaden received the "Go" signal, a U-2 equipped with an A-2 camera and flown by pilot Hervey Stockman took off on a course that took it over Poznan, Poland, where riots had occurred on 28-30 June. After Poznan, Stockman headed for Belorussia, where he turned north to Leningrad. The last leg of the mission took the U-2 over the Soviet Baltic states before returning to Wiesbaden. The main target of this mission was the naval shipyards in Leningrad, center of the Soviet Union's submarine construction program. Mission 2013's route also overflew a number of major military airfields to make an inventory of the new Bison jet-engine heavy bomber.[24]

The second overflight, on the following day, continued the search for Bison bombers. Pilot Carmine Vito's route was similar but somewhat to the south of Stockman's and also flew farther east, more than 200 kilometers past Moscow. Although the Soviet

---

[23] Bissell interview by Welzenbach (S); Cunningham interview (TS Codeword).

[24] [Redacted] *National Photographic Interpretation Center: The Years of Project HTAUTOMAT, 1956-1958*, Directorate of Science and Technology Historical Series NPIC-3, December 1974, 6 vols (hereafter cited as *NPIC History*), vol. 1, p. 20 (S); Mission folder 2013 (4 July 1956), OSA records, job 67-B-328, box 7 (TS Codeword). Note on mission numbers: each proposed mission received a number, but not all of these missions were flown.

capital was almost completely hidden by clouds, the A-2 camera with haze filters took some usable photographs of the city. These turned out to be the only U-2 photographs of Moscow because no other mission was sent over the Soviet capital. Among the key targets photographed during mission 2014 were the Fili airframe plant, where the Bison was being built; the bomber arsenal at Ramenskoye, where the Bisons were tested; the Kaliningrad missile plant; and the Khimki rocket-engine plant.[25]

When Allen Dulles returned to work on Thursday, 5 July 1956, he asked Bissell if any overflights had taken place during the Independence Day holiday. One had been made on the fourth and another just that morning, Bissell replied. (Because of the six-hour time difference, the 5 July flight was safely back in Wiesbaden by the time Dulles spoke to Bissell.) When Dulles asked the routes of these missions, Bissell told him that they had overflown both Moscow and Leningrad. "Oh my Lord," Dulles exclaimed, "do you think that was wise the first time?" "Allen," Bissell replied, "the first is the safest."[26]

President Eisenhower also wanted to know the results of the 4 and 5 July flights, but his principal concern was whether there had been any indication that either flight had been discovered or tracked by radar. Eisenhower told Colonel Goodpaster "to advise Mr. Allen Dulles that if we obtain any information or warning that any of the flights has been discovered or tracked, the operation should be suspended." Goodpaster called both Dulles and Bissell and was told that reports on tracking or attempted interception of the U-2s would not be available for another 36 hours. Later that day the two CIA officials met with Goodpaster to ask if flights could continue in the meantime. Goodpaster replied that

---

[25] *NPIC History,* vol. 1, p. 21 (S); Mission folder 2014 (5 July 1956), OSA records, job 67-B-328, box 7 (TS Codeword).

[26] Bissell interview by Welzenbach (S).

his understanding of the President's directive was that the operation should continue "at the maximum rate until the first evidence of tracking was received."[27]

Although President Eisenhower had originally spoken of suspending the overflights if they were "discovered or tracked," his main concern was to learn if the Soviets could track U-2 missions, meaning that they could follow the flight on their radar screens for most or all of the missions and thus have numerous opportunities to attempt interception. Certainly the President hoped that U-2 flights could not even be detected, but reports received on the 20 June overflight of Eastern Europe had already indicated that this goal was unrealistic. The President's emphasis therefore shifted to tracking. If the Soviets could successfully track U-2 missions, he wanted the overflights halted.[28] Reports on Soviet radar coverage of the first two overflights of the Soviet Union became available on 6 July. These reports showed that, although the Soviets did detect the aircraft and made several very unsuccessful attempts at interception, they could not track U-2s consistently. Interestingly, the Soviet radar coverage was weakest around the most important targets, Moscow and Leningrad, and the Soviets did not realize that U-2s had overflown these two cities.[29]

Detachment A carried out three more overflights of the Soviet Union during the 10-day period authorized by the President. Two of the missions (2020 and 2021) took place on a single day, 9 July 1956. They covered much of Eastern Europe, and the Ukraine and Belorussia in the Soviet Union. Unfortunately, a broken cam-

[27] Andrew J. Goodpaster, Memorandum for the Record, 5 July 1956, WHOSS, Alpha, DDEL (TS).

[28] Gen. Andrew J. Goodpaster, interview by Donald E. Welzenbach and Gregory W. Pedlow, Washington, DC, 8 July 1987 (S).

[29] Mission folders 2013 (4 July 1956) and 2014 (5 July 1956), OSA records, job 67-B-328, box 7 (TS Codeword).

Additional Overflights, 9-10 July 1956

	Mission 2020	9 July 1956
Mission 2021	9 July 1956
Mission 2023	10 July 1956

Secret NOFORN

724744 (B00997) 4-92

era shutter ruined much of the photography of one of the flights. The third mission (2023), on the following day, included the Crimean Peninsula.[30]

The film from the first overflight (4 July) was flown to the United States immediately after the U-2 landed at Wiesbaden. Several members of the Photo Intelligence Division were on hand when the film was developed to check on the results. Also present was James Baker, who had accepted an offer by project officials to get a firsthand look at how the new A-2 lenses were working.[31]

The photos from July overflights were generally good, despite occasional problems caused by cloud cover. The huge amount of film taken by these missions provided more information about the Soviet Union's ability to track and intercept U-2s. Photointerpreters examining the films eventually discovered the tiny images of MiG-15s and MiG-17s beneath the U-2s in various pursuit and attack attitudes: climbing, flipping over, and falling toward Earth. It was even possible to determine their approximate altitudes. These photographs showed that the Soviet air defense system was able to track U-2s well enough to attempt interception, but they also provided proof that the fighter aircraft available to the Soviet Union in 1956 could not bring down a U-2 at operational altitude.[32]

One problem with early U-2 photography became apparent only after the first films were developed. If there was surface water on the runway at Wiesbaden when the U-2 took off, the camera windows became begrimed. Although the water dried during the flight, the oily scum it left behind degraded the photographic image. To combat this problem, AQUATONE ground crews took brooms and spent several hours before takeoff sweeping puddles

---

[30] Mission folders 2020 (9 July 1956), 2021 (9 July 1956), and 2023 (10 July 1956), OSA records, job 67-B-328, box 7 (TS Codeword).

[31] Cunningham interview (TS Codeword).

[32] Lundahl and Brugioni interview (TS Codeword).

of water from the runway to be used by the U-2. Kelly Johnson eventually designed a jettisonable cover for the camera windows, which was released at the same time as the pogos so that it could be recovered and reused.[33]

SOVIET PROTEST NOTE

The 4 and 5 July overflights brought a strong protest from the Soviet Union on 10 July in the form of a note handed to the US Embassy in Moscow. The note said that the overflights had been made by a "twin-engine medium bomber of the United States Air Force" and gave details of the routes flown by the first two missions. The note did not mention Moscow or Leningrad, however, because the Soviets had not been able to track these portions of the overflights. The Soviet note stated that the flights could only be evaluated as "intentional and conducted for the purposes of intelligence." As soon as the note arrived at the White House on the evening of 10 July 1956, Colonel Goodpaster called Bissell and told him to stop all U-2 overflights until further notice. The next morning Goodpaster met with Bissell to review the U-2 situation. Bissell said three additional flights had taken place since the missions mentioned in the Soviet note but added that no more were planned.[34]

Later Eisenhower told Goodpaster that he "didn't like a thing" about the Soviet note and was going to discuss the matter with Secretary of State Dulles. With the strong approval of President Eisenhower, Goodpaster informed DCI Dulles that "there is to be no mention of the existence of this project or of operations incident to it, outside the Executive Branch, and no mention within the

---

[33] Baker interview (S).

[34] "Alleged Violations of Soviet Territory: Soviet Note of July 10, 1956 with U.S. Reply," *US Department of State Bulletin,* 30 July 1956, pp. 191-192; Andrew J. Goodpaster, Memorandum for the Record, 11 July 1956, WHOSS, Alpha, DDEL (TS).

Executive Branch to others than those who directly need to know of the operation, as distinguished from output deriving from it."[35]

During these initial overflights, the U-2 flew above 69,000 feet and could be seen only fleetingly by pilots of the Soviet interceptor aircraft. Thus, it appears that the Soviet claim that the intruder was a twin-engine bomber was probably based on the assumption that this was another overflight by a reconnaissance version of the twin-engine Canberra bomber, similar to the RAF overflight of Kapustin Yar in 1953. The US reply, sent to the Soviets on 19 July, truthfully denied that any US "military planes" had overflown the Soviet Union on the days in question. Meanwhile, on 16 July the Polish Ambassador to the United States delivered an oral protest concerning overflights of Poland on 20 June and 2 July. This was followed by a protest note from the Czechoslovak Government on 21 July. No formal reply was sent to the two Soviet satellite states.[36]

The details of the flightpaths listed in the Soviet and Polish protests, along with the subsequent photographic evidence of Soviet interception attempts, made it clear that U-2s could not fly undetected over the Soviet Union or Eastern Europe and could even be tracked for extended periods of time. This news greatly disturbed President Eisenhower. In a meeting with Allen Dulles on 19 July 1956, the President recalled how he had been told that "not over a very minor percentage of these (flights) would be picked up." He went on to question "how far this should now be pushed, knowing that detection is not likely to be avoided." After discussing the possibility of basing U-2s in the Far East, Presi-

---

[35] Andrew J. Goodpaster, Memorandum for the Record, 11 July 1956, WHOSS, Alpha, DDEL (TS).

[36] "Alleged Violations of Soviet Territory: Soviet Note of July 10, 1956 with U.S. Reply," *US Department of State Bulletin,* 30 July 1956, pp. 191-192; *OSA History,* chap. 11, pp. 32-33 (TS Codeword).

dent Eisenhower went on to say that he had "lost enthusiasm" for the U-2 activity. He noted that, if the United States were on the receiving end of a Soviet overflight operation, "the reaction would be drastic." The President was also concerned that the American public might learn of the overflights and be shocked that their country had violated international law. He stated, "Soviet protests were one thing, any loss of confidence by our own people would be quite another."[37]

The President's rapid disenchantment with the project was not lost on Richard Bissell. Fearing for the U-2 program's survival, he met with the Land committee in early August 1956 to urge them to help make the U-2 less vulnerable to radar pulses. His goal was to reduce the aircraft's radar cross section so that it would be less susceptible to detection. Edward Purcell had some ideas on this and suggested that he supervise a new project in the Boston area to explore them. At the direction of the Land committee, Bissell set in motion a project known as HTNAMABLE to establish a proprietary firm called the Scientific Engineering Institute (SEI) in Cambridge. Former Air Force Col. Richard S. Leghorn headed the SEI operation for the Agency when it began on 26 November 1956. SEI was staffed by several MIT scholars who conducted studies and experiments into radar-absorbing materials and techniques proposed by Purcell. The effort, known as Project RAINBOW, got under way by the end of the year.[38]

THE END OF THE BOMBER GAP
During the three-week period of 20 June to 10 July 1956, U-2s had made eight overflights beyond the Iron Curtain, including five

---

[37] Andrew J. Goodpaster, Memorandum for the Record, 19 July 1956, WHOSS, Alpha, DDEL (TS).

[38] Records of Scientific Engineering Institute (Project HTNAMABLE), OSA records (TS Codeword).

over the Soviet Union. PID's photointerpreters were busy until the end of August with their initial evaluation of the photography obtained by these flights. Their efforts were complicated by the division's move on 9 July from Que Building to the Steuart Building, but, when the photointerpreters were finished, they were able to write "finis" to the controversy over Soviet bomber strength.

Although the Air Force had claimed that the Soviet Union possessed almost 100 of the new Myasishchev-4 (Bison) heavy bombers, U-2 photography proved this assertion wrong. There were no Bison bombers at any of the nine long-range bomber bases photographed by the July missions. DCI Allen Dulles was particularly impressed by the photographs of the Soviet bomber bases, which in later years he called "million-dollar" photography. The actual value of the U-2 photos was probably even greater because, on the strength of their evidence, the White House was able to deny Air Force requests for additional B-52 bombers to "catch up" to the Soviets.[39]

Because of the need to protect the source of the information about Soviet bomber strength, the controversy surrounding this issue did not immediately die down. In November 1956, when the CIA began providing new Bison production figures based on U-2 photography without identifying the source, some members of Congress— unaware of the existence of the U-2—questioned the motivation behind the reduced estimates. They suggested that either the earlier estimates of Soviet bomber strength had been inflated to increase Air Force appropriations or the new estimates had been reduced by White House direction in order to hold down military expenditures. No one in the White House, the CIA, or the Air Force could reveal that U-2 photographs had actually provided the primary evidence for this change in the estimates.[40]

---

[39] *NPIC History,* vol. 1, p. 23 (S).

[40] John Prados, *The Soviet Estimate: U.S. Intelligence Analysis and Russian Military Strength* (New York: Dial Press, 1982), pp. 45-47.

The need to keep the existence of the U-2 program secret caused problems even within the CIA itself. The Office of Security sharply restricted the number of persons who could be cleared for access to U-2 photography. The special clearance was granted on a "slot" basis, and only the person assigned to a particular position or "slot" could have the clearance. The U-2 photographs were kept in a secure room, and only those with special clearances were admitted to the room. In addition, the Office of Security considered U-2 information too sensitive to use in CIA publications. As a result, many analysts did not have access to information that would have greatly aided the production of intelligence estimates.[41]

TACTICAL INTELLIGENCE FROM U-2s
DURING THE SUEZ CRISIS

Although U-2s had ceased flying over the Soviet Bloc because of President Eisenhower's standdown order, they could still be used elsewhere in the world. The Middle East would be the next area for U-2 operations. On 26 July 1956, Egyptian President Gamal Abdel Nasser nationalized the Suez Canal Company in retaliation for the decision by the United States and the United Kingdom to withdraw financial support for the Aswan Dam project. Nasser's action provoked an international crisis that would have a permanent effect on the U-2 program.

Long before the Suez Crisis developed, the CIA had planned to deploy U-2s in Turkey for use in the Soviet overflight program. On 1 May 1956, US Charge d'Affaires Foy D. Kohler approached Turkish Prime Minister Adnan Menderes on this matter. He told the Prime Minister that the effort was a continuation of the GENETRIX program, during which balloons had been released from Turkey, and involved aircraft that could fly 10,000 feet higher than any Soviet plane. Menderes gave his approval immediately. At the

---

[41] Lundahl and Brugioni interview (TS Codeword).

Bases for U-2 Operations in the Middle East, 1956

Secret NOFORN

724745 (B00952) 4-92

time of the Suez takeover, however, the second contingent of U-2 aircraft and pilots was still being trained in Nevada. This unit would not be ready for redeployment before the end of August and would not become established at Incirlik airbase near Adana, Turkey, until early September 1956. The Agency referred to the AQUATONE detachment at Adana as Detachment B, cryptonym KWCORK; the Air Force covername was Weather Reconnaissance Squadron Provisional 2; and the unit's unofficial name was Tuslog Detachment 10-10. By whatever name, the Adana detachment became the mainstay of U-2 activity for the next three and a half years.[42]

---

[42] *OSA History,* chap. 11, pp. 9, 39-40; chap. 12, pp. 5, 12 (TS Codeword).

The fast-moving events of the Suez Crisis would not wait for Detachment B pilots to complete their training. With tension growing between Egypt and the Suez Canal Company's former owners, the United Kingdom and France, as well as between Egypt and Israel, US military and foreign policy planners needed immediate information about developments in the eastern Mediterranean. Detachment A was, therefore, assigned the first Middle East overflights. On 29 August, U-2 missions 1104 and 1105 left Wiesbaden and overflew the eastern Mediterranean littoral, starting with Greece, then Egypt, Israel, Lebanon, Syria, and Turkey. Because these target areas were beyond the round trip range of the Wiesbaden-based U-2s, the planes landed at Adana for refueling. The next day, the same two planes, with different pilots, took off from Adana and overflew the same Middle East territory, this time including the Gaza Strip, before returning to Wiesbaden. The film contained evidence of large numbers of British troops on Malta and Cyprus and [redacted].

As the situation around Suez grew more tense, the Eisenhower administration decided to release some of the U-2 photos to the British Government. On 7 September, James Reber, chairman of the Ad Hoc Requirements Committee, and Arthur Lundahl, chief of the Photo Intelligence Division, flew to London, taking with them photos of the eastern Mediterranean area, including the Suez Canal, taken on 30 August. These were the first and the only photos of the Middle East that the President authorized to be given to the British during the 1956 crisis.[43]

The Eisenhower administration viewed the developments in the eastern Mediterranean with great concern. To keep the President and Secretary of State abreast of developments in the area, Deputy Director for Intelligence Robert Amory established on 12 September a multiagency group known as the PARAMOUNT Committee to monitor the situation on a round-

---

[43] Lundahl and Brugioni interview (TS Codeword); *NPIC History,* vol. 1, pp. 56-58 (S).

the-clock basis. The PARAMOUNT Committee worked inside PID headquarters in the Steuart Building. Composed of members from CIA, State, NSA, Army, Navy, and Air Force, this committee met daily—frequently several times a day—to produce reports based on information obtained from U-2 photography, communications and electronic intelligence, and agents. The photointerpreters working for the PARAMOUNT committee also came from several agencies: the CIA, the Army, and the Navy.[44]

The Suez Crisis was a major turning point in the use of the U-2 airplane. Before this crisis, the U-2 had been seen solely as a collector of strategic intelligence, with high-quality results considered more important than speed. U-2 film had, therefore, been returned to the manufacturer for optimum development and then interpreted in Washington using the most up-to-date devices. Now, because of the Middle East crisis, Project AQUATONE was expected to perform like a tactical reconnaissance unit, developing film immediately after landing for instant interpretation or "readout." Photo-Intelligence Division personnel assigned to Project HTAUTOMAT (U-2 film exploitation), therefore, had to arrange for forward processing of the U-2 film to avoid unacceptable delays in providing intelligence on tactical developments around Suez.

PID acted quickly to carry out its new assignment. Lundahl and Reber flew from the United Kingdom to US Air Force Europe headquarters in Wiesbaden on 12 September to make arrangements for processing and interpreting U-2 film in West Germany. They had been preceded by [redacted] chief of PID's Special Projects Branch. Following detailed discussions with Air Force photo-intelligence personnel, the CIA representatives arranged to use a portion of a nearby Air Force photo laboratory for developing U-2 film. With the assistance of [redacted] chief of the HTAUTOMAT photo laboratory, and Air Force personnel, [redacted] had the lab ready

---

[44] *NPIC History,* vol. 1, pp. 47-49, 54-56 (S).

for processing on the following day, when the next U-2 mission returned from the Middle East. After quickly developing the film, [redacted] and his joint staff of CIA and armed forces personnel studied it for indications of British and French preparations for hostilities and sent their first report to Washington on 15 September.

Although the Air Force provided considerable assistance in establishing [redacted] photo laboratory, Air Force officials did not like the idea of CIA personnel controlling overseas photo processing and interpretation centers, which were normally under Air Force control. Further negotiations led to a CIA-Air Force agreement at the end of October, under which the Air Force would name the commanding officer for such installations and the CIA would designate the deputy, who was responsible for technical and intelligence matters.[45]

PID soon added two photointerpreters and a lab technician to the West German operation, which continued to develop and interpret U-2 photography of the Middle East throughout September and October 1956. This unit's timely and accurate information enabled the PARAMOUNT Committee to predict the joint Israeli-British-French attack on Egypt three days before it took place.

[Redacted]. During the rest of the month, Detachment A pilots flew another eight missions over the Middle East. By this time, the new Detachment B in Turkey was ready for operations, and it was better positioned to provide coverage of the Middle East. Detachment B began flying missions in September and soon became the primary detachment for Middle East overflights, conducting nine out of the 10 such missions flown in October.[46]

Detachment B's first U-2 flight, on 11 September 1956, made passes over [redacted]. The next flight, more than two weeks later,

---

[45] Ibid., pp. 49-52 (S).

[46] *OSA History,* chap. 19, annex 120, "CIA U-2 Missions Flown, 1956-1968," pp. 1-2 (TS Codeword).

covered much the same ground but flew as far west as [redacted]. Both were "special" missions aimed at [redacted].

Other U-2 photographs revealed the presence [redacted]. The Anglo-French military buildup greatly irritated President Eisenhower, who considered these activities a violation of the 1950 Tripartite Declaration, in which the United States, the United Kingdom, and France had agreed to maintain the status quo in armaments and borders in the Middle East [redacted].

U-2 photography continued to keep the President and other key officials well informed about the progress of the crisis. [Redacted]. Secretary of State John Foster Dulles told the President on 28 October that he believed an Israeli attack on Jordan was imminent, adding that he thought the British and French would take advantage of such an attack to occupy the Suez Canal.[47]

The 10-day Middle East war began on the afternoon of 29 October 1956 with Israeli paratroop drops in the Sinai peninsula, followed by mobile columns striking deep into Egyptian territory. The next day, 30 October, Francis Gary Powers conducted mission 1314. [Redacted] where he photographed black puffs of smoke from the fighting between Israel and Egypt. Adana-based U-2s were in the air for the next two days filming the Suez Canal area [redacted].

The United Kingdom and France entered the fray on the evening of 31 October with bombing raids against major Egyptian airfields. The Anglo-French bombing campaign continued for the next 48 hours. Early on the morning of 1 November, an Adana-based U-2, piloted by William Hall, took off to gather intelligence on the [redacted]. Hall flew south [redacted] where he made several passes to obtain complete coverage of the Israeli-Egyptian fighting there. He then headed west to Cairo passing directly over the main Egyptian airbase at Almaza, where he filmed neatly arranged rows of Egyptian military aircraft. Continuing

---

[47] Telephone calls, 28 October 1956, DDE Diary, DDEL.

past Cairo to film another airfield, Hall turned southeast and then north to fly along the Nile, again crossing directly over Almaza. The photography from this leg of the mission revealed the burning wreckage of the Egyptian aircraft. During the short period of time that had passed between Hall's two passes, a combined Anglo-French air armada had attacked the airbase. When shown the before and after photos of Almaza, President Eisenhower told Arthur Lundahl: "Ten-minute reconnaissance, now that's a goal to shoot for!"[48] Eisenhower was pleased with the aerial photography but angered by what it depicted: an Anglo-French attack on Egypt. He quickly called for a cease-fire and denied the United Kingdom any further U-2 photographs of the Middle East.

The 1 November mission over Cyprus and Egypt also photographed Anglo-French preparations to invade Egypt. President Eisenhower was informed of this impending invasion on Sunday, 4 November. On the following day, British and French paratroopers dropped near Port Said at the north end of the Suez Canal. This action prompted Soviet Premier Nikolai Bulganin to send messages to France, Britain, and Israel warning that the Soviet Union was ready to use force to crush the aggressors.[49]

Early on the morning of election day, 6 November, the Anglo-French invasion armada arrived at Port Said and began landing troops. Back in Washington President Eisenhower met with Allen Dulles to discuss the deepening international crisis. Worried that the Soviet Union might be poised to intervene in the war, the President ordered Dulles to have the Adana-based U-2s fly over Syria to see whether the Soviets were moving planes to Syrian airbases

---

[48] Lundahl and Brugioni interview (TS Codeword); Beschloss (*Mayday*, p. 138) mistakenly identifies this quote as coming from the British, but they did not receive copies of these photos.

[49] Donald Neff, *Warriors at Suez: Eisenhower Takes America into the Middle East* (New York: Simon and Schuster, 1981), p. 403.

in preparation for a strike against the forces attacking Egypt. The answer to Eisenhower's question came much sooner than expected because on the previous day a U-2 had already overflown Syria before making a run across northern Egypt. The film from this flight had reached Wiesbaden for processing and readout during the night. The results were in the hands of the PARAMOUNT Committee by midmorning on 6 November, while the President was motoring to Gettysburg to cast his ballot. By the time the President returned to the White House by helicopter at noon, Colonel Goodpaster was waiting for him with an answer: there were no Soviet aircraft in Syria. Because of the President's concern about possible Soviet moves, Syria was the target of 14 additional U-2 flights between 7 November and 18 December 1956.[50]

The increasing reliance on Adana-based U-2s for coverage of the Middle East during the Suez Crisis made it difficult for the photointerpreters to supply timely information. When Detachment B aircraft returned to their base at Adana, there were no film-processing facilities available, and the film had to be flown to Wiesbaden, adding a 10- to 15-hour delay. During the gradual buildup of the crisis, this delay had been tolerated, but, once actual hostilities broke out, US decision makers needed a more rapid response. On 29 October, Richard Bissell ordered Lundahl to establish a film-processing facility at Adana. Two PID employees went to Adana on 13 November to set up the facility, and two photointerpreters moved from Wiesbaden to Adana to help in the effort. Forward processing was, however, hampered by the location of the Adana facility on a flat, arid plain in southern Turkey, 35 miles from the Mediterranean at the very end of a long supply line.

The PID team obtained and outfitted a trailer for film processing, but many problems had to be overcome. The first major problem was

---

[50] Memorandum of Conference, 6 November 1956, Eisenhower Diary, Whitman file, DDEL (U); *OSA History,* chap. 19, annex 120, p. 3 (TS Codeword).

obtaining enough clean water. Detachment B personnel, therefore, purchased large amounts of borax locally for use in purifying water. In fact, they bought so much borax on the local market that one of them was arrested by the Turkish police, who believed he was using the chemical to make drugs. It was also difficult to obtain a constant source of developers and fixers for processing the U-2 film, since the large Air Force supply facility at Wheelus AFB in Libya refused to provide the needed photographic chemicals. When PID personnel accompanied processed film from Turkey to the United States, they returned to Turkey sitting atop cartons of chemicals for the next day's processing. At first, film was developed in improvised tanks using flimsy wooden spools and hand-turned cranks to move the film through the solutions. Later, the Adana facility moved from its trailer to a building and received more up-to-date processing equipment. As was the case with the photo lab in Germany, the Adana lab's personnel came from the Agency and the armed forces.[51]

The need to produce very timely intelligence diminished after the British and French agreed to a cease-fire on 7 November 1956. By the end of the month, foreign troops began evacuating Egyptian territory, and the pressure on the Adana photointerpretation unit eased. The facility remained in existence, however, and was used twice in December 1956 and 11 times in the first half of 1957. It was then placed in caretaker status, for emergency use only.

RENEWED OVERFLIGHTS OF THE SOVIET UNION
Throughout the fall of 1956, U-2s provided valuable coverage of the Middle East crisis, but they were not conducting their original mission of strategic reconnaissance of the Soviet Union. President Eisenhower had halted all such overflights by his order of 10 July, and, in the months that followed, he remained unconvinced by CIA arguments in favor of a resumption of overflights. On

---

[51] *NPIC History,* vol. 1, pp. 53-54 (S); Lundahl and Brugioni interview (TS Codeword).

17 September 1956, DDCI Cabell and Richard Bissell went to the White House to ask President Eisenhower to authorize more flights over the Soviet Union. Adm. Arthur W. Radford, Chairman of the Joint Chiefs of Staff, also attended the meeting. Bissell and Defense Department representatives reviewed the valuable intelligence from the July U-2 flights, and Bissell then informed Eisenhower that many important intelligence requirements remained unfilled. To fill these requirements, Bissell noted, would require photography of approximately 15 separate areas of the Soviet Union. Pleading for the authority to resume overflights, Bissell stressed that conditions for photography were becoming less favorable as the days grew shorter. While the U-2 was then still safe from interception, he added, it might not be in the future.[52]

President Eisenhower acknowledged the value of the U-2 but emphasized that the international political aspects of overflights remained his overriding concern. He said he would talk further with John Foster Dulles about the matter, noting that the Secretary of State had at first seemed to belittle the political risk but had later found it increasingly worrisome.

A little more than two weeks later, on 3 October, when the President again met with Bissell, Cabell, and Radford, John Foster Dulles was also present. In opening the meeting, Eisenhower said he had become discouraged regarding Project AQUATONE. Although he had been assured that "there would be a good chance of not being discovered on most, if not all, operations, just the opposite had proved true." The President observed that arguments in favor of resuming U-2 operations did not take world opinion into consideration. He added that great efforts had been made for many years "to create an opinion in the world that we are not truculent and do not

---

[52] Andrew J. Goodpaster, Memorandum of Conference, 17 September 1956, WHOSS, Alpha, DDEL (TS).

want war," and, if knowledge of the U-2 overflights got out, world opinion would view them as "provocative and unjustified."[53]

Secretary of State Dulles said that, although he essentially agreed with the President's comments, he thought that "really important results" might be obtained by a seven to 10-day operation. He, nevertheless, questioned the long-term value of the results. DDCI Cabell replied that U-2 photographs would be useful much longer than the Secretary of State had implied because they would establish a reference bank of geographic and manmade features. Siding with Cabell, Admiral Radford pointed out the need for more intelligence to make estimates better.

President Eisenhower was not convinced by these arguments. Although willing to consider extensions of the radar-seeking ferret flights he had authorized along the Soviet borders, he remained opposed to penetration flights over the Soviet Union.

Events in Eastern Europe in the fall of 1956 helped to change the President's mind. In October the Soviet Union backed away from a confrontation with nationalist Communist leaders in Poland only to find itself facing a similar situation in Hungary, where mass demonstrations led to the formation of a new government under Imre Nagy on 23 October 1956. Soviet troops and tanks temporarily withdrew from Budapest while awaiting reinforcements. By early November, however, the Kremlin leadership decided that events in Hungary were getting out of hand—particularly when Premier Nagy announced his nation's withdrawal from the Warsaw Pact—and ordered Soviet troops to suppress the Hungarian uprising. Although President Eisenhower deplored the Soviet intervention, he turned down CIA requests for permission to airdrop arms and supplies to the Hungarian rebels. In fact, the President forbid all overflights of that nation, including those by U-2 aircraft, and none was made.[54]

---

[53] Andrew J. Goodpaster, Memorandum for the Record, 3 October 1956, WHOSS, Alpha, DDEL (TS).

[54] Cunningham interview (TS Codeword).

Although President Eisenhower had not been willing to allow overflights during the Hungarian crisis, the Soviet Union's actions in Hungary convinced him to authorize renewed over-flights of the Soviet Bloc, a decision that was made easier by his reelection by a large margin in early November. Initially, how-ever, the President only authorized overflights of Eastern Europe and Soviet border regions, not the deep penetration overflights that had been requested by CIA. At a 15 November 1956 meeting with Acting Secretary of State Herbert Hoover, Jr. (John Foster Dulles was recovering from cancer surgery), JCS Chairman Adm. Arthur Radford, DCI Allen Dulles, and Richard Bissell, Eisen-hower explained why he refused to allow overflights of the Soviet Union: "Everyone in the world says that, in the last six weeks, the United States has gained a place it hasn't held since World War II. To make trips now would cost more than we would gain in form of solid information." Hoover agreed and noted, "If we lost a plane at this stage, it would be almost catastrophic." Torn between his desire to maintain a "correct and moral" position and his wish to know what the Soviet Union was up to, the Presi-dent finally authorized several overflights of Eastern Europe and the Soviet border, "but not the deep one," adding that the aircraft should "stay as close to the border as possible."[55]

The first of these flights, mission 4016 on 20 November 1956, was the first overflight of Soviet territory since 10 July. This mission left Adana and flew east over Iran, then reversed and flew west along the Soviet-Iranian border to Soviet Arme-nia, where it crossed into the Soviet Union and photographed Yerevan. An electrical malfunction then forced the pilot, Francis Gary Powers, to return to Adana. Soviet interceptor aircraft made

---

[55] Andrew J. Goodpaster, Memorandum of Conference with the President, November 15, 1956, WHOSS, Alpha, DDEL (TS); Ambrose, *Eisenhower: The President*, p. 374.

several unsuccessful attempts to reach this U-2, and the Soviet Government sent a secret protest note to Washington.[56]

On 10 December, Bulgaria was the target of two U-2 missions, one (4018) from Detachment B at Adana and another (2029) from Detachment A at Giebelstadt. Bulgarian fighter aircraft made 10 different attempts to intercept the first mission, but the flight proceeded without difficulty.[57]

The second flight came close to crashing but not through the efforts of interceptors. The pilot of mission 2029 was Carmine Vito, who had flown the first U-2 mission over Moscow on 5 July. He was known to his colleagues as the Lemon-Drop Kid because he always carried these hard candies in the knee pocket of his flight suit. Despite warnings to all pilots about the danger of opening the helmet faceplate at high altitudes, several pilots were known to do so. Some ate candy bars; Vito favored lemon drops. On the morning of 10 December, while Vito was undergoing prebreathing, the Air Force enlisted man who oversaw his preflight regimen placed an L-pill in the righthand knee pocket of Vito's flight suit, unaware that this pocket also contained Vito's supply of lemon drops. After he took off, Vito began indulging in his habit of sucking lemon drops. About midway into the mission, he opened his faceplate and popped into his mouth what he thought was another lemon drop. After closing the faceplate, he began sucking on the object and thought it strange that it had no flavor and was much smoother than the previous lemon drops. Although tempted to bite down, Vito decided instead to reopen his faceplate and see what it was he had in his mouth. Spitting the object into his hand, he saw that he had been sucking on the L-pill with its lethal contents of potassium cyanide. Just a thin layer of

---

[56] Mission folder 4016, 20 November 1956, OSA records, job 67-B-972, box 7 (TS Codeword).

[57] Mission folders 2029 (10 December 1956) and 4018 (10 December 1956), OSA records, job 67-B-328, box 7 and job 67-B-972, box 7 (TS Codeword).

glass had stood between him and death. The loss of his aircraft over Bulgaria would have exposed the U-2 program to worldwide publicity and would probably have resulted in an early end to overflights.[58]

Detachment A's security officer overheard Vito relating the L-pill story to a fellow pilot several days later and promptly reported the conversation to headquarters. When details of Vito's close call reached Washington, James Cunningham immediately ordered L-pills placed in boxes so that there would be no chance of mistaking them for anything else. The L-pill continued to be available for another three years. Then in January 1960, the commander of Detachment B, Col. William Shelton, raised an important question that had never been considered: what would happen if an L-pill with its volatile contents accidentally broke inside the cockpit of a U-2? Realizing that such an accident would result in the death of the pilot, James Cunningham ordered the destruction of all L-pills and then turned to the Technical Services Division (TSD) for a better idea. By this time the state of the art in lethal devices was a needle poisoned with algal, an extremely deadly shellfish toxin. The needle was hidden in a tiny hole in a silver dollar supplied by Cunningham. Only one poison-needle coin was made because Cunningham decided that, if any pilot had to use it because of capture, there would probably not be any more overflights.[59]

Although the U-2 overflights of Eastern Europe in late 1956 caused renewed Soviet protests, the sharpest protest came on 15 December 1956, after three specially modified USAF RB-57D bombers photographed the city of Vladivostok in a high-speed

---

[58] Cunningham interview (TS Codeword); Carmine Vito, interview by Donald E. Welzenbach, Washington, DC, 7 May 1986 (S).

[59] Cable from Detachment B to Development Projects Division (DPD), 4 January 1960; cable from DPD to Detachment B, 7 January 1960, OSA records, job 67-B-972, box 18, "Operation KNIFE EDGE" (TS Codeword).

dash over the Far Eastern coast of the Soviet Union (as part of the Air Force's Operation BLACK KNIGHT). President Eisenhower had approved the mission after being told by the Air Force that the high-speed RB-57Ds would probably not be detected.[60]

Reacting strongly to the Soviet protest, the President told Secretary of State Dulles on 18 December that he was going to "order complete stoppage of this entire business." As for a reply to the Soviet protest, Dulles said, "I think we will have to admit this was done and say we are sorry. We cannot deny it." Dulles noted that "our relations with Russia are pretty tense at the moment." Eisenhower agreed, noting that this was no time to be provocative. He then instructed Colonel Goodpaster to call Secretary of Defense Wilson, Joint Chiefs of Staff Chairman Radford, and DCI Dulles to order: "Effective immediately, there are to be no flights by US reconnaissance aircraft over *Iron Curtain* countries."[61]

Flights along the borders of Iron Curtain countries continued, however, and, on 22 December 1956, Detachment B flew the First mission (4019) by a U-2 equipped for electronic intercept. The electronic-detection equipment known as the System-V unit (see appendix C) was installed in the bay normally used by the main camera, and the plane flew along the Soviet border from the Black Sea to the Caspian Sea and on to Afghanistan. The System-V unit worked well.[62]

---

[60] Goodpaster interview (S).

[61] Telephone calls 18 December 1956, DDE Diary, DDEL (U); Andrew J. Goodpaster, Memorandum for the Record, 18 December 1956, WHOSS, Alpha, DDEL (TS, downgraded to S); the Soviet protest note of 15 December 1956 and the U.S. reply of 11 January 1957 are contained in "Alleged Overflight of Soviet Area by American Planes." *US Department of State Bulletin,* vol. 36, 28 January 1957, p. 135. Although Dulles's initial inclination had been to offer an apology, the U.S. reply stated that the "only authorized United States Air Force flights in the general area of the Sea of Japan were normal training activities."

[62] Mission folder 4019 (22 December 1956), OSA records, job 67-B-972, box 7 (TS Codeword).

Early in 1957, a mission along the Soviet border accidentally turned into an overflight. On 18 March 1957, a U-2 collecting electronic intelligence along the Soviet southern border entered Soviet airspace because of compass error compounded by a slight error in the pilot's dead reckoning. Because of heavy cloud cover, the pilot, James W. Cherbonneaux, did not realize he was over the Soviet Union until he saw Soviet fighters attempting to intercept him. These attempts at interception once again demonstrated the Soviets' ability to track the U-2 and their inability to harm it.[63]

At this point in early 1957, the U-2 program was in limbo. Although the President would not allow U-2s to fly their primary mission of reconnaissance of the Soviet Union, he did not cancel the program and continued to authorize flights along Soviet borders. The CIA's overhead reconnaissance program also faced a renewed bid by the Air Force, which now had its own growing U-2 fleet, to gain control of the overflight program in the spring of 1957. The uncertainty surrounding the future of the project made planning and budgeting extremely difficult. In April 1957, Richard Bissell asked the DCI and DDCI to push for a decision on whether the U-2 program was to continue in civilian hands and what its scope was to be. In briefing papers prepared for the DCI, Bissell argued for maintaining a nonmilitary overflight capability, which could "maintain greater security, employ deeper cover, use civilian pilots, keep the aircraft outside military control, and, therefore, make possible more plausible denial of US military responsibility in the face of any Soviet charges." In urging the resumption of overflights, Bissell stated that four U-2 missions over border regions of the Soviet Union or Eastern Europe had been detected by the Soviets without causing any diplomatic protest. He also noted that the

---

[63] Information supplied by James W. Cherbonneaux to Donald E. Welzenbach (S); Mission folder 4020 (18 March 1957), OSA records, job 67-B-972, box 7 (TS Codeword).

President's Board of Consultants on Foreign Intelligence Activities had unanimously recommended the resumption of overflights.[64]

All of these issues were discussed on 6 May 1957, when President Eisenhower met with Deputy Secretary of Defense Donald Quarles, Air Force Chief of Staff Nathan Twining, Acting Secretary of State Christian Herter, and three CIA officials—DCI Dulles, DDCI Cabell, and Richard Bissell. The President expressed concern about the impact of overflights on US-Soviet relations and about possible Soviet responses such as closing off access to Berlin. Although remaining opposed to flights over most of the Soviet Union, Eisenhower finally agreed to permit some flights over peripheral areas such as Kamchatka Peninsula and Lake Baikal, as well as the Soviet Union's atomic testing area at Semipalatinsk. Such overflights could be staged from Pakistan if the Pakistani Government consented. The President rejected the Air Force's request to take over the U-2 program, stating that he preferred to have the aircraft manned by civilians "during operations of this kind."[65]

The President had once again agreed to allow overflights of the Soviet Union, although only over certain areas, because the need to learn more about the capabilities and intentions of the Soviet Union was too compelling. In particular, the President and top administration officials wanted to gather more data on the Soviet Union's missile program, a subject for which considerable Soviet boasting—but no hard data—was available.

Even after he had authorized the resumption of overflights, President Eisenhower maintained tight control over the program. He personally authorized each overflight, which meant that Richard Bissell would bring maps to the White House with the proposed routes marked on them for the President to examine. More than once, accord-

---

[64] *OSA History,* chap. 4, pp 15-16, annex 22 (TS Codeword).

[65] Andrew J. Goodpaster, Memorandum of Conference with the President, 6 May 1957 (TS); "Record of Action—Meeting of May 6, 1957," WHOSS, Alpha, DDEL (TS).

ing to Bissell, Eisenhower spread the map out on his Oval Office desk for detailed study, usually with his son John (an Army officer serving as a White House aide) and Colonel Goodpaster looking over his shoulder. On occasion, the President would pick up a pencil and eliminate a flight leg or make some other correction to the flight plan.[66]

RADAR-DECEPTIVE "DIRTY BIRDS"

One additional reason why President Eisenhower had again authorized overflights of the Soviet Union was renewed CIA promises that Soviet detection or tracking of the U-2 was unlikely. At the 6 May 1957 meeting with the President, Richard Bissell reported on the progress that had been made in developing radar camouflage and absorption devices for the U-2. Once these devices were installed on the operational U-2s, he explained, the majority of incidents would be undetected."[67]

"Trapeze" antiradar attachments to the U-2

---

[66] Bissell interview by Welzenbach (S); Beschloss, *Mayday*, p. 140.
[67] Andrew J. Goodpaster, Memorandum of Conference with the President, 6 May 1957 (TS); "Record of Action—Meeting of May 6, 1957," WHOSS, Alpha, DDEL (TS).

Work on methods of reducing the U-2's vulnerability to radar detection had begun in the fall of 1956 as the result of President Eisenhower's disenchantment with the overflight program following Soviet detection and tracking of the first series of U-2 missions. The CIA proprietary firm Scientific Engineering Institute was conducting this research under a project codenamed RAINBOW. SEI Chief Engineer Dr. Franklin A. Rodgers, formerly of MIT, converted the theories of Harvard physicist Edward Purcell into systems that could be used on aircraft. SEI's radar-deception system consisted of a series of attachments to the U-2. First bamboo poles and later fiberglass rods were attached to the wings, where they would not interfere with the control surfaces. At the ends of these poles, completely circling the aircraft, was a small-gauge wire with precisely spaced ferrite beads. The wire and beads were supposed to capture incoming 70-MHz radar pulses and either trap them in the loop or weaken them so much that they would not register as a valid radar return. This configuration was called the trapeze and was not very successful.

A second approach, tested in early 1958, involved the use of plastic material containing a printed circuit designed to absorb radar pulses in the 65- to 85-MHz range. Nicknamed "wallpaper," this material was glued to parts of the U-2's fuselage, nose, and tail. Although the "trapeze" and "wallpaper" systems provided protection against some Soviet radars, the systems proved ineffective against radars operating below 65-MHz or above 85-MHz. Furthermore, both of these additions degraded the U-2's performance. The weight and drag of "trapeze" reduced the aircraft's operating ceiling by 1,500 feet, and "wallpaper" sometimes caused engines to overheat.[68]

SEI's research results were tested by another firm known as Edgerton, Germeshausen & Grier (EG&G), which was also com-

---

[68] Records of the Scientific Engineering Institute (Project HTNAMABLE), OSA records (TS Codeword).

posed of MIT faculty members. Under an Air Force contract to evaluate radars, EG&G operated a small testing facility at Indian Springs, Nevada, not far from Area 51. Although Kelly Johnson had been closely involved with the radar deception project since its early days, he cooperated reluctantly because he disliked adding attachments that made his aircraft less airworthy. (Johnson's dislike of the antiradar attachments was reflected in the unofficial nickname for aircraft that had been so modified—"dirty birds.") After Lockheed mechanics had mounted the various RAINBOW devices on the prototype U-2, a Lockheed test pilot would fly the plane over EG&G's Indian Springs installation. This was little more than a series of radar sets and a trailer containing instrumentation. EG&G technicians could thus record and evaluate the U-2's radar returns as it traversed a specified course over their facility.[69]

This method of testing radar-deceptive modifications proved both time consuming and dangerous. During a test flight on 2 April 1957, the "wallpaper" modification acted as insulation around the engine of the U-2 known as article 341, causing it to overheat and flameout. Unable to restart the power plant, Lockheed test pilot Robert Sieker bailed out but was struck and killed in midair by the U-2's tailplane. The aircraft crashed in an area of Nevada so remote that Area 51 search teams needed four days to locate the wreckage. The extensive search attracted the attention of the press, and a 12 April 1957 article in the *Chicago Daily Tribune* was headlined, "Secrecy Veils High-Altitude Research Jet; Lockheed U-2 Called *Super Snooper.*"[70]

Because of its large wingspan, an out-of-control U-2 tended to enter a classical flat spin before ground contact. This slowed descent and actually lessened the impact. If there was no fire after

---

[69] References to EG&G programs for the U-2 are contained in the later Convair contracts for Projects FISH and KINGFISH. OSA records, job 67-B-415, box 1 (TS Codeword).

[70] Accident folder, crash of 2 April 1957, OSA records (S).

impact, the remains of crashed U-2s were often salvageable, as was the case with the wreckage of article 341. Kelly Johnson's crew at the Skunk Works used the wreckage, along with spares and salvaged parts of other crashed U-2s, to produce another flyable airframe for about $185,000.[71] The U-2's ability to survive a crash in fairly good condition should have been noted by the Development Projects Staff for consideration in its contingency plans for a loss over hostile territory because the equipment on board the aircraft could easily compromise the weather research cover story.

The loss of one of Lockheed's best test pilots, as well as the prototype "dirty bird" U-2, led Kelly Johnson to suggest that Lockheed install a large boom at the Indian Springs radar test facility. Using the boom, which could lift entire airframes 50 feet in the air, technicians could change the airframe's attitude and run radar tests almost continuously without having to fuel and fly the plane.[72]

By the summer of 1957, testing of the radar-deception system was complete, and in July the first "dirty bird" (DB) arrived at Detachment B. The first operational use of this aircraft occurred on 21 July 1957 in mission 4030 over Iran, Iraq, and Syria. On 31 July, the same aircraft made a run over the Black Sea. There were a total of nine DB missions over the USSR. The antiradar system did not prove very effective, and its use was curtailed in May 1958.[73]

THE NEW DETACHMENT C

On 8 June 1957, a U-2 took off from Eielson Air Force Base in Alaska to conduct the first intentional overflight of the Soviet Union since December 1956. This mission broke new ground in two respects: it was the first overflight conducted from American soil and the first by the new Detachment C.

---

[71] Lockheed contracts, OSA Records (S).

[72] Ibid. (S).

[73] Cunningham interview (TS Codeword).

Detachment C (known officially as Weather Reconnaissance Squadron, Provisional-3) was composed of the third group of pilots to complete their training in Nevada. In the autumn of 1956, this third detachment needed a new base because Area 51 was about to become the training site for a large number of Air Force pilots who would fly the 29 U-2s purchased by the Air Force. The Agency decided that the best location for Detachment C would be the Far East and began looking for bases there.

Even without the arrival of the Air Force pilots, Detachment C could not have stayed in Nevada much longer. In June 1957, the entire facility had to be evacuated because the Atomic Energy Commission was about to conduct a series of nuclear tests whose fallout was expected to contaminate the Groom Lake facility. All remaining CIA personnel, materiel, and aircraft were transferred to Edwards AFB, California, and became known as Detachment G.

The search for a new home for Detachment C led the Agency to ask the Air Force in the autumn of 1956 for permission to locate the detachment at Yokota AFB, Japan. Because Yokota was already the base for one covert project (the very secret Air Force Project BLACK KNIGHT using RB-57s), Air Force Chief of Staff Twining did not wish to locate another one there and denied the request. The Agency then turned to the Navy, which granted permission for Detachment C to use the Naval Air Station at Atsugi, Japan. The Japanese Government received no notification of the proposed deployment because at that time it had no control over activities involving US military bases in Japan. Deployment of Detachment C began in early 1957 but was complicated by a recent decision to permit the families of Project AQUATONE employees to accompany them on overseas tours. As a result, program managers had to find housing facilities on the base or in nearby communities, not an easy task in crowded Japan.[74]

---

[74] *OSA History,* chap. 15, pp. 2, 16-19; chap. 16, p. 1 (TS Codeword).

Detachment C began conducting missions in June 1957 after several aircraft and pilots flew to Eielson Air Force Base near Fairbanks, Alaska. Air Force radar order-of-battle reports and NSA studies had revealed that the radar network in the Soviet Far East, with antiquated radar sets and personnel of a lower caliber than those in the western Soviet Union, was relatively ineffective. To take advantage of these weaknesses, Detachment C staged three missions from Alaska into the Soviet Far East. The first, on 7/8 June (the aircraft crossed the international date line during the flight), was unable to photograph its target, the ICBM impact area near Klyuchi on the Kamchatka Peninsula, because of bad weather and, therefore, never entered Soviet airspace. A second attempt to photograph Klyuchi on 19/20 June was marred by a camera malfunction that ruined every third frame of photography. This flight was tracked by Soviet radars, but there was no attempt at interception. After a pause of almost three months during which Detachment C received a dirty-bird U-2, the detachment's third mission over Klyuchi on 15/16 September 1957 achieved excellent results. The radar-deception devices proved ineffective, however, as the U-2 was tracked by Soviet radar and trailed by five fighters.[75]

DETACHMENT B FLIGHTS FROM PAKISTAN

The most important series of overflights in the summer of 1957 were those that Detachment B staged to gather intelligence on the Soviet Union's guided missile and nuclear programs. President Eisenhower had approved these overflights at the meeting on 6 May 1957, [redacted].

[Redacted]. The airfield at Peshawar, a more desirable location, was not available because of repair work. Detachment B at Ankara ferried four of its U-2s, two of which were dirty birds, to Lahore.

---

[75] Mission folders 6002 (8 June 1957), 6005 (20 June 1957) and 6008 (16 September 1957), OSA records, job 67-B-328, box 7 (TS Codeword).

A C-124 brought in eight pilots and ground crews to prepare for missions over the Soviet Union and the People's Republic of China (PRC) beginning on 4 August (Operation SOFT TOUCH). During a 23-day period, these aircraft made nine flights: seven over the USSR and two over the PRC. Although one of the seven flights over the USSR was a failure because the camera malfunctioned after taking only 125 exposures, the remaining missions over Central Asia were a complete success, producing a bonanza of information that kept scores of photointerpreters busy for more than a year.[76]

The 5 August flight, a dirty bird piloted by Buster Edens, was the first to photograph the major Soviet space launch facility east of the Aral Sea in Kazakhstan. None of the mission planners was certain just where the range was located, so the U-2 pilot followed the rail lines in the area. As a result, the plane did not pass directly over the rangehead and obtained only oblique photography.

Although known in the West today as Tyuratam, this missile installation had no name when it was first photographed in August 1957. In preparation for a briefing to President Eisenhower on the SOFT TOUCH photography, Dino Brugioni, an assistant to PID chief Arthur Lundahl, examined all the existing maps of the area to see if he could find a place name for the missile base. Only one map, made by the Germans during World War II, showed a community in the vicinity of the missile facility. The settlement's name was Tyuratam, which means "arrow burial ground" in the Kazakh language, and this was the name Brugioni gave the missile base. Official Soviet releases concerning this base have always referred to it as Baykonur, but the community of Baykonur is actually more than 200 miles north of Tyuratam.[77]

While PID was still analyzing the SOFT TOUCH photography, the Soviet Union announced the successful launch

---

[76] *OSA History,* chap. 12, pp. 19-20 (TS Codeword); *NPIC History,* vol. 1, pp. 159-161.

[77] Lundahl and Brugioni interview (TS Codeword).

Operation SOFT TOUCH Overflights, August 1957

Mission 4035   5 August
Mission 4036   8 August
Mission 4039   12 August
Mission 4045   21 August
Mission 4048   21 August
Mission 4049   22 August
Mission 4050   22 August
Mission 4051   22 August
Mission 4058   28 August

Secret NOFORN

724747 (B00851) 4-92

of an intercontinental ballistic missile (ICBM) from Baykonur (Tyuratam). On 26 August 1957, the Soviet news agency TASS stated that a "super-long-range multistage intercontinental ballistic rocket" had been successfully tested, adding "it is now possible to send missiles to any part of the world."[78] The Soviet announcement made the intelligence community want even more information on Tyuratam, and a second U-2 piloted by Edwin K. Jones flew over the area on 28 August 1957, just one week after the Soviet ICBM launch. This mission obtained excellent vertical photographs of the main launch complex, and photointerpreters soon determined that the Soviets had only one launchpad at Tyuratam. The base was not photographed again until 9 July 1959, at which time it still had only one launch pad, although two more were under construction.[79]

On 20 and 21 August 1957, U-2s conducted the first overflights of the Soviet nuclear testing grounds at Semipalatinsk, north-northwest of Lake Balkhash. The first mission, piloted by Sammy V. C. Snider, passed over part of the proving grounds, flew on to Novokuznetsk, and then proceeded to Tomsk, where it began its return leg that included coverage of a very large uranium-processing facility at the new city of Berezovskiy. In the second mission, James Cherbonneaux flew directly over the Semipalatinsk proving grounds only four hours before a half-megaton device was detonated. In fact, the U-2 unknowingly photographed the aircraft that was to drop the nuclear device. These photographs also revealed evidence of a recent, low-yield, above-ground nuclear test [redacted].

On its way to Semipalatinsk, the 21 August mission flew a search pattern over the western end of Lake Balkash looking for another Soviet missile-related installation and made the first

---

[78] "Is Russia Ahead in Missile Race?" *US News and World Report*, 6 September 1957, pp. 30-33.
[79] Mission folders 4058 (28 August 1957) and 4125 (9 July 1959), OSA records, job 67-B-972, boxes 8 and 11 (TS Codeword).

photographs of what was later determined to be the new missile test center at Saryshagan. This facility was used to test radars against incoming missiles fired from Kapustin Yar, 1,400 miles to the west. Saryshagan later became the center for the development of the Soviet Union's advanced antiballistic missile (ABM) weapon system.

On 23 August 1957, DDCI Cabell, Richard Bissell, and Air Force Chief of Staff Twining met with President Eisenhower to report on the results of Operation SOFT TOUCH. They showed the President some of the photographic results of the earlier missions and reported on the effects of the antiradar measures. Although the antiradar measures had not proved successful, the photographic yield from the missions was extremely valuable. Bissell then informed the President that the SOFT TOUCH operation was just about to conclude with the transfer of the aircraft back to Adana. He asked permission for one of the U-2s to make another overflight of the Soviet Union on this return trip, but the President denied the request, not wishing to conduct any more overflights than were necessary.[80]

THE DECLINE OF DETACHMENT A

During the summer of 1957, all overflights of the Soviet Union were conducted by either Detachment B or Detachment C. Detachment A in Germany was a less desirable starting point for overflights of the Soviet Union because such missions had to cross Eastern Europe first, increasing the likelihood of detection and diplomatic protests. Furthermore, the Soviet Union's air defense and radar networks were strongest along its western borders, so Detachment B missions over the southern portion of the Soviet Union and Detachment C missions in the Far East were less risky than those conducted by Detachment A. Finally, the main target

---

[80] Andrew J. Goodpaster, Memorandum for the Record, 23 August 1957, WHOSS, Alpha, DDEL (TS).

of U-2 photography after the bomber issue receded was Soviet missile and nuclear progress. The testing areas for these weapons were located in the vast open spaces of the south-central and eastern portions of the Soviet Union, which lay beyond the range of Detachment A's aircraft.

The decline in importance of Detachment A had begun with the President's standdown order of 10 July 1956. During the next three months, the detachment conducted only 11 missions, all over the Mediterranean region rather than the original target of the Soviet Union, and the slow pace of activity and change in mission adversely affected pilot morale. One of the detachment's aircraft was lost in a crash on 17 September, killing pilot Howard Carey and garnering unwanted publicity. Conditions improved when the detachment moved to the newly renovated facility at Giebelstadt in early October 1956, but security now became a problem there. Detachment A personnel discovered that a long, black Soviet-Bloc limousine was parked at the end of the Giebelstadt runway whenever the U-2s took off.[81]

During the next year, Detachment A mounted only four overflights. The first two were over Eastern Europe: one over Bulgaria on 10 December 1956 and the other over Albania on 25 April 1957. Then a long period of inactivity followed, ending with a third mission on 11 October 1957, which conducted electronic surveillance of Soviet naval maneuvers in the Barents Sea. The final overflight of Detachment A, mission 2040 on 13 October 1957, flew north over [redacted].

Although the final missions of Detachment A achieved excellent results, project headquarters had already decided that Western Europe was not a satisfactory location for overflights of the Soviet Union and had notified Detachment A on 20 September 1957 that its operations would cease in November. By 15 November 1957,

---

[81] *OSA History,* chap. 11, pp. 41-42 (TS Codeword).

all of the detachment's personnel and aircraft had returned to the United States. During Detachment A's 17-month period of operations, seven pilots had flown a total of 23 missions: six over the Soviet Union, five over Eastern Europe, and most of the remaining 12 missions over the Mediterranean area.[82]

[Redacted].

DECLINING OVERFLIGHT ACTIVITY

Operation SOFT TOUCH (4-27 August 1957) proved to be the high water mark of U-2 operations against the Soviet Union. Detachment B staged one more overflight on 10 September 1957, when a U-2 piloted by William Hall flew from Adana to photograph the Kapustin Yar Missile Test Range for the first time since the RAF's overflight in 1953, obtaining photographs of a large medium-range ballistic missile (MRBM) on the launchpad. Six days later Detachment C conducted its successful overflight of the ICBM impact site at Klyuchi, and October saw the final two overflights of Detachment A. After these missions, penetration overflights became a rarity. There would be only six more during the next 32 months: one, in 1958; two, in 1959: and three, in 1960 (one of which was unsuccessful). During this period, President Eisenhower did authorize a number of flights along Soviet border areas that occasionally penetrated short distances inside the border, but the Chief Executive had become extremely wary of authorizing "deep penetration" overflights, which invariably brought protests from Moscow.

The border flights took place under tight controls. Beginning in the fall of 1957, all messages from Washington to Adana giving coordinates for flights along the Soviet border contained the statement: "This is not a penetration overflight" and warned about flying too close to Soviet borders. The Soviets even attempted to shoot down U-2s flying well within international airspace

---

[82] *OSA History,* chap. 11, p. 44; chap. 19, annex 120 (TS Codeword).

above the Black Sea, as was the case on 27 October 1957, when electronic intelligence equipment on a U-2 flight over the Black Sea that never violated Soviet airspace revealed 12 attempts at interception by Soviet fighters.[83]

The sole U-2 overflight of 1958 was conducted by a dirty bird from Detachment C. On 1 March 1958, mission 6011 overflew the Soviet Far East and photographed the Trans-Siberian Railroad, Sovetskaya Gavan', the Tatar Strait, and a strange installation at Malaya Sazanka, which was eventually determined to be a structure for mating nuclear devices with their detonators. This was the first and only U-2 overflight of the Soviet Union staged from Japan.[84]

On 5 March 1958, the Soviet Union delivered a vigorous protest concerning this mission, prompting President Eisenhower to tell Colonel Goodpaster on 7 March to inform the CIA that U-2 flights were to be "discontinued, effective at once."[85] This standdown was to last more than 16 months, until July 1959. The Soviets had not been fooled by the antiradar devices carried by mission 6011, as was demonstrated by the detailed information about the mission contained in a Soviet aide-memoire delivered on 21 April 1958. It was clear that dirty bird aircraft were not effective and that Soviet radar operators had little difficulty in tracking them. At this point, the Agency abandoned the use of the antiradar devices on the U-2. As a substitute, Lockheed began working to develop a paint with radar-suppressant qualities, but this project also proved unsuccessful.

The U-2s were not the only cause for the Soviet protests that so vexed the President. On 27 June 1958 [redacted]. Ten days later the Air Force began launching balloons designed to fly across the

---

[83] Mission folder 4061 (27 October 1957), OSA records, job 67-B-972, box 8 (TS Codeword).

[84] Mission folder 6011 (1 March 1958), OSA records, job 67-B-972, box 13 (TS Codeword).

[85] Andrew J. Goodpaster, Memorandum for the Record, 7 March 1958, WHOSS, Alpha, DDEL (TS, declassified).

Soviet Union and Eastern Europe. This new balloon project (known as WS-461L) had been authorized by President Eisenhower on 25 June after Deputy Secretary of Defense Donald Quarles argued that a small number of balloons should be launched to take advantage of a newly discovered change in the west-to-east jet stream. Normally, this fast-moving air current stayed at an altitude of 55,000 feet, but, during June and July, it turned abruptly upward over the Bering Sea just west of Alaska, climbed to 110,000 feet, and then reversed direction. One of the key arguments that convinced the President to approve the project was Quarles's claim that the balloons' "chance of being detected is rather small and their identification or shootdown practically nil."[86]

Release of the balloons took place from an aircraft carrier in the Bering Sea on 7 July 1958. Nothing was heard about them until 28 July, when Poland sent a note protesting the overflight of a US-made, camera-carrying balloon that had fallen to earth in central Poland. The loss of this balloon was because of human error. Each balloon was equipped with a timing device that would cause it to drop its camera and film payload after crossing the target areas. An Air Force technician aboard the aircraft carrier had calculated that the balloons should cross the Eurasian landmass in about 16 days. Thus, he adjusted regulators aboard the balloons to cause automatic descent after 400 hours aloft. When bad weather delayed the launch for three successive days, however, the technician forgot to reset the timing devices. As a result, one payload fell into Poland. None of the three WS-461L balloon payloads was recovered.[87]

The Polish protest was quickly followed by a Soviet note protesting the balloons' violation of the Soviet Union's airspace. Several months later, the Soviets placed the US balloon and pho-

---

[86] Andrew J. Goodpaster, Memorandum for the Record, 25 June 1958, WHOSS, Alpha, DDEL (TS).

[87] Donald E. Welzenbach, "Observation Balloons and Weather Satellites," *Studies in Intelligence* 30 (Spring 1986): pp. 26-28 (S).

tographic equipment on display in Moscow for the world's press. President Eisenhower was angry that the Defense Department's assurances that the balloons would not be detected had proved false. Even worse, one of the balloons had been recovered by the Poles because the Air Force had disobeyed his instructions for the balloon project. When the Air Force had proposed the use of timers to bring down the balloons at the end of the mission, Eisenhower had said no, fearing that a malfunction could cause the balloons to come down prematurely. Furious at the Air Force's insubordination, the President ordered General Goodpaster on 29 July 1958 to tell the Air Force that "the project is to be discontinued at once and every cent that has been made available as part of any project involving crossing the Iron Curtain is to be impounded and no further expenditures are to be made."[88]

Two days later Eisenhower followed up this order with a formal memorandum to Secretary of Defense Neil McElroy telling him that "there is disturbing evidence of a deterioration in the processes of discipline and responsibility within the armed forces." He cited, in particular, "unauthorized decisions which have apparently resulted in certain balloons falling within the territory of the Communist Bloc" and overflights over routes "that contravened my standing orders."[89]

On 2 September 1958, there was another violation of Soviet airspace when an unarmed Air Force EC-130 on an electronic intelligence collection mission crossed from Turkey into Soviet Armenia and was shot down by Soviet fighter aircraft. Six of the men on board were killed and the remaining 11 were never heard

---

[88] Andrew J. Goodpaster, Memorandum for the Record, 29 July 1958, WHOSS, Alpha, DDEL (S); Goodpaster interview (S).
[89] Quoted in Ambrose, *Eisenhower: The President*, pp. 475-476.

from again, despite State Department attempts to get the Soviet Union to reveal their fate.[90]

President Eisenhower was disturbed by the increased super-power tension that had resulted from violations of Soviet airspace by US balloons and aircraft because he still hoped to enter into arms limitation negotiations with the Soviets. On 8 September 1958, the United States sent a note to the Soviet Union calling for a Soviet answer to US proposals for a "study of the technical aspects of safeguards against the possibility of surprise attack." One week later the Soviets agreed to participate and suggested that the talks begin in Geneva on 10 November 1958. President Eisenhower was also attempting to persuade the Soviet Union to begin talks aimed at eliminating the atmospheric testing of nuclear weapons. These efforts began with a 22 August 1958 offer to suspend US nuclear tests for one year on the condition that the Soviet Union also refrain from further tests and join in negotiations. On 30 August, Soviet Premier Nikita Khrushchev accepted the proposal and agreed to start talks on 31 October 1958 in Geneva. When the talks began, however, the Soviets refused to agree to a test ban and carried out nuclear tests at Semipalatinsk on 1 and 3 November. Nevertheless, during the late summer and early autumn of 1958, President Eisen-hower, determined to reduce to a minimum any aggravation of the Soviets, kept the U-2 overflight program in limbo.[91]

In November 1958, relations with the Soviet Union wors-ened after Khrushchev precipitated a new crisis over West Berlin by announcing plans to sign a peace treaty with East Germany by May 1959. He stated that such a treaty would terminate Allied rights in West Berlin. Four days later, Soviet troops began harass-ing US Army truck convoys on the highways leading from West

---

[90] "US Representations to the Soviet Government on C-130 Transport Shot Down by Soviet Fighter Aircraft," *US Department of State Bulletin,* 23 February 1959, pp. 262-271; Beschloss, *Mayday,* p. 159.

[91] Ambrose, *Eisenhower: The President*, pp. 489-491.

Germany to West Berlin. Although this new Berlin crisis never became as threatening as the blockade of 1948-49, President Eisenhower wished to avoid any actions that would provoke the Soviets. Tension over West Berlin was, therefore, an additional reason for continuing to keep the U-2 away from the Soviet Bloc.[92]

CONCERNS ABOUT SOVIET COUNTERMEASURES AGAINST THE U-2

Another reason for President Eisenhower's growing reluctance to authorize flights over the Soviet Union may have been concern that the Soviets were developing countermeasures that would enable them to shoot down a U-2. Before the program started, Richard Bissell had estimated that the U-2 would be able to fly over the Soviet Union with impunity for only about two years. This period was already over, and the Soviets were working frantically to devise a means to stop U-2 overflights. From the very beginning, Soviet air defense units had not only tracked U-2s with radars, but had also made repeated efforts to shoot them down with antiaircraft weapons and interceptor aircraft. In 1956 such attempted interceptions had involved primarily MiG-15s and MiG-17s, which could barely reach 55,000 feet. The advent of MiG-19s and MiG-21s, which could climb even higher, provided a greater threat for U-2 pilots.

Realistic training for pilots learning to intercept the U-2 became possible after the Soviets developed a new high-altitude aircraft, the Mandrake, which was actually an improved version of the Yakovlev-25 all-weather interceptor. The Mandrake used a high-lift, low-drag wing design similar to that employed by the U-2, but its twin engines made it heavier. The Mandrake's operating altitude was 55,000 to 65,000 feet, and its maximum altitude was 69,000, far less than the 75,000 feet reached by the U-2. Like the

---

[92] Ibid., pp. 502-504.

U-2, the Mandrake's wings would not tolerate great stresses, so it could not be used as an attack aircraft at the high altitudes at which both planes operated. Between 1957 and 1959, Yakovlev built 15 to 20 of these aircraft in two versions: the Mandrake-R or YAK-25RM and the Mandrake-T, sometimes called the YAK-26. These high-altitude aircraft were used to overfly the Middle East, India, China, and Pakistan, as well as border regions of NATO nations in Europe during the late 1950s and early 1960s. It is not believed that Mandrakes ever attempted to overfly the continental United States.[93]

Beginning in late 1957, the Mandrake served as a practice target for pilots of high-performance Soviet MiG-19 and MiG-21 interceptors. The Soviet technique that most concerned U-2 pilots was the "snap up" or power dive and zoom climb. In this maneuver, ground-based radar operators would direct the interceptor aircraft along the same flight path as the U-2. When the MiG pilot achieved the same compass heading as the U-2 flying more than 10,000 feet above him, he would put his aircraft into a shallow dive to pick up speed, apply full throttle to the engine, then pull back on the stick and zoom as high as he could. In this manner the Soviet pilot hoped to come up directly beneath the U-2 so he could use his guns and missiles against the shiny U-2 etched in silver against the dark blue-black of space. Using this maneuver, some MiGs were able to climb as high as the U-2 but seldom got very close. At this height the MiGs were completely out of control; their small, swept-back wings provided insufficient lift; and their control surfaces were too small to maintain aircraft stability. U-2 pilots often spotted MiGs that reached the apex of their zoom climbs and then fell away toward the earth. The US pilots' greatest fear was that one of the MiGs would actually collide with a U-2 during a zoom climb.[94]

---

[93] "Yakovlev Yak-25RM Mandrake," *Jane's Defence Weekly*, vol. 3, no. 7, 16 February 1985.

[94] Information supplied by Jacob Kratt and James Cherbonneaux to Donald E. Welzenbach, May 1986.

U-2 pilots complained that they felt like ducks in a shooting gallery under these circumstances and suggested that the underside of the silvery aircraft be camouflaged in some manner. Kelly Johnson had originally believed the U-2 would fly so high that it would be invisible, thus eliminating the need to paint the aircraft and thereby avoiding the added weight and drag that paint produced. The paint penalty was calculated to be a foot of altitude for every pound of paint. A full coat of paint cost the U-2 250 feet of altitude, substantially less than the 1,500-foot penalty paid for the addition of dirty bird devices.

By late 1957, Johnson agreed that something had to be done. After a series of tests over Edwards AFB, Lockheed began coating the U-2s with a standard blue-black military specification paint on top and a lighter cloud-blue paint below. Subsequent tests over Nevada revealed that the U-2s were less conspicuous when painted all over with a matte-finish blue-black color, which helped them blend with the dark canopy of space.[95]

MORE POWERFUL ENGINES FOR THE U-2

Less conspicuous paints were not the only answer to the growing threat of Soviet interceptors. A more powerful engine would increase the U-2's maximum altitude, which was the surest way to protect the aircraft from all Soviet threats. During late 1958 and early 1959, Lockheed began refitting the Agency's 13 remaining U-2s—originally the Agency had taken delivery of 20 planes and the Air Force of 31—with the more powerful Pratt & Whitney J75-P13 jet engine. This new power plant generated 4,200 pounds more thrust while adding only 2,050 pounds more weight. With its greater power, the engine permitted the U-2 to reach operational altitude more quickly, thereby reducing the telltale contrails that the U-2 produced as it passed through the tropopause at 45,000 to

---

[95] Lockheed contracts, OSA records (S).

55,000 feet. With the new engine, U-2 passed through this portion of the atmosphere faster and did so before entering hostile airspace, thus reducing the chance of visual detection. The J75 power plant also made it possible for the U-2 to carry a larger payload and gain another 2,500 feet in altitude, permitting it to cruise at 74,600 feet. The new engines were in very short supply because of the needs of the Air Force's F-105 construction program, but Colonel Geary used his Air Force contacts to obtain an initial supply of 12 engines. The Air Force never equipped its original U-2s with the J75 engines.[96]

Detachment C in Japan received the first of these re-engined aircraft, known as U-2Cs, in July 1959, and two more arrived in Turkey for Detachment B in August. All Agency U-2s had the new engines by the summer of 1962, but by then only seven CIA U-2s remained in service.

INTERVENTION IN LEBANON, 1958

Although the U-2 was used less and less for its original role of gathering strategic intelligence on the Soviet Bloc, it had acquired the new mission of providing US decisionmakers with up-to-date information on crisis situations all around the world. The first use of the U-2 to gather tactical intelligence occurred during the 1956 Suez Crisis. Afterward, U-2s from the Turkish-based Detachment B conducted periodic overflights to monitor the situation in the troubled Middle East, and they became especially active during the summer of 1958.

On 15 July 1958, President Eisenhower ordered US troops to land in Lebanon in response to a request for assistance by Lebanese President Camille Chamoun. Three months earlier, Eisenhower had turned down a similar request because the rioting that had led President Chamoun to ask for American aid had died down before intervention became necessary. In July, however, President Eisenhower saw the overall situation in the Middle East as much more threatening. On 14 July forces aligned toward Egyptian President

---

[96] *OSA History,* chap. 16, p. 8 (TS Codeword); Geary interview (S).

Gamal Abdel Nasser overthrew the Government of Iraq and assassinated the royal family. Long concerned by the growing influence of Nasser, who had close ties to the Soviet Union and now headed both Egypt and Syria in the new United Arab Republic, President Eisenhower decided that US intervention was necessary to stabilize the situation in Lebanon and to show Nasser that the United States was willing to use force to defend its vital interests in the region. Before intervening in Lebanon, the United States consulted with the United Kingdom, which also decided to intervene in the Middle East by sending paratroopers to assist the Government of Jordan on 17 July.

With US Marines and Army troops deployed in a potentially hostile situation in Lebanon, US military commanders and intelligence community analysts immediately requested tactical reconnaissance flights to look for threats to the US units and evidence that other Middle Eastern countries or the Soviet Union might be preparing to intervene. The U-2s of Detachment B in Turkey carried out these missions.

Because tactical reconnaissance required an immediate readout of the films taken, the Photographic Intelligence Center (the new name for the Photo-Intelligence Division from August 1958) quickly reopened the film-developing unit at Adana and staffed it with lab technicians and photointerpreters. Throughout the summer of 1958, Detachment B U-2s brought back photography of military camps, airfields, and ports of those Mediterranean countries receiving Soviet arms. The detachment also kept a close watch on Egyptian-based Soviet submarines, which posed a threat to US 6th Fleet ships in the Mediterranean. In addition, U-2s flew occasional electronic intelligence collection missions along the Soviet border and over the Black Sea without entering Soviet airspace. In late August, as the crisis in the Middle East eased, the United States began withdrawing its 14,300 troops. It was not until 25 October, however, that the last American soldier left Lebanon.[97]

---

[97] Ambrose, *Eisenhower: The President*, pp. 462-473.

BRITISH PARTICIPATION IN THE U-2 PROJECT

Shortly after the withdrawal of US troops from Lebanon, a new group of pilots joined the U-2 project. In November 1958, four RAF officers arrived at Detachment B at Adana, thus beginning the United Kingdom's participation in U-2 operations. The British had first become involved in the U-2 project in September 1956, when the United States supplied them with photography from U-2 missions. To handle U-2 material, the British created a new control system, which later merged with the US control system. By 1957 cooperation between the United Kingdom and the United States had expanded to include frequent consultation between the require-ments and photointerpretation organizations of both countries. James Reber and Arthur Lundahl made periodic trips to the United Kingdom for discussions with Alan Crick's UK Requirements Committee (generally known as the Crick Committee, later as the Joint Priorities Committee), the Joint Intelligence Committee, the Joint Air Reconnaissance Intelligence Center, and MI-6.[98]

The idea of using British pilots in the U-2 program first arose in the spring of 1957, when Richard Bissell—upset that his aircraft had not been allowed to fly over the Soviet Union since the December 1956 standdown—was searching for ways to reduce the political risks of overflights and thus obtain more frequent authorization for missions over the Soviet Union. One of his proposals was to use non-US pilots—possibly British—to increase the possibility of plausible denial in the event of a loss. At a meeting with key CIA, Defense Department, and State Depart-ment officials on 6 May 1957, President Eisenhower approved the concept of British participation in the U-2 project.[99]

---

[98] See, for example, the trip reports of the Ad Hoc Requirements Committee in the COMIREX records, IC Staff (TS Codeword).

[99] Andrew J. Goodpaster, Memorandum of Conference with the President, 6 May 1957 (TS); idem, "Record of Action—Meeting of May 6, 1957," WHOSS, Alpha, DDEL (TS).

During the next six months, Dulles and Bissell met with Sir Dick White, head of MI-6, and Air Vice Marshal William M. L. MacDonald, Assistant Chief of the Air Staff for Intelligence, on several occasions to discuss the proposal in general terms. At first the CIA did not push the proposal too hard because at the same meeting in which he approved British participation, President Eisenhower had consented to the resumption of U-2 missions over the Soviet Union, resulting in 10 overflights during the summer and early fall of 1957. But when flights ceased in October, the thought of British participation became more attractive. By early 1958, Bissell was pressing the British to begin training pilots in the U-2 even though no final political decision on their participation had been made. On 7 February 1958, Bissell instructed the [redacted] to ask Air Vice Marshal MacDonald if the RAF was prepared to select a group of pilots for the U-2 project. MacDonald agreed to Bissell's proposal and began recruiting RAF pilots to fly the U-2.[100]

In June 1958, representatives from the British Air Ministry came to project headquarters for an orientation and then sat down with CIA officials to work out an agreement on plans and procedures for the joint project. The two sides decided to establish a small RAF contingent that would be integrated into and supported by Detachment B at Adana. The British missions would be operationally controlled by CIA project headquarters. Soon afterward four British pilots began training in Texas. One of these pilots, Squadron Leader Christopher H. Walker, died in a training accident in July 1958. Because of the addition of RAF officers to the program, Project AQUATONE received a new codename, CHALICE. By the end of November 1958, three RAF pilots and a flight surgeon joined Detachment B at Adana with Turkish approval.

Formal approval by the political leaders of the United Kingdom and the United States had come several months earlier.

---

[100] *OSA History,* chap. 13, pp. 1-2 (TS Codeword).

On 27 August 1958, Prime Minister Harold Macmillan gave his approval to British participation in the project as long as he had the right to approve or disapprove all operational flights by RAF pilots. On the same day, President Eisenhower gave his approval in principle for the joint project.[101]

Both sides stood to gain from the joint nature of the U-2 project. For Richard Bissell, British participation was a means to gain an additional source of authorization for overflights of the Soviet Union. Six months earlier, Bissell had cabled to [redacted] that he wanted British participation because it would "facilitate operations by them at times or under circumstances beyond the scope of authority accorded by US political authorities."[102]

President Eisenhower viewed British participation as a way to confuse the Soviets as to the sponsorship of particular overflights and also to spread the risk in the event of a loss. Furthermore, he was used to working closely with the British from his wartime experience and believed that their involvement in the U-2 program was a natural aspect of their alliance with the United States.[103]

On the British side, participation in U-2 flights was a logical extension of the close cooperation that already existed between the two countries on the U-2 program. The direct involvement of the British also enabled them to conduct additional flights in areas such as the Middle East that were of more intelligence interest to the United Kingdom than to the United States. The British also may have reasoned that direct participation in the program was the best way to ensure that they had a right to share in the U-2's take. Otherwise, the United States might decide at some point to cut off the flow of U-2 photography, as it had done during the 1956 Suez Crisis.

By November 1958, British pilots had joined Detachment B, and arrangements had been made for the title to the aircraft

---

[101] Ibid., pp. 5-6 (TS Codeword).

[102] Ibid., p. 1 (TS Codeword).

[103] Goodpaster interview (S).

they would be using to be transferred on paper to the British Government. In a final exchange of letters between President Eisenhower and Prime Minister Macmillan in December, the President summarized the lines of authority for the joint program: "British missions are carried out on your authority and are your responsibility just as our activities are authorized and controlled here in accordance with the procedures I have established. In this sense, it could be said that we are carrying out two complementary programs rather than a joint one."[104]

Richard Bissell had achieved his goal of gaining another source of approval for overflights of the Soviet Union. In late 1959 and early 1960, this arrangement proved its value when British pilots conducted two highly successful missions over Soviet missile testing facilities at a time when President Eisenhower had not authorized an overflight for almost six months (see chapter 4). Most flights by the RAF pilots in Detachment B, however, took place in the Middle East, where the United Kingdom carried out 27 missions during the two years its pilots took part in overflights.

In Britain, the cover story for the RAF participation in the U-2 program was that British fliers were being trained to fly high-altitude weather-sampling missions for the RAF weather service. To support this cover, a U-2 was ferried to Watton RAF Base, England, in early May 1959, and used to fly weather missions on 7 and 8 May before returning to Adana. Two more weather-sampling flights took place over England on 5 and 6 October 1959.

THE U-2 PROJECT AT THE BEGINNING OF 1959
Early 1959 saw Detachment B aircraft active primarily over Middle Eastern countries, with occasional overflights of Albania to check for reported Soviet missile installations. Detachment C mainly collected high-altitude weather data, although it also flew two missions

---

[104] *OSA History,* chap. 13, p. 10-11 (TS Codeword).

over Tibet and Southwest China (see chapter 5). The overflight program against the Soviet Union seemed to be at a standstill, but pressures within the government were building to resume deep-penetration flights to resolve the growing "missile-gap" controversy.

Organizationally, the U-2 project underwent a major change after Richard Bissell became CIA's Deputy Director for Plans on 1 January 1959. At first glance, Bissell's selection seems unusual because he had spent most of his Agency career heading the U-2 project, but his first major assignment had been coordinating support for the operation that overthrew the leftist Government of Guatemala in 1954. Furthermore, Bissell's U-2 project was the major covert collector of intelligence against the CIA's primary target, the Soviet Union.

During his years as head of the Development Projects Staff (DPS), Bissell had opposed proposals to bring all Agency air activities together into a single office, fearing that he would lose control of the U-2 project. Once he became Deputy Director for Plans, his viewpoint changed; he was now in a position to consolidate all air activities under his own control. On 16 February 1959, the DPS became the Development Projects Division (DPD) of the Directorate of Plans (at the time known as the Deputy Directorate/Plans or DDP). Despite the tremendous increase in the scope of his duties after assuming control of the DDP, Bissell retained personal control of his previous Development Projects Staff projects: the U-2 program, another project to develop a photosatellite, and a third project to design a follow-on aircraft for the U-2 (OXCART). Although the amalgamation of all Agency air operations and the transfer of the U-2 project to the DDP made sense, the question remained as to whether one individual could effectively control all these different activities.

4

The Final Overflights
of the Soviet Union,
1959-1960

THE U-2 AND THE "MISSILE-GAP" DEBATE
Despite President Eisenhower's reluctance to send U-2s over the
Soviet Bloc, he once again authorized overflights in the summer
of 1959, after a pause of more than a year. The overriding factor
in his decision was the growing "missile-gap" controversy, which
had its roots in a series of dramatic Soviet announcements during
the second half of 1957. The first announcement revealed the
successful test of an intercontinental ballistic missile in August.
Then in October, the Soviets announced the successful orbiting
of the world's first artificial earth satellite, Sputnik. One month
later the Soviets orbited a second satellite containing a dog and
a television camera. To many Americans, including some influential members of Congress, the Soviet Union's space successes
seemed to indicate that its missile program was ahead of that of
the United States. By the spring of 1958, after the United States
had successfully launched several satellites, fears of a space

technology gap between the two superpowers had eased. By the end of the year, however, new concerns arose that the Soviet Union was producing a missile arsenal that would be much larger than that of the United States. This was the famous missile gap that received widespread publicity beginning in early 1959.[1]

The missile-gap controversy was fueled by Soviet boasts about the success of their missile program. On 4 December 1958, a Soviet delegate to the Geneva Conference on Surprise Attack stated: "Soviet ICBMs are at present in mass production." Five days later, Soviet Premier Nikita Khrushchev asserted that the Soviet Union had an ICBM capable of carrying a 5-megaton nuclear warhead 8,000 miles. These statements seemed all the more ominous because, during this same month of December, the first attempt to launch the new US Titan ICBM failed. In reality, all of the Soviet statements were sheer propaganda: they had encountered difficulties with the SS-6 ICBM, and the program was at a standstill. As a result, there were no ICBM launches from Tyuratam between 29 May 1958 and 17 February 1959, a space of almost nine months.[2]

To conceal the difficulties in their missile program, Soviet leaders continued to praise its alleged successes. At the beginning of February 1959, Khrushchev opened the Soviet Communist Party Congress in Moscow by claiming that "serial production of intercontinental ballistic rockets has been organized." Several months later Soviet Defense Minister Rodion Malinovsky stated that these missiles were capable of hitting "precisely any point" and added, "Our army is equipped with a whole series of intercontinental, continental and other rockets of long, medium and short range." When asked at a press conference to comment on

---

[1] For an overview of the controversy, see Roy E. Licklider, "The Missile Gap Controversy," *Political Science Quarterly* 85 (1970):600-615.

[2] Lawrence Freedman, *US Intelligence and the Soviet Strategic Threat*, 2nd ed. (Princeton: Princeton University Press, 1986), pp. 69-70.

Malinovsky's statement, President Eisenhower replied, "They also said that they invented the flying machine and the automobile and the telephone and other things... Why should you be so respectful of this statement this morning, if you are not so respectful of the other three?"[3] Nevertheless, the Soviet statements were taken at face value by most Americans, including many members of the intelligence community.

As concern about Soviet missile progress increased, even the interruption in Soviet ICBM testing was seen as evidence of a Soviet advantage. Although the CIA correctly reasoned that the Soviets were experiencing difficulties in developing an operational ICBM, the Air Force assumed that the Soviets had halted testing because the missile was ready for deployment.[4]

The controversy intensified early in February 1959, when Secretary of Defense Neil H. McElroy testified before the Senate Preparedness Investigating Committee on Soviet missile capabilities for the next few years. McElroy told the Senators that in the early 1960s the Soviet Union might have a 3 to 1 advantage over the United States in operational ICBMs. McElroy stressed that the gap would be temporary and that at its end the United States would enjoy a technological advantage because it was concentrating on developing the more advanced solid-fueled missiles rather than increasing the number of obsolescent liquid-fueled missiles, but it was his mention of a 3 to 1 missile gap that made the headlines. Administration critics such as Senator Stuart Symington quickly charged that the actual gap would eventually be even larger.[5]

Faced with rising public and Congressional concern about the missile gap, Defense Department officials pressed President

---

[3] Ford Eastman, "Defense Officials Concede Missile Lag," *Aviation Week,* 9 February 1959, pp. 26-27.

[4] Freedman, *US Intelligence*, p. 70.

[5] "What About the Missile Gap?" *Time,* 9 February 1959, pp. 11-13.

Kelly Johnson (right) with members of the initial Lockheed U-2 flight test and engineering team. Courtesy of Chris Pocock

Aircraft Assembly In Hangar, Watertown.

A U-2 assembled in one of the hastily-built hangars at Watertown Strip. Courtesy of Chris Pocock

One of the first U-2s on the lakebed at "The Ranch" in Nevada, with ground vehicles attending. Courtesy of Chris Pocock

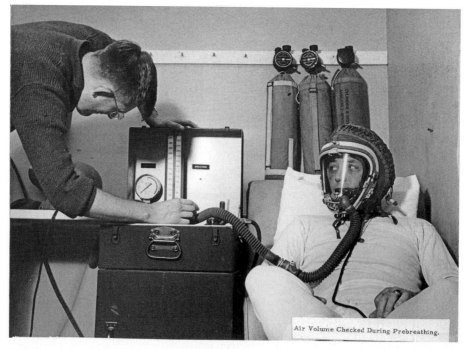

U-2 pilots pre-breathed pure oxygen for an hour before each flight to high altitude. Courtesy of Chris Pocock

The A-2 camera fit that was flown on the first overflights of the Soviet Union is loaded into the "Q-bay" of the U-2: three Hycon 24-inch framing cameras in fixed left, right, and vertical positions. Courtesy of Chris Pocock

The four U-2s of Detachment A flying over their first home at Wiesbaden airbase in West Germany. Courtesy of Chris Pocock

Edwin Land, founder of the Polaroid Company, headed the advisory panel that recommended to President Eisenhower that a radically new high-altitude spyplane be built to overfly the Soviet Union. Courtesy of Chris Pocock

Richard Bissell organized and ran Project AQUATONE for the CIA. Courtesy of Chris Pocock

Part of the navigation map carried by Gary Powers on his first overflight of the Soviet Union in November 1956. The flight lines were designed to provide maximum coverage of the areas of interest below. Courtesy of Chris Pocock

The MiG-19 was the latest Soviet interceptor in 1956—but it could not reach the U-2 flying at 70,000 feet or higher. Courtesy of Chris Pocock

The prototype U-2 crashed in April 1957 during a flight to test radar-absorbent coatings. Courtesy of Chris Pocock

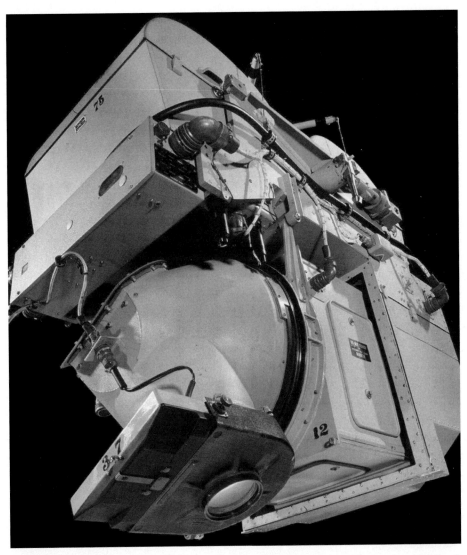

The definitive U-2 camera used on later overflights was the Hycon B, a 36-inch framing system with a lens that rotated through seven "stop-and-shoot" positions. Courtesy of Chris Pocock

The Tyuratam missile test base was a key objective for the U-2 overflights. This image shows a launch pad for the first Soviet ICBM that was designated SS-6 in the West. Courtesy of Chris Pocock

The SA-2 surface-to-air missile that eventually shot down a U-2 was first shown in public two and a half years earlier, in this Moscow parade.
Courtesy of Chris Pocock

U-2 mission 8009 in February 1960 overflew the Soviet aircraft factory at Kazan'. On the snow-covered ramp (bottom of picture) could be seen a new type of swept-wing bomber. It was not formally revealed as the Tu-22 for another 18 months. Courtesy of Chris Pocock

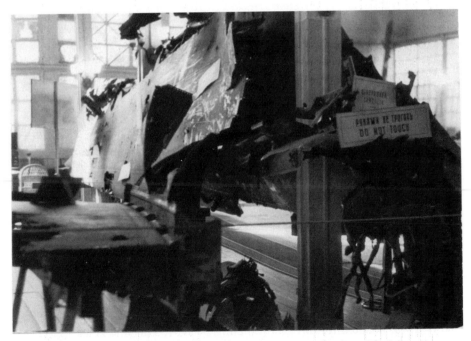

Wreckage of article 360 (shot down on 1 May 1960) displayed in Moscow. Courtesy of Chris Pocock

CIA U-2 on a test flight in the early 1960s. Courtesy of Chris Pocock

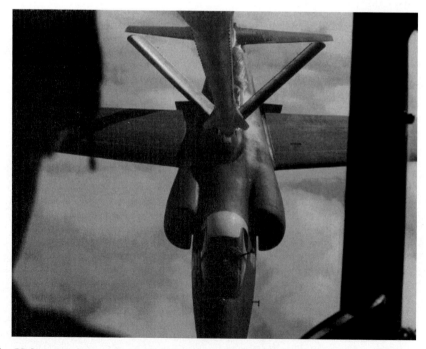

The U-2 was adapted for in-flight refueling in 1961. This one is taking on fuel from a US Air Force KC-135. Courtesy of Chris Pocock

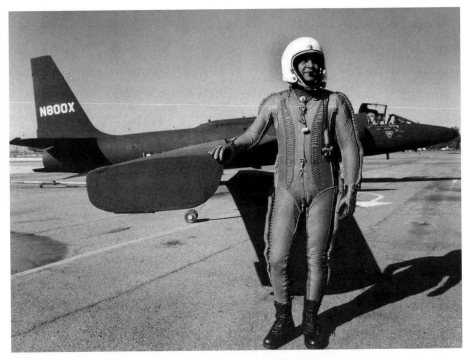

Francis Gary Powers poses in a partial pressure suit by a U-2 after his return from the Soviet Union in 1962. Courtesy of Chris Pocock

Before Taiwan began flying the U-2 high over China in 1962, it was already flying low over the mainland in another joint reconnaissance operation with the CIA that used P2V Neptune maritime patrol aircraft. Courtesy of Chris Pocock

The U-2 was adapted for operation from US Navy aircraft carriers in 1963-64. This aircraft made the first takeoff and then flew approach trials to the USS Kitty Hawk in August 1963. Courtesy of Chris Pocock

The SA-2 continued to threaten U-2 overflights in the 1960s. A US Air Force pilot was shot down over Cuba in October 1962, and five nationalist Chinese pilots fell victim to the same system over China from 1962 to 1967. Courtesy of Chris Pocock

The first four U-2s to be shot down over China on display in Beijing.
Courtesy of Chris Pocock

The enlarged and improved U-2R was flown for the first time in August 1967.
Courtesy of Chris Pocock

A U-2R of Detachment H, also known as the 35th Squadron of the Republic of China Air Force (ROCAF), at Taoyuan airbase. Courtesy of Chris Pocock

Like the U-2 before it, the A-12 was assembled and test-flown at Groom Lake, where this line-up is seen in April 1964. Courtesy of Chris Pocock

After a short-lived operational career, the A-12 fleet was retired in 1968 and placed in storage at Palmdale. Courtesy of Chris Pocock

Desktop model of the CIA's AQUILINE reconnaissance drone developed in the mid-late 1960s and disguised to look like a bird of prey.
Courtesy of Chris Pocock

Eisenhower to authorize renewed overflights to gather up-to-date information about the status of the Soviet missile program. Following a National Security Council meeting on 12 February, Chairman of the Joint Chiefs of Staff Twining, Secretary of Defense McElroy, and Deputy Secretary of Defense Quarles stayed behind to talk to the President about overflights. They hoped that the need to refute criticism of the missile gap from Symington and other Democratic Senators would persuade the President to loosen his policy on the use of the U-2. McElroy pointed out that no matter how often Allen Dulles briefed these critics, they would not believe his reassurances about the absence of a missile gap without positive proof such as photographs. More overflights would be needed to obtain the kinds of photographs required.

The President was not swayed by these arguments. Noting that the reconnaissance satellite project was "coming along nicely," he stated that U-2 flights should be "held to a minimum pending the availability of this new equipment." Quarles objected that the satellites would not be ready for up to two years, but the President replied that this did not matter because the Soviets would not be able to build a first-strike force of ICBMs in the near future. President Eisenhower finally conceded that "one or two flights might possibly be permissible," but he ruled out "an extensive program." In light of the "crisis which is impending over Berlin" he did not want to be provocative.[6]

As the missile-gap controversy raged, President Eisenhower stuck to his refusal to permit overflights of the Soviet Union, although the Soviet Union's resumption of ICBM testing almost persuaded him to change his mind. On 10 April 1959, the President tentatively approved several overflights, but, on the

---

[6] Andrew J. Goodpaster, Memorandum for the Record, 12 February 1959, WHOSS, Alpha, DDEL (TS); Ambrose, *Eisenhower: The President*, pp. 513-514; Beschloss, *Mayday*, p.173.

following day, he called in McElroy and Bissell to inform them that he was withdrawing his authorization, explaining that "there seems no hope for the future unless we can make some progress in negotiation." Eisenhower remained worried by "the terrible propaganda impact that would be occasioned if a reconnaissance plane were to fail." Although he agreed that new information was necessary, especially in light of the "distortions several senators are making of our military position relative to the Soviets," Eisenhower believed that such information would not be worth "the political costs."[7]

The President remained willing to consider flights that did not overfly Soviet territory, and in June he authorized two electronic intelligence collection missions along the Soviet-Iranian border. The two missions of Operation HOT SHOP took place on 9 and 18 June 1959. The first of these missions was noteworthy because it involved both an Agency U-2 and an Air Force RB-57D Canberra. The two aircraft cruised along the Soviet border and made the first telemetry intercept ever from a Soviet ICBM during first-stage flight, 80 seconds after launch.[8]

Efforts to persuade the President to authorize penetration missions continued. On 7 July 1959, Allen Dulles and Richard Bissell met with Eisenhower to discuss the possibility of a penetration flight to gather intelligence on the Soviet missile program. Discussions continued the following day with the addition of Secretary of State Herter, who stated in support of the CIA proposal that "the intelligence objective outweighs the danger of getting trapped." The strong backing of the proposed overflight

---

[7] Quoted in Ambrose, *Eisenhower: The President*, pp. 514-515; Beschloss, *Mayday*, p. 176.
[8] Mission folders 4120 (9 June 1959) and 4121 (18 June 1959), OSA records, job 67-B-972, boxes 10 and 11 (TS Codeword).

by both CIA and the State Department finally convinced President Eisenhower to approve the mission.[9]

On 9 July 1959, more than 16 months after the previous overflight of the Soviet Union, a U-2 equipped with a B camera left Peshawar, Pakistan, flew over the Urals, and then crossed the missile test range at Tyuratam. This mission, known as Operation TOUCHDOWN, produced excellent results. Its photography revealed that the Soviets were expanding the launch facilities at Tyuratam. While this overflight was under way, another U-2 flew a diversionary mission along the Soviet-Iranian border.[10]

Despite its success, this overflight remained an isolated incident. President Eisenhower was unwilling to authorize additional overflights of the Soviet Union, in part because he did not wish to increase tension before Premier Khrushchev's visit to the United States scheduled for 15-27 September 1959. Nevertheless, the President still wanted as much intelligence on the Soviet missile program as possible. Because the Soviets were conducting an extensive program of missile tests in mid-1959, Eisenhower authorized a steady stream of the less provocative electronic intelligence (ELINT)-gathering missions (14 in all) along the Soviet border during the remainder of the year.[11]

Within the United States, concern about the Soviet missile program continued to grow. On 12 September 1959 the Soviets scored another space success when their Luna 2 rocket reached the moon, and Khrushchev stressed this success when he arrived in the United States three days later. He also boasted of Soviet missile progress in private conversations with President

---

[9] Andrew J. Goodpaster, Memorandum for the Record, 7 July 1959 (TS); idem, Memorandum of Conference with the President, 8 July 1959, WHOSS, Alpha, DDEL (TS).

[10] Mission folder 4125 (9 July 1959), OSA records (TS Codeword).

[11] *OSA History,* chap. 19, annex 120, pp. 12-14 (TS Codeword).

Eisenhower, while making no mention of overflights by the United States. After the trip was over, Khrushchev and other leading Soviet officials continued to make exaggerated claims about the extent of their missile force, adding to the confusion and concern within the US intelligence community. Thus in November 1959, Soviet Premier Khrushchev told a conference of journalists, "Now we have such a stock of rockets, such an amount of atomic and hydrogen weapons, that if they attack us, we could wipe our potential enemies off the face of the earth." He then added that "in one year, 250 rockets with hydrogen warheads came off the assembly line in the factory we visited."[12] Because the Soviet Union had been launching at least one missile per week since early fall, US policymakers placed great weight on his remarks.

Despite the intelligence community's intense interest in the Soviet Union's nuclear and missile programs, President Eisenhower did not authorize any more overflights of the Soviet Union during the remainder of the year. On the other hand, he raised no objections to (and probably welcomed) the first British overflight of the Soviet Union in December 1959. For almost a year, the RAF pilots of Detachment B had been ready to fly over the Soviet Union, but Prime Minister Harold Macmillan had not previously authorized any such missions because of his own visit to the Soviet Union, several international meetings, and other state visits. As a result, British U-2 missions had been confined to the Middle East. Now that the Prime Minister's approval had been obtained, Detachment B conducted Operation HIGH WIRE with an RAF pilot. Squadron leader Robert Robinson left Peshawar on 6 December and overflew Kuybyshev, Saratov Engels Airfield, and the Kapustin Yar Missile Test Range before landing at Adana. The mission photog-

---

[12] William E. Borrows, *Deep Black: Space Espionage and National Security* (New York: Random House, 1987), p. 101.

raphy was excellent, but it did not provide intelligence on Soviet ICBMs, which were tested at Tyuratam, not Kapustin Yar.[13]

Because there had been so few overflights in 1958 and 1959, many questions about the Soviet missile program remained unanswered. Within the intelligence community there was still considerable disagreement over the size of the Soviet missile force. Thus, during testimony before the US Senate in January 1960, DCI Allen Dulles, Secretary of Defense Thomas Gates, and Air Force Chief of Staff Nathan Twining each gave different figures for the number of deployed Soviet missiles. Although the CIA figures were based on evidence gained from overflights, Dulles could not reveal this fact to the Senate and, therefore, faced very sharp questioning.[14]

As a result of these Senate hearings, Dulles was determined to obtain permission for more overflights in order to settle the missile-gap question once and for all and end the debate within the intelligence community. To accomplish this, Dulles proposed photographing the most likely areas for the deployment of Soviet missiles. At this time there was still no evidence of SS-6 ICBM deployment outside the Tyuratam missile test range. Because the SS-6 was extremely large and liquid fueled, analysts believed these missiles could only be deployed near railroads. Existing U-2 photography showed railroad tracks going right to the launching pad at the test site. Dulles, therefore, argued that SS-6 installations could easily be located by flying along railroad lines. Dulles was supported by members of the President's Board of Consultants on Foreign Intelligence Activities. At a meeting of the board on 2 February 1960, Gen. James Doolittle urged President Eisenhower to use overflights of the Soviet Union to the

---

[13] *OSA History,* chap. 11, p. 33 (TS Codeword); Mission folder 8005 (6 December 1959), OSA records, job 67-B-972, box 13 (TS Codeword).

[14] Licklider, "Missile Gap Controversy," pp. 608-609.

maximum degree possible. The President's response, as summarized in General Goodpaster's notes of the meeting, showed that the upcoming summit meeting was already an important factor in his attitude toward U-2 flights: "The President said that he has one tremendous asset in a summit meeting, as regards effect in the free world. That is his reputation for honesty. If one of these aircraft were lost when we are engaged in apparently sincere deliberations, it could be put on display in Moscow and ruin the President's effectiveness."[15]

A few days later, another U-2 took to the sky on a mission over the Soviet Union. As in December, the pilot was British, and the mission had been ordered by Prime Minister Macmillan. On 5 February 1960, a Detachment B U-2C with squadron leader John MacArthur at the controls left Peshawar, Pakistan, to conduct Operation KNIFE EDGE. The plane overflew the Tyuratam Missile Test Range, headed northwest to Kazan', and then turned south, photographing long stretches of the Soviet rail network. The excellent photography from this mission did not reveal a single missile site, but analysts did discover a new Soviet bomber, dubbed the BACKFIN, at Kazan'.[16]

Despite the outcome of this mission, the missile-gap debate continued. The Air Force still insisted that the Soviets had deployed as many as 100 missiles. The Army, Navy, and CIA, however, doubted that any had been deployed, because none could be found. Additional U-2 photography was needed to settle the debate. In mid-February, President Eisenhower reviewed plans for four additional U-2 missions. The success of the two British missions, along with the absence of Soviet protests, made the President more willing to consider a resumption of US overflights, and he agreed to

---

[15] Ambrose, *Eisenhower: The President*, p. 568; Beschloss, *Mayday*, p. 233.
[16] Mission folder 8009 (5 February 1960), OSA records, job 67-B-972, box 13 (TS Codeword); *OSA Chronology*, p. 25 (TS Codeword).

allow one mission to be flown during the month of March. The President's continued restrictions upon the use of the U-2 disturbed DCI Dulles, who sent a memorandum to the National Security Council on 1 March 1960 asserting that the cardinal objective of obtaining information on Soviet missile deployment could be better achieved if the U-2 were given freer rein.[17]

In authorizing another overflight of the Soviet Union, President Eisenhower directed that it be conducted before 30 March. Because of complications in getting permission from Pakistan to use the airfield at Peshawar, however, the mission could not be staged in March, and the President agreed to extend his deadline until 10 April 1960. One day before the expiration of this deadline, a U-2 equipped with a B-camera took off from Peshawar on the last successful overflight of the Soviet Union, Operation SQUARE DEAL. As had been the case during the previous two overflights, a second U-2 flew a diversionary mission along the Soviet-Iranian border. After leaving Peshawar, mission 4155 headed first for Saryshagan, where it obtained the first pictures of two new Soviet radars, the HEN HOUSE and HEN ROOST installations. The U-2 then flew to the nuclear testing site at Semipalatinsk. Returning to the Saryshagan area, it crisscrossed the railroad network there and then proceeded to Tyuratam, where it photographed a new two-pad, road-served launch area that suggested a new Soviet missile was in the offing.[18]

In his memoirs Nikita Khrushchev remarked that this U-2 should have been shot down, "but our antiaircraft batteries were caught napping and didn't open fire soon enough." Khrushchev explained that Soviet missile designers had developed a

---

[17] *OSA Chronology*, p. 25 (TS Codeword); Philip K. Edwards, "The President's Board: 1956-60," *Studies in Intelligence* 13 (Summer 1969): 118 (S).

[18] Mission folder 4155, 9 April 1960, OSA records, job 67-B-328, box 6 (TS Codeword).

high-altitude antiaircraft missile and batteries of this missile had been deployed near known targets of the U-2.[19]

The CIA already had strong indications of improvements in the Soviet air defense system, and early in 1960 the Development Projects Division had asked Air Force experts at the Air Technical Intelligence Center (ATIC) for a frank assessment of Soviet capabilities against the U-2. On 14 March 1960, Col. William Burke, acting chief of the DPD, relayed the ATIC assessment to Richard Bissell:

> *The greatest threat to the U-2 is the Soviet SAM. Although the ATIC analysis concedes a remote possibility that the SAM may be less effective than estimated, their present evaluation is that the SAM (Guideline) has a high probability of successful intercept at 70,000 feet providing that detection is made in sufficient time to alert the site.[20]*

One of the reasons why Operation SQUARE DEAL had been selected for the 9 April flight was that mission planners believed that penetration from the Pakistan/Afghanistan area offered the greatest chance of escaping detection by the Soviet air defense system. Colonel Burke's 14 March letter recommending SQUARE DEAL as the preferred route for the next overflight had stated, "There is a reasonable chance of completing this operation without detection." Escaping detection had become important

---

[19] Nikita S. Khrushchev, *Khrushchev Remembers: The Last Testament* (Boston: Little, Brown, & Co., 1974), pp. 443-444.

[20] Memorandum for Richard M. Bissell, Deputy Director (Plans), from Col. William Burke, Acting Chief, DPD, "Evaluation of Proposed CHALICE Operations," 14 March 1960, IC Staff, COMIREX records, job 33-T-123A, box 10, "CHALICE (General)" (TS Codeword).

Operation SQUARE DEAL, 9 April 1960

Secret NOFORN

because, if the Soviet SAMs received sufficient advanced warning, they posed a major threat to the U-2.

CIA hopes that flights from Pakistan or Afghanistan might go undetected proved false. On the 9 April overflight, the U-2's ELINT-collection unit (System VI) indicated Soviet tracking at a very early stage of the mission. Although the Soviets failed to intercept the U-2, their success at tracking it should have served as a warning against future overflights from Pakistan (or anywhere else, for that matter). On 26 April 1960, Colonel Burke informed Richard Bissell that "experience gained as a result of Operation SQUARE DEAL indicates that penetration without detection from the Pakistan/Afghanistan area may not be as easy in the future as heretofore."[21] Unfortunately, neither Colonel Burke nor Richard Bissell took the logical step of recommending the cessation of overflights now that the risks had increased substantially. The lure of the prospective intelligence gain from each mission was too strong, and the Soviets' lack of success at interception to date had probably made the project staff overconfident. Furthermore, both DCI Allen Dulles and the President's Board of Consultants on Foreign Intelligence Activities were pressing for more photos of the Soviet Union in order to settle the missile-gap debate raging in the intelligence community and Congress.

THE LAST OVERFLIGHT: OPERATION GRAND SLAM
Even before the 9 April overflight took place, President Eisenhower had consented on 28 March to an additional overflight during the month of April. His willingness to allow yet another overflight was strengthened when the Soviet Union did not pro-

---

[21] Memorandum for Richard M. Bissell, Deputy Director (Plans), from Colonel Burke, Acting Chief, DPD, "Operational Priority of Proposed CHALICE Missions," 26 April 1960, IC Staff, COMIREX records, job 33-T-123A, box 10, "CHALICE (General)" (TS Codeword).

test the 9 April mission. As Presidential science adviser George Kistiakowsky later remarked about the lack of protest, "This was virtually inviting us to repeat the sortie."[22]

Although President Eisenhower had authorized another overflight for April, he left the designation of its targets up to the experts at the CIA. Of the three missions that remained under consideration, one—Operation SUN SPOT—would overfly southern targets, Tyuratam and Vladimirovka, while the other two would cover railroad networks in the north-central portion of the Soviet Union. The intelligence community had been interested in this area ever since late 1959, when there were indications that the Soviets were building an SS-6 launch facility there. This was the first indication that SS-6s might be located anywhere other than Tyuratam testing facility, where the missiles were launched from a general purpose launching pad. The intelligence community was anxious to obtain photography of a deployed SS-6 site because it could provide exemplars for photointerpreters to use in searching subsequent overhead photography for similar installations.[23]

The two proposed overflights that would cover the northern railroad lines received the strongest consideration. Both plans contained new features. Operation TIME STEP called for a U-2 to take off from the USAF base at Thule, Greenland, which would be the first overflight staged from this base. The aircraft would then fly over Novaya Zemlya on its way to cover the railroad lines from the Polyarnyy Ural Mountains to Kotlas. The return flight would be over Murmansk with the landing to take place at either Bodo or Andoya on Norway's northeast coast. The other proposed overflight, Operation GRAND SLAM, was the first U-2 mission planned to transit the Soviet Union; all previous missions had penetrated

---

[22] George B. Kistiakowsky, *A Scientist at the White House* (Cambridge: Harvard University Press, 1976), p. 328.
[23] *OSA History,* chap. 12, pp. 35-36 (TS Codeword).

not more than halfway and then left in the general direction from which they came. GRAND SLAM proposed to fly across the Soviet Union from south to north, departing from Peshawar, Pakistan, and landing at Bodo, Norway. The mission would overfly Tyuratam, Sverdlovsk, Kirov, Kotlas, Severodvinsk, and Murmansk.

The two preferred missions both required the use of the airfield at Bodo, which had been authorized by senior Norwegian intelligence and military officers. Because the Bodo airfield was involved in NATO maneuvers taking place in the Barents Sea area, Bissell informed the White House that neither mission could be flown before 19 April. Once the maneuvers ended, bad weather over the Soviet Union kept the mission from taking place when it was originally scheduled. Richard Bissell, therefore, asked President Eisenhower for more time, and, on 25 April, General Goodpaster relayed the President's instructions to Bissell that "one additional operation may be undertaken, provided it is carried out prior to May 1. No operation is to be carried out after May 1."[24] The President did not want to fly missions any later than that because the Paris Summit was scheduled to begin on 16 May 1960.

By this time, CIA planners were concentrating on Operation GRAND SLAM as the most likely route for the proposed mission because it offered the best chance of photographing suspected locations of Soviet ICBM sites. The other proposed overflight, Operation TIME STEP out of Greenland, was more likely to run into bad weather (which would affect both navigation and photography) because the flightpath would remain above 60° north latitude during the entire mission. Furthermore, mission planners opposed this route because of its greater risk. In his letter to Richard Bissell on 14 March 1960, Colonel Burke stated:

---

[24] Ambrose, *Eisenhower: The President*, p. 569; Beschloss, *Mayday*, p. 10.

Operation "TIME STEP" is our last choice because we can assume, with a 90 percent probability of being correct, that we will be detected on entry, tracked accurately throughout the period in denied territory (approximately four hours), and will evoke a strong PVO [Soviet Air Defense] reaction. This flight plan would permit alerting of SAM sites, and pre-positioning of missile equipped fighters in the Murmansk area (point of exit) thus enhancing the possibility of successful intercept. In addition, we must assume that even were the Soviets unable to physically interfere with such an incursion, sufficient evidence will be available to permit them to document a diplomatic protest should they desire to do so.[25]

The concerns raised by Colonel Burke about TIME STEP should also have been raised about Operation GRAND SLAM, which would be the most adventuresome overflight to date because it proposed covering so much of the Soviet Union. If the Soviets could track the U-2 early in the mission, they would have plenty of time to prepare to intercept the aircraft.

The pilot selected for Operation GRAND SLAM was Francis Gary Powers, the most experienced U-2 pilot in the program. Powers had joined the project in May 1956 and had flown 27 operational missions in the U-2, including one each over the Soviet Union and China as well as six along the Soviet border.

To prevent the U-2 from being seen at Peshawar, project managers decided to ferry the aircraft from Adana to Pakistan the night before the scheduled flight. Once the plane was refueled and

---

[25] Memorandum for Richard M. Bissell, Deputy Director (Plans), from Col. William Burke, Acting Chief, DPD, "Evaluation of Proposed CHALICE Operations," 14 March 1960, IC Staff, COMIREX records, job 33-T-I23A, box 10, "CHALICE (General)" (TS Codeword).

its camera was loaded, it would take off at daybreak, with little if any exposure to local residents because of darkness and its short stay—less than six hours on the ground. Originally scheduled for Thursday, 28 April, GRAND SLAM was canceled because of bad weather over the northern Soviet Union. This had been the case for the past several weeks. When this flight was canceled, the U-2 returned to Adana before sunrise. That evening the U-2 flew back to Peshawar for another attempt to stage the mission early on the 29th, but bad weather again forced cancellation of the mission, and the U-2 returned to Adana. Because of continued bad weather over the target areas, no mission was planned for Saturday, 30 April."[26]

Meanwhile, the plane ferried to Peshawar on 27 and 28 April had accumulated so many hours of flight time that it had to be removed from service for periodic maintenance. A different aircraft was, therefore, ferried to Peshawar on Saturday night, 30 April. This aircraft, article 360, had made a crash landing in Japan during the previous September (see chapter 5). Although it had been refurbished by Lockheed and now had the more powerful J75 engine that would give it greater altitude, pilots did not completely trust this aircraft and considered it a "hangar queen." As Powers noted in his memoirs, "Its current idiosyncrasy was one of the fuel tanks, which wouldn't feed all its fuel."[27] The aircraft was equipped with a B-model camera, a System-VI electronic intelligence unit, and a System-IXB device, which generated false-angle information in response to the radar pulses used by some Soviet airborne-missile fire-control systems.

Operation GRAND SLAM, mission 4154 and the 24th deep-penetration overflight of the Soviet Union, began almost 30 minutes late on Sunday, 1 May 1960, a delay due to difficulty in getting takeoff approval from Washington. This delay was caused

---

[26] Mission folder 4154 (1 May 1960), OSA records (TS Codeword).
[27] Powers, *Operation Overflight*, p. 76.

by communications problems that are typical at sunrise and sunset during spring and autumn, when the ionosphere will not support reliable communications. In attempting to relay the authorization message, the radio operator in Adana was unable to reach the base in Peshawar, whose codename was HBJARGON. Realizing that neither the prearranged nighttime nor daytime frequencies were working, the operator began sending a message in the clear, using one of the guard frequencies in the transition area between the daytime and nighttime frequencies. The radio operators at Peshawar kept hearing the Morse code letters JGOHB, JGOHB as they tuned from one prearranged frequency to the other. Then one of the Peshawar operators decided to tune in the guard frequency where the Morse transmission was strongest, He was able to discern a break in the letters, making the message read "HBJGO HBJGO." The Peshawar operators realized this stood for "HBJARGON Go." The detachment chief. Col. William Shelton, who had been waiting anxiously inside the radio van for a "Go" or "No Go" message, leaped from the van and ran across the field to give the signal for takeoff to Powers, who was sitting in the U-2C at the end of the runway.[28]

Powers started his takeoff roll at 0159Z on 1 May 1960. Once airborne, Powers guided his aircraft toward Afghanistan. Following standard operating procedure, Powers clicked his radio switch when he reached penetration altitude of 66,000 feet, which signaled the operations unit at Peshawar that everything aboard the aircraft was working and the mission would proceed as planned. Aside from this simple signal, Powers and all U-2 pilots maintained strict radio silence during penetration missions.

Powers' first target was the Tyuratam Missile Test Range after which he headed for Chelyabinsk, just south of Sverdlovsk. The planned route would take him over Kyshtym, Sverdlovsk,

---

[28] Richard K. Pero, "Message Received—Unfortunately," *Studies in Intelligence* 27 (Winter 1983):29 (S).

northwest to Kirov, north over Yur'ya and Plesetsk, then to Severodvinsk, northwest to Kandalaksha, north to Murmansk, and, finally, west to Bodo, Norway.

May Day turned out to be a bad time to overfly the Soviet Union. On this major holiday, there was much less Soviet military air traffic than usual, so Soviet radars could easily identify and track Powers' U-2. In addition, the Soviets responded to the intrusion by ordering a ban on civilian air traffic in a large portion of the Soviet Union. Soviet radar began tracking the U-2 when it was still 15 miles south of the Soviet-Afghan border and continued to do so as the aircraft flew across the Central Asian republics. When Powers reached the Tashkent area, as many as 13 Soviet interceptor aircraft scrambled in an unsuccessful attempt to intercept his plane.

Powers never made it past Sverdlovsk. Four and a half hours into the mission, an SA-2 surface-to-air missile detonated close to and just behind his aircraft and disabled it 70,500 feet above the Sverdlovsk area. The plane began spiraling down toward the ground and Powers looked for a way out. Unable to use the ejection seat because centrifugal force had thrown him against the canopy, he released the canopy and prepared to bail out, waiting to arm the destruction device at the last minute, so that it would not go off while he was still in the plane. When he released his seatbelt, however, he was immediately sucked out of the aircraft and found himself dangling by his oxygen hose, unable to reach the destruction switches. Finally, the hose broke and he flew away from the falling aircraft. After he fell several thousand feet, his parachute opened automatically, and he drifted to earth where he was quickly surrounded by farmers and then by Soviet officials.[29] His aircraft

---

[29] Powers, *Operation Overflight*, pp. 82-84; Beschloss, *Mayday*, pp. 26-28; Transcript of Debriefing Tapes of Francis Gary Powers, 13 February 1962, Board of Inquiry on the Conduct of Francis Gary Powers, Operations MUD-LARK files, OSA records, job 74-B-605, box 6 (S).

had not been destroyed by the crash, and the Soviets were able to identify much of its equipment when they put it on display 10 days later. Even if Powers had been able to activate the destruction device, however, it would not have destroyed the aircraft. The small explosive charge was only designed to wreck the camera.

How had the Soviets succeeded in downing the U-2? Although some CIA project officials initially wondered if Powers had been flying too low through an error or mechanical malfunction, he maintained that he had been flying at his assigned altitude and had been brought down by a near miss of a Soviet surface-to-air missile. This turned out to be the case, for in March 1963, the US air attache in Moscow learned that the Sverdlovsk SA-2 battery had fired a three-missile salvo that, in addition to disabling Powers' plane, also scored a direct hit on a Soviet fighter aircraft sent aloft to intercept the U-2.[30] Mission planners had not known about this SAM site before the mission because they always laid out flight plans to avoid known SAM sites.

THE AFTERMATH OF THE U-2 DOWNING

The first indication that something was wrong with Powers' mission came even before he was overdue at Bodo, Norway. The CIA Operations Center learned on 1 May at 0330 hours Washington time that the Soviets had discontinued radar tracking of the flight's progress two hours earlier (0529Z), southwest of Sverdlovsk. Although there was no word from the Soviet Union concerning the missing U-2, key project personnel assembled in the Agency control center that morning (with the exception of Bissell, who was out of town and did not arrive until 1530) to analyze the latest information and discuss courses of action. They quickly estab-

---

[30] Cunningham interview, 4 October 1983 (TS Codeword); *OSA History,* chap. 14, p. 55 (TS Codeword).

lished a new project, known as Operation MUDLARK, to gather and evaluate all available information about the downed U-2.[31]

Bissell and the other project officials did not know whether Powers was dead or if the plane and camera had been destroyed, but they believed that there was no way that a pilot could survive a crash from an altitude above 70,000 feet. They, therefore, decided to stick with the standard cover story for U-2 flights: that they were weather flights staged by the National Aeronautics and Space Administration (NASA)—originally the National Advisory Committee for Aeronautics, renamed in 1958. This cover story had been approved by the President in 1956.

By the end of the day, the Operation MUDLARK officials had prepared a statement based on the standard cover story but modified to fit the available information on Powers' flight and to show Adana as the aircraft's base in order to conceal Pakistan's role in the mission. This revised cover story, along with a mission flight plan consistent with it, was sent to the field commander at Adana, to Air Force Europe headquarters. [Redacted] to replace the cover story that had been prepared and distributed in advance of the mission. The first announcement of the new cover story came late on 2 May by the Adana base commander, but it did not appear in print until the following day. On Tuesday, 3 May, NASA released a statement about a high-altitude weather plane that was missing on a flight inside Turkey. The statement had been designed to provide an explanation for the presence of wreckage inside the Soviet Union by noting that "the pilot reported over the emergency frequency that he was experiencing oxygen difficulties."[32] Thus, if the Soviets protested and pointed to wreckage inside their borders, NASA could claim that the pilot

---

[31] Geary interview (S).

[32] Beschloss, *Mayday*, p. 39.

had lost consciousness and the aircraft had then flown into the Soviet Union before crashing.

This statement had been prepared for a "best case" scenario, that is to say, one in which neither the pilot nor the plane and film survived. However, pilots had bailed out from extremely high altitudes and survived, and there was even evidence from previous U-2 crashes that much of the aircraft itself could be salvaged. The small destructive charge aboard the U-2 was not sufficient to destroy much more than the camera. The tightly rolled film, which could reveal the exact purpose of the mission even if the pilot and aircraft did not survive, was very hard to destroy. Kelly Johnson later conducted an experiment that revealed film taken out of a completely burned-out aircraft could still provide usable imagery.[33] After almost four years of successful U-2 missions, Richard Bissell and the rest of the Development Projects Division had become overconfident and were not prepared for the "worst case" scenario that actually occurred in May 1960. This failure played directly into the hands of Soviet Premier Nikita Khrushchev, who shrewdly decided to release information about the downed U-2 a little at a time, thereby encouraging the United States to stick with its vulnerable cover story too long. As he later wrote, "Our intention here was to confuse the government circles of the United States. As long as the Americans thought the pilot was dead, they would keep putting out the story that perhaps the plane had accidentally strayed off course and been shot down in the mountains on the Soviet side of the border."[34] The first word from the Soviet Union came on Thursday, 5 May, when Premier Khrushchev announced to a meeting of the Supreme Soviet that a US "spyplane" had been downed near Sverdlovsk. He made no mention of the fate of its pilot.

---

[33] Geary interview.

[34] Khrushchev, *Khrushchev Remembers: The Last Testament*, p. 507.

Khrushchev's announcement aroused considerable interest in the media in the United States, and that same day the State Department and NASA issued another statement that continued the "weather plane" cover story, adding that the pilot became lost during a routine mission near the Caucasus Mountains. Soon afterward, the US Ambassador to Moscow cabled a report to the State Department indicating that the pilot might be alive after all. Two days later, on 7 May 1960, Khrushchev confirmed this report by revealing that the U-2 pilot was alive and had admitted his mission of spying on the Soviet Union.

This revelation completely demolished the US cover story, and senior administration officials then debated what the appropriate course of action should be. Allen Dulles offered to take responsibility for the overflight and resign, but President Eisenhower did not want to give the world the impression that he was not in control of his administration. On Wednesday, 11 May, the President read a statement to the press in which he assumed full responsibility for the U-2 mission but left open the question of future overflights, even though four days earlier he had approved the recommendation of his key foreign policy advisers to terminate all provocative intelligence operations against the Soviet Union.[35]

The U-2 affair had its greatest consequences when the long-awaited summit meeting in Paris began less than a week later on 16 May. Soviet Premier Khrushchev insisted on being the first speaker and read a long protest about the overflight, ending with a demand for an apology from President Eisenhower. In his reply Eisenhower stated that overflights had been suspended and would not be resumed, but he refused to make a formal apology. At that point the summit ended, as did all hopes for a visit to the Soviet Union by President Eisenhower.

---

[35] *OSA History*, chap. 14, pp. 14-16 (TS Codeword); Beschloss, *Mayday*, pp. 43-66, 243-258.

THE WITHDRAWAL OF THE OVERSEAS DETACHMENTS

The loss of Powers' U-2 ultimately resulted in the end of Detachment B in Turkey. As soon as the Development Projects Division learned that Powers was alive in Soviet hands, it immediately evacuated the British pilots from Adana to protect the secret of their involvement in the project. Project officials hoped that flights might eventually resume from Adana, but President Eisenhower's order ending overflights of the Soviet Union made this very unlikely. Less than four weeks later, a coup ousted the government of Turkish Premier Adnan Menderes on the night of 27 May 1960. Because the new government had not been briefed on the U-2, Project Headquarters refused to allow any U-2 flights from Adana, even those necessary for maintaining the aircraft's airworthiness. As a result, no more U-2s flew out of Adana. Instead of being ferried home, three of the four remaining U-2s were disassembled and loaded aboard C-124 cargo planes for the return trip to the United States.[36]

The fourth U-2 remained inside a hangar at Incirlik airbase for several years, looked after by a skeleton crew, in case the Adana installation needed to be reactivated. Finally the decision was made to close down the Adana U-2 facility. During Detachment B's 44 months of active existence, 21 pilots had flown its aircraft, including four RAF pilots and three pilots transferred from the deactivated Detachment A. Fourteen Detachment B pilots were later assigned to other U-2 detachments, but the closing down of Detachment B marked the end of Britain's direct involvement in U-2 operational overflights. A four-man unit of RAF U-2 pilots was stationed at Detachment G, Edwards AFB, until the end of the CIA U-2 program in 1974, but RAF pilots never again conducted an overflight in an Agency U-2.

---

[36] *OSA History,* chap. 12, pp. 46-47 (TS Codeword).

The loss of Powers' U-2, the resultant failure of the Paris Summit, and the end of U-2 operations in Turkey were just the first in a series of setbacks for the U-2 program. On 8 July 1960, the Japanese Government, faced with growing anti-American sentiment and complaints in the press about the presence of "spyplanes" on Japanese territory, asked the United States to remove the U-2s. The very next day the CIA closed Detachment C; its U-2s were dismantled and returned to the United States aboard C-124s.[37]

In the midst of the furor in Japan, on 1 July 1960, just six weeks after the Paris Summit, Soviet fighter aircraft shot down an Air Force RB-47 on an electronic intelligence collection mission over international waters near the Soviet Union's Kola Peninsula. Two survivors were captured. The Soviet Union claimed that the aircraft had violated its airspace, while the United States denounced the Soviets for downing the plane over international waters. The acrimony exacerbated an already tense international atmosphere.[38]

One additional blow to the U-2 program came in the summer of 1960. NASA, concerned about the damage to its reputation from its involvement in the U-2 affair and hoping to obtain international cooperation for its space program, decided to end its support of the cover story that U-2s were conducting weather research under its auspices.[39]

---

[37] *OSA Chronology*, p. 28 (TS Codeword).

[38] "Mystery of the RB-47," *Newsweek*, 25 July 1960, pp. 36-37; "Nikita and the RB-47," *Time*, 25 July 1960, pp. 30-31.

[39] At a meeting of high-level CIA, NASA, and State Department officials on 31 May 1960, NASA was willing to continue its association with U-2 flights for the time being, but the Administrator of NASA, Dr. Keith Glennan, believed that his agency "would be well advised to disengage from the U-2 program as rapidly as possible." James A. Cunningham, Memorandum for the Record, "Telephone Conversation with Dr. Hugh Dryden, Deputy Director, NASA," 1 June 1960, DPD chrono file #4553-60, OSA records (S).

These developments resulted in a complete halt to all U-2 operations from overseas bases for more than six months. Pilots and aircraft from Detachments B and C were consolidated into Detachment G at Edwards Air Force Base, California, the unit formed after the CIA had vacated the Nevada testing site in 1957 as a result of AEC nuclear testing. Detachment G now comprised eight pilots from Detachment B and three pilots from Detachment C. Because Powers' capture had compromised Project CHALICE, the Agency assigned a new cryptonym to the U-2 effort; henceforth, it was called Project IDEALIST.[40]

THE FATE OF FRANCIS GARY POWERS

Downed U-2 pilot Francis Gary Powers underwent extensive interrogation at the hands of the Soviets. His instructions from the CIA on what to do in the event of capture were meager, and he had been told that he might as well tell the Soviets whatever they wanted to know because they could get the information from his aircraft anyway. Nevertheless, Powers tried to conceal as much classified information as possible while giving the appearance of cooperating with his captors. To extract the maximum propaganda value from the U-2 Affair, the Soviets prepared an elaborate show trial for Powers, which began on 17 August 1960. Powers continued to conceal as much information as possible, but, on the advice of his Soviet defense counsel, he stated that he was sorry for his actions. The Soviet court sentenced him to 10 years' "deprivation of liberty," with the first three to be spent in prison.[41]

During the next 18 months, confidential negotiations to obtain the release of Powers took place as the United States explored the possibility of trading convicted Soviet master spy Rudolf Abel for

---

[40] *OSA History,* chap 12, pp. 47-49; chap. 16, p. 10 (TS Codeword).

[41] Powers, *Operation Overflight,* pp. 160-192; Beschloss, *Mayday,* pp. 331-335.

Powers. These negotiations were conducted by Abel's court-appointed defense counsel, former OSS lawyer James Donovan, in correspondence with Abel's "wife" (probably his Soviet control) in East Germany. In November 1961, Acting DCI Pearre Cabell wrote to Secretary of State Dean Rusk supporting such a trade, and on 10 February 1962 the actual exchange took place in the middle of the Glienecke Bridge connecting East and West Berlin. As part of the deal, American graduate student Frederick Pryor, who had been jailed in East Germany for espionage, was released at another location.

After Powers returned to the United States, he underwent extensive debriefing, for many questions about his mission remained unanswered. To conduct the debriefing, the Agency immediately reconvened the Damage Assessment Team that had met for two months in the summer of 1960 to estimate what Powers knew about the overflight program and could have told Soviet interrogators. Given Powers' long involvement with the U-2 program, the team had concluded in 1960 that his knowledge was extensive and he had probably revealed most of it to the Soviets. After two weeks of debriefing Powers in February 1962, however, the team found that the damage was much less than had been estimated, and they were quite satisfied with Powers' behavior.[42] After reading the debriefing reports, Allen Dulles expressed support of Powers' actions and told Powers, "We are proud of what you have done," but Dulles had already resigned as DCI in November 1961.[43] The new DCI, John A. McCone, demanded a closer look at Powers' actions and set up a Board of Inquiry headed by retired Federal Judge E. Barrett Prettyman. After eight days of hearings and deliberation, the board reported on 27 February that Powers had acted in accordance with his instructions and had "complied with his obligations as an

---

[42] James J. White, "Francis Gary Powers——The Unmaking of a Hero, 1960-1965," (draft), CIA History Staff, 1974, p. 19 (S).

[43] Powers, *Operation Overflight*, p. 307.

American citizen during this period." The board, therefore, recommended that he receive his back pay.

The Prettyman Board's finding was based on a large body of evidence indicating that Powers was telling the truth about the events of 1 May 1960: the testimony of the experts who had debriefed Powers after his return; a thorough investigation of Powers' background with testimony by doctors, psychiatrists, former Air Force colleagues, and his commander at Adana; Powers' own testimony before the board; the results of a polygraph examination that he had volunteered to undergo; and the evidence provided by photographs of the wreckage of his aircraft, which Kelly Johnson had analyzed and found consistent with Powers' story. Nevertheless, DCI McCone remained skeptical. He asked the Air Force to convene its own panel of experts to check Johnson's assessment of the photographs of the U-2. The Air Force quickly complied, and the panel supported Johnson's findings. McCone then seized upon the one piece of evidence that contradicted Powers' testimony—a report by the National Security Agency (NSA) that suggested that Powers may have descended to a lower altitude and turned back in a broad curve toward Sverdlovsk before being downed—and ordered the Prettyman Board to reconvene on 1 March for another look at this evidence. The board remained unconvinced by NSA's thin evidence and stuck to its original findings. A few days later, on 6 March 1962, Powers appeared before the Senate Armed Services Committee, which commended his actions. The Senate Foreign Relations Committee also held brief hearings on the U-2 Affair, with DCI McCone representing the CIA.[44]

Although all of these inquiries found Powers to have acted properly, they did not release many of their favorable findings to the public, which had received a very negative image of Powers' behav-

---

[44] Beschtoss, *Mayday*, p. 352-354; Thomas Powers, *Man Who Kept the Secrets*, p. 328; Prettyman Board, DCI records (S).

ior from sensational press reports and statements by public figures who were not aware of (or chose to ignore) the truth about Powers' actions while in captivity. One member of the Senate Foreign Relations Committee, Senator John J. Williams, expressed concern about the impact of this silence on Powers' reputation in a question to DCI McCone on 6 March 1962: "Don't you think he is being left with just a little bit of a cloud hanging over him? If he did everything he is supposed to do, why leave it hanging?"[45] Doubts about Powers did remain in the public mind because he received no public recognition for his efforts to withhold information from the Soviets. He was also snubbed by President Kennedy, who one year earlier had warmly welcomed two Air Force RB-47 fliers released by the Soviet Union. McCone remained hostile to Powers, and in April 1963 he awarded the Intelligence Star to all of the U-2 pilots except Powers. Finally on 25 April 1965, just two days before McCone's resignation became effective, Powers received the Star (which was dated 1963 on the back) from DDCI Marshall S. Carter.[46]

Powers' return from captivity raised the question of what his future employment should be. This issue had already been discussed one year earlier by John N. McMahon, executive officer of the DPD, who noted that he and Col. Leo P. Geary (the Air Force project officer) were concerned about a major dilemma for the CIA and the US Government: "On the one hand we have gone to considerable lengths to prove that the U-2 program was a civilian undertaking and not military aggression; on the other hand there is on file a document that assures Francis Gary Powers that if he so desires he may be *reinstated* into the USAF." On 21 March 1961 McMahon wrote:

---

[45] United States Congress, Senate, Foreign Relations Committee, *Executive Sessions of the Senate Foreign Relations Committee (Historical Series)*, vol. 12, 86th Congress, Second Session, "Report on the U-2 Incident," 6 March 1962, p. 265 (declassified 1982).

[46] *OSA History* chap. 14, p. 54 (TS Codeword); Beschloss, *Mayday*, p. 397.

If we grant him [Powers] the right that is now his, namely reinstatement in the Air Force, then we would be subjecting ourselves to probable adverse propaganda by the USSR. Admitting little appreciation for the finer points of political and psychological warfare, should Francis Gary Powers return to the USAF I suspect that the Soviets would have a "PP" field day illustrating our big lie. The question then, since we cannot permit Powers to return to the USAF, is what do we do with him.[47]

Despite this negative recommendation, the Air Force agreed on 4 April 1962 to reinstate Powers effective 1 July, a decision that was approved by the Agency, State Department, and White House. Then Powers' divorce proceedings began, and the Air Force, concerned about adverse publicity, postponed reinstatement until the end of the proceedings. In the meantime Powers began working for Lockheed as a U-2 pilot. In March 1963, he met with Colonel Geary to discuss his future plans and decided to stay with Lockheed.[48] Powers remained at Lockheed until U-2 testing ceased in September 1969. Earlier in the year, he had published an account of his experiences on the U-2 project under the title *Operation Overflight*. Later he flew a light plane as a traffic reporter for a Los Angeles radio station and then a helicopter for a television station. On 1 August 1977, he and a cameraman from the station died when his helicopter crashed on the way to an assignment.[49]

---

[47] John N. McMahon to Chief, Cover Staff, DPD, 21 March 1961, Operation MUDLARK files, OSA records, job 74-B-605, box 6 (S).

[48] *OSA History,* chap. 14, p. 52 (TS Codeword).

[49] Beschloss, *Mayday*, pp. 396-401. Beschloss claims that Powers was fired by Lockheed for criticizing the Agency in his memoirs (which he had shown to the Agency in draft form), but Kelly Johnson's "U-2R Log" records on 25 September 1969: "We have no flight test activity at all. I must let Gary Powers go. Have protected him for about seven years, but he doesn't have an ATR (Air Transport Rating), so we have no other job for him—not even flying the Beechcraft."

CHANGES IN OVERFLIGHT PROCEDURES
AFTER MAY 1960

One of the most important changes in the overflight program after the loss of Francis Gary Powers' U-2 was the institution of more formal procedures for the approval of U-2 missions. During the first four years of U-2 activity, very few members of the Eisenhower administration had been involved in making decisions concerning the overflight program. The President personally authorized all flights over the Soviet Union and was consulted by Richard Bissell and either the DCI or the DDCI about each such proposed mission. In addition to CIA officials, the President's discussions of individual U-2 missions or of the program as a whole generally included the Secretary of State or his Under Secretary, the Chairman of the Joint Chiefs of Staff, the Secretary of Defense or his deputy, and the President's secretary, Colonel (later General) Goodpaster.

The approval process under President Eisenhower was thus very unstructured. There was no formal approval body charged with reviewing overflight proposals: the President kept this authority in his hands and simply consulted with selected cabinet officials and advisers before reaching a decision. In 1959 the U-2 program had gained a second approval authority when British Prime Minister Harold Macmillan became the approval authority for missions conducted by the RAF pilots in Detachment B.

The loss of Powers' U-2 in May 1960 led to major changes in the approval process. For all practical purposes, Prime Minister Macmillan ceased to be a source of approval because the RAF pilots who remained in the U-2 program did not conduct any more operational missions (although the use of British pilots was considered on several occasions). In the United Slates the approval process became more formal as the National Security Council became involved. Henceforth, proposed missions had to be submitted to the National Security Council (NSC) Special Group for approval. In the early 1960s, the Special Group consisted of the DCI, the Deputy Secretary of Defense, the Under Secretary of State, and the Military Adviser to the President. After the Military Adviser, Gen. Maxwell Taylor, became Chairman of the Joint Chiefs of Staff in 1962, his place on the Special Group was taken by McGeorge Bundy, the President's Special Assistant for National Security Affairs.[50]

Before requesting permission from the Special Group for a U-2 mission over denied territory, the CIA prepared a detailed submission giving justification for the proposed mission and maps showing the targets to be photographed, flight times, and emergency landing sites. Such submissions came to be known as "black books" because they were placed in black, looseleaf binders. The decision of the Special Group was generally final, although on occasion controversial issues were presented to the President for his decision.

This approval process did not come into play immediately after May 1960 because there was a long pause in U-2 operations as the detachments returned from overseas. It was not until late October 1960 that the next U-2 operation occurred, this time over Cuba. By this time the full approval procedure had been established, and the Special Group approved the mission (see chapter 5).

The approval process was not the only part of the U-2 program that changed after May 1960. The process for establishing requirements for overhead reconnaissance missions also became more formal. In August 1960 the US Intelligence Board

---

[50] The Special Group, which had been created by NSC Intelligence Document 5412/2 in 1955 to oversee covert activities, was originally known as the 5412 Committee. Later the Special Group became known as the 303 Committee and then the 40 Committee. United States Congress, Senate, Select Committee to Study Governmental Operations with Respect to Intelligence Activities, *Foreign and Military Intelligence*, book 1 (Washington, DC: US Government Printing Office, 1976), pp. 48-53.

took over the Ad Hoc Requirements Committee and merged it with the Satellite Intelligence Requirements Committee to form the Committee on Overhead Reconnaissance. DCI Directive 2/7 tasked COMOR with the "coordinated development of foreign intelligence requirements for overhead-reconnaissance projects over denied areas." The DCID defined "overhead reconnaissance" to include "all reconnaissance for foreign-intelligence purposes by satellite, or by any vehicle over denied areas, whether by photographic, ELINT, COMINT, infrared, RADINT, or other means." The only exception to COMOR's area of responsibility was "reconnaissance and aerial surveillance in direct support of actively combatant forces."[51]

By this time the Air Force had developed a large overhead reconnaissance program of its own, including a fleet of U-2s, and, occasionally, there were conflicts between the areas of responsibility of COMOR and the military services for collection requirements. The Air Force had already won a major victory in 1958, when it claimed that the White House had given responsibility for peripheral reconnaissance of the Soviet Union to the military. DCI Dulles, who was always reluctant to become involved in matters that seemed to lie in the military's area of responsibility, did not resist this claim, and the Ad Hoc Requirements Committee stopped preparing requirements for peripheral flights. This ended a major requirements committee study, which sought to estimate what could be gained from U-2 oblique photography along the entire border of the Soviet Union.[52] The last CIA U-2 mission along the Soviet Union's coasts occurred on 22 June 1958; thereafter, the only peripheral missions conducted by

---

[51] DCID 2/7, effective 9 August 1960 (S).
[52] Memorandum for DCI McCone from James Q. Reber, Chairman, COMOR, "Proposed Procedures for Approval of Critical Reconnaissance," 21 March 1962, COMIREX records (TS Codeword).

the CIA were those along the Soviet Union's southern border with Iran and Afghanistan from bases in Pakistan and Turkey under covert arrangements with the host governments.

Until the spring of 1961, there was virtually no coordination of military reconnaissance activities, even within the individual services. Each commander of a Theater or a Unified and Specified Command conducted his own independent reconnaissance activities. To meet the growing need for overall coordination of these activities at the national level, the Joint Chiefs of Staff (JCS) established the Joint Reconnaissance Center (JRC) under the J-3 (Operations) of the Joint Staff. The JRC immediately began to coordinate and obtain approval for approximately 500 missions per month, assigning each a risk factor of Critical, Sensitive, Unique, or Routine. The IRC then prepared a monthly Activities Book giving details of the proposed missions and briefed the Joint Chiefs of Staff on the more risky missions. The CIA received a copy of the Activities Book.

Most military reconnaissance missions were approved or disapproved at the JCS level, but the most sensitive missions were submitted through the Secretary of Defense to the Special Group for approval. In addition to this Department of Defense approval path, the military services could also submit requirements through the DCI using their representatives on COMOR. As a result, the military services had two channels for submitting reconnaissance missions to the Special Group. The Agency had only one—COMOR.[53]

The main conflicts between the requirements committee and the military services arose over missions in the Far East. In the early 1960s, North Vietnam had not been designated a denied area by the US Intelligence Board (USIB), so the military services could plan missions there without consulting COMOR. Such mis-

---

[53] Ibid. (TS Codeword).

sions, however, came very close to China, which was a denied area and, therefore, came under COMOR's area of responsibility. Once the war in Southeast Asia escalated in 1964, the military services received responsibility for the entire area (see chapter 5).

To reduce the number of disputes between the competing CIA and Air Force reconnaissance programs and to manage the growing satellite program, the two agencies worked out an agreement to provide overall coordination for reconnaissance activities at the national level. The first such interagency agreement came in the fall of 1961, and it was followed by three additional agreements during the next four years.[54]

Interest in coordinating the reconnaissance efforts of the military services and the CIA also affected the field of photographic interpretation. In the wake of the loss of Francis Gary Powers' U-2 on 1 May 1960, the President's Board of Consultants on Foreign Intelligence Activities (PFIAB) had urged the establishment of an interagency group to study ways to improve the entire US intelligence community. Formed on 6 May 1960, the Joint Study Group on Foreign Intelligence Activities met for the next seven months under the leadership of Lyman Kirkpatrick, CIA Inspector General. One of the study group's key recommendations in the report it issued in December 1960 was the creation of a national photointerpretation center that would bring together photointerpreters from the Agency and the military services. The report further recommended that the CIA be placed in charge of the new center. Ignoring Air Force claims that it should head such a center, President Eisenhower approved the report's recommendation, and, on 18 January 1961, National Security Council Intelligence Directive (NSCID) No. 8 established the National Photographic

---

[54] Problems of classification prevent a more detailed discussion of this aspect of the reconnaissance program, which will be covered in a future history of satellite reconnaissance at a higher level of classification.

Interpretation Center (NPIC). Henceforth, the director of NPIC would be designated by the DCI and approved by the Secretary of Defense, and the deputy director would come from one of the military services. The first director of NPIC was Arthur S. Lundahl, head of the CIA's Photo-Intelligence Division.[55]

One additional major change in the U-2 program in the years immediately following the May Day incident—although not directly related to the loss of Powers' U-2—was the departure of Richard Bissell from the CIA and the subsequent reorganization of the Agency's reconnaissance and scientific activities. The roots of Bissell's downfall went back to 1 January 1959, when he became Deputy Director for Plans and decided to place all Agency air assets in the DDP in order to maintain control of his overhead reconnaissance projects (the U-2 and its two proposed successors, the OXCART aircraft and the reconnaissance satellite). The previously independent Development Projects Staff became the Development Projects Division (DPD) of the DDP and now controlled all Agency air operations, including air support for covert operations. As a result, U-2s were occasionally employed for gathering intelligence to support DDP operations in addition to their primary mission of gathering strategic and tactical intelligence.

Although the reorganization made sense in terms of increasing the efficiency of Agency air operations, the use of the U-2 to support covert action disturbed Bissell's backers among the scientists advising Presidents Eisenhower and Kennedy, especially James Killian and Edwin Land. They were concerned that Bissell was becoming too involved in covert action and was not able to devote sufficient time to the overhead reconnaissance program. Then came the disastrous Bay of Pigs invasion in April 1961, which discredited Bissell with the Kennedy administration

---

[55] Lundahl and Brugioni interview (TS Codeword).

in general and the two scientists in particular. Later that year, Bissell lost another important source of support when Allen Dulles resigned as DCI in November 1961. During his final months as the Deputy Director for Plans, Bissell found himself involved in a major struggle with Killian and Land, who were serving on President Kennedy's Foreign Intelligence Advisory Board (successor to the Eisenhower administration's President's Board of Consultants on Foreign Intelligence Activities). These two influential Presidential advisers strongly advocated removing the Agency's overhead reconnaissance programs from the DDP and placing them in a new, science-oriented directorate, but Bissell resisted this proposal. With his position in the Agency becoming increasingly untenable, Bissell resigned on 17 February 1962, after turning down an offer from the new DCI, John A. McCone, to become the CIA's first Deputy Director for Research.[56]

Two days after Bissell's departure, the new Directorate came into existence, and it absorbed all of the Development Projects Division's special reconnaissance projects. Only conventional air support for the Clandestine Services remained with the DDP in the new Special Operations Division. The U-2 program was no longer connected with covert operations.

The first half of 1962 was a confusing period for the Development Projects Division. After losing the individual who had created and supervised it for seven years, the DPD also lost its feeling of autonomy when it was transferred from its own building to the new CIA Headquarters at Langley. Soon afterward, Col. Stanley W. Beerli, who had headed the DPD since 1960, returned to the Air Force. Then on 30 July 1962, the overhead reconnaissance projects underwent a major reorganization with the formation of

---

[56] Killian interview (S); Land interview (TS Codeword); Richard M. Bissell to John A. McCone, 7 February 1962, DCI records, job 80-B-1676R, box 18, folder 10 (S).

the new Office of Special Activities (OSA) to replace the DPD. The original organization of OSA with 10 division or staff heads reporting directly to the director of the office (at that time known as the Assistant Director for Special Activities) proved too cumbersome, and, on 30 September 1962, a reorganization divided most of these offices between two major subordinates, the Deputy for Technology and the Deputy for Field Activities. The Office of Special Activities (OSA) continued to control reconnaissance activities and related research and development after the Directorate of Research was enlarged and renamed the Deputy Directorate for Science and Technology (DDS&T) on 5 August 1963 (along with the other Directorates, DDS&T dropped the "Deputy" from its title in 1965 and became known as the Directorate of Science and Technology). In 1965 the head of OSA received a new title, Director of Special Activities. The Office of Special Activities remained in control of the CIA's overhead reconnaissance activities until 1974, when the Agency ended its involvement with manned reconnaissance aircraft.[57]

---

[57] *OSA Chronology*, pp. 34-35 (TS Codeword).

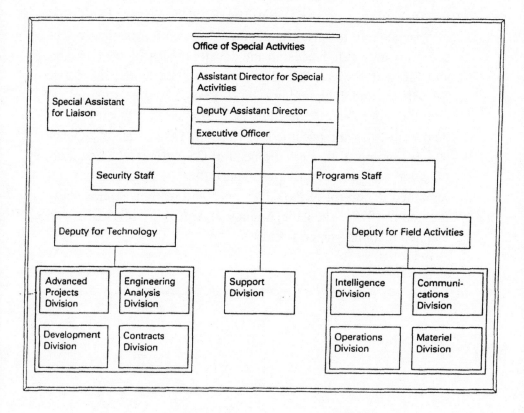

5

U-2 Operations after May 1960

The loss of Francis Gary Powers' U-2 over the Soviet Union on 1 May 1960 marked the end of the aircraft's use over the Soviet Bloc. Soon after the May Day incident, President Eisenhower ordered an end to overflights. Similarly, his successor, John F. Kennedy, told a 25 January 1961 press conference, "I have ordered that the flights not be resumed, which is a continuation of the order given by President Eisenhower in May of last year." This was not a binding pledge, as John A. McCone (who became DCI in November 1961) pointed out to President Kennedy's successor, Lyndon B. Johnson, on 15 January 1964 in response to the new President's request for information on U-2 overflight policies:

> *Contrary to popular assumption, President Kennedy did not make any pledge or give an assurance, at least publicly, that there would be no further overflights. He limited his response to a statement that he had ordered*

that the flights not be resumed. An order, obviously, is
valid only until countermanded.[1]

Technically, McCone was correct, but no President was likely
to order a resumption of overflights of the Soviet Union without
very good reason, and such a situation never developed, in part
because satellite photography gradually began to fill the gap left
by the end of U-2 coverage.

Although there were several proposals to resume overflights
of the Soviet Union in the years that followed, none reached the
mission planning stage. The Kennedy administration came closest to resuming overflights of the Soviet Union during the Berlin
Crisis in the summer and fall of 1961. On 14 September 1961,
Kelly Johnson noted in his project log:

Have had request from Mr. Bissell to propose ways
and means for increasing safety of the U-2 on proba-
ble overflights....It seems that President Kennedy, who
publicly stated that no U-2's would ever be over Rus-
sia while he was president, has requested additional
flights. Some poetic justice in this.[2]

---

[1] Memorandum for President Johnson from DCI McCone, "Response to
Query Concerning U-2 Overflight Policy," 15 January 1964, DCI records, job
80-B-1676R, box 17, folder 14 (TS Codeword).

[2] Johnson, "Log for Project X," 14 September 1961. In preparation for the
possible resumption of overflights, Kelly Johnson began thinking about what to
do in a worst case scenario like that of 1 May 1960. He noted in the project log
on 21 September 1961: *One of the greatest technical problems and, of course, a*
great moral one, is how we insure destroying the aircraft and the pilot should the
mission fail. I have proposed a time-altitude fusing setup for multitude bombs,
that looks like it should do the trick. Beerli [Col. Stanley Beerli, USAF, Director
of the Office of Special Activities] doesn't want anything to do with this, but we
will go ahead and develop it in case someone decides it is necessary.

One week later Colonel Geary called to order Lockheed to upgrade six older U-2s into U-2Cs with the more powerful engines on a priority basis, even if it meant taking people off the work on the successor aircraft in order to speed up the conversions.

Shortly thereafter, the resumption of overflights became a major topic of discussion within the intelligence community. On 25 September 1961, the Committee on Overhead Reconnaissance prepared a detailed "Justification for U-2 Photography over the USSR," which argued in favor of U-2 missions over selected, high-priority targets such as ICBM complexes. The COMOR paper stated that satellite photography did not provide sufficient detail to answer many critical questions about the Soviet ICBM program. To back up this contention, the report placed U-2 and satellite photography of the same Soviet targets side by side, clearly demonstrating the far superior resolution of the U-2's cameras. Not all members of COMOR supported the resumption of overflights, however. When COMOR formally recommended this course of action to the USIB on 1 October 1961, the State Department and CIA members dissented, having found "insufficient justification for resuming U-2 overflights of the USSR at this time."[3]

Nothing came of the proposal to resume overflights in the fall of 1961, as both the USIB and the Special Group came out against it, but, as long as U-2 photography remained clearly superior to satellite photography, the thought of obtaining U-2 coverage of the Soviet Union remained tempting. In February 1962, the USIB seriously considered a COMOR proposal to send a U-2 over Kamchatka to photograph Soviet antiballistic-missile facilities but finally decided to wait for the results

---

[3] Memorandum for USIB from COMOR, "Justification for U-2 Photography over the USSR," 25 September 1961, IC Staff, COMIREX records, job 33-T-123A, box 10, "COMOR (General)" (TS Codeword); Memorandum for USIB front COMOR, "Requirements for Resumption of U-2 Overflights of the USSR," 1 October 1961, IC Staff, COMIREX records, job 33-B-119A, box 1 (TS Codeword).

of an Air Force peripheral mission. The board later accepted DCI McCone's recommendation to seek satellite rather than U-2 coverage of the area.[4]

With both the CIA and the State Department strongly opposed to sending the highly vulnerable U-2 over the Soviet Union, prospects for resuming flights remained slight unless the international situation worsened to such a degree that overflights would be worth the risks involved. Since this never happened, Francis Gary Powers' flight on 1 May 1960 proved to be the last CIA overflight of the Soviet Bloc. Yet, the U-2 remained useful, for it could operate successfully in other areas with less developed radar and air defense systems. After May 1960, the main focus of U-2 activity shifted to two new areas: Latin America, where U-2s would play an extremely important role during the early 1960s, and the Far East, where CIA U-2s were active from 1958 until 1974, when the Agency's involvement in manned reconnaissance finally ended.

U-2 OPERATIONS IN LATIN AMERICA
U-2 Support to the Bay of Pigs Invasion
During late summer 1960, the Directorate of Plans was planning a counterrevolutionary invasion of Cuba for the following year. To

---

[4] Memorandum for the Special Group from COMOR, "Illustrations of Policy Restraints on the Collection of Information through Overflight of Denied Areas during 1962," 14 December 1962, IC Staff, COMIREX records, job 33-B-119A, box 1 (TS Codeword); James S. Lay, "The United States Intelligence Board, 1958-1965," (draft) CIA History Staff MS-2, 1974, p. 385 (TS Codeword). One year later Saryshagan was the topic of US Intelligence Board deliberations. In October 1963 the board asked COMOR to prepare recommendations on the need for an electronic intelligence-gathering mission against the Soviet ABM installations at Saryshagan. The proposed mission would not however, violate Soviet airspace; instead, the U-2 would fly over the portion of the People's Republic of China closest to Saryshagan. Lay, "USIB History," pp. 393-94 (TS Codeword).

support this effort, the Agency asked the National Security Council's Special Group to approve U-2 overflights of Cuba. Known as Operation KICK OFF, these flights were designed to obtain intelligence on Cuban air and ground order of battle and to provide geographic data for choosing an invasion site.

To allay fears that mechanical problems could lead to the loss of a U-2 over Cuba, the submission to the Special Group for overflights emphasized that, if a U-2 had a flameout anywhere over Cuba, it could still glide back and make a safe landing in Florida. The Special Group approved Operation KICK OFF but stipulated that only two overflights could be made. Detachment G staged the Cuban missions from Laughlin AFB near Del Rio, Texas, a base used by SAC U-2 aircraft. Agency photointerpreters went to Del Rio to read out the photography after these missions. The two flights, on 26 and 27 October 1960, were very long missions, covering 3,500 miles and lasting over nine hours. Because of cloud cover over Cuba, the results of both missions were poor. The Agency, therefore, asked the Special Group to approve additional missions. After receiving authorization, Detachment G conducted three missions (Operation GREEN EYES) on 27 November and 5 and 11 December 1960 with good results.

Overflights of Cuba continued under the new administration of President Kennedy. Under the codename Operation LONG GREEN, two overflights on 19 and 21 March 1961 photographed Cuba extensively to aid the final preparations for the invasion. Two weeks later Detachment G again deployed from Edwards AFB, California, to Laughlin AFB, Texas. Beginning on 6 April, Detachment G U-2s made 15 flights over Cuba to provide photographic coverage of the ill-fated Bay of Pigs invasion and its aftermath. These flights were known as Operation FLIP TOP.[5]

---

[5] *OSA History,* chap. 16, pp. 13-15 (TS Codeword).

Aerial Refueling Capability for the U-2

Long missions conducted over Cuba in late 1960 and over Southeast Asia in early 1961 pointed out the need to increase the range of the U-2. In May 1961, Lockheed began modifying Agency U-2s so that they could be refueled in flight to extend their operating range. The six Agency aircraft that were modified to achieve this capability received the designation U-2F. All Agency U-2 pilots then underwent training in the techniques of in-flight refueling.

Refueling a U-2 in flight was a very delicate task. When fully loaded with fuel, KC-135 tankers found it difficult to reduce airspeed to 200 knots, the safest speed for refueling a U-2. As for the U-2s, they were in a very vulnerable position when approaching a tanker at 200 knots because their frail wings could not stand much stress. As a result, U-2 pilots had to approach the KC-135 tankers very carefully in order to avoid the vortexes from the wingtips of the tanker and the turbulence caused by the four large jet engines. During the first few years of refueling operations, two U-2s crashed after their wings broke off as they crossed into the turbulent area behind the tankers; one of the pilots was killed.[6]

The in-flight refueling capability was a useful modification to the U-2, but it could not dramatically extend mission length. The main limiting factor remained pilot fatigue, which prevented missions from lasting longer than approximately 10 hours.

U-2 Coverage during the Cuban Missile Crisis

Cuba remained a high-priority target even after the Bay of Pigs invasion failed in April 1961. Soon afterward, Detachment G U-2s began flying monthly missions over Cuba in a program known as Project NIMBUS. Most of the flights were staged from Laughlin AFB, Texas, but three were flown from Edwards AFB, California, using in-flight refueling to extend the range of the air-

---

[6] Ibid., p. 11-12 (TS Codewords).

craft. By the spring of 1962, having received reports of increased Soviet activity in Cuba, the CIA requested permission for additional photographic coverage of the island. The Special Group authorized increasing the number of Cuban overflights to at least two per month, beginning in May 1962. At the same time, the National Photographic Interpretation Center began publishing a *Photographic Evaluation of Information on Cuba* series.[7]

By early August 1962, CIA analysts had noted a substantial increase in Soviet arms deliveries to Cuba during the preceding weeks. The first U-2 overflight in August, mission 3086 on the 5th, flew too soon to detect the Soviet construction program just getting under way at various sites in Cuba. A second mission (3088) was originally set for 8 August, but bad weather forced repeated postponements until 29 August. This mission's photography provided the first hard evidence of the nature of the Soviet buildup in Cuba. Two days after the mission, the CIA reported in the *President's Intelligence Checklist* that there were at least eight surface-to-air missile (SA-2) sites in the western half of Cuba.[8]

On 5 September the next U-2 overflight (mission 3089) provided more evidence of the Soviet buildup. The mission's photography showed three more SAM sites and also revealed a MiG-21, one of the newest Soviet fighter aircraft, at the Santa Clara airfield.

The discovery of SAMs in Cuba had a twofold effect on the US reconnaissance effort over Cuba. First, it added substance to DCI McCone's fears that Cuba might become a base for Soviet medium-range ballistic missiles (he argued that SAM sites would only be set up to protect high-priority facilities such as missile

---

[7] Ibid., pp. 19-20 (TS Codeword).

[8] Richard Lehman, "CIA Handling of the Soviet Buildup in Cuba, 1 July-16 October 1962," 14 November 1962 (Hereafter cited as Lehman Report), DCI records, job 80-B-1676R, box 17, folder 18 (TS Codeword).

bases). At this time, however, McCone's suspicions were not shared by other officials in the Agency or the administration. The second and most significant effect of the discovery of SAMs in Cuba was to make the administration far more cautious in its use of U-2s for reconnaissance of the island. As the loss of Francis Gary Powers' U-2 in May 1960 had demonstrated, the U-2 was very vulnerable to the SA-2 missile.

Within the administration, concern mounted about the U-2's vulnerability to SAMs in Cuba and the possibility that a loss could cause a major diplomatic crisis. Such fears increased as the result of two incidents in other parts of the world. On 30 August 1962, a SAC U-2 on a peripheral reconnaissance mission overflew Sakhalin Island in the Far East, prompting a Soviet protest on 4 September. The United States apologized for the intrusion. Then on 8 September, a U-2 with a Nationalist Chinese pilot was shot down over the People's Republic of China (this CIA reconnaissance program is discussed later in this chapter in the section on Asian operations). Increasing concern about U-2 vulnerability led to an impromptu meeting on 10 September 1962 of Secretary of State Dean Rusk, National Security Adviser McGeorge Bundy, and DDCI Marshall S. Carter (in place of the DCI, who was on his honeymoon in France). The Secretary of State objected to the CIA's plans for two extended overflights covering the remaining areas of Cuba not covered by the last two missions. Rusk wanted peripheral flights over international waters kept separate from overflights of Cuban territory. He argued that the loss of an aircraft on a mission that combined both types of flights would make it difficult for the United States to stand on its rights to fly over international waters. Bundy and Carter therefore agreed to split the proposed reconnaissance program into four missions: two overflights and two peripheral flights, all planned for maximum safety. The overflights were thus designed to be quick "in-and-out" operations across the

U-2 Overflights of Cuba, August - October 1962

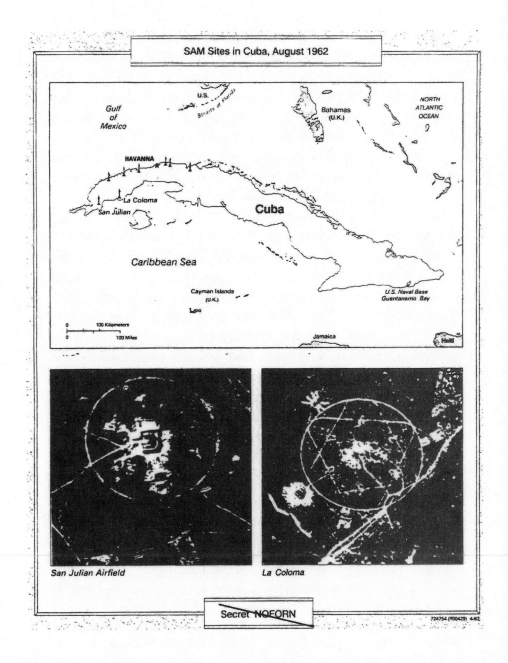

SAM Sites in Cuba, August 1962

San Julian Airfield

La Coloma

Secret NOFORN

724754 (R00429) 4-82

narrow width of the island instead of flights along the entire length of Cuba, as had been the case previously. As an additional precaution, flightpaths would be laid out to avoid known SAM sites. Although these changes greatly reduced the danger to the U-2, they slowed the gathering of information on the Soviet buildup by reducing each mission's coverage.[9]

To ensure that the photographs taken by these missions were of the highest quality, the CIA decided to conduct flights only when the weather along the flight routes was less than 25 percent overcast. Weather proved to be a major problem during the month of September. Unfavorable forecasts (along with a brief standdown of U-2 overflights after the loss of the Nationalist Chinese U-2) prevented the launching of any missions from 6 through 16 September. Moreover, when mission 3091 finally flew on 17 September, the favorable weather forecast proved inaccurate and heavy clouds prevented the mission from obtaining usable photography. Bad weather continued to rule out missions until 26 September, when mission 3093 covered eastern Cuba and found three additional SAM sites. Three days later mission 3095 flew over the Isle of Pines and Bay of Pigs area, finding one more SAM site and a coastal-defense cruise missile site.[10]

---

[9] Lehman Report, pp. 12-13 (TS Codeword).

[10] DCI John A. McCone, Memorandum for the Record, "U-2 Overflights of Cuba, 29 August through 14 October 1962," 27 February 1963, DCI records, job 80-B-1676R, box 17, folder 18 (S). Although this DCI memo states that "the delay in completing the photographic coverage was due solely to the unfavorable weather predicted during this period," a more contemporary COMOR memo reported a standdown of U-2 overflights until 16 September as a result of the loss of mission No. GRC-127 over China on 8 September. Memorandum for DDCI Carter from James Q. Reber, Chairman, COMOR, "Historical Analysis of U-2 Overflights of Cuba," 24 October 1962, IC Staff, COMIREX records, job 33-B-122A, box 1, "Cuba Requirements, 1961-63" (TS Codeword).

The cautious series of U-2 flights in September had turned up many more SAM sites but no concrete evidence of the presence of surface-to-surface missiles. Growing impatient with the restrictions that had been placed on U-2 overflights of Cuba, DCI McCone told the Special Group on 4 October 1962 that their policy of avoiding SAM sites had restricted the Agency to using the U-2 only in Cuba's southeastern quadrant. He questioned "whether this was a reasonable restriction at this time, particularly since the SAM's were almost certainly not operational."[11] The Special Group then requested the preparation of an overall program for reconnaissance of Cuba in time for its next meeting on 9 October.

In the meantime, CIA U-2s continued the reconnaissance program that the Special Group had approved in September. In early October two peripheral missions—3098 along the southeastern coast on 5 October and 3100 along the northern coast on 7 October—discovered an additional five SAM sites. This brought the total to 19, but there was still no evidence of surface-to-surface missiles.

Evidence was mounting that the portion of Cuba that the September and early October missions had avoided was the most likely location for Soviet medium-range ballistic missiles (MRBMs). On 6 October 1962, the Committee on Overhead Reconnaissance recommended frequent and regular coverage of Cuba, pointing in particular to the need for renewed coverage of western Cuba:

The absence of coverage of the western end since August 29, coupled with the rate of construction we have observed, means that there may well be many

---

[11] Minutes of the Special Group meeting, 4 October 1962, in Memorandum for DCI McCone from J. S. Earman, Inspector General, "Handling of Raw Intelligence Information During the Cuban Arms Buildup," 20 November 1962, DCI records, job 80-B-1676R, box 17 (TS Codeword).

more sites now being built of which we are unaware. Ground observers have in several recent instances reported sightings of what they believe to be the SS-4 (SHYSTER) MRBM in Cuba. These reports must be confirmed or denied by photo coverage.[12] Attached to this memorandum was a list of targets, with the area around San Cristobal at the top.

On 9 October the Special Group met to discuss COMOR's recommendations, the most important of which was a U-2 flight over the "suspect MRBM site as soon as weather permits." This mission was also designed to pass over one of the SA-2 sites that was thought to be most nearly operational in order to determine the status of SA-2 defenses of Cuba. If this overflight did not provoke an SA-2 reaction, the study recommended "maximum coverage of the western end of the island by multiple U-2s simultaneously."[13] Because the danger posed by the SA-2 sites was one of the major topics at the Special Group meeting, DCI McCone brought along Col. Jack C. Ledford (USAF), head of the Office of Special Activities, who presented a vulnerability analysis that estimated the odds of losing a U-2 over Cuba at 1 in 6. The Special Group approved the recommended flight over San Cristobal.

As the Special Group meeting was breaking up, Deputy Secretary of Defense Roswell Gilpatric and the Air Force representative questioned the adequacy of the Agency's cover story, which was that its pilots were Lockheed employees on a ferry flight to Puerto Rico. The Air Force and DOD representatives argued that it would be better to use Air Force pilots and state in the event of a mishap that the overflight was a routine Air Force peripheral surveillance mission that had gone off course. McCone

---

[12] Lehman Report, p. 30 (TS Codeword).
[13] Ibid., p. 31 (TS Codeword).

then asked Colonel Ledford's opinion of the proposed change. Ledford agreed that the DOD cover story was better but pointed out that the SAC U-2s were much more vulnerable than those of the Agency, which had superior electronic countermeasures and a higher maximum altitude. Ledford then suggested that Air Force pilots use Agency aircraft after receiving familiarization training. After leaving the Special Group meeting, McCone and Gilpatric met with President Kennedy, who approved the San Cristobal mission and the use of Air Force pilots.[14]

Two days later (11 October), Air Force and CIA representatives met to discuss the change in cover stories. Herbert Scoville, CIA Deputy Director for Research, agreed that in the long run the Air Force cover story was best but emphasized that an Air Force pilot should not be used until he had received adequate training. The conversation then turned to the issue of who would run the next mission, the CIA or the Air Force. Strongly favoring Air Force control of the U-2 missions over Cuba, the DOD representatives called DCI McCone and obtained his consent. Shortly thereafter, McCone left Washington for California and did not return until 14 October. Air Force control of the Cuban overflights became official on 12 October, when President Kennedy transferred "responsibility, to include command and control and operational decisions, with regard to U-2 reconnaissance overflights of Cuba" from the CIA to the Department of Defense.[15] The Air Force then asked to borrow two of CIA's U-2Cs.

---

[14] Brig. Gen. Jack C. Ledford, USAF Ret., interview by Gregory W. Pedlow, Washington, DC, 20 February 1987 (S); Memorandum for DCI McCone from Herbert Scoville, Jr., Deputy Director (Research), "The Chronology of Events Leading to the Transfer of Cuban Overflight Responsibility," 28 February 1963, DCI records, job 80-B-1676R, box 17, folder 18 (S).

[15] Memorandum for DCI McCone from McGeorge Bundy, "Reconnaissance Overflights of Cuba," 12 October 1962, DCI records, job 80-B-1676R, box 17, folder 18 (TS).

The Acting DCI, Lt. Gen. Marshall S. Carter, US Army, reacted strongly to the Air Force takeover of a major CIA operation. At one point he remarked, "I think it's a hell of a way to run a railroad. It's perfectly obviously a geared operation to get SAC in the act."[16] In a series of conversations with high-ranking Air Force and administration officials, Carter argued against changing command and control of the flights at such a crucial time. The Agency operation, Carter pointed out, was already in place and working well, whereas the Air Force lacked experience in controlling U-2 overflights, particularly with the U-2C, which was not in the Air Force inventory. Carter also emphasized that Air Force pilots lacked experience with the more powerful J75 engines in the U-2C. He told Roswell Gilpatric, "To put in a brand new green pilot just because he happens to have on a blue suit and to completely disrupt the command and control and communication and ground support system on 72 hours' notice to me doesn't make a God damn bit of sense, Mr. Secretary."[17] DDCI Carter admitted that the Air Force's cover story was probably better than the CIA's but suggested at one point, "Let's take one of my boys and put him in a blue suit."[18] Realizing, however, that the pilot would probably have to come from the Air Force, Carter concentrated his efforts on trying to convince DOD and administration officials to conduct an orderly transition by allowing the CIA to continue its operation for a few weeks using an Air Force pilot, and the Air Force gradually taking over command and control. Carter's efforts were in vain. The Air Force insisted on immediate control of the operation, and administration officials were unwilling

---

[16] Telephone conversation between DDCI Carter and McGeorge Bundy, 13 October 1962, DCI records, job 80-B-1676R, box 17, folder 18 (TS Codeword).
[17] Telephone conversation between DDCI Carter and Roswell Gilpatric, 12 October 1962, DCI records, job 80-B-1676R, box 17, folder 18 (TS Codeword).
[18] Telephone conversation between DDCI Carter and Gen. William McKee, 12 October 1962, DCI records, job 80-B-1676R, box 17, folder 18 (TS Codeword).

to become involved in what they perceived as a jurisdictional dispute. Presidential Assistant for National Security Affairs McGeorge Bundy told DDCI Carter that "the whole thing looks to me like two quarreling children."[19] Furthermore, no one wanted to speak out against a decision that the President had already made.

Once the decision was clearly irrevocable, the Agency gave its complete support to the Air Force in preparing for the upcoming overflight. A SAC U-2 pilot had already arrived unannounced at the CIA's U-2 Detachment at Edwards Air Force Base on 11 October, and the CIA U-2 detachment put him through a hasty training program to familiarize him with the U-2C. By Sunday, 14 October 1962, the weather over Cuba had cleared, and the first SAC overflight of the island took place.

When the U-2 returned, its film was rushed to the National Photographic Interpretation Center. By the evening of 15 October, photointerpreters had found evidence of the presence of MRBMs in the San Cristobal area. NPIC Director Arthur Lundahl immediately notified DDI Ray Cline, who in turn notified DDCI Carter (DCI McCone had again left town). As the readout progressed and the evidence became firmer, the DDI notified National Security Adviser Bundy and Roger Hilsman of the Department of State's Bureau of Intelligence and Research, who informed Secretary of State Dean Rusk. On the following morning, 16 October, DDCI Carter briefed the President on the results of the 14 October mission.[20]

Now that the presence of Soviet medium-range surface-to-surface missiles in Cuba had been confirmed, the rules

---

[19] Telephone conversation between DDCI Carter and McGeorge Bundy, 12 October 1962, DCI records, job 80-B-1676R, box 17, folder 18 (TS Codeword).
[20] For a more detailed account of NPIC's discovery of the Soviet missiles in Cuba, see Dino Brugioni, *The Cuban Missile Crisis—Phase 1, 29 August—16 October 1962*, DDS&T Historical Series, NPIC-1 (CIA: NPIC, 1971) (S).

for U-2 mission approval changed. The Strategic Air Command received blanket approval to fly as many missions as needed to cover Cuba completely, without again consulting the Special Group. During the week that followed the discovery of the missiles, SAC U-2s conducted multiple missions each day. U-2 photography was supplemented by low-level photography taken by high-performance Navy and Air Force aircraft. Throughout the remainder of the Cuban Missile Crisis, the Agency's U-2 pilots remained idle, but the photointerpreters at NPIC did yeoman service in studying the thousands of feet of film returned by Air Force and Navy reconnaissance aircraft. President Kennedy used NPIC photographs to illustrate his address to the nation on 22 October 1962, when he revealed the Soviet missile buildup in Cuba and declared his "naval quarantine" to prevent the shipment of offensive weapons to Cuba.

On 27 October, at the height of the crisis, one of the U-2Cs lent by the Agency to the Air Force was shot down over Cuba, killing the pilot, Maj. Rudolph Anderson. This loss again illustrated the U-2's vulnerability to the SA-2 missile. Nevertheless, SAC U-2 overflights continued, both during and after the crisis. Responsibility for photographic coverage of Cuba remained with the Air Force; Agency pilots never flew another mission over the island.

Although SAC carried out most of the U-2 activity during the Cuban Missile Crisis, the Agency's U-2 missions had made vital contributions during the initial stages of the crisis. In all, Project IDEALIST pilots had spent 459 hours overflying Cuba during 1961 and 1962. They had provided concrete evidence of the Soviet buildup on the island, evidence that was simply not available through any other means. Although by late 1962 photographic satellites had become an integral part of the overhead collection program, only U-2s could provide the highly detailed photography that photointerpreters needed to spot the early stages of work on missile sites. Attempts had been made to photograph

Cuba with satellites, but to no avail because the satellites' normal orbits placed them over Cuba at the wrong time of day, after clouds had formed.

U-2s over South America
Agency U-2s again conducted operations in the Western Hemisphere in December 1963. The Directorate of Plans had requested photographic coverage of Venezuela and neighboring British Guiana because of guerrilla activities conducted by a pro-Castro movement inside Venezuela. Supplies for this movement appeared to be coming across the border from British Guiana. On 30 November 1963, the NSC Special Group approved overflights of the British Guiana–Venezuela border to determine the scope and rate of buildup of guerrilla forces. The Special Group stipulated that the entire effort was to be conducted without the knowledge of either the British or the Venezuelans.

Within three days, several Detachment G aircraft and pilots deployed to Ramey AFB, Puerto Rico, from which they made six flights over the border areas between 3 and 19 December 1963 in an operation known as SEAFOAM. The results of the effort were inconclusive, and the task force returned to Edwards AFB on 22 December.[21]

U-2 OPERATIONS IN ASIA
Detachment C and the Indonesian Revolt of 1958
U-2 operations in Asia began even before the end of overflights of the Soviet Bloc. By 1958 the Eisenhower administration, although very reluctant to approve U-2 flights over or near Soviet and East European borders, was not averse to using the spyplanes in the Third World, where radar detection was unlikely. Thus, in the spring of 1958, Agency U-2s from

---

[21] *OSA History,* chap. 16, pp. 35-36 (TS Codeword).

Detachment C conducted a major reconnaissance effort over Indonesia, Operation ROBIN HOOD.

Long unhappy with President Achmed Sukarno's perceived sympathy to Communism and his institution of "guided democracy" in Indonesia, the CIA, after consultation with the State Department, began in early 1957 to supply financial assistance to a group of dissident Indonesian Army officers on the island of Sumatra. By 25 September 1957, the National Security Council had become concerned with the course of events in Indonesia and on its recommendation President Eisenhower authorized the Agency to "employ all feasible covert means" to support the dissidents. Planning for increased aid of all types began immediately, and in January 1958 a US arms shipment for the dissidents arrived in Sumatra. Then on 10 February, the situation came to a head. While Sukarno was out of the country on a state visit to Japan, the dissident army colonels, without consulting CIA, organized a Revolutionary Council in Padang, West Sumatra, and demanded the abolition of President Sukarno's "guided democracy." Five days later, this council proclaimed itself the new "Revolutionary Government" of Indonesia. President Sukarno's armed forces responded swiftly to this threat. In late February the Indonesian Air Force began bombing dissident strongholds, and by mid-March government forces were conducting an all-out air-sea-land drive against the rebel-held areas in central Sumatra. Although the Sumatran rebels were falling back, additional unrest broke out over 1,800 miles away in the islands of Celebes (Sulawesi), and CIA quickly began supplying weapons to these dissidents, too.[22]

---

[22] [Redacted] *Covert Support to Indonesian Revolutionary Government, 1957-1958*, 2 vols, Clandestine Service Historical Series, CSHP-53 (CIA: History Staff, 1970) (S); John Prados, *Presidents' Secret Wars: CIA and Pentagon Covert Operations Since World War II* (New York, William Morrow: 1986), pp. 133-144.

Increasingly involved in Indonesia, the Agency urgently needed accurate information on the situation there. As in previous crises, U-2s flew reconnaissance missions. On 24 March 1958,

Detachment C and the Indonesian Revolt, 1958

TOKYO
Japan
Atsugi

China

East China Sea

India

Okinawa

TAIPEI

Macau VICTORIA
(Port.) Hong Kong
(U.K.)

Taiwan

Burma

HANOI
NORTH
VIENTIANE VIETNAM

Laos

Luzon

Philippine Sea

RANGOON

Thailand
BANGKOK

South China

Foward processing center established, 28 March

Cubi Point Naval Air Station
Clark Airbase
MANILA

Detachment C moved from Japan, 24 March

Cambodia SOUTH
VIETNAM

Sea

Philippines

PHNOM PENH
SAIGON

JESSELTON
BRUNEI
Brunei (U.K.)
North Borneo
(U.K.)

KUALA LUMPUR
Malaya

Sarawak (U.K.)

KUCHING

Borneo

CIA support for captured island, 27 April

Morotai

SINGAPORE
Singapore
(U.K.)

CIA arms delivery, mid-April

Dissident uprising, 10 February

Padang

Government troops retake city, 17 April

Sumatra

Celebes

HOLLANDIA

Terr. of New Guinea (Th. Terr.)

US advisors evacuated, 1 May

I n d o n e s i a

Ambon
Capture of Allen Pope, 17 May

DJAKARTA

Java

DILI

Terr. of Papua (Austr.)

Portuguese Timor
(Port.)

INDIAN OCEAN

Australia

0   300   600 Kilometers
0   300   600 Miles

724755 (f00427) 4-92

the Development Projects Staff moved the entire complement of Detachment C's pilots and planes from Japan to a base more easily accessible to Indonesia: Cubi Point Naval Air Station in the Philippines. Cubi Point was far from any facility that could develop and interpret the U-2 photographs, so two Photo-Intelligence Division employees went to Clark Airfield, just 30 minutes by air from Cubi Point, to establish a forward processing center. They arrived on 28 March and had the photo lab ready to go on the following day.[23]

The first U-2 mission over Indonesia took place on 28 March 1958. By 12 June, when the operation was phased out, Detachment C U-2s had flown 30 missions over the major islands of Indonesia. Sanitized photos from these missions were used to brief members of the DDP's Covert Action Staff (CAS), who were in charge of a small force of World War II–vintage aircraft such as P-51s and B-26s used to support the rebel troops. The CIA's proprietary, Civil Air Transport, supplied the aircraft, which were based on the Indonesian island of Morotai and flown by mercenary pilots. Desperately short of pilots, the CAS asked if some of the U-2 pilots with experience in World War II aircraft could be detailed to the Morotai effort. Although such a request represented an improper use of the highly trained U-2 pilots and posed a potential threat to the entire U-2 program if one of them were captured, Richard Bissell agreed to send pilots James Cherbonneaux and Carmine Vito to help. Both were experienced with World War II aircraft, although Vito had never flown the rebels' fighter aircraft, the P-51 Mustang. After arriving on Morotai, Cherbonneaux explained to Vito how to fly the fast and powerful Mustang while the two were sitting at a makeshift bar on the edge of the airfield.

---

[23] *OSA History,* chap. 15, pp. 25-26 (TS Codeword).

Several days later, when Cherbonneaux was off the island on another mission, a flight of Indonesian twin-engine bombers of Czechoslovak manufacture was spotted making its way toward the island. Exclaiming, "I'm not going to sit around and wait to be bombed," Vito had a Filipino mechanic start up a P-51 sitting on the tarmac. In his first and only flight in a P-51, Vito managed to get the plane off the ground. Once he was airborne and turned in the direction of the lumbering bombers, they all took flight in as many directions as there were aircraft. After firing a few .50-caliber rounds in the direction of the closest bomber, Vito circled the field and landed the aircraft safely.[24]

Agency efforts in support of the rebel government proved fruitless. By early May, Central Government forces had taken most of the remaining rebel strongholds, and the Sumatran rebellion was deteriorating into small-scale guerrilla activity. Then on 18 May, an American mercenary pilot, Allen Lawrence Pope, was shot down on a bombing mission over Ambon Island. Pope's capture ended Allen Dulles's enthusiasm for the effort, and President Eisenhower also wanted no more part of it. The US Government rapidly withdrew its support, and the remaining remnants of the rebellion collapsed. Four years later, the Indonesians freed Pope after Attorney General Robert Kennedy personally appealed to President Sukarno.

When the revolt ended, the U-2s returned to Atsugi. On the way back, one of the planes, which was equipped with a System-V electronic intelligence unit, flew along the coast of China to gather data on Communist Chinese radars.[25]

---

[24] Information supplied by Carmine Vito and James Cherbonneaux to Donald E. Welzenbach, May 1986.
[25] Mission folder 1773, (10 June 1958), OSA records, job 67-B-328, box 7 (TS Codeword); *OSA History,* chap. 15, pp. 25-26 (TS Codeword).

China Offshore Islands Dispute of 1958

During the summer of 1958, tension between the People's Republic of China and Nationalist China (Taiwan) increased to such an extent that on 18 June Detachment C mounted a U-2 mission to film the Chinese mainland coast and adjacent island areas. On 11 August, People's Liberation Army (PLA) artillery began bombarding the offshore islands of Quemoy and Little Quemoy, where the Nationalists had stationed large numbers of troops to ward off any invasion. On 23 August the Communists increased the shelling. After five days of intense bombardment, which made resupply of the islands from Taiwan impossible, the PLA commander ordered the Nationalist garrisons to surrender, intimating that an invasion was imminent. The Nationalists refused to surrender and received support from the United States in the form of warships from the 7th Fleet, which began escorting Nationalist ships carrying supplies to the beleaguered garrisons.

During this period, Detachment C U-2s flew four missions over the mainland, searching for troop movements that would indicate that the PRC was planning to invade the islands. Photos from these missions showed no evidence of a PRC buildup, but the atmosphere in the region remained tense. Detachment C U-2s flew two more missions (9 September and 22 October) to monitor PRC troop movements and again found no indications of preparations for an invasion. The Offshore Islands Crisis receded in late October 1958 after the PRC learned that it would not receive support from the Soviet Union if the crisis escalated into a confrontation with the United States.[26]

While the Offshore Islands Crisis was still in progress, Detachment C began conducting flights in support of its weather reconnaissance cover story. On 14, 15, and 16 July 1958, U-2s flew high above Typhoon Winnie, which was causing great dam-

---

[26] *OSA History,* chap. 15, p. 27 (TS Codeword).

age on Taiwan. These missions provided the first photography ever obtained of such a massive storm system. Photographs of the storm were the subject of articles in the magazine *Weatherwise* and the 21 July edition of *Aviation Week*. In September, Detachment C aircraft photographed two more typhoons.

U-2 Support for DPP Operations in Tibet

The consolidation of all Agency air activities under the DDP in 1959 led to increased involvement of the U-2 program with clandestine efforts against Communist governments. One important area of DDP activity during this period was Tibet. In March 1959, the PLA suppressed an uprising against the Chinese occupation of Tibet, and several thousand Tibetans fled the country along with their spiritual leader, the Dalai Lama. Afterward, Agency operatives from the DDP's Far East Division began training some of these Tibetan refugees for paramilitary operations inside Tibet. Once the Tibetans completed their training, FE Division planned to parachute them back into Tibet. Such missions, however, required detailed maps and aerial photographs of the areas of operation. Richard Bissell, therefore, obtained permission from the President to use Detachment C U-2s to provide the necessary photography.

Operation MILL TOWN, as the reconnaissance missions over Tibet were known, consisted of two missions staged from Cubi Point Naval Air Station on 12 and 14 May 1959. The photography revealed that Communist China had built new roads with supply and defense points. Agency photointerpreters also discovered two large new airfields at elevations above 13,000 feet. Later in the year, the Far East Division needed photographs and maps of another area of Tibet. To conceal the target of this new operation, which was codenamed SOUTH GATE, the Development Projects Division planned and flew a total of six missions covering much of Southeast Asia—Vietnam, Laos, Cambodia [redacted] — as well as the desired area in Tibet. Only four of the missions involved the area of operational interest. Five of the flights took place between 29 August and 9 September, and one additional flight (Operation QUICK KICK) followed on 4 November. All of these missions were "Fast Move" operations in which necessary supplies and personnel flew to a remote staging area in a C-130, where they rendezvoused with a U-2 that had been ferried in. The staging base in this case was Ta Khli, Thailand. These flights did not go unnoticed; on 13 September 1959, Hong Kong's *China Post* published a story headlined "U-2 of USAF Said Reconnoitering Red China at Unreachable Altitude."[27]

U-2Cs for Detachment C

Late in 1958, Lockheed began refitting the Agency's 13 remaining U-2s with the more powerful Pratt & Whitney J75/P-13 jet engine. The first of these U-2Cs arrived at Detachment C in the summer of 1959. During a test flight of this aircraft (article 360) on 24 September 1959, the pilot decided to set a new altitude record. Although the plane was equipped with a camera, it carried no film and did not have a full load of fuel, which made it considerably lighter than an operational U-2C. As a result, the plane reached 76,400 feet—the highest altitude achieved by any of the original U-2 aircraft. In the process, however, the aircraft consumed more fuel than was called for in the test flight plan, causing the engine to flame out during the return to base. The pilot then made an emergency wheels-up landing at a glider-club strip near Fujisawa, south of Atsugi.

The crash did not cause any injuries or serious damage to the aircraft, but it did bring unwanted publicity to the U-2 program. Much of the publicity resulted from the actions of Detachment

---

[27] Ibid., chap. 18, pp. 6-7, 12; chap. 15, p. 29 (TS Codeword).

C's security unit, whose conspicuous Hawaian shirts and large pistols drew the attention of Japanese reporters. One reporter even flew over the area in a helicopter, taking pictures of the U-2. These photographs appeared in many Japanese newspapers and magazines.[28]

U-2 Crash in Thailand

Flights by Detachment C U-2s over Tibet and western China continued during the first half of 1960 under Operation TOPPER. The first mission on 30 March was very successful. The second mission on 5 April took good photographs but encountered mechanical problems. At the start of the mission, the landing-gear doors failed to close completely, resulting in increased drag and higher fuel consumption. With no fuel gauge to warn the pilot of the critical fuel situation, the aircraft ran out of fuel far short of Ta Khli, forcing the pilot to make a crash landing in a rice paddy. The area was inaccessible to large vehicles, and the plane, article 349, had to be cut into pieces in order to remove it. With the help of local villagers, the retrieval team dissassembled the aircraft for transport to the base, where the pieces were loaded onto a C-124 under cover of darkness. The crash and subsequent recovery of the U-2 did not attract the attention of the press; there was only one report in a local Thai newspaper, which simply referred to the crash of a jet plane. In appreciation for the assistance provided by the villagers, [redacted] gave the headman funds to build a new school.[29]

End of Detachment C Operations

The loss of two aircraft in slightly more than six months left Detachment C with just two aircraft. Fortunately, the level of mis-

---

[28] Ibid., chap. 15, p. 30 (TS Codeword).
[29] Ibid., chap. 15, pp. 32-33 (TS Codeword).

sion activity remained low because Detachment C was no longer conducting overflights of the Soviet Union.

One important remaining mission was high-altitude air sampling (HASP), in which specially equipped U-2s gathered upper-altitude air samples to look for evidence of Soviet nuclear testing. The direction of the prevailing winds made Detachment C ideally situated for this activity, which began in the fall of 1958 and continued in 1959. In late April 1960, Detachment C was preparing to stage to the Philippines to conduct additional air-sampling missions, when the loss of Powers' U-2 temporarily halted all U-2 activities.

The publicity generated by the U-2 incident stirred considerable controversy in Japan, and there were soon demonstrations against the continuing presence of U-2s in Japan. On 6 June 1960, project headquarters decided on a phased-out withdrawal of Detachment C between 15 July and 1 September, but this timetable had to be accelerated when the Japanese Government formally requested the removal of the U-2s on 8 July.[30]

Detachment G Missions over Laos and North Vietnam
In the aftermath of the Powers loss, both of the overseas U-2 detachments returned to the United States and their aircraft and personnel were incorporated into Detachment G at Edwards Air Force Base in California. This detachment was now responsible for providing coverage in Asia, and its first mission came in Laos. After the neutralist Laotian Government of Souvanna Phouma collapsed in early December 1960, reports began circulating that leftist antigovernment forces were using Soviet arms. Then on 30 December, a new Laotian Government appealed for UN aid against what it said was an invasion from North Vietnam and possibly Communist China. Alarmed over the possibility of the civil

---

[30] Ibid., chap. 15, pp. 33-36 (TS Codeword).

war expanding because of the introduction of foreign troops, the Eisenhower administration ordered Detachment G to gather more information on the events in Southeast Asia.

Five Detachment G pilots and planes were ferried to Cubi Point Naval Air Station in the Philippines to conduct an operation known as POLECAT. During the period 3 to 18 January 1961, these U-2s made seven flights over Laos and North Vietnam. To search for the reported foreign troops, these missions concentrated on the lines of communications leading into Laos from North Vietnam and China. In addition, the U-2s scanned North Vietnamese airfields for Soviet aircraft to determine the magnitude of the airdrop operation allegedly supporting the Pathet Lao troops. NPIC sent photointerpreters to Clark Air Force Base in the Philippines to obtain an immediate readout of the results of each mission. The photography did not substantiate the Laotian claims, and on 26 January the Laotian Government retracted its charges of a foreign invasion. Detachment G's U-2s returned to California in early February 1961.[31]

During the final stages of Operation POLECAT, there was a major threat to the security of the mission. The film from the flights made on 16 and 18 January had been sent to the United States for duplicate processing. Afterward the film was put aboard an Agency C-47 on 14 March to ferry it to Washington. During the flight one of the aircraft's engines failed, forcing the crew to jettison 43 boxes of highly classified film over mountainous terrain around Williamsport, Pennsylvania, to keep the craft airborne. After making an emergency landing at the Scranton-Wilkes-Barre Airport, the pilot reported the incident to Headquarters. The Office of Security immediately contacted the Pennsylvania State Police, who sealed off the wooded area. Agency security officers soon

---

[31] Ibid., chap 16, p. 17 (TS Codeword).

arrived to search for the boxes. They recovered all 43 containers; not one had broken.[32]

Detachment G's only other activity during the summer of 1961 was a solitary overflight of North Vietnam, known as Operation EBONY. In preparation for this mission, a U-2 deployed to Cubi Point on 13 August 1961. Two days later it successfully conducted the overflight and subsequently returned to the United States.[33]

New Detachment on Taiwan

Long before the Nationalist Chinese became involved in the U-2 program, they were flying covert reconnaissance missions for the CIA. In 1952 the CIA began recruiting Nationalist Chinese crews to replace US personnel from the proprietary firm Civil Air Transport, who had been flying Agency aircraft to drop leaflets, agents, and supplies over the Chinese mainland. This project (BGMARQUE) also provided photographic coverage of the rail line from Shanghai to the border with French Indochina. CIA-sponsored aerial reconnaissance over the mainland increased substantially in 1955 with the establishment of Project STPOLLY, which used Agency aircraft with Nationalist Chinese crews to gather Signals Intelligence (SIGINT) and conduct psychological warfare against the People's Republic of China. At first the SIGINT equipment was installed in World War II-vintage aircraft such as PB-4Ys and B-17s, but in 1958 the project received a new aircraft procured covertly by the Agency from Lockheed, the P2V7, with an extremely sophisticated airborne SIGINT system. STPOLLY added the more advanced Lockheed P3A in 1963. Between 1955 and 1967, when the CIA terminated the project, STPOLLY conducted 399 overflights of the People's Republic of China, losing a total of eight aircraft and crews.

---

[32] Ibid., chap. 7, p. 24 (TS Codeword).
[33] Ibid., chap. 16, p. 18 (TS Codeword).

In addition to CIA-sponsored aerial reconnaissance projects, the Nationalist Chinese Air Force had its own reconnaissance capability with US-supplied RB-57 aircraft. In 1958 the US Air Force proposed supplying the Nationalist Chinese Government with the most advanced reconnaissance aircraft available, the U-2. The CIA opposed a reconnaissance aircraft Nationalist Chinese U-2 program because such flights would destroy the existing unclassified cover for the U-2. In discussions with the Air Force, DDCI Cabell only consented to having Nationalist pilots trained to fly U-2s so that they would be ready in case they were needed in the future; he opposed any Nationalist overflights. The training of the Nationalist Chinese pilots began in March 1959. By the end of the year, there was a group of trained pilots ready for operations, and DCI Dulles met with the Joint Chiefs of Staff to discuss the program's future. Dulles reaffirmed the Agency's opposition to Nationalist Chinese U-2 missions, and the Air Force, which had wanted the Nationalists to be allowed to begin operations, reluctantly agreed to wait until conditions were favorable.[34] The situation changed radically in May 1960 after the loss of Powers' U-2 destroyed the existing cover story for U-2 operations. Now there was no longer any reason not to use the Nationalist pilots. In addition, the Agency soon found itself in need of a base of operations in the Far East after Detachment C had to leave Japan.

During discussions with Nationalist officials on 6 May 1960, the [redacted] raised the possibility of assigning U-2s to the Chinese Air Force. Two weeks later, [redacted] approached [redacted] informally to propose that the U-2 aircraft based in Japan be moved to Taiwan. This was followed three days later by an official offer [redacted]. President Eisenhower learned of

---

[34] Andrew J. Russo, *Low-Level Technical Reconnaissance Over Mainland China (1955-1966)* (draft), Clandestine Services Historical Program, CSHP-2.348 (CIA: History Staff, 1972) (S).

Nationalist China's proposal on 18 June. Several weeks later, Richard Bissell suggested that two U-2s be turned over to the Nationalists for use in overflying the mainland. The project would be conducted along the lines of Project STPOLLY.[35]

On 26 August 1960, President Eisenhower and the State Department approved Bissell's proposal to turn U-2s over to the Nationalist Chinese rather than move an American detachment to Taiwan. Using Nationalist pilots for overflights had the advantage of providing complete deniability for the United States, even if an aircraft was lost over hostile territory. The U-2s would belong to Nationalist China and would have Nationalist pilots, and there was no overt US involvement with the overflights. In reality, however, the United States would maintain strict control over the missions to be flown.[36]

On 7 December 1960, two U-2s were officially licensed for export to Nationalist China as part of a new effort codenamed TACKLE. These planes came from the Agency's U-2 inventory and arrived in Taiwan on 14 December. Within the Agency the Nationalist pilots and aircraft were known as Detachment H, and they were based at the Nationalist Chinese Air Force Base at T'ao-yuan. One of the U-2s was painted with the Nationalist Chinese insignia, and the other was left unmarked so that it could also be used by Agency pilots as needed. The planes were maintained by Lockheed mechanics under contract to the CIA. The Agency attempted to maintain at least two U-2s in Detachment H, so lost or damaged aircraft were replaced from the Agency's inventory.

During 1961, Detachment H conducted training missions with both U-2s, and one Nationalist pilot was killed in a crash on 19 March. Although the detachment was ready to begin operations, the new Kennedy administration was not yet ready to authorize

---

[35] OSA History, chap. 17, pp. 1-7 (TS Codeword).
[36] Ibid., chap. 17, pp. 12-13, 44 (TS Codeword).

overflights of the PRC. In a 3 March 1961 meeting between State Department and CIA officials to discuss the possibility of such overflights, Under Secretary of State Chester Bowles noted that "the President was feeling his way on the international scene, and time was needed to evaluate the new Sino-Soviet posture with relation to the United States."[37] In July 1961 the USIB considered the possibility of conducting overflights of the PRC, but the State Department remained opposed.

By the fall of 1961, interest in overflights of the PRC was growing because of indications that the Chinese were making progress in nuclear energy and missile development. As a result, on 4 October 1961 PFIAB recommended the initiation of a limited number of U-2 photographic missions over the Chinese mainland. The President approved the board's recommendation.

Because the US–Nationalist Chinese overflight program (Project TACKLE) was a joint effort, both countries participated in the approval process and also shared in the results of the missions. The USIB COMOR established the requirements for Detachment H's overflights, which had to be approved by the NSC's Special Group (5412 Committee) and the President. The Nationalist Chinese Government also approved all missions flown by its pilots. Under the terms of an agreement reached with the Nationalist Chinese Government, film from the overflights of the mainland would be processed in the United States, with a duplicate positive copy returned to Nationalist China within 10 days. NPIC was responsible for the initial reporting on these missions.[38]

---

[37] James A. Cunningham, Jr., Assistant Chief, DPD-DD/P, Memorandum for the Record, "TACKLE STPOLLY Briefing for State Department Officials," 6 March 1961, IC Staff, COMIREX records, job 33-B-119A, box 1, "IDEAL-IST/TACKLE, 1961" (S).

[38] *OSA History,* chap. 17, pp. 18-19, annex 107 (TS Codeword).

Project TACKLE overflights began early in 1962. Following a 5 January Special Group decision to approve three missions, a Detachment H U-2 with a Nationalist Chinese pilot flew its first mission over the PRC's missile-testing range at Shuangchengzi on 12 January 1962. Unfortunately, because of faulty navigation or faulty maps, the aircraft was poorly positioned and obtained only oblique, rather than vertical, photography of the range. En route to and from Shuangchengzi, the U-2 overflew Fukien and Chekiang Provinces looking for suspected deployed missiles, but none could be found in the mission photography.[39]

The second Project TACKLE mission took place on 23 February 1962, when a U-2 overflew the PRC's nuclear weapons establishment at Lan-chou. Photography from this mission revealed that the installation was at least two years away from operational capacity. Two more missions on 13 and 26 March flew over K'un-ming and central China covering numerous airfields that had been discovered in satellite photography. The U-2 photographs showed more detail than the satellite pictures, thereby, providing additional intelligence data, particularly for air order of battle. In addition to the primary targets already described, the initial series of Project TACKLE missions obtained photography of the submarine construction facilities at Shanghai and Wu-ch'ang, which showed a low level of activity. Other photographs revealed tremendous expansion of the industrial complexes at Nanking and Ch'ang-sha and the presence of a previously unknown industrial area at Chiang-yu.[40]

---

[39] Ibid., chap. 17, p. 45 (TS Codeword); Mission folder GRC100 (12 January 1962), OSA records, job 67-B-972, box 19 (TS Codeword). Note: The numbers for missions flown by Nationalist Chinese pilots began with GRC (Government of the Republic of China).

[40] *OSA History,* chap. 17, p. 45 (TS Codeword); Mission folders GRC102 (23 February 1962), GRC104 (13 March 1962), and GRC106 (26 March 1962), OSA records, job 67-B-972, box 19 (TS Codeword).

Initial Overflights of China, January - March 1962

Mission GRC 100 13 January 1962
Mission GRC 102 23 February 1962
Mission GRC 104 13 March 1962
Mission GRC 106 26 March 1962

Secret NOFORN

Encouraged by the success of the first TACKLE missions, COMOR recommended in May 1962 that Detachment H cover as many as possible of the highest priority industrial and airfield targets in northeast China and the missile test ranges in north China. COMOR noted that, with the exception of the areas around Peiping and the Shuangchengzi missile test range, the chances of a U-2 being downed were low. The USIB concurred with COMOR's recommendations, and Detachment H therefore conducted three more overflights of the PRC during the month of June.[41]

Before the month was over, however, another confrontation between Nationalist China and the PRC over the Formosa Strait erupted. The Nationalist Government reported a massive buildup of PRC troops and aircraft in Fukien Province opposite the Nationalist-held Quemoy and Ma-tsu Islands. Secretary of Defense Robert McNamara immediately ordered U-2 coverage of the Strait area to determine the extent of the PRC buildup. In response, Detachment H flew six missions over the Strait between 25 June and 28 July 1962. To speed up the readout of this photography, the films were processed at the Asian Photographic Interpretation Center (ASPIC) at Yokota, Japan, a joint military-CIA endeavor. The U-2 coverage ended in late July when it became apparent that the PRC did not intend to mount an invasion of the offshore islands.[42]

The pace of Detachment H missions slowed considerably in August 1962; the sole Project TACKLE overflight covered Peiping and Manchuria. The following month the detachment mounted two missions, one over south China on the eighth and the second over Kiangsu Province on the ninth. Unfortunately, mechanical difficulties led to the loss of the latter aircraft near Lu-shan. A flameout forced the U-2 down to an altitude where PRC interceptors were able to hit the U-2 with an air-to-air rocket. The Nationalist Chi-

---

[41] Lay, "USIB History," vol. 2, pp. 385-386 (TS Codeword).
[42] *OSA History,* chap. 17, p. 46 (TS Codeword).

nese pilot parachuted and was captured. At this point, President Kennedy ordered a standdown of overflights of the PRC.[43]

Following the capture of the Nationalist Chinese U-2 pilot, the People's Republic of China accused the United States of masterminding the overflights, but the State Department denied any involvement. Nationalist China then revealed that the United States had granted it a license to purchase two U-2 aircraft. In a 13 September 1962 response to the Chinese protest, President Kennedy denied any responsibility for the sale of the U-2s to Taiwan, noting that the sale had occurred under the previous administration. He stated that there were no current plans to sell any more U-2s to Nationalist China. Eight months later, however, the President approved an export license for the delivery of another U-2 to Taiwan. Such licenses were needed only for cover purposes. The Agency continued to maintain two U-2s on Taiwan, bringing new ones in to replace aircraft lost in training or on missions.

Detachment H resumed overflights of mainland China in December 1962, but its missions now concentrated on the southern portion where there were fewer radars and SAM sites. During December 1962 and January 1963, the detachment conducted two successful overflights of Sichuan, but a mission over south China had to be aborted prematurely. The results of Detachment H's continuing coverage of the People's Republic of China remained of considerable interest to the United States. On 17 December 1962, the Special Group approved plans for fiscal year 1963/64 that included requirements for photo coverage of mainland China and for maintaining at least two operational U-2 aircraft in Detachment H.[44]

---

[43] Ibid., pp. 46-47 (TS Codeword); Mission folders GRC125 (11 August 1962), GRC126 (8 September 1962), and GRC127 (9 September 1962), OSA records, job 67-B-972, boxes 20 and 21 (TS Codeword).

[44] *OSA History*, chap. 17, pp. 48-49 (TS Codeword); Mission folders GRC134 (25 December 1962), GRC136 (28 December 1962), and GRC138 (20 January 1963), OSA records, job 67-B-972, box 21, and job 66-B-664, box 1 (TS Code word).

Use of Detachment H Aircraft by US Pilots

Detachment H's importance did not lie solely in the missions carried out by its Nationalist Chinese pilots against targets in mainland China; the detachment also provided aircraft for use by American pilots flying missions in other parts of Asia. Indochina was an area of particular interest as American involvement there began growing during the early 1960s. Beginning in February 1962, Detachment G pilots went to T'ao-yuan to use the unmarked Project TACKLE U-2 for overflights of North Vietnam. During the first half of 1962, Detachment G pilots made seven overflights of North Vietnam from the Tao Yuan base. Thereafter, Detachment G pilots could use their own aircraft because the unit began staging teams and aircraft from Edwards AFB to Ta Khli AFB in Thailand.

Between 1962 and 1964, Agency U-2s staged a total of 36 photographic missions over North and South Vietnam. By April 1964, however, photographic requirements were changing from strategic reconnaissance to tactical support as the Viet Cong became more active, taking advantage of the weakness of the South Vietnamese central government following the coup that overthrew President Ngo Dinh Diem in 1963 and subsequent coups by disgruntled army officers. During this period the South Vietnamese "strategic hamlet" concept began breaking down, and the Viet Cong forces stepped up the pace of their attacks. As a result of the increasing level of combat in Indochina, the USIB gave responsibility for aerial reconnaissance of the areas where fighting was taking place to the SAC. Henceforth, SAC U-2s would be used over South Vietnam, parts of Cambodia within 30 miles of South Vietnam, all of Laos south of Paksane, and all of North Vietnam within 30 miles of South Vietnam or the coast. The remaining portions of Indochina remained the responsibility of the Agency's U-2s. Then in August 1964, following the Gulf of Tonkin Resolution, the Air Force assumed responsibility for all of Indochina.[45]

---

[45] *OSA History,* chap. 16, pp. 18-19 (TS Codeword).

U-2s in India

In October 1962, the People's Republic of China launched a series of massive surprise attacks against India's frontier forces in the western provinces of Jammu and Kashmir and in the North-East Frontier Agency (NEFA). The Chinese overran all Indian fortifications north of the Brahmaputra Valley before halting their operations.

The Indian Government appealed to the United States for military aid. In the negotiations that followed, it became apparent that Indian claims concerning the extent of the Chinese incursions could not be reliably evaluated. US Ambassador John Kenneth Galbraith, therefore, suggested to the Indian Government that US aerial reconnaissance of the disputed areas would provide both governments with a more accurate picture of the Communist Chinese incursions. On 11 November 1962, Prime Minister Jawaharlal Nehru consented to the proposed operation and gave the United States permission to refuel the reconnaissance aircraft (U-2s) in Indian airspace.[46]

In late November, Detachment G deployed to Ta Khli, Thailand, to carry out the overflights of the Sino-Indian border area. Since the U-2s were not authorized to overfly Burma, they had to reach the target area via the Bay of Bengal and eastern India and, therefore, required midair refueling.

Because of severe winter weather conditions, the first flight did not take place until 5 December. Poor weather and air turbulence hampered the mission, and only 40 percent of the target area could be photographed. A second mission on 10 December was more successful, but the U-2 experienced rough engine performance because of icing of the fuel lines.[47]

---

[46] Ibid., chap. 16, pp. 26-27 (TS Codeword).

[47] Ibid., p. 28 (TS Codeword); Mission folders 3201 (5 December 1962) and 3203 (10 December 1962), OSA records, job 67-B-972, box 26 (TS Codeword).

Detachment G U-2s made four more overflights of the Sino-Indian border areas in January 1963, which led to a PRC protest to India. Photography from these missions was used in January and again in March 1963 to brief Prime Minister Nehru, who then informed the Indian Parliament about Communist Chinese troop movements along the border. Although Nehru did not reveal the source of his intelligence, a UPI wire story surmised that the information had been obtained by U-2s.

The United States had provided photographic coverage of the border area to India for two reasons. First of all, US policymakers wanted a clear picture of the area under dispute. In addition, the intelligence community wanted to establish a precedent for overflights from India, which could lead to obtaining a permanent staging base in India for electronic reconnaissance missions against the Soviet ABM site at Saryshagan and photographic missions against those portions of western China that were out of range of Detachment H. In April 1963, Ambassador Galbraith and the Chief of Station at New Delhi made the first official request to India for a base. The following month, President Kennedy agreed to DCI McCone's suggestion to raise the question of a U-2 base in India when he met with India's President Savepalli Radhakrishnan on 3 June. This meeting resulted in an Indian offer of an abandoned World War II base at Charbatia, south of Calcutta.[48]

The Charbatia base was in poor condition and needed considerable renovation before it could be used for U-2 operations. Work on the base by the Indians took much longer than expected, so Detachment G continued to use Ta Khli when it staged four sorties over Tibet from 29 September to 10 November 1963. In addition to the coverage of the Sino-Indian border during this series of flights, the U-2s also photographed all of Thailand to produce a photomap of the border regions as a quid pro quo for

---

[48] *OSA History,* chap. 16, p. 30 (TS Codeword).

the Thai Government. During one of these photomapping missions, a U-2 pilot conducted the longest mission ever recorded in this aircraft—11 hours and 45 minutes. At the end of this flight on 10 November 1963, the pilot was in such poor physical condition that project managers prohibited the scheduling of future missions longer than 10 hours.[49]

Charbatia was still not ready in early 1964, so on 31 March 1964 Detachment G staged another mission from Ta Khli. The first mission out of Charbatia did not take place until 24 May 1964. Three days later Prime Minister Nehru died, and further operations were postponed. The pilots and aircraft left Charbatia, but other equipment remained in place to save staging costs. In December 1964, when Sino-Indian tensions increased along the border, Detachment G returned to Charbatia and conducted three highly successful missions, satisfying all of COMOR's requirements for the Sino-Indian border region. By this time, however, Ta Khli had become the main base for Detachment G's Asian operations, and Charbatia served merely as a forward staging base. Charbatia was closed out in July 1967.[50]

Increasing Responsibilities, Inadequate Resources in Asia

The main focus of Agency U-2 activity in Asia remained the U-2s of Detachment H on Taiwan. In March and April 1963, the USIB met to consider COMOR proposals for aerial reconnaissance of Laos, North Vietnam, North Korea, and the People's Republic of China. All of COMOR's intelligence requirements could best be met by the U-2 because heavy cloud cover made it difficult to obtain satellite photography of the region. At the 28 May 1963 meeting of the Special Group, DCI McCone requested author-

---

[49] Mission folder 3238 (10 November 1963), OSA records, job 67-B-972, box 29 (TS Codeword).

[50] *OSA History,* chap. 16, pp. 30-34 (TS Codeword).

ization for a series of overflights to meet these requirements and stressed the need for additional intelligence on the atomic energy facilities of the PRC. The Special Group then established a "bank" of four authorizations for overflights of the PRC, subject to monthly review by the Group.[51]

As a result of the increasing intelligence community interest in the Far East, both Agency U-2 detachments became very active in the region. Detachment G conducted a number of missions over the border areas of China, North Vietnam, and Laos during April and May of 1963. At the same time, Detachment H became more adventurous, sending U-2s deeper and deeper into the PRC. These missions included renewed overflights of the missile test range near Baotou and the Lan-chou nuclear facilities, as well as targets in northern China, Manchuria, and west-central China (as far as Koko Nor).

The increased level of U-2 activity in the Far East during the spring of 1963 exposed a serious weakness in Projects IDE-ALIST and TACKLE, a shortage of aircraft. The Agency only had seven flyable U-2s when the TACKLE overflights of the PRC began in January 1962, and one of these aircraft had already been lost during an overflight in September 1962. To deal with this shortage, DCI McCone asked Defense Secretary McNamara and the Joint Chiefs of Staff on 10 June 1963 to transfer two U-2s from the Air Force to the CIA. The Defense Department quickly approved this request. Before the two Air Force aircraft were placed in service, however, the Agency had them upgraded with J75/P-13A engines and various electronic devices, a process that took more than four months.[52]

As overflights over the PRC increased, so did concern about the growing number of Chinese surface-to-air missile sites. The

---

[51] Lay, "USIB History," vol. 3, pp. 391-392 (TS Codeword).

[52] *OSA History,* chap. 16, p. 10 (TS Codeword).

Office of Special Activities, therefore, got permission from the Defense Department to equip Project TACKLE aircraft with System-XII SAM-warning units. These devices alerted the pilot that his aircraft was being tracked by the FAN SONG acquisition radar, part of the SA-2's electronic targeting system. The System-XII units also recorded each radar-tracking sequence. Analysis of these recordings revealed changes in the FAN SONG radar's characteristics, information that proved useful in designing electronic-countermeasure (ECM) devices for US aircraft operating over Vietnam during the late 1960s.[53]

Despite the addition of System-XII in the spring of 1963, the Nationalist Chinese-piloted U-2s of Project TACKLE had far fewer ECM devices than other Agency U-2s. Project IDEALIST aircraft possessed a complete suite of ECM gear in addition to the previously mentioned System-XII unit. Among this ECM equipment was a device that told the pilot that an SA-2 missile had been launched (nicknamed the "Oscar-Sierra" unit, which was the acronym for the expletive U-2 pilots used when they learned that an SA-2 missile was on the way: "Oh, shit!") and a System-XIII unit that produced false-angle returns to the homing radar aboard the approaching missile in an effort to steer it away from the aircraft. The Defense Department opposed installing such devices aboard Detachment H's U-2s, for fear they could fall into Communist hands.

The danger posed by the growing number of SA-2 sites in the PRC was clearly demonstrated on 1 November 1963, when a second Project TACKLE U-2 was lost near the Kiangsi-Chekiang border on its way back from photographing the PRC's Shuangchengzi missile test range. As was the case after the first operational loss over China in September 1961, President Kennedy ordered a standdown of overflights of mainland China. This standdown lasted almost five months.

---

[53] Ibid., chap. 17, p. 50 (TS Codeword).

As a result of this second loss over the PRC, the Office of Special Activities began installing a new 30-channel telemetry system aboard Detachment H U-2s to monitor various aircraft functions. Known as BIRDWATCHER, this unit periodically broadcast a burst of data to the airbase that launched the U-2. This data burst contained a status report on all the major systems aboard the plane, such as airspeed, altitude, exhaust temperature, fuel supply, film supply, and oxygen supply. BIRDWATCHER provided project managers with a benchmark of aircraft performance that could be used to determine if a lost plane had been shot down at altitude or had suffered mechanical failure.[54]

BIRDWATCHER'S first operational use came on 16 March 1964, when overflights resumed with a mission over southern China. The PRC was now a high-priority target for the U-2 because more data were needed to prepare National Intelligence Estimates due in the autumn. Of particular concern was the PRC's nuclear program. Despite the high priority of its missions, Detachment H's resources remained scarce. It was short of both pilots and planes and never had more than three U-2s or six qualified Nationalist Chinese pilots at any one time. By the spring of 1964, crashes during training and the two losses over the mainland had reduced Detachment H to only two qualified pilots, one of whom suffered from ulcers and a nervous disorder. Indeed, this pilot had every reason to be nervous; he flew three of the next four Detachment H overflights and became the third Nationalist Chinese pilot to be shot down over the mainland.

This loss came on 7 July 1964. The Nationalist Chinese pilot's last transmission was that his System-XII unit had alerted him that he was being tracked by the FAN SONG radar. BIRD-WATCHER data revealed that the aircraft was at penetration altitude and all systems were normal when the pilot made this

---

[54] Ibid., p. 51, 53 (TS Codeword).

report. Project managers presumed that the U-2 was downed by a direct hit or near miss by an SA-2 missile.[55]

President Johnson ordered a standdown of overflights of the PRC. This standdown was welcomed by the Nationalist Chinese Government, which told the Taiwan Chief of Station that it wanted "to let some time go by" before more overflights were scheduled. The Nationalists pointed out that the only remaining qualified U-2 pilot had "disqualified" himself because of nervous tension. No new pilots could be qualified for U-2 flights before mid-August.

The Nationalists then demanded faster and higher flying aircraft as well as better antimissile equipment for the planes. This request led some CIA personnel to suspect that Nationalist China had learned about Project OXCART, the successor to the U-2 that was still undergoing testing. Despite the Nationalists' request for better ECM equipment, the Defense Department remained reluctant to authorize the use of the System-XIII false-angle radar jammer on Project TACKLE U-2s. The Defense Department feared that the loss of this device with its highly advanced traveling-wave tube (TWT) would enable Communist Bloc technicians to devise countermeasures and also learn how to produce the highly efficient TWT themselves. As an incentive for the Nationalist Chinese to agree to more overflights, the CIA agreed to permit them to process the U-2 film on Taiwan and to use their own photointerpreters to exploit the film along with US photointerpreters.

To counter the shortage of pilots in Detachment H, DCI McCone suggested to the Special Group on 6 August 1964 that civilian CIA pilots be used to fly missions over mainland China. The

---

[55] *OSA History,* chap. 17, pp. 53-55 (TS Codeword); Mission folder C174C (7 July 1964), OSA records, job 66-B-664, box 7 (TS Codeword). Note: beginning in 1964 Nationalist Chinese mission numbers began with "C" instead of "GRC."

group agreed that the matter should be taken up with President Johnson. On the following day, however, Presidential National Security Assistant McGeorge Bundy informed McCone that, because Secretary of State Rusk and Secretary of Defense McNamara opposed the idea, he would not take it up with the President.[56]

Advanced ECM Equipment for Detachment H

Demand for overhead photography of the PRC continued to grow, spurred in part by the results of earlier U-2 missions that revealed the presence of Soviet-made MiG-21s in the PRC. In addition, there were indications that Communist China might be producing its own SAMs. Furthermore, satellite photography revealed that preparations for the first Chinese nuclear test were almost complete at the Lop Nor test site.

The need for photographs of the Lop Nor site was considered so urgent that the Defense Department finally relented and permitted the System-XIII false-angle device jammer to be installed in Project TACKLE aircraft, with the proviso that it not be turned on until after the pilot had been alerted by System-XII that he was being tracked by FAN SONG radars. Photographing Lop Nor, however, was not a simple task. Located more than 2,000 miles west-northwest of Taiwan, Lop Nor lay beyond the round trip range of T'ao-yuan-based U-2s and in-flight refueling was not possible. Lop Nor was closer to Ta Khli, Thailand, only 1,650 miles northwest of that base, and much closer to Charbatia, India, which lay only 1,200 miles south of the testing site.

After refusing DCI McCone's suggestion to stage a Lop Nor overflight from Charbatia using a CIA civilian pilot, President Johnson approved a proposal to send a Project TACKLE unit to Ta Khli for the mission to Lop Nor. A Detachment H U-2 with a Nationalist Chinese pilot deployed to Ta Khli in mid-October

---

[56] *OSA History,* chap. 17, pp. 58-59 (TS Codeword).

to prepare for the overflight. Before mission preparations could be completed, however, the Chinese detonated their first nuclear weapon on 16 October 1964, and the mission was canceled.[57]

The first overflight of Communist China since the 7 July 1964 loss was a 31 October mission over Lan-chou. By mid-November, three more overflights had taken place, one over North Korea and northern China and two over southern and central China. An overflight of Manchuria on 9 December 1964 brought back photos of a G-class ballistic-missile submarine. By this time, the mass of data being provided by Project TACKLE overflights was overwhelming the analysts of the Office of Research and Reports (ORR). An ORR memorandum from 11 January 1965 reported that analysis of the "large backlog of unexploited photography on Chinese Communist ground force installations...would require about two man-years work, backed up by a larger expansion of photointerpretation effort."[58]

[Redacted].

The loss of yet another U-2 and its pilot made Nationalist Chinese officials reluctant to resume overflights of the mainland. They insisted that their U-2 pilots be given permission to turn on the System-XIII false-angle device during the entire time they were over hostile territory, not just after they had been alerted by the System-XII radar-detection device. The Defense Department acceded to these demands in order to keep the TACKLE flights going. In addition, the Project TACKLE U-2s began receiving even more advanced ECM equipment.[59]

With their demands met, Nationalist Chinese officials again consented to overflights by Detachment H, and operations

---

[57] Lay, "USIB History," vol. 6, pp. 751, 753-755.

[58] ORR, Memorandum for the Record, 11 January 1965, OSA records (TS Codeword).

[59] Ibid., chap. 17, pp. 59-61 (TS Codeword).

resumed in February 1965 with three missions over the mainland. By this time US interest in the People's Republic of China was very high because of the PRC's development of nuclear weapons. The Special Group, therefore, approved an extensive reconnaissance program directed against the PRC. By the end of the year, Detachment H had flown 30 missions, the highest annual total during the entire program.

The level of activity declined during 1966, with only 10 missions flown over the mainland. Detachment H also suffered the loss of two more aircraft and pilots in crashes during training missions in 1966. In the fall of that year, joint US-Nationalist Chinese relations in the field of overhead reconnaissance were further strained by the unilateral US decision to kill the longstanding program of low-altitude nighttime overflights of the mainland (STPOLLY).[60]

[Redacted].

The entire U-2 overflight program was temporarily halted in early November 1967 after an Air Force U-2 in Vietnam was discovered to have cracks in its wing. All Air Force and CIA U-2s were ordered back to Lockheed for ultrasonic inspection of the wings and other stress points to check on metal fatigue. Upon completion of this inspection, both the Air Force and the Agency resumed their overflight activity.[61]

The End of U-2 Overflights of Mainland China

Project TACKLE mounted a mission over northeastern China on 13 December 1967 and an overflight of central China on 5 January 1968. Later that month the Far East became very tense when North Korea seized the US electronic intelligence ship Pueblo on 23 January. One week later the Viet Cong and North Vietnamese launched

---

[60] Ibid., chap.19, annex 120, pp.22-24; chap.17, p.69 (TS Codeword).
[61] *OSA History*, chap. 16, p. 44 (TS Codeword).

their Tet offensive in South Vietnam. The 303 Committee (the new name for the Special Group after 1964) decided on 1 February 1968 to suspend a group of overflights scheduled for February and called for mission-by-mission approval "during this period of tension." The committee approved one additional overflight of southern China, which was flown by Detachment H on 16 March 1968, and two overflights of Cambodia, carried out on 27 March and 3 April 1968 by Detachment G in its first operations since early 1966. These three missions turned out to be the last overflights by U-2s in the Far East. By this time U-2 flights over the PRC had become so dangerous that the State Department opposed further overflights, and on 10 April 1968 the 303 Committee decided not to approve any mission that would fly closer than 20 miles from the coast of China.

One reason why Detachment H's overflights were stopped was the steady increase in the PRC's ability to track and engage U-2s, as evidenced by its success in downing five U-2s. By 1968 PRC radars along the coast opposite Taiwan were keeping a close watch on U-2 activity from the T'ao-yuan base and actively tracked U-2s as soon as they became airborne. The U-2s then had to face a growing PRC air defense system that not only consisted of SA-2 missiles but also the fast and high-flying MiG-21. The PRC's MiG-21 pilots had become adept at the power-zoom technique and were threatening almost every U-2 mission. The risks to U-2s now seemed too great.[62]

The decision to end Asian overflights was also rooted in the Johnson administration's change in its whole approach to the war in Indochina in the spring of 1968. On 31 March 1968, the President limited the bombing of North Vietnam in order to improve the chances for peace talks. The end of flights over the People's

---

[62] OSA, "Chronology of Events Leading to Present Impasse on Resumption of TACKLE Overflights of Mainland China," December 1968, OSA records (TS).

Republic of China was viewed as another way to improve the peace process.

During its six years of overflight operations, Project TACKLE had been extremely active, staging a total of 104 flights over the People's Republic of China. These missions had brought back huge amounts of data about the PRC but not without a price: five Project TACKLE aircraft had been downed by the PRC, with two of the pilots killed and the other three captured (although later returned). In addition, five other Nationalist Chinese pilots had been killed in training accidents.

Overflights by Project TACKLE

Fiscal Year	Overflights
Total	104
1962	18
1963	17
1964	13
1965	30
1966	10
1967	14
1968	2

Peripheral Missions by Detachment H

Detachment H did not cease its activities following the termination of overflights of mainland China. Its next U-2 mission took place on 18 May 1968. This was an electronic intelligence mission that, in accordance with the new guidelines, never came closer than 20 miles to the Chinese coast. All future Detachment H missions against the PRC also conformed with this restriction but were still the target of interception attempts by PRC MiG-21s or hastily erected SAM sites on offshore islands. The use of peripheral missions prevented any further losses, although one aircraft crashed into the sea from unknown causes shortly after taking off to start a mission on 5 January 1969. Another pilot was killed on 24 November 1970 in a crash during a routine training mission.[63]

The level of activity gradually increased during the remaining years of Project TACKLE, as can be seen in the table below.

The U-2s flying these missions were generally equipped with the B or the newly designed 48-inch H cameras to obtain oblique photography and with various signal-intelligence-gathering systems. Beginning in May 1971, Project TACKLE began using a new communications-intelligence collection package known as LONG SHAFT. This system was used on 32 occasions through 12 December 1973, when the LONG SHAFT collection program ended.

Project TACKLE Peripheral Missions. 1969-1974

Fiscal Year	Missions
1969	9
1970	14
1971	19
1972	23
1973	31
1974	17

Once the United States began seeking a rapprochement with the People's Republic of China, Detachment H U-2s came under more and more restrictions. Soon after the impending visit of President Richard M. Nixon to the PRC was announced, U-2 missions were ordered to stay even farther away from the mainland: 25 nautical miles instead of the previous 20. During the months of

---

[63] "Office of Special Activities History, April 1969 to Phase-Out," (draft; hereafter cited as "OSA History-2") (CIA: DS&T, 1974), chap. 3, pp. 36-42 (TS Codeword).

February and March 1972, when the President's visit took place, Detachment H ceased all operational missions.[64]

In March 1973, the TACKLE agreement with the Nationalist Chinese was renegotiated. Although no end date was set, the agreement contained a termination clause that would become effective three months after notification by either party. This clause provided more flexibility to the United States, which could now end the Nationalist Chinese U-2 program whenever US foreign policy considerations made such a step desirable.

Operation SCOPE SHIELD over North Vietnam

In addition to the Project TACKLE peripheral missions against the PRC, Detachment H (with Agency rather than Nationalist Chinese pilots) flew a series of missions known as Operation SCOPE SHIELD to gather intelligence on activities in North Vietnam. The Indochina area had become the responsiblity of the Air Force in 1964, but, under the terms of the cease-fire agreement negotiated with North Vietnam in January 1973, US military flights in the area were forbidden. The Nixon administration, therefore, tasked the CIA with monitoring North Vietnam's compliance with the cease-fire accords.

The Agency dispatched several pilots to Taiwan under the cover of Lockheed employees working on a government contract to check weather conditions. Their highly sensitive missions had to remain at least 15 nautical miles away from the North Vietnamese coast, and they initially flew at low altitude in a deceptive direction in order to avoid PRC radars. These constraints made the missions difficult because at low altitude the U-2 consumed more fuel and encountered more turbulence and the pilots' pressure suits tended to overheat.

---

[64] Ibid., pp. 44-45 (TS Codeword).

The first mission on 30 March 1973 was only marginally successful because of cloud cover and haze, which prevented it from photographing most of its targets. A second mission on the following day had somewhat better luck with the weather, but problems with the film processing reduced the mission's coverage. Afterward, the monsoon season prevented any further missions until 21 July 1973. This mission obtained usable photography of SAM sites and North Vietnamese supply operations, although the resolution was not as high as it should have been because the H camera lens had not been properly focused. The last SCOPE SHIELD mission, on 6 January 1974, finally succeeded in obtaining high-quality photography. The mission provided complete coverage of shipping in Haiphong Harbor, SAM defenses, and North Vietnamese naval order of battle.[65]

IMPROVEMENTS IN U-2 TECHNOLOGY
Modification of U-2s for Aircraft Carrier Deployment
In mid-1963, the Office of Special Activities set in motion Project WHALE TALE to examine the possibility of adapting the U-2 aircraft for operations from an aircraft carrier. In the past, protest notes from the Soviet Union to Turkey and Pakistan and from Communist China to India had been responsible for interrupting overflight operations. CIA planners believed that, if U-2s could be modified to operate from aircraft carriers, the United States could avoid the political problems involved in seeking permission to base U-2s in other nations. Kelly Johnson began working on changes to the aircraft, and Office of Special Activities Deputy Director James A. Cunningham, Jr., a former Marine Corps aviator, asked the Navy for assistance.

The first test of the U-2's capability for carrier operations took place in August 1963 from the USS Kitty Hawk operating

---

[65] Ibid., pp. 48-51 (TS Codeword).

in the Pacific Ocean off San Diego, California. A U-2C, which had been loaded aboard the carrier at North Island Naval Base, took off from the flight deck with a full load of fuel and was airborne within 321 feet. No assistance from catapults was necessary. Although the takeoff was very successful, the attempted landing was not. The aircraft bounced, hit hard on one wing tip, and then just barely managed to become airborne again before reaching the end of the deck. Kelly Johnson realized that the airframe would have to be altered in order to make carrier landings possible. These alterations involved strengthening the landing gear, installing an arresting hook at the rear of the fuselage, and fitting "spoilers" on the wings to cancel the aerodynamic lift once the aircraft was over the flight deck. Aircraft thus modified were designated U-2G. While several aircraft underwent these modifications, Detachment G pilots began undergoing training in landing on aircraft carriers. The first successful carrier landing took place on 2 March 1964.[66]

Use of Carrier-Based U-2 to Film a French Nuclear Test Site

Within a few months after the completion of carrier testing, one of the carrier-modified U-2s conducted an operation in the Pacific. Its mission was to gather information on the activities of an ally. In December 1963, France had announced its intention to detonate a hydrogen device over Mururoa Atoll in the Tuamotu Archipelago area of French Polynesia but had given no specific date for the event. The Committee on Overhead Reconnaissance had been following French nuclear developments since September 1963, when it had apprised the USIB of the need for overflights of this South Pacific area. At that time the USIB decided against recom-

---

[66] "U-2 Aircraft Carrier Operations: Project 'WHALE TALE,' Operation FISH HAWK," DS&T, 1964, pp. 1-13 (TS Codeword); Johnson, "Log for Project X," 5 August 1963 and 2 March 1964.

mending such overflights because of State Department concern about potential political difficulties with France in the event the mission was discovered.

Following reports of a buildup of French troops and technical personnel in neighboring Tahiti, the Special Group on 24 April 1964 approved a mission to overfly the atoll to check for activity. This required photography with a resolution better than the 3 to 5 feet possible with the standard B-model camera that had been in use since October 1956. Work on a very-high-resolution camera had begun in early 1963, when the Agency contracted with the Itek Corporation to modify for placement in the U-2 a camera that had been developed for the satellite program. Known as the Delta-II, or the 112A, this device could photograph a 28-kilometer swath with 26° convergent stereoscopic lenses, resulting in a 70° lateral coverage and a ground resolution of 10 inches. This camera was installed in a Detachment H U-2 and used on two missions conducted over Indochina in late December 1963. Resolution was not as high as had been expected, and the unit was returned to Itek for modifications. By early 1964, the 112A had been reworked and was now known as the 112B. In tests it had proved capable of providing photography with resolution in the 10- to 12-inch range.

Detachment G conducted Operation FISH HAWK in May 1964 by sending two pilots, an NPIC photointerpreter, and a U-2G equipped with the Itek 112B camera to make the first operational U-2 flights from an aircraft carrier. On 19 May the U-2 took off from the USS Ranger and overflew the French atomic test area. As soon as the aircraft returned to the Ranger, the film was developed in the carrier's photo lab, and the NPIC photointerpreter then read out the film to see if the photography met the requirements for resolution and quality. A second U-2 flight carried out a similar mission on 22 May. The photography provided all the detail needed to identify the preparations for the nuclear test that occurred later that year.[67]

There was never another Agency U-2 mission from an aircraft carrier. Although the idea of using a floating airbase to avoid political sensitivity proved feasible, the cost did not. Aircraft carriers are enormously expensive to operate and require an entire flotilla of vessels to protect and service them. The movement of large numbers of big ships is difficult to conceal and cannot be hastily accomplished, while the deployment of a solitary U-2 to a remote airfield can take place overnight.

A New Version of the U-2

By the summer of 1966, the number of flyable Agency U-2s had dwindled to six—two at Detachment H in Taiwan and four at Detachment G in California—with three more at Lockheed undergoing repair. The Agency had originally ordered 20 U-2s in 1954-55 (the Air Force had purchased another 31 of these planes), and Kelly Johnson's crew at the Skunk Works had managed to assemble four additional craft for the Agency from leftover spare parts and usable sections of crashed aircraft. This brought the total number of U-2s acquired by the Agency to 24, for an average cost of $812,500 each.

At this point, the DCI and the Secretary of Defense on 1 August 1966 decided to place an order with Lockheed for eight more aircraft to be used in the Agency and Air Force U-2 programs—a completely new version of the aircraft. Kelly Johnson had been working on ways to improve the performance of the U-2 since early 1965 because he was concerned that all the modifications and additions to the aircraft over the years had made it so heavy that it had lost almost half of its range and sev-

---

[67] "U-2 Aircraft Carrier Operations: Project 'WHALE TALE,' Operation FISH HAWK," DS&T, 1964, pp. 17-25.

eral thousand feet in cruising altitude.[68] The new model, known as the U-2R, had a longer fuselage and a wider wingspan than the original U-2. The U-2R's wings were 103 feet long with 1,000 square feet of lifting surface, in contrast to the U-2C's 80-foot wings with only 600 square feet. The longer fuselage of the U-2R made it possible to provide two pressurized bays with an additional 2.2 cubic meters of equipment space and also achieve a better weight distribution. The net result of all these improvements was a much better performing aircraft. No longer did the U-2 pilot have to worry about keeping the aircraft's speed at altitude within a 6-knot window in the stall/buffet corner of the flight envelope. The envelope was now extended to 20 knots, which greatly improved flyability.

The U-2R used the upgraded Pratt & Whitney J75/P-13B engine and was able to fly higher—in excess of 74,000 feet—and faster—Mach 0.72 (410 knots), which is 12 knots faster than the U-2C. When flying at the higher altitude, however, the U-2R's range was less than the U-2C's. The restart capability of the P-13B engine was significantly better than the P-13A power plant. As a result, the U-2R could be restarted at 54,000 feet, which was 10,000 feet higher than the U-2C. Francis Gary Powers was one of the Lockheed test pilots who checked out this new aircraft when it first took to the air on 28 August 1967. The last of the U-2Rs was delivered on 11 December 1968.

The increased performance of the U-2R did not come cheaply. At $7.1 million per aircraft, the new models cost almost 10 times as much as the original U-2s. Much of the increased cost was due to inflation, but some was the result of technological advances. The initial order for eight of the new version of the U-2 was followed on 23 November 1966 by an order from the DCI

---

[68] Johnson, "Log for Project X," 2 February 1965, June to October 1965, 20 October 1965; Johnson, "U-2R Log," January to August 1966.

and the Secretary of Defense for four more. This brought the total number of U-2Rs purchased by the CIA and the Air Force to 12.[69]

In addition to a new aircraft, the U-2 program received a new camera. Agency managers felt that, because the B camera was now 10 years old, the U-2R needed a camera that incorporated the many important advances that had occurred in recent years. The 112B—the modified version of the satellite program's stereo camera that had been used in the U-2G—had not proved totally successful. Despite its stereo capability, this camera's shorter focal length could not provide the scale of imagery needed to obtain the highly technical data desired by analysts. As a result, the Office of Special Activities asked the Hycon Manufacturing Company of Pasadena, California, to adapt its successful high-resolution 48-inch 9- by 9-inch format camera developed for the OXCART aircraft for use in the U-2R. This camera was actually a very advanced version of the original B camera with a new lens designed by James Baker. The new camera was designed to resolve objects smaller than 4 inches.

Hycon began work on the HR-333 camera in 1966. Unlike the OXCART camera, the new unit was to use the split 18- by 18-inch format of the B camera, so the lens had to be redesigned. James Baker's contribution to this effort was a 48-inch f/5.6 system that provided remarkably sharp imagery. Hycon completed the camera in time for it to be installed in the first U-2Rs delivered to the Agency in 1968; it is known as the H camera.[70]

Replacement of the Original U-2s with U-2Rs

As the new U-2Rs began coming off the production line at Lockheed in the autumn of 1968, CIA and the Department of Defense

---

[69] *OSA History,* chap. 5, pp. 34-36 (TS Codeword); "OSA History-2," chap. 5, pp. 1-2 (TS Codeword).
[70] "OSA History-2," chap. 5, pp. 10-12.

had to decide who would get the new aircraft. At a meeting on 13 November, DCI Richard Helms and Secretary of Defense Robert McNamara agreed that the Air Force and the Agency would each get six U-2Rs. The six older U-2s remaining from the original 1954-55 production were to be kept in flyable condition and be used as replacements if newer models were lost.

Despite the greatly increased capabilities of the new model of the U-2, the era of overflights of hostile territory was over. The U-2R would have six years of useful service with the Agency, but its missions did not include penetration flights over hostile territory.

THE FINAL YEARS OF THE U-2

When the OXCART's brief operational career with the Agency ended in 1968, the U-2 was once again the center of the Agency's manned reconnaissance program. But by this time, reconnaissance aircraft had declined in importance as collection systems. Over-flights were a thing of the past. Although Project TACKLE U-2s with Nationalist Chinese pilots were still flying missions targeted against the People's Republic of China, these missions did not overfly PRC territory. Increasingly, Agency U-2s flew missions that did not involve intelligence collection requirements.

Support to Other Agencies

Beginning in 1964, the Agency conducted a program known as RED DOT for the Department of Defense. RED DOT involved the development and testing of various color, black and white, and infrared films, emulsions, and processing techniques for use in manned and unmanned high-altitude reconnaissance systems. From 1968 until 1974, Detachment G U-2s photographed areas within the United States that were analagous to portions of the Soviet Union in order to test films and techniques for spotting certain targets. This analogous filming was particularly valuable in connection with agricultural areas and nuclear test sites.

Some U-2 missions supported agencies outside the intelligence community. In 1968 and 1969, Detachment G U-2s flew high-altitude photographic missions in conjunction with the Apollo VII and IX spaceflights in response to a NASA request. These flights provided photography of the western United States for comparison with the photography taken by the Apollo crews. The Department of the Interior also requested U-2 support in early 1969 to help determine the extent of damage caused by a leak in an offshore oil well in California's Santa Barbara Channel. After preliminary assessment of the film at NPIC, the mission photography was given to the US Geological Survey for further study.

Also in early 1969, Detachment G began providing coverage of the western United States at the request of the Department of Commerce. U-2s filmed the Sierra snowfield to aid hydrologists in forecasting snowmelt and flooding potentials. Later that year, Detachment G supported the Office of Emergency Preparedness by photographing 61,000 square miles of the southern United States as part of a Hurricane Baseline Survey. These photographs could be used for future damage assessment following a major hurricane. A subsequent mission in fiscal year 1971 continued the Hurricane Baseline Survey by photographing the Gulf Coast. When a major earthquake struck the Los Angeles area on 9 February 1971, Detachment G U-2s flew four sorties to obtain damage-assessment photos.[71]

Subsequent missions in support of Federal agencies included COMPASS TRIP in fiscal year 1973, when Agency U-2s photographed poppy fields that had been planted by the Bureau of Narcotics in order to provide a standard for comparison with sat-

---

[71] Ibid., chap. 3, pp. 3-29 (TS Codeword).

ellite imagery. In the following year, U-2s assisted the Corps of Engineers in conducting a geological survey.

Overseas Deployment Exercises and Missions

With the exception of the Chinese Nationalist-piloted U-2s of Detachment H, all of the Agency's U-2 assets were concentrated in Detachment G in California. To test the ability of Detachment G to respond to a crisis in Europe or the Middle East, the Agency staged an overseas deployment exercise known as SCOPE SAINT each year (unless there was an actual operational deployment, as was the case in 1970, 1973, and 1974). The first of these exercises, SCOPE SAINT-I, took place on 9 October 1968, when Detachment G deployed a U-2G to the [redacted]. The U-2 conducted several training flights and then returned to California. SCOPE SAINT-II followed in April 1969 and demonstrated the feasibility of employing a C-141 aircraft to accompany a U-2 in flight to its destination. The C-141 carried support equipment to the [redacted]. In October 1969, the third of these exercises took place at a different location. [Redacted].

No overseas deployment exercise was necessary in 1970, for elements of Detachment G actually deployed overseas to provide photography of the Middle East. At the time, President Nixon's National Security Adviser, Henry A. Kissinger, was mediating between the Arabs and Israelis in order to obtain a cease-fire along the Suez Canal, where a virtual undeclared war was taking place. Once agreement was reached in August, Kissinger promised both sides that the United States would monitor the agreed upon 32-mile pullback from the waterway. Originally, Kissinger intended for photosatellites to do the monitoring. One satellite was tasked to photograph the Suez Canal area on 10 August, but the quality of its imagery lacked the detail needed to discover such small targets as gun emplacements and jeeps.

In early August, Kissinger asked the Air Force to provide U-2s to overfly the Canal, but the Air Force demurred, saying it would take several weeks to move a U-2 detachment from Del Rio, Texas, to the Middle East. At this point, DCI Helms told an NSC meeting that the Agency's Detachment G at Edwards Air Force Base could deploy aircraft to [redacted] and begin filming the Suez area within the week, and it did. In fact, the first U-2 arrived in [redacted] only 71 hours after receiving notification to deploy. Between 9 August and 10 November 1970, Agency U-2s flew 29 missions over the cease-fire zone as part of Project EVEN STEVEN. Most flights used the B camera, but 12 were equipped with the new, high-resolution H camera. The EVEN STEVEN U-2s also employed a dozen electronic-intelligence-collection packages, from System-X to System-XXIV. After 10 November 1970, Air Force SR-71s took over the task of photographing the cease-fire zone.[72]

The Middle East was again the cause of a Detachment G deployment in October 1973, when another Arab-Israeli war broke out. Two U-2s deployed to the [redacted] on 7 and 8 October 1973, to be ready for possible coverage of the conflict. Detachment G received no such tasking, however, and the last of the aircraft returned to California on 13 November. The 1973 war did lead to the overseas deployment of Detachment G U-2s in 1974, when the CIA was tasked to monitor the Israeli-Egyptian and later the Israeli-Syrian disengagement areas. On 21 April 1974, a Detachment G U-2 with appropriate support elements arrived at Akrotiri, Cyprus, to conduct Operation OLIVE HARVEST. Between 12 May and 28 July, the detachment conducted six overflights of the disengagement areas. During these missions the electronic warning systems of the U-2 registered numerous radar lockons, but no surface-to-air missiles were fired. On 1 August 1974, responsibility for the OLIVE HARVEST missions as well as the aircraft

---

[72] Ibid., pp. 15-20 (TS Codeword).

itself came into the hands of the Air Force as part of the transfer of the entire Agency U-2 program at that time.[73]

The Phaseout of the Office of Special Activities

The Agency's U-2 program had been under review since the autumn of 1969 to determine if it should be continued along with the larger Air Force U-2 program. In December 1969, President Nixon decided to keep the Agency's program in existence through 1971 and asked for a formal review by the 40 Committee (the new name for the 303 Committee/Special Group). In August 1970, the committee recommended continuing the program through fiscal year 1972. On 12 August 1972, the 40 Committee again favored continuation of the CIA U-2 program. This recommendation was motivated primarily by a desire not to alienate the Nationalist Chinese Government by eliminating Project TACKLE. In June 1973, however, DCI James R. Schlesinger informed the 40 Committee that this project could be terminated without causing major difficulties with the Nationalist Chinese. On 30 August 1973, the 40 Committee approved the CIA's plans to terminate the U-2 program effective 1 August 1974. The Air Force would assume funding responsibility for the four U-2R aircraft assigned to the Agency and would take physical possession of them then or shortly thereafter. On 1 April 1974, Ambassador Walter P. McConaughy informed the Nationalist Chinese Government of the US intention to end the U-2 project, and the two countries then worked out a schedule for phasing out Project TACKLE.[74]

The transfer of all Agency U-2s to the Air Force eliminated Detachments G and H. Their parent organization, the Office of Special Activities, began its phaseout immediately thereafter. The 20-year career of the U-2 with the CIA had come to an end.

---

[73] Ibid., pp. 31-34 (TS Codeword).
[74] Ibid., chap. 10, pp. 1-4 (TS Codeword).

6

The U-2's Intended Successor: Project OXCART, 1956-1968

Before the U-2 became operational in June 1956, CIA project officials had estimated that its life expectancy for flying safely over the Soviet Union would be between 18 months and two years. After overflights began and the Soviets demonstrated the capability of tracking and attempting to intercept the U-2, this estimate seemed too optimistic. By August 1956, Richard Bissell was so concerned about the U-2's vulnerability that he despaired of its ability to avoid destruction for six months, let alone two years.

To extend the U-2's useful operational life, project officials first attempted to reduce the aircraft's vulnerability to detection by Soviet radars. Project RAINBOW's efforts to mask the radar image of the U-2 not only proved ineffective, but actually made the aircraft more vulnerable by adding extra weight that reduced its maximum altitude. Because Soviet radar operators continued to find and track U-2s equipped with antiradar systems, the CIA canceled Project RAINBOW in May 1958.

Long before the failure of Project RAINBOW, Richard Bissell and his Air Force assistant, Col. Jack A. Gibbs, had begun to look for a more radical solution to the problem of Soviet radar detection—an entirely new aircraft. In the late summer of 1956, the two officials visited a number of airframe contractors in a search for new ideas. Among the more unusual was Northrop Aviation's proposal for a gigantic aircraft with a very-high-lift wing. Because it would not be made of metal, the wing would require a type of bridge truss on its upper side to give it rigidity. The proposed aircraft would achieve altitudes of 80,000 to 90,000 feet but only at subsonic speeds, just enough to keep it airborne.[1]

The slow-flying Northrop design did not solve the problem of radar detection, and in 1957 the emphasis switched to supersonic designs. In August 1957, the Scientific Engineering Institute (SEI), a CIA proprietary firm that had been working on ways to reduce the U-2's vulnerability to radar, began to investigate the possibility of designing an aircraft with a very small radar cross section. SEI soon discovered that supersonic speed greatly reduced the chances of detection by radar.[2] From this point on, the CIA's attention focused increasingly on the possibility of building an aircraft that could fly at both extremely high speeds and high altitudes while incorporating the best ideas in radar-absorbing or radar-deflecting techniques.

THE EVALUATION OF DESIGNS FOR A SUCCESSOR TO THE U-2

By the autumn of 1957, Bissell and Gibbs had collected so many ideas for a successor to the U-2 that Bissell asked DCI Dulles for permission to establish an advisory committee to assist in the selection process. Bissell also felt that the support of a committee

---

[1] Donovan interview (S).

[2] [Redacted] "The OXCART Story," *Studies in Intelligence* 15 (Winter 1971):2 (S).

of prominent scientists and engineers would prove useful when it came time to ask for funding for such an expensive project. Edwin Land became the chairman of the new committee, which included some of the scientists and engineers who had served on previous advisory bodies for overhead reconnaissance: Edward Purcell, Allen F. Donovan, H. Guyford Stever, and Eugene P. Kiefer. The Air Force's chief scientist, Courtland D. Perkins, was also a member. The committee first met in November 1957 and held six more meetings between July 1958 and the late summer of 1959. The meetings usually took place in Land's Boston office and almost always included the Air Force's Assistant Secretary for Research and Development, Dr. Joseph V. Charyk, and his Navy counterpart, Garrison Norton. Designers from several aircraft manufacturers also attended some of the meetings.[3]

The two most prominent firms involved in the search for a new aircraft were Lockheed, which had designed the successful U-2, and Convair, which was building the supersonic B-58 "Hustler" bomber for the Air Force and also working on an even faster model known as the B-58B "Super Hustler." Early in 1958, Richard Bissell asked officials from both firms to submit designs for a high-speed reconnaissance aircraft. During the spring and summer of 1958, both firms worked on design concepts without government contracts or funds.

Following extended discussions with Bissell on the subject of a supersonic successor to the U-2, Lockheed's Kelly Johnson began designing an aircraft that would cruise at Mach 3.0 at altitudes above 90,000 feet. On 23 July 1958, Johnson presented his new high-speed concept to Land's advisory committee, which expressed interest in the approach he was taking. At the

---

[3] Clarence L. Johnson, Report No. SP-1362, "History of the OXCART Program," Lockheed Aircraft Corporation, Burbank, CA, 1 July 1968, p.1 (TS Codeword).

Johnson's first drawing of the "U-3" (A-1); revised version of the A-1 same meeting, Navy representatives presented a concept for a high-altitude reconnaissance vehicle that examined the possibility of developing a ramjet-powered, inflatable, rubber vehicle that would be lifted to altitude by a balloon and then be propelled by a rocket to a speed where the ramjets could produce thrust. Richard Bissell asked Johnson to evaluate this concept, and three weeks later, after receiving more details from Navy representatives, Kelly Johnson made some quick calculations that showed that the design was impractical because the balloon would have to be a mile in diameter to lift the vehicle, which in turn would need a wing surface area greater than one-seventh of an acre to carry the payload.[4]

By September 1958, Lockheed had studied a number of possible configurations, some based on ramjet engines, others with both ramjets and turbojets. Personnel at Lockheed's Skunk Works referred to these aircraft concepts as "Archangel-1," "Archangel-2," and so forth, a carryover from the original nickname of "Angel" given to the U-2 during its development. These nicknames for the various designs soon became simply "A-1," "A-2," etc.

In September 1958, the Land committee met again to review all the concepts then under consideration and to winnow out the few that were most practicable. Among the concepts rejected were the Navy's proposal for an inflatable, ramjet-powered aircraft, a Boeing proposal for a 190-foot-long hydrogen-powered inflatable aircraft, and a Lockheed design for a hydrogen-powered aircraft (the CL-400). The committee examined two other Kelly Johnson designs at this meeting—a tailless subsonic aircraft with a very-low-radar cross section (the G2A) and a new supersonic design (the A-2)—and did not accept either one, the former because of

---

[4] Clarence L. Johnson, "Development of the Lockheed SR-71 Blackbird," *Studies in Intelligence* 26 (Summer 1982):4 (U); Johnson, "Archangel log," 23 July 1958, 14 August 1958.

its slow speed and the latter because of its dependence on exotic fuels for its ramjets and its overall high cost. The committee approved the continuation of Convair's work on a ramjet-powered Mach 4.0 "parasite" aircraft that would be launched from a specially configured version of the B-58B bomber. The design was termed a parasite because it could not take off on its own but needed a larger aircraft to carry it aloft and accelerate it to the speed required to start the ramjet engine. The Convair design was called the FISH.[5]

Two months later, after reviewing the Convair proposal and yet another Lockheed design for a high-speed reconnaissance aircraft (the A-3), the Land committee concluded in late November 1958 that it would indeed be feasible to build an aircraft whose speed and altitude would make radar tracking difficult or impossible. The committee, therefore, recommended that DCI Dulles ask President Eisenhower to approve further pursuit of the project and to provide funds for additional studies and tests.[6]

On 17 December 1958, Allen Dulles and Richard Bissell briefed the President on the progress toward a successor to the U-2. Also present were Land and Purcell from the advisory committee, Presidential Science Adviser James Killian, and Air Force Secretary Donald Quarles. DCI Dulles reviewed the results of the U-2 missions to date and stated his belief that a successor to the U-2 could be used all over the world and "would have a much greater invulnerability to detection."

Bissell then described the two competing projects by Lockheed and Convair, noting that the chief question at the moment

---

[5] *OSA History,* chap. 20, p. 8 (TS Codeword); Johnson, "Archangel log," 17-24 September 1958.

[6] *OSA Chronology,* p. 21 (TS Codeword); [Redacted] "OXCART Story," p. 3 (S); *OSA History* chap. 20, p. 8 (TS Codeword); Johnson, "Archangel log," 12 November 1958.

Convair FISH

Kelly Johnson's A-2 Design

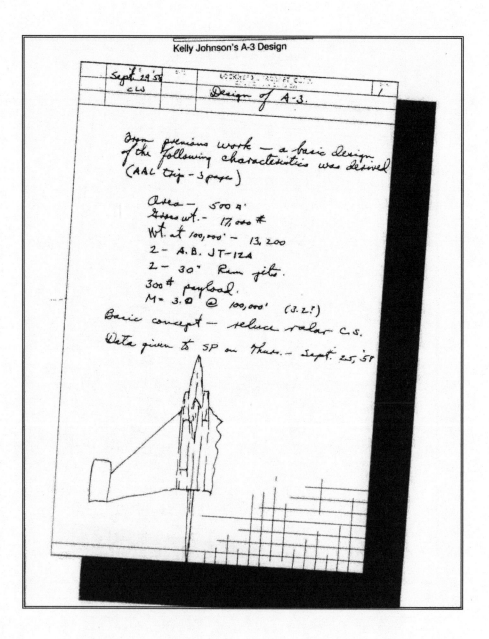

Kelly Johnson's A-3 Design

was whether to use air launch or ground takeoff. The next phase, he added, would be detailed engineering, at the end of which it was proposed that 12 aircraft be ordered at a cost of about $100 million.

Although President Eisenhower supported the purchase of this type of aircraft, he questioned the plan to procure any before they had been tested. Promising that more thought would be given to the matter before such an order was placed, Secretary Quarles noted that CIA, the Defense Department, and the Bureau of the Budget were working on a funding plan for the project. The President suggested that the Air Force "could support the project by transferring some reconnaissance money." At the close of the meeting, Eisenhower asked the group to return after completing the next work phase to discuss further stages of the project with him.[7]

COMPETITION BETWEEN LOCKHEED AND CONVAIR
With funding for the proposed new type of aircraft now available, Richard Bissell asked Lockheed and Convair to submit detailed proposals. During the first half of 1959, both Lockheed and Convair worked to reduce the radar cross section of their designs, with assistance from Franklin Rodgers of the Scientific Engineering Institute. In pursuing his antiradar studies, Rodgers had discovered a phenomenon that he believed could be used to advantage by the new reconnaissance aircraft. Known as the Blip/Scan Ratio but also referred to as the Rodgers' Effect, this phenomenon involved three elements: the strength of a radar return, the altitude of the object being illuminated by the radar, and the persistence of the radar return on the radar screen (Pulse-Position Indicator display).

---

[7] Andrew J. Goodpaster, "Memorandum of Conference with the President, 17 December 1958, 10:26 a.m.," 22 December 1958, WHOSS, Alpha, DDEL (TS).

Most tracking radars in the late 1950s swept a band of sky 30° to 45° wide and 360° in circumference. Any object encountered in this area reflected the radar pulse in a manner directly proportional to its size—the larger the object, the stronger the returning radar signal. This return appeared on the cathode-ray tube of the radar screen as a spot or blip, and the persistence of this blip on the radar screen also depended on the strength of the radar return, with blips from larger objects remaining on the screen longer. During the late 1950s and early 1960s, a human radar operator watched the radar screen and kept track of the blips that indicated aircraft within the radar's field of view.

Rodgers determined that a high-altitude object moving two to three times as fast as a normal aircraft would produce such a small blip with so little persistence that the radar operator would have great difficulty tracking it, if indeed he could even see it. Rodgers estimated that for an aircraft to take advantage of this Blip/Scan Ratio phenomenon it must fly at altitudes approaching 90,000 feet and have a radar cross section of less than 10 square meters, preferably not much over 5 square meters. However, for a Mach 3.0 aircraft to achieve such a small radar cross section, its designers would have to make many concessions in its structural design and aerodynamics.[8]

By the summer of 1959, both firms had completed their proposals. In early June, Lockheed submitted a design for a ground-launched aircraft known as the A-11. It would have a speed of Mach 3.2, a range of 3,200 miles, an altitude of 90,000 feet, and a completion date of January 1961. Kelly Johnson had refused to reduce the aerodynamics of his design in order to achieve a greater antiradar capability, and the A-11's radar cross

---

[8] Unnumbered Convair document on the Blip/Scan Ratio or Rodgers' Effect (TS).

section, although not great, was substantially larger than that of the much smaller parasite aircraft being designed by Convair.[9]

The Convair proposal called for a small, manned, ramjet-powered, reconnaissance vehicle to be air launched from one of two specially configured Convair B-58B Super Hustlers. The FISH vehicle, a radical lifting body with a very-small-radar cross section, would fly at Mach 4.2 at 90,000 feet and have a range of 3,900 miles. Two Marquardt ramjets would power its Mach 4.2 dash over the target area. Once the FISH decelerated, two Pratt & Whitney JT-12 turbojets would bring it back to base. The ramjet exit nozzles and wing edges would be constructed of Pyroceram, a ceramic material that could withstand the high temperatures of very high speeds and would absorb radiofrequency energy from radar pulses. Convair stated that the FISH could be ready by January 1961.[10]

Convair's proposal depended on two uncertain factors. First and foremost was the unproven technology of ramjet engines. At the time, no aircraft in existence could carry a large, ramjet-powered craft into the sky and then accelerate to sufficient speed for the ramjet engines to be ignited. Since ramjet engines had only been tested in wind tunnels, there was no available data to prove that these engines would work in the application proposed by Convair. The second uncertain factor was the B-58B bomber that was supposed to achieve Mach 2.2 before launching the FISH above 35,000 feet. This version of the B-58 was still in the design stage.

Convair's proposal suffered a major setback in June 1959, when the Air Force canceled the B-58B project. Conversion of the older, slower B-58A into a supersonic launching platform for

---

[9] Johnson, "Archangel log," December 1958-July 1959.

[10] *OSA History,* chap. 20, p. 12 (TS Codeword); Convair Division, General Dynamics Corporation, "Project FISH Status Review," 9 June 1959 (S).

the FISH was ruled out by the high cost and technical difficulties involved. Moreover, the Air Force was unwilling to part with two aircraft from the small inventory of its most advanced bomber. Even had the B-58B program not been canceled, however, the FISH proposal would probably not have been feasible. Convair engineers had calculated that the added weight of the FISH would prevent the B-58B from achieving the speed required to ignite the parasite aircraft's ramjet engines.

The Convair proposal was therefore unusable, but the Lockheed design with its high radar cross section was also unacceptable to the Land committee. On 14 July 1959, the committee rejected both designs and continued the competition. Lockheed continued to work on developing a design that would be less vulnerable to detection, and Convair received a new CIA contract to design an air-breathing twin-engine aircraft that would meet the general specifications being followed by Lockheed.[11]

Following recommendations by the Land committee, both Lockheed and Convair incorporated the Pratt & Whitney J58 power plant into their designs. This engine had originally been developed for the Navy's large, jet-powered flying boat, the Glenn L. Martin Company's P6M Seamaster, and was the most powerful engine available. In 1958 the Navy had canceled the Seamaster program, which had left Pratt & Whitney without a buyer for the powerful J58 engine.[12]

Although the Land committee had not yet found an acceptable design, it informed President Eisenhower on 20 July 1959 that the search was making good progress. Concerned about the U-2's vulnerability to detection and possible interception and

---

[11] *OSA History,* chap. 20, p. 15 (TS Codeword).

[12] Cunningham interview, 4 October 1983 (TS Codeword); Joseph V. Charyk, interview by Donald E. Welzenbach, tape recording, Washington, DC, 5 December 1984 (TS Codeword).

Lockheed A-11

aware that the photosatellite project was encountering significant problems, the President gave his final approval to the high-speed reconnaissance aircraft project.[13]

THE SELECTION OF THE LOCKHEED DESIGN

By the late summer of 1959, both Convair and Lockheed had completed new designs for a follow-on to the U-2. Convair's entry, known as the KINGFISH, used much of the technology developed for the F-102, F-106, and B-58, including stainless steel honeycomb skin, planiform wing design, and a crew capsule escape system, which eliminated the need for the pilot to wear a

---

[13] Andrew J. Goodpaster, "Memorandum of Conference with the President," 20 July 1959, WHOSS, ALPHA, DDEL (TS).

pressurized suit. The KINGFISH had two side-by-side J58 engines inside the fuselage, which significantly reduced the radar cross section. Two additional important design features that contributed to a small radar return were Convair KINGFISH fiberglass engine inlets and wings whose leading edges were made of Pyroceram.[14]

Lockheed's new entry was much like its first, but with several modifications and a new designator, A-12. It, too, would employ two of the powerful J58 engines. Lockheed's major innovation in reducing radar return was a cesium additive in the fuel, which decreased the radar cross section of the afterburner plume. This improvement had been proposed by Edward Purcell of the Land committee. Desiring to save weight, Kelly Johnson had decided not to construct the A-12 out of steel. Traditional lightweight metals such as aluminum were out of the question because they could not stand the heat that would be generated as the A-12 flew at Mach 3.2, so Johnson chose a titanium alloy.

On 20 August 1959, Lockheed and Convair submitted their proposals to a joint Department of Defense, Air Force, and CIA selection panel. As the table shows, the two aircraft were similar in performance characteristics, although the Lockheed design's specifications were slightly better in each category. The Lockheed design was also preferable in terms of overall cost. In the vital area of vulnerability to radar detection, however, the Convair design was superior. Its smaller size and internally mounted engines gave it a smaller radar cross section than the Lockheed A-12.[15]

---

[14] Convair Division, General Dynamics Corporation, "KINGFISH Summary Report," 1959 (S). Kelly Johnson was very skeptical of the Convair design, noting in the Archangel project log on 1-20 August 1959: "Convair have promised substantially reduced radar cross section on an airplane the size of our A-12. They are doing this, in my view, with total disregard for aerodynamics, inlet and afterburner performance."

[15] *OSA History,* chap. 20, pp 18-19 (TS Codeword).

Convair KINGFISH

Comparison of Lockheed and Convair Designs

	Lockheed A-12	Convair KINGFISH
Speed	Mach 3.2	Mach 3.2
Range (total)	4,120 nm	3,400 nm
Range (at altitude)	3,800 nm	3,400 nm
Cruising Altitude		
Start	84,500 ft.	85,000 ft.
Midrange	91,000 ft.	88,000 ft.
End	97,600 ft.	94,000 ft.
Cost summary (for 12 aircraft without engines)	$96.6 million	$121.6 million

Some of the CIA representatives initially favored the Convair KINGFISH design because of its smaller radar cross section, but they were eventually convinced to support the Lockheed design by the Air Force members of the panel, who believed that Convair's cost overruns and production delays on the B-58 project might be repeated in this new project. In contrast, Lockheed had produced the U-2 under budget and on time. Another factor favoring the A-12 was security. Lockheed had experience in running a highly secure facility (the Skunk Works) in which all of the key employees were already cleared by the Agency.

Despite its vote in favor of the Lockheed proposal, the selection panel remained concerned about the A-12's vulnerability to radar detection and therefore required Lockheed to prove its concept for reducing the A-12's radar cross section by 1 January 1960. On 14 September 1959, the CIA awarded a four-month contract to Lockheed to proceed with antiradar studies, aerodynamic structural tests, and engineering designs. This research and all later work on the A-12 took place under a new codename, Project OXCART, established at the end of August 1959 to replace its more widely known predecessor, Project GUSTO.[16] The CIA's project manager for OXCART was John Parangosky, who had long been associated with the U-2 program.

EFFORTS TO REDUCE THE A-12'S RADAR CROSS SECTION

During the spring of 1959, Kelly Johnson's Skunk Works crew—which then numbered only 50—had begun building a full-scale mockup of the proposed aircraft. The mockup was to be tested for its radar cross section by Edgerton, Germeshausen & Grier (EG&G) in cooperation with the Scientific Engineering Institute at a small testing facility at Indian Springs, Nevada. Lockheed objected to this site because its pylon would not support the full-scale mockup and because the facilities were in full view of a nearby highway. On 10 September 1959, EG&G agreed to move its radar test facility to the former U-2 testing site at Area 51 of the Atomic Energy Commission's Nevada Proving Grounds.[17]

When the new radar test facility with its larger pylon was ready, Johnson put the A-12 mockup on a specially designed trailer truck that carried it from Burbank to Area 51. By 18 November 1959, the mockup was in place atop the pylon, and radar testing could begin. These tests soon proved that Lockheed's concept of shape, fuel additive, and nonmetallic parts was workable, but it would take more than 18 months of testing and adjustment before the OXCART achieved a satisfactory radar cross section.

It was in the course of this radar testing that the OXCART received its characteristic cobra-like appearance. Edward Purcell and Franklin Rodgers had come up with a theory that a continuously curving airframe would be difficult to track with a radar pulse because it would present few corner reflectors or sharp angles

---

[16] Parangosky interview (S); *OSA History,* chap. 20, pp. 19-21 (TS Codeword).

[17] *OSA History,* chap. 20, p. 22 (TS Codeword).

from which pulses could bounce in the direction of the radar. To achieve the continuously curving airframe, Kelly Johnson added thin, curved extensions to the engine housings and leading edges of the wings and eventually to the fuselage itself, creating what is known as a chine on each side. At first Johnson was concerned that these additions might impair the airworthiness of the plane, but wind tunnel testing determined that the chines actually imparted a useful aerodynamic lift to the vehicle. Because titanium was very brittle and therefore difficult to bend, Johnson achieved the necessary curvature by combining triangular-shaped pieces of titanium called fillets. These fillets were glued to the framework of the chines with a special adhesive, epoxy resin.

On later OXCART models the fillets were made from electrically resistive honeycomb plastic with a glass-fiber surface that would not melt at high speed. When struck by a radar pulse, the composite chines tended to absorb the pulse rather than reflect it. A similar approach was used for the leading edges of the wings. Again electrically resistive honeycomb material was fabricated into triangular shapes, known as wing teeth, and fitted into the titanium wings. Both the metal and composite fillets and teeth were held in place with the newly developed epoxy cements.

The greatest remaining area of concern in the A-12's radar cross section was the two vertical stabilizers. To reduce radar reflections, Kelly Johnson canted the stabilizers inward 15° and fabricated them out of resin-impregnated nonmetallic materials. Once these changes were completed, the only metal in each vertical stabilizer was a stainless steel pivot. The Air Force, which later ordered several versions of the OXCART aircraft for its own use, never adopted the laminated vertical stabilizers.[18]

---

[18] Johnson, "Development of Lockheed SR-71," pp. 6-7; *OSA History,* chap. 20, p. 35 (TS Codeword).

Antiradar features of the A-12

THE OXCART CONTRACT

By mid-January 1960, Lockheed had demonstrated that its concept of shape, fuel additive, and nonmetallic parts would reduce the OXCART's radar cross section substantially. Richard Bissell, however, was very upset to learn that the changes had led to a reduction in the aircraft's performance, which meant it would not be able to attain the penetration altitude he had promised to President Eisenhower. Kelly Johnson then proposed to reduce the aircraft's weight by 1,000 pounds and increase the fuel load by

2,000 pounds, making it possible to achieve the desired target altitude of 91,000 feet. Afterward, he noted in the project log: "We have no performance margins left; so this project, instead of being 10 times as hard as anything we have done, is 12 times as hard. This matches the design number and is obviously right."[19]

These changes satisfied Bissell, who notified Johnson on 26 January that the CIA was authorizing the construction of 12 of the new aircraft. The actual contract was signed on 11 February 1960. Lockheed's original quotation for the project was $96.6 million for 12 aircraft, but technological difficulties eventually made this price impossible to meet. Recognizing that fabricating an aircraft from titanium might involve unforeseen difficulties, the CIA included a clause in the contract that allowed costs to be reevaluated. During the next five years, this clause had to be invoked on a number of occasions as the A-12's costs soared to more than double the original estimate.[20]

NEW TECHNOLOGIES NECESSITATED BY OXCART'S HIGH SPEED

According to the specifications, the OXCART aircraft was to achieve a speed of Mach 3.2 (2.064 knots or 0.57 miles per second, which would make it as fast as a rifle bullet), have a range of 4,120 nautical miles, and reach altitudes of 84,500 to 97,600 feet. The new aircraft would thus be more than five times as fast as the U-2 and would go almost 3 miles higher.

One major disadvantage of the OXCART's great speed was high temperatures. Flying through the earth's atmosphere at Mach 3.2 heated portions of the aircraft's skin to almost 900°F. An aircraft operating at these high speeds and high temperatures required fuels, lubricants, and hydraulic fluids that had not yet

---

[19] Johnson, "Archangel log," 21 January 1960.
[20] *OSA History,* chap 20, pp. 27-29, 33-34, 36 (TS Codeword).

been invented. The OXCART's fuel requirement called for a low-vapor-pressure fuel with a low volume at operating temperatures; the fuel would also be used as a heat sink to cool various parts of the aircraft. The J58 engines required lubricants that did not break down at the very high operating temperatures of Mach 3.2 speeds. This requirement led to the invention of synthetic lubricants. Lockheed also had to search long and hard for a hydraulic fluid that would not vaporize at high speed but would still be usable at low altitudes. Finding a suitable hydraulic pump was just as difficult. Kelly Johnson finally modified a pump that was being developed for North American's B-70 bomber project.[21]

Some of the greatest problems related to the high speeds and high temperatures at which the OXCART operated resulted from working with the material chosen for the airframe—titanium. After evaluating many materials, Johnson had chosen an alloy of titanium (B-120) characterized by great strength, relatively light weight, and good resistance to high temperatures, but high in cost. As strong as stainless steel, titanium weighed slightly more than half as much. Obtaining sufficient quantities of titanium of a quality suitable for fabricating aircraft components proved very difficult because methods for maintaining good quality control during the milling of titanium were not fully developed. Up to 80 percent of the early deliveries from Titanium Metals Corporation had to be rejected. It was not until 1961, when company officials were informed of the objectives and high priority of the OXCART program, that problems with the titanium supply ended. Even after sufficient high-quality titanium was received, Lockheed's difficulties with the metal were not over. Titanium was so hard that tools normally used in aircraft fabrication broke; new ones therefore had to be devised. Assembly line production

---

[21] Johnson, "Development of Lockheed SR-7l," pp. 11-12.

was not possible, and the cost of the program mounted well above original estimates.[22]

The high temperatures that the OXCART would encounter also necessitated planning for the pilot's safety and comfort because the inside of the aircraft would be like a moderately hot oven. To save weight, Kelly Johnson did not attempt to insulate the interior of the aircraft. The pilot would therefore have to wear a type of space suit with its own cooling, pressure control, oxygen supply, and other necessities for survival.

DESIGNING THE OXCART'S CAMERAS

Providing cameras for the A-12 posed a number of unique problems. In late 1959, OXCART managers asked Perkin-Elmer, Eastman Kodak, and Hycon to develop three different photographic systems for the new aircraft. These cameras would provide a range of photography from high-ground-resolution stereo to extremely-high-resolution spotting data.

The Perkin-Elmer (P-E) entry, known as the Type-I camera, was a high-ground-resolution general stereo camera using an f/4.0 18-inch lens and 6.6-inch film. It produced pairs of photographs covering a swath 71 miles wide with an approximately 30-percent stereo overlap. The system had a 5,000-foot film supply and was able to resolve 140 lines per millimeter and provide a ground resolution of 12 inches.

To meet severe design constraints in the areas of size, weight, thermal environment, desired photographic resolution, and coverage, Perkin Elmer's Dr. Roderick M. Scott employed concepts never before used in camera systems. These included the use of a reflecting cube rather than a prism for the scanner, a concentric film supply and takeup system to minimize weight shift, a

---

[22] [Redacted] "OXCART Story," p. 5 (S); *OSA History,* chap. 20, p. 33 (TS Codeword).

constant-velocity film transport that provided for the contiguous placement of stereo images on one piece of film, and airbars for the film transport and takeup systems.[23]

Eastman Kodak's entry, called the Type-II camera, was a high-convergent stereo device using a 21-inch lens and 8-inch film. It produced pairs of photographs covering a swath 60 miles wide with an approximately 30-percent stereo overlap. It had an 8,400-foot film supply and was able to resolve 105 lines per millimeter and provide a ground resolution of 17 inches.

The Hycon entry, designed by James Baker and known as the Type-IV camera, was a spotting camera with extremely-high-ground resolution. In fact, it was an advanced version of the highly reliable B camera developed for the original U-2 program. It used a 48-inch Baker-designed f/5.6 lens to focus images onto 9.5-inch film. Like the B camera it could provide seven frames of photography covering a swath 41 miles wide with stereo overlap on 19 miles of the swath. The Hycon camera carried the largest film supply of the three cameras, 12,000 feet. It was able to resolve 100 lines per millimeter and provide a ground resolution of 8 inches. A version of this 48-inch Hycon camera, known as the H camera, later saw service in U-2R aircraft.

Each of the three camera systems had unique capabilities and advantages, so all three were purchased for the OXCART. Before they could be effectively employed in the aircraft, however, new types of camera windows were needed. The OXCART's camera windows had to be completely free from optical distortion. Achieving this goal was difficult in a window whose exterior would be subjected to temperatures of 550°F while the interior surface would be only 150°F. After three years and the expenditure of $2 million in research and development, the Corning Glass

---

[23] *OSA History,* chap. 20, p. 26 (TS Codeword); [Redacted] "OXCART Story," p. 4 (S).

Works, which had joined this effort as a Perkin-Elmer subcontractor, solved the problem of producing a camera window that could withstand tremendous heat differentials. Its quartz glass window was fused to the metal frame by an unprecedented process involving high-frequency sound waves.[24]

Later in the program, the OXCART received yet another camera system. In 1964 the Texas Instruments Corporation developed an infrared camera for Project TACKLE U-2s that were being used to determine whether the People's Republic of China was producing weapons-grade nuclear material. This stereo device, known as the FFD-4, was adapted for use in OXCART. The camera had an effective focal length of 50 inches and a 150-foot supply of 3.5-inch film. The camera's resolution was 3°C thermally, 1 milliradian spatially, and 60 feet on the ground. It could be used for both day and night imagery collection.

CHOOSING PILOTS FOR OXCART

Just as in the U-2 program, the Air Force provided considerable support to Project OXCART, including training, fuel storage, and weather service. One of the most important areas of support was the provision of pilots; all of the OXCART pilots came from the Air Force. Prospective pilots had to be qualified in the most advanced fighters and be emotionally stable and well motivated. In contrast to 1955, when cover considerations had limited the U-2 pilot selection process to individuals with reserve commissions, the Air Force was able to devise personnel and cover procedures that enabled both regular and reserve officers to volunteer to become OXCART pilots. Because of the limited size of the A-12 cockpit, they had to be under six feet tall and weigh less than 175 pounds. Following extensive physical and psychological screening, 16 potential nominees were selected for intensive

---

[24] Baker interview (S); [Redacted] "OXCART Story," pp. 5-6 (S).

security and medical screening by the Agency. By the end of this screening in November 1961, only five individuals had been approved and had accepted the Agency's offer of employment on a highly classified project involving a very advanced aircraft. A second search and screening raised the number of pilots for the OXCART to eleven. The thorough screening process produced an elite group of pilots: all but one of these 11 officers eventually became generals. The new pilots transferred from military to civilian status and received compensation and insurance arrangements somewhat better than those of the U-2 pilots.[25]

SELECTION OF A TESTING SITE FOR THE OXCART

From the very beginning, it was clear that Lockheed could not test the OXCART aircraft at its Burbank facility, where the runway was too short and too exposed to the public. The ideal testing site would be far removed from metropolitan areas, away from civil and military airways, easily accessible by air, blessed with good weather, capable of accommodating large numbers of personnel, near an Air Force installation, and having a runway at least 8,000 feet long. But no such place was to be found.

After considering 10 Air force bases programmed for closing, Richard Bissell decided to upgrade the Area 51 site in Nevada where the U-2 had been tested. Although its personnel accommodations, fuel storage capacity, and runway length were insufficient for the OXCART program, the site's remote location would greatly ease the task of maintaining the program's security, and a moderate construction program could provide adequate facilities. Construction began in September 1960; a C-47 shuttle service ferried work crews from Burbank to Las Vegas and from Las Vegas to the site.

---

[25] [Redacted] "OXCART Story," pp. 6-7 (S); *OSA History,* chap. 20, pp. 48-50 (TS Codeword); Geary interview with Pedlow (S).

The new 8,500-foot runway was completed by 15 November 1960. Kelly Johnson had been reluctant to have a standard Air Force runway with expansion joints every 25 feet because he feared the joints would set up undesirable vibrations in the speedy aircraft. At his suggestion a 150-foot wide runway was therefore constructed of six 25-foot-wide longitudinal sections, each 150 feet long but staggered. This layout put most of the expansion joints parallel to the direction of aircraft roll and reduced the frequency of the joints.

Additional improvements included the resurfacing of 18 miles of highway leading to the base so that heavy fuel trucks could bring in the necessary fuel. The need for additional buildings on the base was met by the Navy. Three surplus Navy hangars were dismantled, moved, and reassembled on the north side of the base, and more than 100 surplus Navy housing buildings were also transported to Area 51. All essential facilities were ready in time for the forecast delivery date of the first A-12 on 1 August 1961.[26]

Unfortunately, this delivery date began to slip further and further into the future. Delays in obtaining the titanium, and later the J58 engines, caused the postponement of the final assembly of the first plane. Eventually, Kelly Johnson and Agency project officials decided to begin testing without waiting for the J58 engines by using Pratt & Whitney J75/19W engines, designed for the Convair F-106, to test the A-12 at altitudes up to 50,000 feet and at speeds up to Mach 1.6. Such a change, however, meant that the engine compartment of the first aircraft had to be reconfigured to accommodate the J75 engine. Lockheed hoped that this substitution would permit the delivery of the first A-12 by 22 December 1961 and its initial test flight by 27 February 1962.

Lockheed ran into so many technological problems with the OXCART effort that by October 1961 its costs had swollen to

---

[26] *OSA History,* chap. 20, pp. 39-40, 43, 51 (TS Codeword); [Redacted] "OXCART Story," pp 7-9 (S).

$136 million and were still climbing. Something obviously had to be done to reduce expenditures. After much refiguring, project officials decided to decrease the number of deliverable aircraft. Amendment No. 11 to the contract reduced from 12 to 10 the number of A-12s, for a total cost of $161.2 million.[27]

The cancellation of these two A-12s was offset by an Air Force order for the development of a supersonic interceptor variant of the A-12 to serve as a replacement for the North American F-108A Rapier interceptor project, which had been canceled in late 1960. With the assistance of the Agency's west coast contracting office, the Air Force entered into an agreement with Lockheed to produce three AF-12 aircraft, based on the A-12 design but modified to carry a second crewman and three air-to-air missiles. This effort was called Project KEDLOCK. The AF-12 (later redesignated the YF-12A) was designed to intercept enemy bombers long before they reached the United States, and initial Air Force plans envisioned a force of up to 100 of these supersonic interceptors. In fact, only three of these planes were built and delivered during the 1963-64 time frame because Secretary of Defense McNamara canceled the program as a cost-cutting measure. The Air Force bore all of the costs of the YF-12A project; CIA was only involved in helping to write "black" contracts.[28]

Lockheed was not the only OXCART contractor having trouble containing costs; Pratt & Whitney was fighting an even bigger battle. In mid-1961, Pratt & Whitney overruns threatened to halt the entire OXCART project. At the suggestion of Cdr. William Holcomb in the office of the Chief of Naval Materiel, Richard Bissell asked the Navy to assist in funding the J58's development. After hearing Bissell and Holcomb's suggestion

---

[27] *OSA History,* chap. 20, pp. 46-47, 51-55 (TS Codeword); [Redacted] "OXCART Story," p. 10 (S).

[28] *OSA History,* chap. 20, pp. 46-47 (TS Codeword).

that the J58 might be used in future Navy aircraft, VAdm. William A. Schoech, Chief of the Navy Materiel Command that had originally financed the J58 engine, authorized the transfer of $38 million in end-of-year funds to the project, thus keeping the OXCART's head above water.[29] As it turned out, the J58 was never used in a Navy aircraft.

DELIVERY OF THE FIRST OXCART

The first A-12, known as article 121, was assembled and tested at Burbank during January and February 1962. Since it could not be flown to the Nevada site, the aircraft had to be partially disassembled and put on a specially designed trailer that cost nearly $100,000. The entire fuselage, without the wings, was crated and covered, creating a load 35 feet wide and 105 feet long. To transport this huge load safely over the hundreds of miles to the site, obstructing road signs were removed, trees were trimmed, and some roadbanks had to be leveled. The plane left Burbank on 26 February 1962 and arrived at Area 51 two days later.

After the fuselage arrived in Nevada, its wings were attached and the J75 engines were installed, but the aircraft was still not ready to be tested. This new delay was caused by leaking fuel tanks, a problem that would never be solved completely. Because the A-12's high speeds heat the titanium airframe to more than 500°F, Lockheed designers had to make allowances for expansion. When the metal was cold, the expansion joints were at their widest. In the fuel tanks, these gaps were filled by pliable sealants, but the fuel for the A-12's engines acted as a strong reducing agent

---

[29] Parangosky interview (S); *OSA History,* chap. 20, p. 55 (TS Codeword). During this period, Kelly Johnson was very disappointed with Pratt & Whitney's work on the J58, particularly when they shocked him in September 1961 with the news that the engine would be overweight, underpowered, and late. Johnson, "Archangel log," 11 September 1961.

that softened the sealants, causing leaks. Thus, when fuel was first poured into the aircraft, 68 leaks developed. Lockheed technicians then stripped and replaced all the sealant, a tedious and time consuming procedure because the sealant required four curing cycles, each at a different temperature over a period of 30 to 54 hours. The engineers were never able to discover a sealant compound that was completely impervious to the jet fuel while remaining elastic enough to expand and contract sufficiently. The A-12's tanks continued to leak, so when it was fueled, it only received enough fuel to get airborne. The plane would then rendezvous with a tanker, top off its tanks, and immediately climb to operating altitude, causing the metal to expand and the leaks to stop.[30]

CHANGES IN THE PROJECT MANAGEMENT

Richard Bissell, whose concern for the viability of the U-2 in 1956 had led to the establishment of Project OXCART and who had directed its growth all along, was no longer in charge when the first OXCART aircraft took to the air. He resigned from the Agency in February 1962, and his departure brought a major reorganization of the reconnaissance program. The Development Projects Division of the Directorate of Plans, with its two aircraft (OXCART and U-2) and its satellite project, were transferred to the new Directorate of Research headed by Herbert (Pete) Scoville. The following year Scoville resigned and this Directorate was reorganized and its name changed to the Directorate of Science and Technology, with Albert (Bud) Wheelon, Jr., as its first head. The overhead reconnaissance projects belonged to the Office of Special Activities, headed by Col. Jack C. Ledford, who now had the title of Assistant Director for Special Activities. These project management changes in the CIA had no immediate impact on the

---

[30] *OSA History,* chap. 20, p. 62 (TS Codeword); [Redacted] "OXCART Story," p. 11 (S).

OXCART project because the aircraft was still in the development stage, handled mainly by the contractors. Moreover, a good deal of continuity was provided by officers who had served for a number of years with the U-2 program and were now involved with OXCART: James Cunningham, the Deputy Assistant Director for Special Activities; Col. Leo Geary, the Air Force's project officer for the two aircraft; and John Parangosky, who oversaw the day-to-day affairs of the OXCART project.

OXCART'S FIRST FLIGHTS

With new sealant in its fuel tanks, the prototype OXCART was ready to take to the air. On 25 April 1962, test pilot Louis Schalk took "article 121" for an unofficial, unannounced flight, which was an old Lockheed tradition. He flew the craft less than two miles at an altitude of about 20 feet and encountered considerable problems because of the improper hookup of several controls. These were promptly repaired and on the next day, 26 April, Schalk made the official 40-minute maiden flight. After a beautiful takeoff, the aircraft began shedding the triangular fillets that covered the framework of the chines along the edge of the aircraft body. The lost fillets, which had been secured to the airframe with epoxy resin, had to be recovered and reaffixed to the aircraft, a process that took the next four days.

Once the fillets were in place, the OXCART's official first flight took place on 30 April 1962, witnessed by a number of Agency personnel including DDR Scoville. Richard Bissell was also present, and Kelly Johnson noted in the project log, "I was very happy to have Dick see this flight, with all that he has contributed to the program."[31] This official first flight was also the first flight with the wheels up. Piloted again by Schalk, the OXCART took off at 170 knots and climbed to 30,000 feet.

---

[31] Johnson, "Archangel log," 30 April 1962.

During the 59-minute flight, the A-12 achieved a top speed of 340 knots. Kelly Johnson declared it to be the smoothest first test flight of any aircraft he had designed or tested. On 2 May 1962, during the second test flight, the OXCART broke the sound barrier, achieving a speed of Mach 1.1.[32]

Four more aircraft, including a two-seat trainer, arrived at the testing site before the end of the year. During the second delivery on 26 June 1962, the extra-wide vehicle carrying the aircraft accidentally struck a Greyhound bus traveling in the opposite direction. Project managers quickly authorized payment of $4,890 for the damage done to the bus in order to avoid having to explain in court why the OXCART delivery vehicle was so wide.

One of the biggest problems connected with flight testing the A-12 was keeping its existence secret. Realizing that the nation's air traffic controllers would be among the first unwitting people to learn about the plane, the Deputy Assistant Director for Special Activities, James Cunningham, had called on Federal Aviation Administrator Najeeb E. Halaby in early 1962 to brief him about the craft's existence and ask his assistance in keeping it secret. Halaby cooperated fully with the Agency and personally briefed all FAA regional chiefs on how to handle reports of unusually fast, high-flying aircraft. Air controllers were warned not to mention the craft on the radio but to submit written reports of sightings or radar trackings. The Air Force gave similar briefings to NORAD, the North American Air Defense Command.[33]

Initial testing could not explore the A-12's maximum potential, since the J58 engine was still not ready. Developing this power plant to OXCART specifications was proving much more

---

[32] *OSA History,* chap. 20, p. 63 (TS Codeword); [Redacted] "OXCART Story," pp 11-12 (S).

[33] [Redacted] "OXCART Story," pp. 10-11 (S); *OSA History,* chap. 20, p. 60 (TS Codeword).

difficult than had been expected because the J58 had to reach performance levels never before achieved by a jet engine, while operating under extremely difficult environmental conditions. To simulate the stress that the J58 would undergo during maximum power output (Mach 3.2 at 97,000 feet), the power plant was tested in the exhaust stream of a J75 engine. In the course of this extremely severe testing, the J58's problems were gradually overcome. By January 1963, Pratt & Whitney had delivered 10 J58 engines to the Nevada testing site. The first flight of an A-12 with two J58 engines took place on 15 January 1963.[34]

SPEED-RELATED PROBLEMS

As J58-equipped A-12s reached higher and higher speeds, more difficulties arose. Major problems developed at speeds between Mach 2.4 and 2.8 because the aircraft's shock wave interfered with the flow of air into the engine, greatly reducing its performance. Solving this problem required long and often highly frustrating experimentation that ultimately required a complete redesign of the air-inlet system that controlled the amount of air admitted to the engine. In the new, adjustable inlet the cone-shaped projection at the front—known as a spike—was designed to move in or out as much as three feet in order to capture and contain the shock wave produced by the aircraft at high speeds, thus preventing the shock wave from blowing out the fire inside the engine.[35]

Another J58 engine problem in early 1963 was foreign object damage. Small objects such as pens, pencils, screws, bolts, nuts, and metal shavings that fell into the engine nacelles during assembly at Burbank were sucked into the power plant

---

[34] William H. Brown, "J58/SR-71 Propulsion Integration," *Studies in Intelligence* 26 (Summer 1982), pp. 17-18 (U); *OSA History* chap. 20, pp. 58, 67 (TS Codeword).

[35] *OSA History,* chap. 20, p. 67 (TS Codeword).

during initial engine testing at Area 51 and damaged impeller and compressor vanes. To control the problem Lockheed instituted a program that included X-rays, shaking of the nacelles, installing screens over various air inlets to the engine, and even having workers wear coveralls without breast pockets. Another source of foreign object damage was trash on the runways. The giant J58 engines acted like immense vacuum cleaners, sucking in anything lying loose on the paving as they propelled the A-12 down the runway for takeoff. To prevent engine damage, Area 51 personnel had to sweep and vacuum the runway before aircraft takeoff.[36]

NEW VERSIONS OF THE OXCART
In 1962 the Agency and the Air Force ordered two more versions of the OXCART (in addition to the A-12 and the YF-12A). One was a modification of the A-12 to carry and launch ramjet-powered, 43-feet-long drones capable of reaching Mach 3.3. The two-seater mothership received the designation M-12; the drone was called the D-21. This project was known as TAGBOARD. The original development of the drones and mothership was sponsored by the CIA, but in June 1963 the project was turned over to the Air Force, which had overall responsibility for unmanned reconnaissance aircraft. Development of the M-12/D-21 combination continued until 1966, when an unsuccessful D-21 launch caused the loss of its mothership and the death of one of the crew members. Afterward the Air Force turned to B-52 bombers to carry the drones.[37]

The second new version of the OXCART was another reconnaissance aircraft. In December 1962 the Air Force ordered six "reconnaissance/strike" aircraft, which were designed to con-

---

[36] Johnson, "Development of Lockheed SR-71," p. 12.
[37] *OSA History*, chap. 20, p. 71; Jay Miller, *Lockheed SR-71 (A12/YF12/D-21)*, Aerofax Minigraph 1 (Arlington, Texas: Aerofax, Inc., 1985), p. 3.

duct high-speed, high-altitude reconnaissance of enemy territory after a nuclear strike. This new aircraft differed from other A-12 versions in that it was longer, had a full-blown two-seat cockpit, and carried a large variety of photographic and electronic sensors. The additional weight of all this equipment gave the Air Force craft a slower maximum speed and a lower operating ceiling than the Agency's A-12. In August 1963, the Air Force added 25 more aircraft to this contract, for a total of 31.[38]

THE QUESTION OF SURFACING A VERSION OF THE OXCART

As the funds being spent on Air Force versions of the OXCART increased dramatically, the Defense Department became concerned that it could not offer any public explanation for these expenditures. At the same time, Agency and Defense Department officials recognized the growing danger that a crash or sightings of test flights could compromise the program. This led the Defense Department in late 1962 and early 1963 to consider surfacing the Air Force's interceptor version of the A-12 to provide a cover for OXCART sightings or crashes and an explanation for the rise in Air Force spending. Some journalists had also become aware of the aircraft's existence, raising concern that the secret would eventually come out in the press. Agency officials remained reluctant to reveal the existence of any version of the A-12, and the issue soon came to the attention of the PFIAB. James Killian and Edwin Land strongly opposed disclosing OXCART's existence, and in January 1963 they presented their views to President Kennedy at a meeting attended by DCI McCone and Defense Secretary Robert McNamara. Killian, Land, and McCone succeeded in persuading the President and Secretary of Defense to keep the OXCART's existence a secret for the time being.

---

[38] *OSA History,* chap. 20, pp. 71-72 (TS Codeword).

Later that year supporters of the idea of surfacing the OXCART found a more powerful argument for their proposal—the need to disseminate the supersonic technology that had been developed for the OXCART. This technology would be invaluable for Air Force projects such as the B-70 bomber and for the civilian supersonic transport (SST) then being discussed in Congress. In the fall of 1963, several Presidential advisers expressed their concern to DCI McCone that Lockheed had received a $700 million head-start in the development of supersonic technology, giving the firm a tremendous advantage over other aerospace companies working on a supersonic transport. McCone passed these concerns on to President Kennedy on 12 November 1963, just 10 days before the fateful trip to Dallas. The President instructed CIA and the Defense Department to develop a plan for surfacing the OXCART but to await further discussions with him before taking any action.[39]

President Lyndon B. Johnson received a detailed briefing on the OXCART program from McCone, McNamara, Bundy, and Rusk on 29 November, after just one week in office. McNamara strongly advocated surfacing a version of the OXCART. McCone was more cautious, calling for the preparation of a statement that could be used when surfacing became necessary but arguing that such a step was not yet needed. Agreeing with McCone's position, President Johnson said the issue should be reviewed again in February.[40]

---

[39] John A. McCone, "Memorandum of Meeting in Cabinet Room for the Purpose of Discussing the Surfacing of the OX," 21 January 1963, DCI records (TS Codeword); idem, Memorandum for the Record, Discussion with the President—October 21st—6:00 p.m., 22 October 1963, DCI records (S); *OSA History,* chap. 20, pp. 73-74 (TS Codeword).

[40] John A. McCone, "Memorandum for the Record, Meeting with the President, Secretary McNamara, Mr. Bundy and DCI," 29 November 1963, DCI records (TS); *OSA History,* chap. 20, p. 73 (TS Codeword).

One additional argument in favor of surfacing the OXCART was the realization that the aircraft could not be used to fly undetected over the Soviet Union. By 1962 the United States had become aware of the effectiveness of a new Soviet radar system, codenamed TALL KING. The introduction of this computer-controlled radar undercut one of the basic premises of the OXCART program, the assumption that radar operators would not be able to track high-flying supersonic targets visually because of their small, nonpersistent radar returns. By coupling a computer to a radar, the Soviets could now weight the individual radar returns and identify those produced by high-flying, very fast objects.[41]

By February 1964 DCI McCone had become convinced that surfacing was necessary. Soviet development of the TALL KING radar system had eliminated his hope that OXCART would eventually be able to carry out its original intended purpose—overflights of the USSR. The final decision on the issue of surfacing the OXCART came at a National Security Council meeting on 29 February 1964, at which all of the participants supported the decision to surface. That same day President Johnson held a news conference at which he announced the successful development of an "advanced experimental jet aircraft, the A-11, which has been tested in sustained flight at more than 2,000 miles per hour and at altitudes in excess of 70,000 feet."[42]

President Johnson had spoken of the A-11 rather than the Agency's A-12, and the aircraft that was actually revealed to the

---

[41] *OSA History,* chap. 20, pp. 147-149 (TS Codeword).

[42] John A. McCone, Memorandum for the Record, "Discussion at the NSC Meeting, Attended by the President, all members and the four members of the President's personal staff, 29 February 1964," 2 March 1964, DCI records (S); Minnich, "OXCART Story," p. 14—erroneously identifies the date as 24 February—(S).

public was the Air Force's YF-12A interceptor, a project that had already been canceled.[43] Following the President's announcement, two of these aircraft were hastily flown to Edwards Air Force Base. From this point on, the Air Force versions of the OXCART were based at Edwards and provided a diversion so that the faster and higher flying A-12s at the Nevada site could continue testing out of the public eye.

The President's announcement did not mention the CIA's involvement in the project, which remained classified, but keeping the Agency's extensive role in the OXCART a secret was not an easy task. The first step had been to separate the Air Force's versions of the A-12 from the Agency's by moving the Air Force aircraft to California. Next, those firms that were to be given the new technology had to be briefed on the program and agree to abide by the same secrecy agreements then in force with Lockheed. Moreover, everyone witting of OXCART (including those no longer associated with the program, such as Allen Dulles, Richard Bissell, and General Cabell) had been briefed about the impending Presidential announcement, so that they would not think that the need for secrecy about OXCART had ended.[44]

The process of surfacing versions of the OXCART continued on 25 July 1964, when President Johnson revealed the existence of a new Air Force reconnaissance aircraft, which he called the SR-71. Actually, the President was supposed to say RS-71 (for "reconnaissance-strike"). Deciding that renaming the aircraft was

---

[43] President Johnson's use of the designator A-11 at the press conference has sometimes been called an error, but Kelly Johnson wrote the President's press release and chose this designator for security reasons because it referred to the earlier version of the aircraft that lacked the radar-defeating modifications of the A-12. Johnson, "Archangel log," 25 February 1964.

[44] *OSA History,* chap. 20, p. 76 (TS Codeword).

easier than correcting President Johnson, the Air Force invented a new category—"strategic reconnaissance"—to explain the SR-71's designation.

ADDITIONAL PROBLEMS DURING FINAL TESTING

The first A-12 crash occurred on 24 May 1963, when a detachment pilot, realizing the airspeed indication was confusing and erroneous, decided to eject. The pilot was unhurt, but the plane was destroyed when it crashed near Wendover, Utah. A cover story for the press described the plane as an F-105. All A-12s were grounded for a week while the accident was investigated. The malfunction was found to be caused by ice that had plugged up a pitot-static tube used to determine airspeed.[45]

Two more A-12s were lost in later testing. On 9 July 1964, article 133 crashed while landing when a pitch-control servo device froze, rolling the plane into a wing-down position. Ejecting from an altitude of 120 feet, the pilot was blown sideways out of the craft. Although he was not very high off the ground, his parachute did open and he landed during the parachute's first swing. Fortunately he was unhurt, and no news of the accident filtered out of the base. Eighteen months later, on 28 December 1965, article 126 crashed immediately after takeoff because of an improperly wired stability augmentation system. As in the previous crash, the pilot ejected safely, and there was no publicity connected with the crash. An investigation ordered by DCI McCone determined that the wiring error had resulted from negligence, not sabotage.[46]

The A-12 made its first long-range, high-speed flight on 27 January 1965. The flight lasted 100 minutes, 75 minutes of which were flown at speeds greater than Mach 3.1, and the air-

---

[45] Ibid., pp. 69-70 (TS Codeword).

[46] Ibid., pp. 80-81 (TS Codeword);[Redacted] "OXCART Story," pp. 17-18 (S).

craft covered 2,580 miles at altitudes between 75,600 and 80,000 feet. By this time, the OXCART was performing well. The engine inlet, camera, hydraulic, navigation, and flight-control systems all demonstrated acceptable reliability.

Nevertheless, as the OXCART began flying longer, faster, and higher, new problems arose. The most serious of these problems involved the aircraft's wiring. Continuing malfunctions of the inlet controls, communications equipment, ECM systems, and cockpit instruments were often attributable to wiring failures. Wiring connectors and components had to withstand temperatures above 800°F, structural flexing, vibration, and shock. Such demands were more than the materials could stand. Not all of the OXCART's problems could be traced to materiel failures, however, and Agency officials believed that careless maintenance by Lockheed employees also contributed to malfunctions.[47]

Concerned that Lockheed would not be able to meet the OXCART's schedule for operational readiness, the Office of Special Activities' Director of Technology, John Parangosky, met with Kelly Johnson on 3 August 1965 to discuss the project's problems. Johnson not only assigned more top-level supervisors to the project but also decided to go to Nevada and take charge of the OXCART's development himself. His presence made a big difference, as can be seen in his notes in the project log:

I uncovered many items of a managerial, materiel and design nature....I had meetings with vendors to improve their operation...Changed supervision and had daily talks with them, going over in detail all problems on the aircraft...Increased the supervision in the electrical

---

[47] *OSA History,* chap. 20, p. 94 (TS Codeword).

group by 500% ....We tightened up the inspection pro-
cedures a great deal and made inspection stick.

It appears that the problems are one-third due to
bum engineering...The addition of so many systems to
the A-12 has greatly complicated the problems, but we
did solve the overall problem.[48]

These improvements in on-site management got the project back on schedule.

By 20 November 1965, the final validation flights for OXCART deployment were finished. During these tests, the OXCART achieved a maximum speed of Mach 3.29, an altitude of 90,000 feet, and sustained flight time above Mach 3.2 of 74 minutes. The maximum endurance test lasted six hours and 20 minutes. On 22 November, Kelly Johnson wrote to Brig. Gen. Jack C. Ledford, head of the Office of Special Activities, stating, "The time has come when the bird should leave its nest."[49]

Three years and seven months after its first flight in April 1962, the OXCART was ready for operational use. It was now time to find work for the most advanced aircraft ever conceived and built.

DISCUSSIONS ON THE OXCART'S FUTURE EMPLOYMENT

Although the OXCART had been designed to replace the U-2 as a strategic reconnaissance aircraft to fly over the Soviet Union, this use had become doubtful long before the OXCART was ready for operational use. The U-2 Affair of 1960 made Presidents very reluctant to consider overflights of the Soviet Union. Indeed, Presidents Eisenhower and Kennedy had both stated publicly

---

[48] Johnson, "Archangel log," 5 August-30 April 1965.
[49] [Redacted] "OXCART Story," p. 23 (S).

that the United States would not conduct such overflights. In July 1962, Secretary of Defense McNamara told DCI McCone that he doubted that the OXCART would ever be used and suggested that improvements in satellite reconnaissance would very likely eliminate the need for the expensive OXCART program. Strongly disagreeing, McCone told McNamara that he had every intention of using OXCART aircraft to fly over the Soviet Union.

McCone raised this issue with President Kennedy in April 1963, at a time when the nation's photosatellites were experiencing a great number of failures and the intelligence community was clamoring for better photography to confirm or disprove allegations of the existence of an antiballistic missile system at Leningrad. Unconvinced by McCone's arguments for OXCART overflights, President Kennedy expressed the hope that some means might be devised for improving satellite imagery instead.[50]

Although overflights of the Soviet Union appeared to be out of the question, the OXCART's eventual employment elsewhere in the world remained a strong possibility, particularly after the Cuban Missile Crisis of October 1962 demonstrated the continuing need for manned strategic reconnaissance aircraft. Since satellites had not been able to supply the kinds of coverage needed, U-2s had carried out numerous overflights of Cuba. Nevertheless, the U-2 remained vulnerable to surface-to-air missiles (as had once again been demonstrated by the downing of a SAC U-2 during the Missile Crisis), and project headquarters had even briefly considered sending the A-12 over Cuba in October 1962,

---

[50] John A. McCone, Memorandum for the Record, "Summary of meeting with Secretary McNamara and Secretary Gilpatric, General Carter and Mr. McCone on 5 July 1962," 6 July 1962, DCI records (S); McCone, Memorandum for the File, "Meeting with the President—5:30—15 Apr 1963 in Palm Beach, Florida," DCI records (S).

even though the aircraft still lacked the required J58 engines and would have had to use much less powerful ones.[51] After the Missile Crisis ended, Air Force U-2s continued to photograph Cuba under a tacit superpower understanding that such monitoring of the withdrawal of the missiles would proceed without interference. But the possibility of future Soviet or Cuban action against the U-2s remained, raising the dismaying prospect that the United States would not be able to tell if the Soviet Union was reintroducing ballistic missiles into Cuba.

Such fears became acute in the summer of 1964 after Soviet Premier Nikita Khrushchev told foreign visitors such as columnist Drew Pearson, former Senator William Benton, and Danish Prime Minister Jens Otto Krag that, once the US elections had been held in November, U-2s flying over Cuba would be shot down. Project headquarters therefore began preparing contingency plans (Project SKYLARK) for the possible employment of OXCART over Cuba, even though the new aircraft was not yet ready for operations. On 5 August 1964, the Acting DCI, Gen. Marshall S. Carter, ordered the project staff to achieve emergency operational readiness of the OXCART by 5 November 1964, in case Premier Khrushchev actually carried out his threat to shoot down U-2s.[52]

To meet this deadline, the Office of Special Activities organized a detachment of five pilots and ground crews to conduct flights to validate camera performance and qualify pilots for Mach 2.8 operations. Simulating Cuban missions during training flights, the detachment demonstrated its ability to conduct overflights of Cuba by the 5 November deadline, which passed without

---

[51] On 23 October 1962 Johnson noted in his "Archangel log" that the performance of an A-12 with J75 engines (as suggested by project headquarters for possible use over Cuba) would be "hardly spectacular."

[52] Johnson, "Archangel log," 17 August 1964; [Redacted] "OXCART Story," p. 19 (S); *OSA History,* chap. 20, p. 81 (TS Codeword).

any hostile action by the Soviets or Cubans. The detachment then worked to develop the capability for sustained operations with its five aircraft. All these preparations were valuable training for the OXCART program, even though the SKYLARK contingency plan was never put into effect. Since U-2s continued to satisfy collection requirements for Cuba, the A-12s were reserved for more critical situations.

When the Agency declared that OXCART had achieved emergency operational status on 5 November 1964, the aircraft was still not prepared for electronic warfare, as only one of the several planned electronic countermeasure devices had been installed. Nevertheless, a senior government panel decided that the OXCART could conduct initial overflights of Cuba without a full complement of warning and jamming devices, should the need for such missions arise.

One reason for the delay in completing OXCART's electronic warfare preparations was the Air Force's concern that OXCART use of existing ECM devices could, in the event of the loss of an OXCART over hostile territory, compromise the ECM equipment used by Air Force bombers and fighters. Even if OXCART's ECM devices were merely similar to military ECM systems, the Air Force still worried that their use would give the Soviets an opportunity to work out countermeasures.

Such concerns led the Agency to an entirely different approach to antiradar efforts in Project KEMPSTER. This project attempted to develop electron guns that could be mounted on the OXCART to generate an ion cloud in front of the plane that would reduce its radar cross section. Although this project proved unsuccessful, the CIA also developed a number of more conventional ECM devices for use in the OXCART.[53]

---

[53] *OSA History,* chap. 20, pp. 149-151 (TS Codeword); Notes on the OXCART project by John Parangosky, OSA records (TS Codeword).

As the OXCART's performance and equipment continued to improve, there was renewed consideration of deploying the aircraft overseas, particularly in Asia, where US military activity was increasing. On 18 March 1965, DCI McCone, Secretary of Defense McNamara, and Deputy Secretary of Defense Vance discussed the growing hazards confronting aerial reconnaissance of the People's Republic of China. In three years the Agency had lost four U-2s over China, and the Air Force had lost numerous reconnaissance drones. The three men agreed to go ahead with all the preparatory steps needed for the OXCART to operate over China so that it would be ready in case the President decided to authorize such missions.

Project BLACK SHIELD, the plan for Far East operations, called for OXCART aircraft to be based at Kadena airbase on Okinawa. In the first phase, three planes would be flown to Okinawa for 60-day periods, twice a year, an operation which would involve about 225 personnel. Later there would be a permanent detachment at Kadena. In preparation for the possibility of such operations, the Defense Department spent $3.7 million to provide support facilities and real-time secure communications on the island by early autumn 1965.[54]

In the summer of 1965, after the United States had begun introducing large numbers of troops into South Vietnam, Southeast Asia became another possible target for the OXCART. Because the continued use of U-2s for reconnaissance missions over North Vietnam was threatened by the deployment of Soviet-made surface-to-air missiles, McNamara asked the CIA on 3 June 1965 whether it would be possible to substitute OXCART aircraft for U-2s. The new DCI, Adm. William F. Raborn, replied

---

[54] *OSA History,* chap. 20, pp. 90-91 (TS Codeword).

that the OXCART could operate over Vietnam as soon as it had passed its final operational readiness tests.[55]

Formal consideration of proposed OXCART missions involved the same approval process that was used for U-2 overflights. In late November 1965, after the OXCART had passed its final validation tests, the 303 Committee met to consider a proposal to deploy the OXCART to Okinawa to overfly Southeast Asia and China. Although the committee did not approve deployment, it ordered the development and maintenance of a quick-reaction capability, ready to deploy to Okinawa within 21 days after notification.

There the matter remained for more than a year. During the first half of 1966, DCI Raborn raised the issue of deploying the OXCART to Okinawa at five separate 303 Committee meetings but failed to win sufficient support. The JCS and the PFIAB supported the CIA's advocacy of OXCART deployment. Top State and Defense Department officials, however, thought that the political risks of basing the aircraft in Okinawa—which would almost certainly disclose it to the Japanese—outweighed any gains from the intelligence the OXCART might gather. On 12 August 1966, the divergent views were presented to President Johnson, who upheld the 303 Committee's majority opinion against deployment for the time being.[56]

The CIA then proposed an OXCART overflight of Cuba in order to test the aircraft's ECM systems in a hostile environment. On 15 September the 303 Committee considered and rejected this idea on the grounds that sending OXCART over Cuba "would disturb the existing calm prevailing in that area of our foreign affairs."[57]

---

[55] [Redacted] "OXCART Story," p. 21 (S).
[56] [Redacted] "OXCART Story," p. 23 (S); *OSA History,* chap. 20, pp. 110-111 (TS Codeword).
[57] *OSA History,* chap. 20, p. 112 (TS Codeword).

With operational missions still ruled out, proficiency training remained the main order of business. This led to improvements in mission plans and flight tactics that enabled the detachment to reduce the time required to deploy to Okinawa from 21 days to 15. Records continued to fall to the OXCART. On 21 December 1966, a Lockheed test pilot flew an A-12 for 16,408 kilometers over the continental United States in slightly more than six hours, for an average speed of 2,670 kilometers per hour (which included in-flight refueling at speeds as low as 970 kilometers per hour). This flight set a record for speed and distance unapproachable by any other aircraft.[58]

Two weeks later, on 5 January 1967, an A-12 crashed after a fuel gauge malfunctioned and the aircraft ran out of fuel short of the runway. Pilot Walter Ray ejected but was killed when he could not become separated from the ejection seat. To preserve the secrecy of the OXCART program, the Air Force informed the press that an SR-71 was missing and presumed down in Nevada. This loss, like the three preceding crashes, did not result from difficulties caused by high-speed, high-temperature flight but from traditional problems inherent in any new aircraft.

Proposals for OXCART operations continued to surface, and in May 1967 the CIA forwarded a detailed request to the 303 Committee to use the OXCART to collect strategic intelligence about a new Soviet missile system. As early as 1962, the intelligence community began to be concerned about the actual purpose of new missile installations that first appeared near Tallinn, Estonia, and soon spread along the northwestern quadrant of the Soviet Union. Attempts to photograph the sites using reconnaissance satellites had been frustrated by the prevailing cloud cover in the region. Because of the lack of accurate information about the missile sites, there was a wide divergence of views within the

---

[58] [Redacted] "OXCART Story," p. 24 (S).

intelligence community about their purpose. These views ranged from the CIA's belief that the installations contained long-range, surface-to-air missiles designed to counter strategic bombers, to the Air Force's contention that Tallinn sites represented a deployed antiballistic missile system.

Photointerpreters insisted that imagery with a resolution of 12 to 18 inches was necessary to determine missile size, antenna pattern, and configuration of the engagement radars associated with the system. Electronic intelligence (ELINT) analysts also needed data about the Tallinn radars, but there were no collection sites that could monitor the Tallinn emanations when the radars were being tested. Moreover, the Soviets never operated the radars in the tracking and lockon modes, a fact that prevented analysts from knowing the frequencies or any other performance characteristics of the radar.

To settle the question of the purpose of the Tallinn installations, Office of Special Activities planners proposed a mission that would use the high resolution of the OXCART's camera along with the U-2's sophisticated ELINT-collection equipment. This project's unclassified name was Project SCOPE LOGIC; its classified title was Operation UPWIND.

The proposed project involved launching an A-12 OXCART aircraft from Area 51 in Nevada and flying it to a Baltic Sea rendezvous with a Project IDEALIST U-2 flying from an RAF facility in Great Britain. The OXCART would fly north of Norway and then turn south along the Soviet-Finnish border. Shortly before Leningrad, the A-12 would head west-southwest down the Baltic Sea, skirting the coasts of Estonia, Latvia, Lithuania, Poland, and East Germany before heading west to return to Area 51. The entire flight would cover 11,000 nautical miles, take eight hours and 38 minutes, and require four aerial refuelings.

Although the A-12 would not violate Soviet airspace during this dash, it would appear to Soviet radar network operators to be headed for an overflight penetration in the vicinity of Leningrad.

It was hoped that the A-12's passage would provoke Soviet air defense personnel to activate the Tallinn system radars in order to track the swift OXCART aircraft. As the A-12 made its dash down the Baltic, its Type-I camera would be filming the entire south coast. If Agency analysts were correct in their assumption that the Tallinn system was designed to counter high-altitude aircraft at long ranges, then the OXCART would be in jeopardy during this dash down the Baltic. Nevertheless, Agency weapons experts believed that the A-12 aircraft's speed and suite of electronic countermeasures would keep it safe from the standard Soviet surface-to-air missile installations.

While the A-12 was conducting its high-speed dash along the Baltic coast of Eastern Europe, the U-2 would be flying farther out to sea, safely beyond the range of all Soviet SAMs. The U-2 would be able to collect the Tallinn radar installation's ELINT emanations.

Agency and Defense Department officials supported the proposed mission, but Secretary of State Dean Rusk strongly opposed it and the 303 Committee never forwarded the proposal to President Johnson.[59] The Tallinn radar installation remained of great interest to the intelligence community, and in the late 1960s the CIA attempted to develop a small, unmanned reconnaissance aircraft that could photograph Tallinn and other coastal areas. The project (AQUILINE) was abandoned in 1971 (see appendix E).

FIRST A-12 DEPLOYMENT: OPERATION BLACK SHIELD

Although the Tallinn mission was still being considered in May 1967, another possible employment for the OXCART came under

---

[59] Memorandum for DDCI R. L. Taylor from C. E. Duckett, DDS&T, "Collection of Photo and ELINT Data on Tallinn Sites Utilizing the OXCART and the U-2," 4 May 1967, DS&T records (TS Codeword).

discussion. This time the proposal was for OXCART to collect tactical rather than strategic intelligence. The cause was apprehension in Washington about the possible undetected introduction of surface-to-surface missiles into North Vietnam. When President Johnson asked for a proposal on the matter, the CIA suggested that the OXCART be used. While the State and Defense Departments were still examining the proposal's political risks, DCI Richard Helms raised the issue at President Johnson's "Tuesday lunch" on 16 May. Helms got the President's approval, and the CIA put the BLACK SHIELD plan to deploy the OXCART to the Far East into effect later that same day.[60]

The airlift of personnel and equipment to Kadena began on 17 May 1967, and on 22 May the first A-12 flew nonstop from Area 51 to Kadena in six hours and six minutes. A second aircraft arrived on 24 May. The third A-12 left on 26 May, but the pilot had trouble with the inertial navigation system and communications near Wake Island. He made a precautionary landing at Wake, where a pre-positioned emergency recovery team was located. The problem was corrected and the aircraft continued its flight to Kadena on the following day.

Before the start of the operation, the CIA briefed a number of key US and Allied officials on the operation. Included were the US Ambassadors [redacted].

By 29 May 1967, 13 days after President Johnson's approval, BLACK SHIELD was ready to fly an operational mission. On 30 May, the detachment was alerted for a mission on the following day. As the takeoff time approached, Kadena was being deluged by rain, but, since weather over the target area was clear, flight preparations continued. The OXCART, which had never operated in heavy rain, taxied to the runway and took off.

---

[60] [Redacted] "OXCART Story," p. 25 (S).

This first BLACK SHIELD mission flew one flight path over North Vietnam and another over the demilitarized zone (DMZ). The mission was flown at Mach 3.1 and 80,000 feet and lasted three hours and 39 minutes. While over North Vietnam, the A-12 photographed 70 of the 190 known surface-to-air missile sites and nine other priority targets. The A-12's ECM equipment did not detect any radar signals during the mission, which indicated that the flight had gone completely unnoticed by both the Chinese and North Vietnamese.

During the next six weeks, there were alerts for 15 BLACK SHIELD missions, seven of which were actually flown. Only four detected hostile radar signals. By mid-July 1967, the BLACK SHIELD missions had provided sufficient evidence for analysts to conclude that no surface-to-surface missiles had been deployed in North Vietnam.[61]

Project Headquarters in Langley planned and directed all operational BLACK SHIELD missions. To ensure secure communications between Headquarters and Kadena [redacted].

A typical mission over North Vietnam required refueling south of Okinawa, shortly after takeoff. After the planned photographic passes, the aircraft withdrew for a second aerial refueling in the Thailand area before returning to Kadena. So great was the plane's speed that it spent only 12.5 minutes over Vietnam during a "single-pass" mission, and 21.5 minutes during a "two-pass" mission. Because of its wide 86-mile turning radius, the plane occasionally crossed into Chinese airspace when getting into position for a second pass.

After the aircraft landed, the camera film was removed and sent by special plane to processing facilities in the United States. By late summer, however, an Air Force photo laboratory in Japan

---

[61] [Redacted] "OXCART Story," pp. 25-28 (S); *OSA History,* chap. 20, pp. 119-124, annex 152 (TS Codeword).

began doing the processing in order to place the photointelligence in the hands of US commanders in Vietnam within 24 hours of a mission's completion.

BLACK SHIELD activity continued unabated during the second half of 1967. From 16 August to 31 December 1967, 26 missions were alerted and 15 were flown. On 17 September one SAM site tracked the vehicle with its acquisition radar but was unsuccessful with its FAN SONG guidance radar. It was not until 28 October that a North Vietnamese SAM site launched a missile at the OXCART. Mission photography documented the event with photographs of missile smoke above the SAM firing site and pictures of the missile and its contrail. Electronic countermeasures equipment aboard the OXCART performed well, and the missile did not endanger the aircraft.

The only time the enemy came close to downing an OXCART was on 30 October 1967. During his first pass over North Vietnam, pilot Dennis Sullivan detected radar tracking. Two SAM sites prepared to launch missiles but neither did. During Sullivan's second pass the North Vietnamese fired at least six missiles at the OXCART, each confirmed by vapor trails on mission photography. The pilot saw these vapor trails and witnessed three missile detonations near but behind the A-12, which was traveling at Mach 3.1 at about 84,000 feet. Postflight inspection of the aircraft revealed that a piece of metal had penetrated the underside of the right wing, passed through three layers of titanium, and lodged against a support structure of the wing tank. The fragment was not a warhead pellet but probably debris from one of the missile detonations that the pilot observed.[62]

BLACK SHIELD missions continued during the first three months of 1968, with four missions flown over North Vietnam out of 14 alerts. The last OXCART overflight of Vietnam took

---

[62] [Redacted] "OXCART Story," p. 28 (S).

place on 8 March 1968. During this same three-month period, the OXCART made its first overflight of North Korea after the USS Pueblo was seized on 23 January 1968. The goal of this mission was to discover whether the North Koreans were preparing any large-scale hostile move in the wake of this incident. When NPIC photointerpreters examined OXCART photography taken on 26 January, they found the missing USS Pueblo in Wonsan harbor.

Secretary of State Dean Rusk was reluctant to endorse a second mission over North Korea for fear of diplomatic reper-cussions should the aircraft come down in hostile territory. The Secretary was assured that the plane could transit North Korea in seven minutes and was unlikely to land in either North Korea or China. The 303 Committee then endorsed a second mission over North Korea, which was flown on 19 February. A third and final overflight of North Korea on 8 May 1968 proved to be the last operational deployment of the OXCART aircraft.[63]

THE END OF THE OXCART PROGRAM

Almost a decade had elapsed between the time when the concept for the OXCART aircraft was first examined and the first A-12 was operationally deployed. Now after only 29 operational mis-sions, the most advanced aircraft ever built was to be put out to pasture. The abandonment of the OXCART did not result from any shortcomings of the aircraft; the causes lay in fiscal pressures and competition between the reconnaissance programs of the CIA and the Air Force.

Throughout the OXCART program, the Air Force had been exceedingly helpful; it gave financial support, conducted the refueling program, provided operational facilities at Kadena, and airlifted OXCART personnel and supplies to Okinawa for the Vietnam and Korean operations. Air Force orders for vari-

---

[63] Ibid., pp. 28-29 (S).

ants of the CIA's A-12— the YF-12A interceptor and the SR-71 reconnaissance aircraft—had helped lower development and procurement costs for the OXCART. Nevertheless, once the Air Force had built up its own fleet of reconnaissance aircraft, budgetary experts began to criticize the existence of two expensive fleets of similar aircraft.

In November 1965, the very month that the A-12 had been declared operational, the Bureau of the Budget circulated a memorandum that expressed concern about the costs of the A-12 and SR-71 programs. It questioned both the total number of planes required for the combined fleets, and the necessity for a separate CIA fleet. The memorandum recommended phasing out the A-12 program by September 1966 and stopping any further procurement of the SR-71 models. The Secretary of Defense rejected this recommendation, presumably because the SR-71 would not be operational by September 1966.[64]

In July 1966, at the Bureau of the Budget's suggestion, a study group was established to look for ways to reduce the cost of the OXCART and SR-71 programs. The study group consisted of C. W. Fischer from the Bureau of the Budget, Herbert Bennington from the Department of Defense, and John Parangosky from CIA. The study group listed three possible courses of action: maintain both fleets, mothball the A-12s but share the SR-71s between CIA and the Air Force, or mothball the A-12s and assign all missions to Air Force SR-71s. On 12 December 1966, four high-level officials met to consider these alternatives. Over the objections of DCI Helms, the other three officials—Deputy Secretary of Defense Cyrus Vance, Bureau of the Budget Director Charles L. Schultze, and Presidential Scientific Adviser Donald F. Hornig—decided to terminate the OXCART fleet. Concerned

---

[64] *OSA History,* chap. 20, p. 130 (TS Codeword); [Redacted] "OXCART Story," p. 30 (S).

that this recommendation would strip the CIA of its supersonic reconnaissance capability, Helms then asked that the SR-71 fleet be shared between CIA and the Air Force.[65]

Four days later, Schultze handed Helms a draft memorandum for the President requesting a decision either to share the SR-71 fleet between CIA and the Air Force or to terminate the CIA capability entirely. Having just received new information indicating that the SR-71's performance was inferior to that of the A-12, Helms asked for another meeting to review this data. His concern was that the SR-71 could not match the photographic coverage that the A-12 could provide. Only one of the SR-71's three camera systems was working anywhere near the original specifications, and that was its Operational Objective system which could only photograph a swath 28 miles wide with a resolution of 28 to 30 inches. The A-12's Type-I P-E camera could photograph a swath 72 miles wide with a nadir resolution of 12 to 18 inches and oblique resolution of 54 inches. Thus, the A-12's camera covered three times as much territory as the SR-71's camera and did so with better resolution. In addition, the A-12 could fly 2,000 to 5,000 feet higher than the SR-71 and was also faster, with a maximum speed of Mach 3.1 compared with the SR-71's Mach 3.0.[66]

In spite of Helms's request and the strength of his arguments, the Bureau of the Budget memorandum was submitted to President Johnson. On 28 December 1966, the President approved the termination of the OXCART program by 1 January 1968.

This decision meant that CIA had to develop a schedule for an orderly phaseout of the A-12. This activity was known as Project SCOPE COTTON. Project headquarters informed Deputy

---

[65] *OSA History,* chap. 20, pp. 130-133 (TS Codeword); [Redacted] "OXCART Story," pp. 30-31 (S).
[66] [Redacted] "OXCART Story," p. 31 (S); *OSA History,* pp. 133-134 (TS Codeword).

Defense Secretary Vance on 10 January 1967 that the A-12s would gradually be placed in storage, with the process to be completed by the end of January 1968. In May 1967, Vance directed that SR-71s would assume responsibility for Cuban overflights by 1 July 1967 and would add responsibility for overflights of Southeast Asia by 1 December 1967. Until these capabilities were developed, OXCART was to remain able to conduct assignments on a 15-day notice for Southeast Asia and a seven-day notice for Cuba.[67]

All these arrangements were made before the OXCART had conducted a single operational mission, which did not occur until 31 May 1967. In the months that followed the initiation of operations in Asia, the OXCART demonstrated its exceptional technical capabilities. Soon some high-level Presidential advisers and Congressional leaders began to question the decision to phase out OXCART, and the issue was reopened.

The CIA contended that the A-12 was the better craft because it flew higher, faster, and had superior cameras. The Air Force maintained that its two-seat SR-71 had a better suite of sensors, with three different cameras (area search, spotting, and mapping), infrared detectors, side-looking aerial radar, and ELINT-collection gear. In an effort to resolve this argument, the two aircraft were pitted against each other in a flyoff codenamed NICE GIRL. On 3 November 1967, an A-12 and an SR-71 flew identical flight paths, separated in time by one hour, from north to south roughly above the Mississippi River. The data collected during these missions were evaluated by representatives of the CIA, DIA, and other Defense Department intelligence organizations.

The results proved inconclusive. Both photographic systems provided imagery of sufficient quality for analysis. The A-12 Type-I camera's 72-mile swath width and 5,000-foot film sup-

---

[67] [Redacted] "OXCART Story," p. 31 (S); *OSA History*, p. 138 (TS Codeword).

ply were superior to the SR-71 Operational Objective camera's 28-mile swath and 3,300-foot film supply. On the other hand, the SR-71's infrared, side-looking aerial radar, and ELINT/COMINT equipment provided some unique intelligence not available from the A-12. Air Force planners admitted, however, that some of this equipment would have to be sacrificed in order to provide the SR-71 with ECM gear.[68]

Although the flyoff had not settled the question of which aircraft was superior, the OXCART did win a temporary reprieve in late November 1967. The Johnson administration decided to keep both fleets for the time being, particularly because the OXCART was actually flying missions over North Vietnam. With expenditures for the Vietnam war rising steadily, the question of reducing the costs of competing reconnaissance programs was bound to surface again. In the spring of 1968, there was yet another study of the OXCART and SR-71 programs. On 16 May 1968, the new Secretary of Defense, Clark Clifford, reaffirmed the original decision to terminate the OXCART program and store the aircraft. President Johnson confirmed this decision on 21 May.[69]

Project headquarters selected 8 June 1968 as the earliest possible date for phasing out all OXCART aircraft. Those A-12s already at the Nevada site were placed in storage, and the aircraft on Okinawa were scheduled to return by 8 June. Unfortunately, tragedy struck before this redeployment took place. On 4 June 1968 during a test flight from Kadena to check out a new engine, an A-12 disappeared 520 miles east of Manila. Search and rescue missions found no trace of the plane or its pilot, Jack W. Weeks. Several days later the remaining two A-12s left Okinawa to join the other eight OXCART aircraft in storage at Palmdale, Cali-

---

[68] Information supplied by James Cunningham to Donald E. Welzenbach.
[69] [Redacted] "OXCART Story," pp. 32-33 (S); *OSA History,* chap. 20, pp. 143-146 (TS Codeword).

fornia. Because the A-12s were smaller than either of the Air Force's versions, the only parts that could be salvaged for Air Force use were the J58 engines. The OXCART's outstanding Perkin-Elmer camera cannot be used in the SR-71 because the two-seater Air Force aircraft has a smaller camera compartment than that of the A-12. Constructed from one of the most durable metals known to man but unable to fly for want of engines, the OXCART aircraft are fated to remain inactive at Palmdale for many, many years.

POSSIBLE SUCCESSORS TO THE OXCART

The OXCART was the last high-altitude reconnaissance aircraft produced for the CIA, although the Office of Special Activities did briefly consider several possible successors to the OXCART during the mid-1960s. The first of these, known as Project ISINGLASS, was prepared by General Dynamics to utilize technology developed for its Convair Division's earlier FISH proposal and its new F-111 fighter in order to create an aircraft capable of Mach 4-5 at 100,000 feet. General Dynamics completed its feasibility study in the fall of 1964, and OSA took no further action because the proposed aircraft would still be vulnerable to existing Soviet countermeasures. In 1965 a more ambitious design from McDonnell Aircraft came under consideration as Project RHEINBERRY (although some of the work seems to have come under the ISINGLASS designation as well). This proposal featured a rocket-powered aircraft that would be launched from a B-52 mother ship and ultimately reach speeds as high as Mach 20 and altitudes of up to 200,000 feet. Because building this aircraft would have involved tremendous technical challenges and correspondingly high costs, the Agency was not wilting to embark on such a program at a time when the main emphasis in overhead reconnaissance had shifted from aircraft to satellites. As a result, when the OXCART program ended in the summer of 1968, no more advanced successor was waiting in the wings—only the veteran U-2.

SUMMARY OF THE OXCART PROGRAM

Intended to replace the U-2 as a collector of strategic intelligence, the OXCART was never used for this purpose. Its brief deployment was strictly for obtaining tactical intelligence and its photographic product contributed very little to the Agency's strategic intelligence mission. By the time OXCART became operational, photosatellite systems had filled the role originally conceived for it. The most advanced aircraft of the 20th century had become an anachronism before it was ever used operationally.[70]

The OXCART did not even outlast the U-2, the aircraft it was supposed to replace. The OXCART lacked the quick-response capability of the smaller craft: a U-2 unit could be activated overnight, and within a week it could deploy abroad, fly sorties, and return to home base. The OXCART planes required precise logistic planning for fuel and emergency landing fields, and their inertial guidance systems needed several days for programming and stabilization. Aerial tankers had to be deployed in advance along an OXCART's flight route and be provisioned with the highly specialized fuel used by the J58 engines. All of this required a great deal of time and the effort of several hundred people. A U-2 mission could be planned and flown with a third fewer personnel.

---

[70] "On 26 January 1967 Kelly Johnson noted on his "Archangel log": *I think back to 1959, before we started this airplane, to discussions with Dick Bissell where we seriously considered the problem of whether there would be one more round of aircraft before the satellites took over. We jointly agreed there would be just one round, and not two. That seems to have been a very accurate evaluation, as it seems that 30 SR-71's give us enough overflight reconnaissance capability and we don't need the additional 10 Oxcart aircraft.*

Although the OXCART program created a strategic recon-naissance aircraft with unprecedented speed, range, and altitude, the program's most important contributions lay in other areas: aerodynamic design, high-impact plastics, engine performance, cameras, electronic countermeasures, pilot life-support systems, antiradar devices, use of nonmetallic materials for major aircraft assemblies, and improvements in milling, machining, and shap-ing titanium. In all of these areas, the OXCART pushed back the frontiers of aerospace technology and helped lay the foundation for future "stealth" research.

7

Conclusion

U-2 OVERFLIGHTS OF THE SOVIET UNION

Before the first U-2 overflights in the summer of 1956, project managers believed that their aircraft could fly virtually undetected over the Soviet Union. They did not expect this advantage to last very long, however, because they also expected the Soviets to develop effective countermeasures against the U-2 within 12 to 18 months. Recognizing that time was against them, the U-2 project managers planned a large number of missions to obtain complete coverage of the Soviet Union as quickly as possible. At this time, the U-2 program focused solely on the collection of strategic intelligence.

Once operations began, however, project managers found themselves operating under severe constraints. Contrary to the CIA's expectations, the U-2 could not fly undetected. Its overflights led to Soviet diplomatic protests and numerous attempts at interception. Not wishing to aggravate the Soviet Union during periods of tension or to harm relations during more favorable intervals, President Eisenhower placed strict limits on overflights, personally authorizing each one and greatly limiting their number. Yet, the President never went so far as to eliminate the overflight program. As Commander in Chief, he valued the intelligence that the U-2 overflights collected, especially at times when the press and Congress alleged that the United States was falling behind the Soviet Union militarily, first in bombers and then in missiles. As a result of the President's ambivalence toward overflights, the years 1956-60 were marked by long periods during which no overflights occurred, followed by brief bursts of activity.

The low level of overflight activity did not prevent the U-2 from accomplishing a lot in the four years it flew over the Soviet Union and Eastern Europe. Twenty-four U-2 missions made deep penetration overflights of the Soviet Union: six by Detachment A from Germany, three by Detachment C from the Far East and Alaska, and 15 by Detachment B from Turkey and Pakistan, including the unsuccessful Powers mission.

The amount of information these missions gathered was impressive. By the summer of 1960, the U-2 project had developed more than 1,285,000 feet of film—a strip almost 250 miles long. The U-2s covered more than 1,300,000 square miles of the Soviet Union, approximately 15 percent of its total area. Information from U-2 photographs was used to prepare 5,425 separate photoanalytical reports.[1]

Numbers alone cannot describe the importance of the U-2 overflight project. In a 28 May 1960 memorandum, after Powers was shot down, DCI Allen W. Dulles described the program's accomplishments: "Five years ago, before the beginning of the U-2 program…half knowledge of the Soviet Union and uncertainty of its true power position posed tremendous problems for the United States. We were faced with the constant risk of exposing ourselves to enemy attack or of needlessly expending a great

---

[1] DCI Allen W. Dulles, Memorandum for Brig. Gen. Andrew J. Goodpaster, "Statistics Relating to the U-2 Program," 19 August 1960, Operation MUDLARK files, OSA records, job 74-B-605, box 2 (TS Codeword).

deal of money and effort on misdirected military preparations of our own." Dulles went on to describe the U-2's contribution in gathering information on four critical aspects of the Soviet Union's power position: its bomber force, its missile force, its atomic energy program, and its air defense system.[2]

The first major contribution of intelligence collected from U-2 overflights was the exposure of the "bomber gap" as a myth. Contrary to the US Air Force's claims, the Soviet Union was not building a large force of long-range bombers. Armed with information from U-2 overflights, President Eisenhower was able to resist pressure to build a large US bomber fleet to meet a nonexistent Soviet threat.

The "bomber-gap" controversy was soon followed by a "missile-gap" controversy, provoked by an extensive Soviet propaganda campaign that claimed a substantial Soviet lead in developing and deploying ICBMs. U-2 missions searched huge stretches of the Soviet Union along the rail network, looking for ICBMs deployed outside the known missile testing facilities. These missions enabled the CIA to conclude, as Dulles explained to Congress in May 1960, that "the Soviet ICBM program has not been and is not now a *crash* program; instead, it is an orderly, well-planned, high-priority program aimed at achieving an early ICBM operational capability."[3] As with the controversy over Soviet bomber strength, information from U-2 photography enabled President Eisenhower to resist pressure to accelerate the US missile deployment program by building obsolescent liquid-fueled missiles rather than waiting to complete the development of more reliable solid-fueled missiles.

---

[2] The original draft of this document was probably written by James Q. Reber. It was then revised by DCI Dulles. "Accomplishments of the U-2 Program," 27 May 1960, Operation MUDLARK files, OSA records, job 74-B-605, box 2 (TS Codeword).

[3] Ibid., p. 3 (TS Codeword).

U-2 missions also gathered considerable data on the Soviet Union's atomic energy program, including the production of fissionable materials, weapons development and testing activities, and the location and size of nuclear weapons stockpile sites. Such U-2 photography also revealed no evidence that the Soviet Union had violated the nuclear testing moratorium.

One of the greatest contributions of the U-2 program was to increase the capabilities of the US deterrent force. Before the U-2 overflights, most target information was based on obsolete materials dating back to World War II or shortly thereafter. With the assistance of U-2 photography, the Defense Department could allocate weapons and crews more efficiently and identify many new targets. U-2 photos also proved invaluable in determining the precise location of targets. One further contribution to the capabilities of the US deterrent force was the information that U-2s collected on the Soviet air defense system. U-2 photography located Soviet fighter airfields and gained intelligence on new fighter models. Special electronic intercept and recording equipment carried on many U-2 missions enabled the CIA to analyze the technical characteristics, operational techniques, and radar order of battle of the Soviet Union's electronic defenses. This information was vital both for planning the routes for US deterrent forces and for developing electronic countermeasures.

The U-2 program not only provided information on individual Soviet weapons systems, but also helped analysts assess basic Soviet intentions, particularly during crisis situations, as Dulles wrote in May 1960:

Whenever the international situation becomes tense because of a problem in some particular area, we are concerned whether the situation might get beyond control—that someone on the other side might suddenly and irrationally unleash big war...Our knowledge of

Soviet military preparations, however, resulting from the overflight program, has given us an ability to discount or call the bluffs of the Soviets with confidence. We have been able to conclude that Soviet statements were more rhetorical than threatening and that our courses of action could be carried through without serious risk of war and without Soviet interference. [4]

Dulles closed his report on the U-2's accomplishments by putting the program in perspective as part of the entire national intelligence effort, noting that "in terms of reliability, of precision, of access to otherwise inaccessible installations, its contribution has been unique. And in the opinion of the military, of the scientists and of the senior officials responsible for our national security it has been, to put it simply, invaluable."

The impact of the U-2 overflights on international relations is harder to measure. On the one hand, the intelligence they gathered was a major factor in keeping the United States from beginning a costly and destabilizing arms race in the late 1950s and early 1960s by showing that the Soviet Union was not engaged in major buildups of strategic bombers and intercontinental ballistic missiles. On the other hand, violations of Soviet airspace by U-2s strained relations with Moscow at times and led to the collapse of the 1960 summit meeting. On balance, however, the impact of the U-2 on superpower relations was positive. Without the intelligence gathered by the U-2, the Soviet Union's strategic military capabilities would have remained a mystery, making it very difficult for the President to resist pressure from the military, the Congress, and the public to carry out major increases in strategic weapons, which would

---

[4] Ibid., pp. 9-10 (TS Codeword).

have poisoned relations with the Soviet Union far more than the small number of overflights did.

PARTICIPATION OF ALLIES IN THE U-2 PROGRAM

From the very beginning of the overflight project, US Allies provided valuable support. Bases in Germany, Turkey [redacted] Pakistan played a major role in overflights of the Soviet Union. Bases in India, Thailand, Japan, and the Philippines greatly assisted operations in Asia. Two Allies—the United Kingdom and Nationalist China—made an even greater contribution to the U-2 program by providing pilots and conducting overflights. British pilots began flying in late 1958 and conducted two important overflights of the Soviet Union in late 1959 and early 1960. After the end of such missions in May 1960, the need for British participation lessened. RAF pilots henceforth flew only training or ferry missions, although their use for operational missions was considered on several occasions.

The end of overflights of the Soviet Union reduced the importance of British participation but resulted in the addition of a new source of pilots when the focus of interest for the U-2 in its strategic-intelligence-gathering role shifted to the People's Republic of China. The United States and Nationalist China had been conducting joint reconnaissance projects over the Chinese mainland since the mid-1950s, and in 1961 the CIA equipped the Nationalist Chinese with the latest in reconnaissance aircraft, the U-2. For the next 12 years, Agency U-2s with Nationalist Chinese pilots brought back large quantities of information on the development of Communist China's armed forces, nuclear technology, and economy. Such information was extremely important to US policymakers. Nationalist China paid a high price in lives for its participation in the U-2 program: seven pilots died (five in training accidents and two on overflights), and another three were captured.

U-2s AS COLLECTORS OF TACTICAL INTELLIGENCE

The low level of mission activity over the project's original target—the Soviet Union—was initially very frustrating for CIA project managers, but the U-2 soon found new missions not originally envisioned for the program. With its strategic-intelligence-collection role often on hold, the U-2 became highly useful as a collector of tactical intelligence during crisis situations.

Beginning with the Suez Crisis of 1956 and continuing with subsequent Middle Eastern wars, a rebellion in Indonesia, Sino-Indian border fighting, and culminating in support to the growing US involvement in Indochina, U-2 photography provided accurate and up-to-date intelligence to US policymakers and field commanders, assisting them in crisis management and the planning of military operations. Agency U-2s also assisted in monitoring cease-fire agreements in the Middle East, with operations occurring after an undeclared war in 1970 and the 1973 Middle East war.

By the time the OXCART became fully operational, manned strategic reconnaissance of the Soviet Union was no longer seriously considered. The political risks were too high, especially since the quality of intelligence from reconnaissance satellites was increasing steadily. Thus, the OXCART's only operational use was for collecting tactical intelligence in the Far East. Like the U-2, the OXCART gathered valuable intelligence during crisis situations. Thus, in January 1968, OXCART photography revealed the location of the USS Pueblo and showed that the North Koreans were not preparing any large-scale military activity in conjunction with the ship's seizure.

ADVANCES IN TECHNOLOGY

One very important byproduct of the CIA's manned reconnaissance program was the many advances in technology that it generated. Thanks to simplified covert procurement arrangements and the lack of detailed and restricting specifications, creative designers such as Kelly Johnson produced state-of-the-art aircraft in record time. The U-2, designed to carry out reconnaissance missions for two years at best, proved so successful that, even after its original area of activity became too dangerous for overflights at the end of four years, the aircraft served the CIA well for another 14 years and still is in service with other government agencies.

The OXCART is an even better example of the technological advances generated by the CIA's reconnaissance program. Although the OXCART was designed almost 30 years ago and first flown in 1962, its speed and altitude have never been equaled. The development of this aircraft also led to the use of new materials in aircraft construction. Unfortunately, the technological breakthroughs that made the OXCART possible took longer than expected. By the time the aircraft was ready for operations, the missions originally planned for it were not practicable. The tremendous technological achievement represented by the OXCART ultimately led to the aircraft's demise by inspiring the Air Force to purchase its own version of the aircraft. The government could not afford to maintain two such similar reconnaissance programs. The elimination of the Agency's OXCART program did not, however, spell the end of the usefulness of the world's most advanced aircraft; its offspring, the SR-71, is still in service.

In addition to the aircraft themselves, many other items associated with the reconnaissance program have represented important advances in technology. The flight suits and life-support systems of the U-2 and OXCART pilots were the forerunners of the equipment used in the space program. Camera resolution improved dramatically as the result of cameras and lenses produced for the CIA's reconnaissance program.

COOPERATION WITH THE AIR FORCE

In this history, which concentrates on the CIA's involvement in overhead reconnaissance, it is easy to overlook the important role that the US Air Force played in the U-2 and OXCART programs. From the very beginnings of the U-2 program in 1954, the Agency and the Air Force were partners in advancing the state of the art in overhead reconnaissance. Air Force personnel served at all levels of the reconnaissance program, from project headquarters to the testing site and field detachments. The Air Force supplied the U-2's engines, at times diverting them from other high-priority production lines. Perhaps most important of all, the Air Force provided pilots for the U-2s after the Agency's original attempt to recruit a sufficient number of skilled foreign pilots proved unsuccessful. Finally, the day-to-day operations of the U-2s could not have been conducted without the help of Air Force mission planners, weather forecasters, and support personnel in the field detachments. The cooperation between the Agency and the Air Force that began with the U-2 and continued with Project OXCART remains a major feature in US reconnaissance programs today.

IMPACT OF THE OVERHEAD RECONNAISSANCE PROGRAM ON THE CIA

CIA's entry into the world of overhead reconnaissance at the end of 1954 ultimately produced major changes in the Agency. Classical forms of intelligence—the use of covert agents and clandestine operations—gradually lost their primacy to the new scientific and technical means of collection. As soon as the U-2 began flying over the Soviet Union, its photographs became the most important source of intelligence available. The flood of information that the U-2 missions gathered led to a major expansion of the Agency's photointerpretation capabilities, which finally resulted in the creation of the National Photographic Interpretation Center to serve the entire intelligence community.

The U-2's tremendous success as an intelligence-gathering system led the Agency to search for follow-on systems that could continue to obtain highly reliable information in large quantities. Thus, the CIA sponsored the development of the world's most advanced aircraft—the OXCART—and also pioneered research into photosatellites. Less than a decade after the U-2 program began, the Agency's new emphasis on technical means of collection had brought about the creation of a new science-oriented directorate, which would ultimately rival in manpower and budget the Agency's other three directorates combined.

The negative aspect of this new emphasis on technology is exploding costs. The Agency's first strategic reconnaissance aircraft, the U-2, cost less than $1 million apiece. With the U-2's successor, the OXCART, each aircraft cost more than $20 million, and the cost explosion has continued with each new generation of reconnaissance satellites.

Perhaps the greatest significance of the CIA's entry into the world of overhead reconnaissance in December 1954 was the new national policy that it signaled. Although US military aircraft had frequently violated Soviet airspace in the decade after World War II, such shallow-penetration overflights, concentrating primarily on order-of-battle data, had been authorized and controlled by US field commanders, not by the President. In the autumn of 1954, however, President Dwight D. Eisenhower—determined to avoid another Pearl Harbor—authorized the construction of a new aircraft designed solely to fly over the Soviet Union and gather strategic intelligence. Peacetime reconnaissance flights over the territory of a potential enemy power thus became national policy. Moreover, to reduce the danger of conflict, the President entrusted this mission not to the armed forces, but to a civilian agency—the CIA. From that time forward, overhead reconnaissance has been one of the CIA's most important missions.

APPENDIX A

ACRONYMS

AEC	Atomic Energy Commission
AFB	Air Force Base
AFDAP	Air Force office symbol for the Assistant for Development Planning under the Deputy Chief of Staff for Development
AMD	Air/Maritime Division
ARC	Ad Hoc Requirements Committee
ARDC	Air Research and Development Command (USAF)
ASPIC	Asian Photographic Interpretation Center
ATIC	Air Technical Intelligence Center (USAF)
BSAP	Boston Scientific Advisory Panel
BUORL	Boston University Optical Research Laboratory
COMINT	Communications Intelligence
COMIREX	Committee on Imagery Requirements and Exploitation
COMOR	Committee on Overhead Reconnaissance
DB	"Dirty Bird"
DCI	Director of Central Intelligence
DCID	Director of Central Intelligence Directive
DDCI	Deputy Director of Central Intelligence
DDI	Deputy Director for Intelligence
DDP	Deputy Director (or Directorate) for Plans
DDS&T	Deputy Director for Science and Technology
DPD	Development Projects Division
DPS	Development Projects Staff
ECM	Electronic Countermeasures
EG&G	Edgerton, Germeshausen & Grier, Incorporated
ELINT	Electronic Intelligence
FCRC	Federally Controlled Research Center
HASP	High-Altitude Air Sampling Program
IAC	Intelligence Advisory Committee
IAS	Indicated air speed
IC	Intelligence community

ICBM	Intercontinental ballistic missile
IR	Infrared
ISP	Intelligence Systems Panel (USAF)
JRC	Joint Reconnaissance Center
MATS	Military Air Transport Service (USAF)
MRBM	Medium-range ballistic missile
NACA	National Advisory Committee for Aeronautics
NAS	Naval air station
NASA	National Aeronautics and Space Administration
NIE	National Intelligence Estimate
NPIC	National Photographic Interpretation Center
NSA	National Security Agency
NSC	National Security Council
NSCID	National Security Council Intelligence Directive
ODM	Office of Defense Mobilization
ORR	Office of Research and Reports
OSA	Office of Special Activities
OSI	Office of Scientific Intelligence
PBCFIA	President's Board of Consultants on Foreign Intelligence Activities
P-E	Perkin-Elmer Company
PFIAB	President's Foreign Intelligence Advisory Board
PI	Photointerpreter
PIC	Photographic Intelligence Center
PID	Photo-Intelligence Division
PSAC	President's Science Advisory Committee
RAF	Royal Air Force
RFP	Request for proposal
SAB	Scientific Advisory Board (USAF)
SAC	Science Advisory Committee
SAC	Strategic Air Command
SA/PC/DCI	Special Assistant to the DCI for Planning and Coordination
SAM	Surface-to-air missile
SEI	Scientific Engineering Institute
SENSINT	Sensitive intelligence (USAF)
SLAR	Side-looking aerial radar
TAS	True air speed
TCP	Technological Capabilities Panel
USIB	United States Intelligence Board
WADC	Wright Air Development Command (USAF)
WRSP	Weather Reconnaissance Squadron, Provisional

APPENDIX B

Key Personnel

AYER, Frederick, Jr.
Special assistant to Trevor Gardner in the Office of the Secretary of the Air Force, Ayer was a strong advocate of overhead reconnaissance by balloons and an early supporter of Lockheed's CL-282 design.

BAKER, James G.
Harvard astronomer and lens designer, Baker was a leading designer of high-acuity aerial lenses during World War II and continued this work after the war. He also headed the Air Force Intelligence Systems Panel and served on the Technological Capabilities Panel's Project Three committee that urged the development of the U-2 aircraft. Baker designed the lenses for the U-2's cameras.

BISSELL, Richard M., Jr.
Head of all CIA overhead reconnaissance programs from 1954 until 1962, a former economics professor at MIT and high official of the Marshall Plan, Bissell became Allen W. Dulles's Special Assistant for Planning and Coordination in January 1954 and received responsibility for the new U-2 project at the end of that year. Later he also headed the first photosatellite project and oversaw the development of the OXCART. In 1959 Bissell became Deputy Director for Plans but kept the reconnaissance projects under his control. He resigned from the CIA in February 1962.

CABELL, George Pearre
Air Force general and DDCI from 1953 until 1962. Because of Cabell's many years of experience in aerial reconnaissance, DCI Dulles delegated most of the responsibility for the reconnaissance projects to him.

CARTER, Marshall S.
Army general who served as DDCI from 1962 until 1965. During the period leading up to the Cuban Missile Crisis, Carter served as Acting DCI on a number of occasions while DCI McCone was out of town. In October 1962 he fought unsuccessfully to keep the CIA involved in flying reconnaissance missions over Cuba. Carter became the Director of the National Security Agency in 1965.

CHARYK, Joseph R.
An aeronautical engineer who had followed careers first in academia and then the aerospace industry, Charyk became the Chief Scientist of the Air Force in January 1959. Five months later he moved up to Assistant Secretary of the Air Force for Research and Development, and the following year he became Under Secretary of the Air Force. In these positions he was involved in coordination with the CIA on both the U-2 and OXCART projects. In 1963 Charyk left government to become the first chairman of the Communications Satellite Corporation.

CUNNINGHAM, James A., Jr.
An ex-Marine Corps pilot, he became the administrative officer for the U-2 project in April 1955. Cunningham handled the day-to-day management of the U-2 program and brought only the more complex problems to Richard Bissell's attention. Later he served as the Deputy Director of the Office of Special Activities and then Special Assistant to the Deputy Director for Science and Technology.

DONOVAN, Allen F.
An aeronautical engineer who had helped to design the P-40 fighter while working at the Curtiss-Wright Corporation, Donovan was one of the founders of the Cornell Aeronautical Laboratory after World War II. He served on several Air Force advisory panels and was a strong advocate of the proposed Lockheed CL-282 aircraft. Later he became vice president of the Aerospace Corporation.

DOOLITTLE, James H.
A vice president of Shell Oil Company and an Army Air Force reserve general, Doolittle headed General Eisenhower's Air Staff during World War II. After the war Doolittle served on many Air Force advisory panels, and in 1954 he chaired a special panel investigating the CIA's covert activities. Doolittle also served on the Technological Capabilities Panel and the President's Board of Consultants on Foreign Intelligence Activities.

DUCKETT, Carl E.

Headed the Directorate of Science and Technology from September 1966 until May 1976, first as Acting Deputy Director and then as Deputy Director beginning in April 1967. During his tenure, the emphasis in the CIA's overhead reconnaissance program shifted from aircraft to satellites.

DULLES, Allen W.

DCI from 1953 until 1961. Although initially reluctant to see the CIA involved in aerial reconnaissance, which he viewed as the military's area of responsibility, Dulles became a strong supporter of the U-2 program when he saw how much intelligence it could gather on the Soviet Union. Because his own interests lay more in the area of human intelligence, he left the management of the reconnaissance program in the hands of DDCI Cabell and project director Richard Bissell.

GARDNER, Trevor

During World War II, Gardner worked on the Manhattan Project, and later he headed the General Tire and Rubber Company before starting his own research and development firm, the Hycon Company, which built aerial cameras. Gardner served as the Secretary of the Air Force's Special Assistant for Research and Development and then as the Assistant Secretary for Research and Development during Eisenhower's first term of office. Gardner's concern about the danger of a surprise attack helped lead to the establishment of the Technological Capabilities Panel. Gardner also urged the building of Lockheed's CL-282 aircraft.

GEARY, Leo P.

Air Force colonel (later brigadier general) who was James Cunningham's Air Force counterpart in the U-2 program. He was instrumental in diverting engines from other Air Force projects for use in the U-2, and his 10 years with the U-2 project provided a high degree of continuity.

GOODPASTER, Andrew J.

An Army colonel who served as President Eisenhower's Staff Secretary from 1954 to 1961. During this period, he was the CIA's point of contact in the White House for arranging meetings with the President on the subject of overhead reconnaissance. Goodpaster's later career included service as the supreme commander of NATO and then commandant of the US Military Academy at West Point.

HELMS, Richard M.

DCI from 1966 to 1973. During his tenure as DCI, the CIA's manned reconnaissance program came under heavy pressure because of competition from the Air Force's reconnaissance program.

JOHNSON, Clarence L. (Kelly)

One of the nation's foremost aeronautical designers, Kelly Johnson graduated from the University of Michigan's School of Aeronautics in 1933 and began working for the Lockheed Aircraft Corporation. During World War II he designed the P-38 fighter, and after the war his design successes continued with the F-104 jet fighter, the Constellation airliner, and the CIA's two strategic reconnaissance aircraft, the U-2 and the OXCART A-12.

KIEFER, Eugene P.

An Air Force officer with a degree in aeronautical engineering who in 1953 informed a friend at Lockheed of the Air Force's search for a high-altitude reconnaissance aircraft, thus, leading to the initial design of the CL-282. After leaving the Air Force, Kiefer became Richard Bissell's technical adviser for the OXCART and photosatellite programs.

KILLIAN, James R., Jr.

President of the Massachusetts Institute of Technology, Killian headed a high-level and very secret study of the nation's ability to withstand a surprise attack. While this project was still under way, he and Edwin Land persuaded President Eisenhower to support the development of a high-altitude reconnaissance aircraft, the U-2. Later, Killian headed Eisenhower's Board of Consultants for Foreign Intelligence Activities, served as his Cabinet-level science adviser, and chaired the President's Science Advisory Board. Killian was also chairman of the President's Foreign Intelligence Advisory Board under John F. Kennedy.

LAND, Edwin H.

An extremely talented inventor famous for the development of polarizing filters and the instant-film camera. Land also devoted considerable time and energy to voluntary government service. During World War II, Land worked for the Radiation Laboratories, and after the war he served on numerous Air Force advisory panels. As the head of the Technological Capabilities Panel's study group investigating US intelligence-gathering capabilities, Land became a strong advocate of the development of a high-altitude reconnaissance aircraft (the CL-282) under civilian rather than Air Force control. Land and James

Killian persuaded President Eisenhower to approve the U-2 project and later the first photosatellite project. Land also served on the President's Board of Consultants for Foreign Intelligence Activities.

LEGHORN, Richard S.

An MIT graduate in physics, Leghorn joined the Army Air Force in 1942 and went to work for reconnaissance expert Col. George Goddard. By the time of the invasion of Europe, Leghorn was chief of reconnaissance for the 9th Tactical Air Force. After the war, Leghorn began preaching the need for "pre-D-day" reconnaissance in order to gather intelligence on the Soviet Bloc. He returned to the Air Force during the Korean war and later worked for Harold Stassen's Disarmament Office. In 1956 he became the head of the Scientific Engineering Institute, an Agency proprietary working on ways to reduce the U-2's vulnerability to radar detection. In 1957 he founded Itek Corporation.

LUNDAHL, Arthur E.

A Navy photointerpreter during World War II and afterward. Lundahl became the chief of the Photo-Intelligence Division in 1953. To support the U-2 project, he established a separate photointerpretation center under Project HTAUTOMAT. Under his leadership the Photo-Intelligence Division grew rapidly and achieved office status as the Photographic Intelligence Center in 1958. In 1961 Lundahl became the first head of the National Photograhic Interpretation Center, which combined the photointerpretation efforts of the CIA and the military services.

McCONE, John A.

DCI from 1961 to 1965. A strong supporter of the CIA's manned reconnaissance program, McCone presided over the OXCART's main period of development and pushed for a greater role for the CIA in its joint reconnaissance programs with the Department of Defense.

MILLER, Herbert I.

Miller worked in the Office of Scientific Intelligence's nuclear branch and became Richard Bissell's first deputy for the U-2 project. He later left the Agency to work for the Scientific Engineering Institute.

NORTON, Garrison

An assistant to Trevor Gardner, Norton became an early supporter of the Lockheed CL-282 and started the CIA's interest in overhead reconnaissance by informing Philip Strong about the aircraft. Norton later became Navy Assistant Secretary for Research and Development and was involved with the OXCART program.

OVERHAGE, Carl F. J.

After working on the development of Technicolor, Overhage went to work for Kodak. He headed the Beacon Hill Panel in 1952 and later became director of Lincoln Laboratories.

PARANGOSKY, John N.

Parangosky worked for Richard Bissell's Development Projects Staff in the mid-1950s. He served as deputy chief of the Adana U-2 unit in 1959 and became project manager of the OXCART program from its inception through the test flight stage.

PERKIN, Richard S.

President of the Perkin-Elmer Corporation, Perkin was a close friend of James Baker and was also a member of several advisory panels, including the BEACON HILL project. He helped Baker decide what cameras to use in the first U-2 aircraft.

POWERS, Francis Gary

An Air Force Reserve Officer who became a CIA U-2 pilot in 1956, Powers flew 27 successful missions before being shot down over the Soviet Union on 1 May 1960. After his return to the United States in exchange for Soviet spymaster Rudolf Abel in 1962, Powers was cleared of all allegations of misconduct in his mission, capture, trial, and captivity. He became a test pilot for Lockheed and later piloted light aircraft and helicopters for radio and television stations. He died in a helicopter crash on 1 August 1977.

PURCELL, Edward M.

A physicist who won a Nobel prize in 1954 for his work in nuclear resonance, Purcell served on a number of advisory bodies, including the USAF Scientific Advisory Committee and Edwin Land's Technological Capabilities Panel study group. It was Purcell's ideas for reducing the radar cross section of the U-2 that led to the OXCART program. Purcell also contributed to the satellite programs.

RABORN, William F., Jr.

DCI from 1965 to 1966, Raborn pushed for the deployment of OXCART to the Far East but failed to sway the top officials of the Johnson administration.

REBER, James Q.

After serving as the Assistant Director for Intelligence Coordination in the early 1950s, Reber became the chairman of the Ad Hoc Requirements Committee in 1955 and continued to chair this committee after it was taken over by the US Intelligence Board in 1960 and renamed the Committee on Overhead Requirements. In 1969 he became the chairman of the USIB's SIGINT Committee.

RODGERS, Franklin A.

Formerly of MIT, Rodgers was the chief engineer at the Scientific Engineering Institute who converted the theories of Edward Purcell into practical systems to reduce the radar image of the U-2 and especially the OXCART.

SCHLESINGER, James R.

DCI from February to July 1973, Schlesinger supported the Nixon administration's proposal to terminate the Agency's U-2 program.

SCOTT, Roderic M.

An engineer with Perkin-Elmer who worked with James Baker in designing the first cameras for use in the U-2, Scott helped design the 30001 camera for the OXCART.

SCOVILLE, Herbert, Jr.

In February 1962 Scoville became the first Deputy Director for Research, which took over control of the Agency's reconnaissance programs from the Deputy Director for Plans. Frustrated by the lack of support from the DCI and the other directorates, he resigned in June 1963.

SEABERG, John

An aeronautical engineer who was recalled to active duty with the Air Force during the Korean war, Seaberg drafted the first specifications for a high-flying jet reconnaissance aircraft in 1953.

STEVER, H. Guyford

A professor of aeronautical engineering at MIT, Stever served on numerous Air Force advisory panels and later became the Air Force's chief scientist.

STRONG, Philip G.

Chief of collection in the Office of Scientific Intelligence, Strong kept himself well informed on developments in overhead reconnaissance and attended many Air Force advisory panel meetings as an observer. In 1954 he learned about the Lockheed CL-282 design and passed the information on to Edwin Land's study group investigating US intelligence-gathering capabilities.

WHEELON, Albert ("Bud") D.

Wheelon became the Deputy Director for Science and Technology in August 1963 following the reorganization and renaming of the Deputy Director for Research. He held this position until September 1966.

APPENDIX C

ELECTRONIC DEVICES CARRIED BY THE U-2

From the beginning the U-2 was envisioned as more than a camera platform. In fact, the U-2 would ultimately carry only five types of photographic equipment but more than 20 different types of electronic devices, some for collecting electronic intelligence (ELINT), others ("ferret" equipment) for gathering intelligence on foreign radars, and a few for self-protection—electronic countermeasures to defeat enemy missile-control radars.

The various electronic, countermeasures and intelligence-gathering systems designed for the U-2 received designations using Roman numerals—Systems I through XXII. The first seven devices were built by the Ramo-Wooldridge firm, now part of the TRW Corporation. System-I used S- and X-band ELINT receivers to collect ground-controlled intercept and air defense signals. Weighing only 7.7 kilograms, this system was aboard all U-2s from 1955 through 1959. System-II, a communications and navigation system, never worked properly and was canceled. System-III, a 16-kilogram VHF recorder for communications intelligence (COMINT), was never used and was transferred to the Navy in 1958. System-IV, a ferret device that recorded electromagnetic energy in the 150- to 4,000-MHz range was used on 16 missions between 1957 and 1959, when it was given to the Air Force. System-V was similar to System-I but covered nine wave bands. The device was so heavy that U-2s using it could not carry a camera system. System-V was used on only three missions and was replaced by the lighter weight System-VI that covered the P-, L-, S-. and X-band frequencies and could be used with either the A or B camera. System VI was used from 1959 through 1966.

The growing need for data on Soviet missile development led to a contract with the firm of Haller-Raymond-Brown (HRB) to build a missile-telemetry intercept system as quickly as possible. The resulting device (System-VII) could record up to 12 minutes of data from six simultaneous frequencies. This unit first saw service on 9 June 1959 and was used on another 22 missions during the next year. Following modifications to make System-VII suitable for use by the Navy, the designation was changed to System-VIII.

System-IX was an electronic-countermeasures (ECM) device for generating false-angle information in response to X-band radar pulses from surface-to-air missile radars. Also known as the Mark-30, the unit was manufactured by the Granger Company. One of these devices was aboard Gary Powers' U-2 when he was shot down.

System-X was a modification of the HRB's System-VII that was specially built in 1962 for a mission over the Soviet Union that never took place. Systems-XI through XV were ECM devices used by U-2s overflying China and North Vietnam during the Vietnam war. System-XVI was a passive ELINT collector.

System-XVII was built by HRB-Singer as a result of an October 1963 USIB requirement for the collection of antiballistic-missile (ABM) data from Saryshagan. The system was to be deployed in a U-2 that would fly over western China, along the Sino-Soviet border, collecting data on the ABMs being tested at Saryshagan. By the time the unit was completed in 1965, however, the tipoff time before test launches had been reduced from almost 24 hours to less than an hour, making it impossible to stage U-2 missions in time to collect the data.

In the late 1960s, additional ECM systems were needed to counter the increasing threats posed by more accurate SAMs and higher flying aircraft. System-XX was specifically designed to counter the acquisition and guidance radars used by MIG aircraft, and System-XXII was an infrared jammer to counter air-to-air missiles. System-XXI, a COMINT package that replaced the much older System-III, was originally developed for the OXCART program and was later adapted for use aboard the follow-on U-2, the U-2R.

APPENDIX D

U-2 Overflights of the Soviet Union,
4 July 1954-1 May 1960

Date	Mission	Pilot	Airfield	Unit	Payload	Route
4 July 1956	2013	Stockman	Wiesbaden	A	A-2	East Germany, Poland, Minsk, Leningrad, Estonia, Latvia, Poland
5 July 1956	2014	Vito	Wiesbaden	A	A-2	East Germany, Warsaw, Minsk, Moscow, Estonia, Latvia, Lithuania, Poland
9 July 1956	2020	Knutson	Wiesbaden	A	A-2	East Germany, Poland, Minsk, Poland
9 July 1956	2021	Overstreet	Wiesbaden	A	A-2	Czechoslovakia, Vienna, Hungary, L'vov, Kiev, Minsk, Poland
10 July 1956	2024	Dunaway	Wiesbaden	A	A-2	Poland, Kishinev, Kerch', Sevastopol', Simferopol', Odessa, Romania, Hungary
20 November 1956	4016	Powers	Adana	B	A-2	Iran, Yerevan, Baku, Astara, Caucasus
18 March 1957	4020	Cherbonneaux	Adana	B	Sys-V	Soviet border to Afghanistan, Azerbaijan, Armenia, Georgia
20 June 1957	6005	Rand	Eielson	C	B	Khaylyulya, Ust'-Kamchatsk, Kozyrevsk, Karaganskiy-Ostrov
5 August 1957	4035	Edens	Lahore	B	B	Afghanistan, Tashkent, Tyuratam, Kazalinsk, Aral Sea
11 August 1957	4039	McMurray	Lahore	B	B	Alma-Ata, Ust'-Kamenogorsk, Sinkiang
21 August 1957	4045	Snider	Lahore	B	A-2	Novokuznetsk, Tomsk
21 August 1957	4048	Jones	Lahore	B	A-2	Lake Balkhash, Karaganda, Omsk, Alma-Ata

U-2 Overflights of the Soviet Union, 4 July 1954-1 May 1960 (continued)

Date	Mission	Pilot	Airfield	Unit	Payload	Route
22 August 1957	4049	Birkhead	Lahore	B	A-2	Merket Bazar, Kuldja, Abakan, Krasnoyarsk, Kansk, Sinkiang
22 August 1957	4050	Cherbonneaux	Lahore	B	A-2	Lake Balkhash, Semipalatinsk, Barnaul, Prokop'yevsk, Novokuznetsk, Leninogorsk
28 August 1957	4058	Jones	Lahore	B	A-2	Dushanbe, Tashkent, Tyuratam, Kazalinsk, Aral Sea
10 September 1957	4059	Hall	Adana	B	A-2	Krasnovodsk, Gur'yev, Astrakhan', Tbilisi
16 September 1957	6008	Baker	Eielson	C	A-2	Kamchatka Peninsula, Milkovo
13 October 1957	2040	Stockman	Giebelstadt	A	A-2	Norway, Finland, Murmansk, Kandalaksha
1 March 1958	6011	Crull	Atsugi	C	A-2	Dal'nerechensk, Khabarovsk, Blagoveshchensk, Belagorsk, Komsomolsk, Sovetskaya Gavan'
9 July 1959	4125	Knutson	Peshawar	B	B	Tyuratam for suspected Sputnik launch
6 December 1959	8005	Robinson[a]	Peshawar	B	B	Kuybyshev, Kapustin Yar, Caucasus
5 February 1960	8009	MacArthur[a]	Peshawar	B	B	Tyuratam, Kazan
9 April 1960	4155	Erickson	Peshawar	B	B	Lake Balkhash, Semipalatinsk, Kyzylespe, Dzhezhkazgan, Tyuratam
1 May 1960	4154	Powers	Peshawar	B	B	Tyuratam, Kyshtym, Sverdlovsk; downed by SAM

[a]RAF pilot

APPENDIX E

Unmanned Reconnaissance Projects
AQUILINE

In the early 1960s, there were many problems in obtaining coverage of hostile territory. The U-2 was too vulnerable to Soviet surface-to-air missiles, as had been demonstrated by losses over the Soviet Union, Cuba, and the People's Republic of China. The OXCART was still under development and even when completed might prove vulnerable to Soviet radars and missiles. Although safe from interception, the newly developed photosatellites could not provide coverage of a desired target on short notice. Because several of the intelligence community's primary targets such as Cuba and the new Soviet radar installation at Tallinn (Estonia) were not located deep in hostile territory, CIA scientists and engineers began to consider the possibility of using small, unmanned aircraft for aerial reconnaissance. They believed that recent advances in the miniaturization of electronic technology would make possible the development of a reconnaissance vehicle with a very-low-radar cross section and small visual and acoustical signatures. Such a vehicle could reconnoiter an area of interest without the hostile country realizing that it had been overflown.

In mid-1965, David L. Christ, chief of the Office of Research and Development's Applied Physics Division, and Frank Briglia of the same office began working on the concept of a small, inexpensive aircraft that would be about the size of a large bird and could carry various payloads for photography, nuclear sensing, and ELINT collection. ORD soon formed a Special Projects Group to develop the aircraft with Briglia as the project manager. Only one firm—the Douglas Aircraft Company—responded favorably to a request for proposal to study the feasibility of a low-altitude reconnaissance system. On 15 November 1965, Douglas received a study contract. This was followed by two Agency contracts on 21 November 1966 for the development of an operational low-altitude intelligence-gathering system. Further contracts followed in 1968 and 1969.

The AQUILINE prototype developed by Douglas Aircraft (which became part of McDonnell-Douglas in 1969 as the result of a merger) was essentially a powered glider with an 8.5-foot wingspan. The aircraft weighed only 105 pounds. AQUILINE's tail-mounted engine drove a two-bladed propeller. Powered by a small 3.5-horse-power two-cycle engine originally developed by the McCullough Corporation for chainsaws, [redacted].

In 1968 tests on an AQUILINE prototype at Randsburg Wash on the US Navy's Naval Ordnance Test Station at China Lake, California, showed that the aircraft was extremely difficult to see. To assist pilots of chase aircraft in keeping AQUILINE in sight, its entire upper surface was painted bright orange; even so, sighting remained difficult.

The testing process was very hard on AQUILINE because it was recovered by flying it into a net close to the ground, which almost always caused some damage to the wings or propeller. As a result, one or more of the aircraft was always being repaired, and eventually three of the five AQUILINE prototypes were destroyed in testing. [Redacted].

At this point the project was turned over to the Office of Special Activities for operational testing [redacted]. Flight tests showed the aircraft to be successful by the standards originally set for the project in 1967, as it flew 130 miles and obtained very high resolution photography of a target before returning successfully to the original launchsite. However, improving AQUILINE sufficiently to make it a practical long-range reconnaissance system was estimated to cost another $35 million and take two to three years. On the recommendation of DDS&T Carl Duckett on 1 November 1971, Project AQUILINE was canceled. [Redacted].

AXILLARY

While Project AQUILINE was still under development, its chief aerodynamicist, Charles N. Adkins, left the program because he believed that its escalating costs would prevent it from ever producing a deployable aircraft. He wanted to build a small, inexpensive remote-controlled aircraft to test a low-cost lightweight autopilot currently being developed by ORD. Under a $5,000 time-and-materials contract with Melpar, Incorporated, Adkins hired a local model aircraft builder to assemble and modify a standard Hawk-750 glider kit and power it with a rear-mounted engine and pusher propeller. Following a series of successful test flights, Adkins installed a small camera and took a number of aerial photographs.

By this time the effort to build a "Miniature Multi-Purpose Airborne Vehicle" had become known as Project AXILLARY. Melpar, Inc., received a second contract for $50,000 to install ORD's autopilot in the aircraft, and the project managers now began searching for a use for their vehicle. The two main possibilites were (1) as a short-range reconnaissance vehicle for use in a peace-monitoring or intelligence-gathering system and (2) as a short-range warhead delivery system. In 1971 the Office of Special Activities evaluated AXILLARY flight-testing and determined that the small model aircraft was not suitable for use as a covert reconnaissance vehicle because of its large radar cross section and significant accoustical signature. The aircraft's radar signature made it potentially useful as a weapons systems, however. ORD suggested that AXILLARY be equipped with a radar-homing unit [redacted] which would make it an inexpensive means for [redacted] surface-to-air missile systems in North Vietnam. The Director of Defense Research and Engineering, John Foster, liked the concept and provided DOD funding for ORD to develop two versions of AXILLARY, one with a radar-homer and one with a television reconnaissance package. The radar homing system proved successful as AXILLARY sought out and destroyed a radar during testing at China Lake Naval Air Station. However, the end of US involvement in Vietnam in early 1973 led to the cancellation of further DOD funding, and AXILLARY was placed on the shelf. [Redacted].

BIBLIOGRAPHY

Published Works Cited

Aart, Dick van der. *Aerial Espionage, Secret Intelligence Flights by East and West*. Shrewsbury, England: Airlife Publishing, 1985.

"AF Cites Red Bomber Progress." *Aviation Week,* 24 May 1954, p. 14.

"Alleged Overflight of Soviet Area by American Planes." *US Department of State Bulletin,* vol. 36, 28 January 1957, p. 135.

"Alleged Violations of Soviet Territory: Soviet Note of July 10, 1956 with U.S. Reply." *US Department of State Bulletin,* 30 July 1956, pp. 191-192.

Alsop, Stewart. *The Center.* New York: Popular Library, 1968.

Ambrose, Stephen E. *Eisenhower.* Vol. 2, *The President.* New York: Simon and Schuster, 1984.

Andrew, Christopher. *Her Majesty's Secret Service: The Making of the British Intelligence Community.* New York: Viking, 1986.

"Aviation Week Story Spurs Debate on US, Red Airpower Positions." *Aviation Week,* 30 May 1955, pp. 13-14.

Beschloss, Michael R. *Mayday: Eisenhower, Khrushchev and the U-2 Affair.* New York: Harper & Row, 1986.

Brown, William H. "J58/SR-71 Propulsion Integration." *Studies in Intelligence* 26 (Summer 1982): pp. 17-18 (Unclassified).

Brugioni, Dino. *The Cuban Missile Crisis-Phase I, 29 August-16 October 1962.* DDS&T Historical Series, NPIC-1 (CIA: NPIC, 1971) (Secret).

Burrows, William E. *Deep Black: Space Espionage and National Security.* New York: Random House, 1987.

"Can Soviets Take the Air Lead? What LeMay, Wilson, lke Say." *US News and World Report,* 11 May 1956, pp. 108-114.

Chronology of the Office of Special Activities, 1954-1968. (CIA: DS&T, 1969) (Top Secret Codeword).

Coughlin, William. "Gardner Defends Greater R&D Spending." *Aviation Week,* 26 September 1955, p. 14.

Eastman, Ford. "Defense Officials Concede Missile Lag." *Aviation Week 9* February 1959, pp. 26-27.

Edwards, Philip K. "The President's Board: 1956-60." *Studies in Intelligence* 13 (Summer 1969): p. 118 (Secret).

Eisenhower, Dwight D. *Waging Peace, 1956-1961.* Garden City, NY: Doubleday, 1965.

Freedman, Lawrence. *US Intelligence and the Soviet Strategic Threat.* 2nd ed. Princeton: Princeton University Press, 1986.

George, A. L. *Case Studies of Actual and Alleged Overflights, 1930-1953.* Rand Study RM-1349. Santa Monica: Rand, 1955 (Secret).

[Redacted]. *The Defector Reception Center Germany, 1951 to 1967.* Clandestine Service Historical Series CSHP-41. CIA: History Staff, 1972 (Secret).

Hotz, Robert. "Firing of 900-Mile Russian Missile Spurs US Changes." *Aviation Week,* 20 February 1956, pp. 26-28.

_____. "Russian Air Force Now Gaining in Quality." *Aviation Week,* 12 March 1956, pp. 286-291.

_____. "Russian Jet Airpower Gains Fast on US." *Aviation Week,* 23 May 1955, pp. 12-15.

"Is Russia Ahead in Missile Race?" *US News and World Report,* 6 September 1957, pp. 30-33.

"Is Russia Really Ahead in Missile Race?" *US News and World Report,* 4 May 1956, pp. 34-35.

"Is Russia Winning the Arms Race?" *US News and World Report,* 18 June 1954, pp. 28-29.

"Is US Really Losing in the Air?" *US News and World Report,* 18 May 1956, pp. 25-27.

Johnson, Clarence L. "Development of the Lockheed SR-7I Blackbird." *Studies in Intelligence* 26 (Summer 1982): p. 4 (Unclassified).

Johnson, Clarence L. with Maggie Smith. *Kelly: More Than My Share of It All.* Washington, DC: Smithsonian Institute Press, 1985.

Khrushchev, Nikita S. *Khrushchev Remembers: The Last Testament.* Boston: Little, Brown, & Co., 1974.

Killian, James R., Jr. *Sputnik, Scientists, and Eisenhower: A Memoir of the First Special Assistant to the President for Science and Technology,* Cambridge: MIT Press, 1977.

Kistiakowsky, George B. *A Scientist at the White House.* Cambridge: Harvard University Press, 1976.

Kleyla, Helen H., and Robert D. O'Hern. *History of the Office of Special Activities, DS&T.* 16 vols. Directorate of Science and Technology Historical Series OSA-l. CIA: DS&T, 1969 (Top Secret Codeword).

Lay, James S. "The United States Intelligence Board, 1958-1965." CIA History Staff MS-2 (draft), 1974 (Top Secret Codeword).

Licklider, Roy E. "The Missile Gap Controversy." *Political Science Quarterly* 85 (1970): pp. 600-615.

[Redacted]. *The National Photographic Interpretation Center.* Vol. 1, *Antecedents and Early Years.* Directorate of Science and Technology Historical Series NPIC-2. CIA: NPIC, 1972 (Secret).

_____. *National Photographic Interpretation Center: The Years of Project HTAUTOMAT, 1956-1958.* 6 vols. Directorate of Science and Technology Historical Series NPIC-3. CIA: NPIC, 1974 (Secret).

Miller, Jay. *Lockheed U-2.* Aerograph 3. Austin, Texas: Aerofax, 1983.

[Redacted]. "The OXCART Story." *Studies in Intelligence* 15 (Winter 1971): pp. 1-34 (Secret).

"Missiles Away." *Time,* 30 January 1956, pp. 52-55.

"Mystery of the RB-47." *Newsweek,* 25 July 1960, pp. 36-37.

"Nikita and the RB-47." *Time.* 25 July 1960, pp. 30-31.

"Office of Special Activities History, April 1969 to Phase-Out." (draft) (CIA: DS&T, 1974), chap. 3. pp. 36-42 (Top Secret Codeword).

Pero, Richard K. "Message Received—Unfortunately." *Studies in Intelligence 27* (Winter 1983): p. 29 (Secret).

Pocock, Chris. *Dragon Lady: The History of the U-2 Spyplane.* Shrewsbury, England: Airlife, 1989.

Powers, Francis Gary, with Curt Gentry. *Operation Overflight.* New York: Holt, Rinehart and Wilson, 1970.

Powers, Thomas. *The Man Who Kept the Secrets: Richard Helms and the CIA.* New York: Alfred A. Knopf, 1979.

Prados, John. *Presidents' Secret Wars: CIA and Pentagon Covert Operations Since World War II.* New York: William Morrow, 1986.

_____. *The Soviet Estimate: U.S. Intelligence Analysis and Russian Military Strength.* New York: Dial Press, 1982.

[Redacted]. *Covert Support to Indonesian Revolutionary Government, 1957-1958.* 2 vols. Clandestine Service Historical Series, CSHP-53. CIA: History Staff, 1970 (Secret).

"Red Air Force: The World's Biggest." *Newsweek,* 23 August 1954, pp. 28-33.

Richelson, Jeffrey. *American Espionage and the Soviet Target.* New York: William Morrow, 1987.

"Russia Parades Airpower as 'Big Stick'." *Aviation Week,* 28 June 1954, p. 15.

[Redacted]. *Low-Level Technical Reconnaissance over Mainland China (1955-66).* Clandestine Services Historical Program, CSHP-2.348. CIA: History Staff, 1972 (Secret).

Stanley, Roy M., II. *World War II Photo Intelligence.* New York: Scribners, 1981.

Sturm, Thomas A. *The USAF Scientific Advisory Board: Its First Twenty Years, 1944-1964.* Washington, DC: USAF Historical Office, 1967.

Twining, Nathan F. *Neither Liberty nor Safety.* New York: Holt, Rinehart & Winston, 1966.

United States Air Force. Project LINCOLN. *BEACON HILL Report: Problems of Air Force Intelligence and Reconnaissance.* Massachusetts Institute of Technology, 15 June 1952 (Secret, downgraded to Confidential).

United States Congress. Senate. Foreign Relations Committee. *Executive Sessions of the Senate Foreign Relations Committee (Historical Series),* vol. 12, 86th Congress, 2nd Session, "Report on the U-2 Incident" 6 March 1962 (declassified 1982).

United States Congress. Senate. Select Committee to Study Governmental Operations with Respect to Intelligence Activities. *Foreign and Military Intelligence.* Book 1. Washington, DC: US Government Printing Office, 1976.

United States Office of Defense Mobilization. Science Advisory Committee. Technological Capabilities Panel. *Meeting the Threat of Surprise Attack,* 14 February 1955. (Top Secret/Restricted Data, downgraded to Secret).

"US Representations to the Soviet Government on C-130 Transport Shot Down by Soviet Fighter Aircraft." *US Department of State Bulletin,* 23 February 1959, pp. 262-271.

Weber, Karl H. *The Office of Scientific Intelligence, 1949-68.* Directorate of Science and Technology Historical Series OSI-1. CIA: DS&T, 1972 (Top Secret Codeword).

Welzenbach, Donald E. "Observation Balloons and Weather Satellites." *Studies in Intelligence* 30 (Spring 1986): pp. 21-28 (Secret).

White, James J. "Francis Gary Powers—The Unmaking of a Hero, 1960-1965." (draft) CIA: History Staff, 1974 (Secret).

Wise, David and Thomas B. Ross. *The U-2 Affair.* New York: Random House, 1962.

Witze, Claude. "Russians Outpacing US in Air Quality, Twining Warns Congress." *Aviation Week,* 27 February 1956, pp. 26-28.

"Yakovlev Yak-25RM Mandrake," *Jane's Defence Weekly,* vol. 3, no. 7, 16 February 85.

Interviews and Speeches

Interview with Robert Amory, Jr., by Donald E. Welzenbach and Gregory W. Pedlow, Washington, DC, 22 April 1987 (Secret).

Interview with James G. Baker by Donald E. Welzenbach, Washington, DC, 24 April 1985 (Secret).

Speech given by Richard Bissell at CIA Headquarters, 12 October 1965 (Top Secret Codeword).

Interview with Joseph V. Charyk by Donald E. Welzenbach. Washington, DC, 5 December 1984 (Top Secret Codeword).

Interview with former U-2 pilots James Cherbonneaux, Carmine Vito, and Hervey Stockman, by Donald E. Welzenbach, Washington, DC, May 1986 (Secret).

Interview with James A. Cunningham, Jr., by Donald E. Welzenbach, Washington, DC, 4 October 1983 (Top Secret Codeword).

Interview with Allen F. Donovan by Donald E. Welzenbach, Corona del Mar, California, 20 May 1985 (Secret).

Interview with Brig. Gen. Leo A. Geary, USAF (Ret.), by Donald E. Welzenbach, 3 April 1986 (Secret).

Interview with Gen. Andrew J. Goodpaster by Donald E. Welzenbach and Gregory W. Pedlow, Washington, DC, 8 July 1987 (Secret).

Speech by Maj. Gen. Patrick J. Halloran (former Air Force U-2 pilot) at the National Air & Space Museum, 24 April 1986 (Unclassified).

Interview with James R. Killian, Jr. by Donald E. Welzenbach, Cambridge, Massachusetts, 2 November 1984 (Secret).

Interview with Edwin H. Land by Donald E. Welzenbach, Cambridge, Massachusetts, 17 and 20 September 1984 (Top Secret Codeword).

Interview with Brig. Gen. Jack C. Ledford, USAF (Ret.), by Gregory W. Pedlow, Washington, DC, 20 February 1987 (Secret).

Interview with Richard S. Leghorn by Donald E. Welzenbach, Washington, DC, 19 August 1985 (Secret).

Interview with Arthur S. Lundahl and Dino Brugioni by Donald E. Welzenbach, Washington, DC, 14 December 1983 (Top Secret Codeword) .

Interview with Garrison Norton by Donald E. Welzenbach, Washington, DC, 23 May 1983 (Secret).

Interview with John Parangosky by Donald E. Welzenbach, 6 March 1986 (Secret).

Interview with James Q. Reber by Donald E. Welzenbach and Gregory W. Pedlow, Washington, DC, 21 May 1987 (Secret).

Interview with Carmine Vito by Donald E. Welzenbach, Washington, DC, 7 May 1986 (Secret).

Interview with John S. Warner, Office of the General Counsel, by Donald E. Welzenbach, Washington, DC, 5 August 1983 (Top Secret Codeword).

INDEX

A

A-1 camera 58–59
A-2 aircraft 272–273
A-2 camera 59, 84, 108, 112, 113
A-3 aircraft 273
A-11 278, 304
A-12 282, 284, 285–287, 288, 290, 292, 294, 295, 296, 297, 299, 300, 301, 302, 304, 305, 306, 308, 309, 311, 314, 315, 316–320, 321, 322, 323, 324, 325
Abel, Rudolf 191–192, 345
Ad Hoc Requirements Committee (ARC) 88, 89, 123, 198, 346
Adana, Turkey 122
Adkins, Charles N. 353
Administration (East) Building 50
advanced antiballistic-missile (ABM) 147
aerial cameras 16, 38, 56, 57, 342
aerial lenses 340
aerial photography 3, 15, 40, 56, 103, 127
aerial tankers 326
aerodynamic lift 258, 286
aerodynamic structural tests 284
aerodynamicist 353
Aerospace Corporation 341
Afghanistan 135, 175, 177, 183, 199
afterburner plume 282
ailerons 55, 75
Air Research and Development Command 7, 9
Air Staff for intelligence 160
Air Weather Service 96, 100

air-inlet system 300
air-to-air missiles 295, 349
air-traffic controllers 79
Air/Maritime Division (AMD) 80
aircraft carrier 151, 257–260
airfields 24, 90, 101, 103, 112, 126, 127, 143, 158, 174, 179, 211, 226, 229, 233, 238, 240, 260, 331
airframe 7, 10, 12, 29, 31, 47, 52, 56, 62, 67, 77, 78, 113, 141, 258, 269, 285, 286, 289, 296, 298
airframe contractors 269
airspace 4, 5, 23, 136, 143, 149–153, 157, 158, 190, 243, 315, 318, 332, 337
airspeed 74, 83, 210, 248, 306
Alaska 141, 143, 151, 329
Albania 148, 162
Albuquerque, New Mexico 82, 85
Allen, Edward L. 25
Almaza Airbase, Egypt 126
altimeters 66
altitude 1–20, 22, 23, 27–31, 39, 41, 43, 46, 54–62, 66, 68–73, 77–79, 81, 83, 86, 87, 92, 94–96, 99–101, 104, 109, 116, 133, 140, 151, 154–157, 162, 175, 182, 183, 185–187, 193, 219, 230, 232, 240, 248, 252, 256, 261, 263, 264, 268–270, 272, 273, 277, 278, 287–289, 294, 297, 298, 302, 304, 306–308, 316, 325, 327, 335, 343, 352
aluminum 282
Ambon Island 227

American Civil War 1
Amory, Robert 123
Anderson, Rudolph 222
Andoya, Norway 178
"Angel" 53, 58, 272
Anglo-French bombing campaign 126
Anglo-Soviet relations 101
antiaircraft missile 175
antiaircraft weapons 99, 154
antiballistic missile system 309, 315
antiradar studies 277, 284
Apollo VII 264
Applied Physics Division 352
AQUATONE 47, 49–53, 65, 70, 73,
    81, 84, 90, 95–96, 99, 102, 107,
    116, 122, 124, 130, 142, 160
AQUILINE 316, 352–353
Arabs 265
Aral Sea 144
Arbenz, Jacobo 19
"Archangel-1" 272
"Archangel-2" 272
Area 51 63, 78, 80, 82, 84, 85, 140,
    142, 285, 293, 294, 296, 301,
    315, 317
Arizona 87
Arkansas 85
arms limitation negotiations 153
arms race 332
Army Air Corps 26, 63
Army Air Force 5, 57, 341, 344
article 121 296, 298
article 126 306
article 133 306
article 341 73, 77, 140, 141
article 345A 87
article 346 87
article 347 109
article 349 231
article 354 87
article 357 87

article 360 182, 230
article number 66
articles 25, 66, 106, 229
Ashford, Douglas E. 36
Asia 144, 200, 210, 223–230, 232,
    233, 242, 245–250, 312, 313,
    323, 333
Asian Photographic Interpretation 240
aspheric lens 60
ASPIC (Asian Photographic
    Interpretation Center) 240
Aswan Dam 121
atmosphere 31, 157, 190, 228, 288
atmospheric testing 153
atomic bomb 24
Atomic Energy Commission (AEC)
    63, 142, 191, 285
atomic energy facilities 246
ATR (Air Transport Rating) 195
Atsugi, Japan 142, 227, 230
Autopilot 83, 353
Aviation Week 229
AXILLARY 353–354
Ayer, Frederick, Jr. 16–18, 43, 340

B
B-model camera 208, 259
B-17 bomber 234
B-26 bomber 226
B-36 bomber 13, 27, 57
B-47 bomber 70
B-52 bomber 25, 47, 120, 301
B-57 bomber 7–11, 16, 18, 29, 43, 79
B-58 bomber 270, 273, 279
B-58 "Hustler" bomber 270
B-58A bomber 279
B-58B "Super Hustler" 270, 279
B-58B bomber 273, 279, 280
B-70 bomber 289, 303
BACKFIN 173
"badlands" 77

Baikal, Lake 137
Baird, Walter 62
Baird Associates 62
Baker, James G. 21, 26, 28–30,
    35–38, 54, 57–62, 116, 262, 291,
    340, 345, 346
Balkhash, Lake 146
ballistic missiles 2, 146, 149, 164,
    211, 217, 251
Baltic Sea 4
Baltic states 112
Baltimore, Maryland 7, 10
Barents Sea 148, 179
barrel rolls 83
Batlin, Alex 72, 73
Bay of Bengal 243
Bay of Pigs 201, 208–210, 216
Baykonur, Soviet Union 144, 146
Beacon Hill 21–23, 25, 29
BEACON HILL Report 21–23, 25, 29
BEACON HILL Study Group 21,
    22, 25
Beechcraft 63, 195
Beerli, Stanley W. 202
Beijing, China (*See* Peiping, China)
Bell Aircraft Corporation 10
Bell Laboratories 22
Bell Telephone Laboratories 35
"bends" 71
Bennington, Herbert 321
Benton, William 310
Berezovskiy, Soviet Union 146
Berlin, Germany 19, 24, 137, 153,
    154, 167, 192, 206
Berlin crisis 154, 206
BGMARQUE 234
BIRDWATCHER 248
Bison bomber 25, 32, 38, 105, 112, 120
Bissell, Richard M., Jr. 18–19, 36,
    46, 47, 49, 50, 52, 62, 63, 65,
    68, 72, 75, 76, 81, 85, 88, 90,
    96, 97, 99, 101, 102, 107, 108,
    109, 112, 113, 117, 119, 128,
    130, 132, 136, 137, 138, 147,
    154, 159, 160, 161, 162, 163,
    168, 175, 177, 179, 186, 187,
    196, 201, 202, 226, 229, 236,
    268, 269, 270, 272, 273, 277,
    287, 288, 293, 295, 297, 298,
    305, 340–345
Bissell's Narrow-Gauge Airline 78
"black books" 197
"black" contracts 295
BLACK KNIGHT 135, 142
Black Sea 92, 135, 141, 150, 158
BLACK SHIELD 312, 316–320
Blip/Scan Ratio 277, 278
BLUE BOOK 78–80
Board of Inquiry 192
Boeing RB-47 3
Boeing KC-135 78
bomb damage 56
bomber 2, 3, 4, 6, 7, 13, 15, 24, 25,
    27, 28, 32, 38, 57, 70, 73, 89,
    105, 106, 112, 113, 117–121,
    134, 148, 173, 227, 270, 273,
    279, 280, 289, 295, 301, 303,
    311, 315, 329, 330, 332
Bomber Gap 38, 119–121, 330
borax 129
Boston, Massachusetts 15, 21, 26,
    29, 32, 59, 62, 119, 270
Boston camera 15
Boston University 26, 29, 59
Bowles, Chester 237
Brahmaputra Valley 243
bridges 90
Briggs School 50
Briglia, Frank 352
British and French fleets 125
British Guiana 223
British Guiana-Venezuela border 223

British overflight of the Soviet Union
  27–28, 170
British Parliament 101
British radar network 101
Brugioni, Dino 144
Budapest, Hungary 131
Budget, Bureau of the 277, 321, 322
Budget, Director of the 47
Buffalo, New York 10, 70
Bulganin, Nikolai 101, 127
Bulgaria 109, 133, 134, 148
Bundy, McGeorge 197, 212, 221,
  250, 303
BUORL 26
Burbank, California 53
Burke, William 175, 177, 179–180

C
C model camera 61
C-124 cargo planes 73, 144, 189,
  190, 231
Cabell, Charles P. 36, 37, 43, 44,
  50, 95, 109, 130, 131, 137, 147,
  192, 235, 340, 342
Cairo, Egypt 126, 127
Calcutta, India 244
California 11, 16, 29, 44, 53, 57, 61,
  62, 142, 191, 209, 210, 219,
  232, 233, 258, 260, 262,
  264–266, 305, 353
California Institute of Technology 32
Cambodia 229, 242, 253
camera lenses 99
camera technicians 85
camera-carrying balloons 17, 22, 27,
  91, 151
cameras 1, 3, 6, 13, 15, 16, 17, 22,
  25, 26, 27, 34, 36–39, 52, 55,
  56–62, 67, 84, 85, 91–94, 99,
  108, 112, 113, 116, 117, 135,
  143, 144, 151, 164, 169, 174,

182, 185–187, 207, 230, 255,
  257, 259, 262, 266, 290–292,
  307, 310, 315, 316, 318,
  322–325, 327, 335, 340, 342,
  343, 345, 346, 348, 353
Canberra 6, 7, 10, 28, 29, 74, 118, 168
Cannon, Clarence 96
Capp, Al 53
cardiovascular system 69
Carey, Howard 87, 148
Carter, John H. (Jack) 11, 12
Carter, Marshall S. 194, 212, 220,
  310, 341
Caspian Sea 135
catheterized 71
cathode-ray tube 278
Caucasus Mountains 188
celestial "fixes" 84
Central Asia 144
Central Asian republics 184
Central Intelligence Agency (CIA)
  16–20, 40–43
  Air Force competition 320
  air operations 163, 201
  General Counsel 52
  Inspector General 200
  proprietary 139, 226
  proprietary firm 119, 139, 234, 269
  U-2 program 189, 267
centrifugal force 184
CHALICE 160, 191
Chamoun, Camille 157
Chance Vought Corporation 9
Charbatia, India 244, 245, 250
Charyk, Joseph V. 270
Chekiang Province 238
Chelyabinsk, Soviet Union 183
Cherbonneaux, James 136, 146,
  226, 227
Chicago Daily Tribune 140
"chimney" 77

China 7, 92, 155, 163, 180, 200, 227, 228–233, 238, 240–242, 244–255, 257, 259, 312, 313, 320, 349, 353, 354
China Lake 353, 354
chine 286
Chinese Communist nuclear tests 251
Chinese mainland 228, 234, 237, 333
Chinese nuclear test 250
Christ, David L. 352
Christian Science Monitor 21–22
Civil Air Transport 226, 234
civilian supersonic transport (SST) 303
CL-282 Project 12–20, 29–31, 34–39, 40–45, 73, 340–344, 347
CL-400 aircraft 272
clandestine operations 19, 336
Clandestine Services 202
Clark Airfield, Philippines 226
Clifford, Clark 324
"coffin corner" 83
Cold War 21
collection requirements 88–90, 198, 263, 311
Columbia Broadcasting System 22
combat aircraft 7, 31
Combined Shipping Adjustment Board 19
Commerce, Department of 264
commercial airliners 78
communications intelligence (COMINT) 198, 324, 348, 349
Communications Satellite Corporation 341
COMPASS TRIP 264
competitive bidding 51, 52
compressor vanes 301
computer-controlled radar 304
computers 59
Congress, United States 51, 95–96, 105, 120, 164, 165, 177, 303, 323, 329, 330, 332

constant-velocity film transport 291
Constellation airliner 12, 343
Contingency Reserve fund 47, 52
contractors 50, 51, 65, 78, 269, 292, 295, 298
contrails 156
Convair 270, 273, 277–284, 294, 325
Convair F-106 294
convective clouds 100
Cornell Aeronautical Laboratory 22, 29, 30, 341
Corning Glass Works 291–292
cosmic-ray effects 100
cover officer 97
covert activities 47, 341
Covert Action Staff (CAS) 226
Crabb, Lionel 101
Crick, Alan 159
Crick Committee 159
Crimean Peninsula 116
Cuba 197, 208–212, 216–219, 221–223, 309–311, 313, 323, 341, 352
Cuban air and ground order of battle 209
Cuban Missile Crisis 61, 210–223, 309, 341
Cubi Point Naval Air Station, Philippines 226, 229, 233
Culbertson, Allman T. 73
Cunningham, James A., Jr. 49, 72, 75, 78, 85, 86, 134, 257, 298, 299, 341, 342
Current Intelligence, Office of 89
Curtiss-Wright Corporation 341
Czechoslovakia 109

D
D-21 aircraft 301
Dalai Lama 229
Dallas, Texas 303
Damage Assessment Team 192
David Clark Company 70

Davis, Saville 21
Dayton, Ohio 6, 9, 79
deep penetration overflights 132, 149, 182
Defector Reception Center (DRC) 3
defectors 3
Defense, Department of 199, 219, 262, 263, 282, 321, 344
Defense, Deputy Secretary of 88, 137, 151, 167, 197, 218, 312, 321
Defense, Secretary of 88, 135, 137, 151, 152, 166, 167, 172, 196, 197, 199, 201, 218, 240, 250, 260, 262, 263, 295, 302, 309, 312, 321, 324
Defense Mobilization, Office of 21
Science Advisory Committee 32, 45
Del Rio, Texas 209, 266
Delta-II camera 259
denied territory 180, 197
Deputy Director of Central Intelligence (DDCI) 36, 44, 50, 95, 109, 130, 131, 136, 137, 147, 194, 196, 212, 220, 221, 235, 340, 341, 342
Detachment A 100–101, 102, 108, 109, 114, 123, 125, 133, 134, 147–149, 189, 329
Detachment B 122, 123, 125, 128, 129, 133, 134, 135, 141, 143–147, 149, 157, 158, 159, 160, 161, 162, 170, 173, 189, 191, 196, 329
Detachment C 141–143, 147, 149, 150, 157, 162, 190, 191, 223–227, 228, 229, 230–232, 235, 329
Detachment G 189, 191, 209, 210, 223, 232–234, 242, 244, 245, 246, 253, 258, 259, 260, 263, 246, 265, 266, 267
Detachment H 236, 237, 238, 240, 241, 242, 244, 245, 246, 247,
248, 249, 250–251, 254–256, 259, 260, 265, 267
Development, Deputy Chief of Staff for 8, 13, 21, 42
Development Planning, Office of 13
Development Projects Division (DPD) 163, 175, 187, 189, 194, 201, 202, 203, 229, 297
Development Projects Staff (DPS) 62, 141, 163, 201, 226, 345
Dirty-Birds (DB) 138–141, 143, 144, 150, 156
Donovan, Allen F. 22, 29, 35, 36, 37, 42, 270, 341
Donovan, James 192
Doolittle, James H. 69, 172, 341
Douglas Aircraft 352
DRAGON 3
DRAGON LADY 84
drivers 66
drone 301, 312
Dryden, Hugh 97, 190
DuBridge, Lee 32
Dulles, Allen 20, 36, 38, 39, 40, 41, 42, 43, 44, 46, 47, 51, 52, 63, 67, 80, 84, 88, 90, 93, 95, 96, 99, 100, 102, 104, 113, 117, 118, 120, 127, 132, 167, 168, 172, 177, 188, 192, 202, 227, 273, 305, 329, 340, 342
Dulles, John Foster 24, 126, 130, 132
Dunaway, Glendon 72

E

Earman, J. S. 217
earth's atmosphere 288
East Berlin riots of June 1953 19
East Germany 107–109, 153, 192, 315
Eastern Europe 2, 92, 95, 97, 107–109, 114, 118, 131, 132, 134, 136, 147, 148, 149, 151, 316, 329
Eastman Kodak 5, 37, 38, 290, 291

eavesdropping 2
EBONY 234
Eden, Anthony 100, 101
Edens, Buster 144
Edgerton, Germeshausen & Grier
    (EG&G) 139, 285
Edwards AFB, California 142, 156,
    189, 209, 210, 223, 242
Eielson AFB, Alaska 141, 143
Eisenhower, Dwight D. 23, 32, 39,
    42–46, 52, 63, 67, 80, 92, 93, 95,
    101–109, 113, 114, 117–119, 121,
    123, 126–132, 135, 137–139, 143,
    144, 147, 149–154, 157–162, 164,
    166–170, 172–174, 177–179,
    188, 189, 196, 200, 201, 202, 205,
    223, 224, 227, 233, 235, 236, 273,
    277, 280, 287, 308, 328, 330, 337,
    341–344
electromagnetic energy 348
electronic countermeasures (ECM)
    219, 247, 311, 316, 319, 327,
    331, 348, 349
electronic intelligence (ELINT) 124,
    136, 150, 152, 158, 168, 169,
    177, 182, 190, 198, 227, 252,
    254, 315, 316, 324, 348
electronic intercept 135, 331
electronic sensors 302
electronic warfare 311
ELINT collection 152, 158, 168,
    190, 266, 315
ELINT emanations 316
ELINT-collection gear 323
ELINT-collection unit (System VI) 177
Emergency Preparedness, Office
    of 264
engine nacelles 300
engineers 8–10, 12, 15, 21, 31, 35,
    37, 51, 53, 54, 61, 68, 77, 270,
    280, 297, 341, 346, 352

English Electric Company 6, 28
epoxy resin 286, 298
EQUINE 91
Ericson, Robert J. 87
espionage 2, 20, 40, 41, 192
Estonia 314, 315, 352
Eurasian landmass 151
Europe 2, 5, 24, 28, 90, 92, 93, 95,
    97, 99, 107–109, 114, 118, 124,
    131, 132, 134, 136, 147, 148,
    149, 151, 155, 186, 265, 316,
    329, 344
EVEN STEVEN 266
Executive Branch 117, 118
exotic fuels 273

F
F-100 fighter 78
F-102 fighter 281
F-104 fighter 12, 53, 343
F-106 fighter 281, 294
F-108A Rapier 295
F-111 fighter 325
Fairbanks, Alaska 143
Fairchild K-19 aircraft 56
FAN SONG acquisition radar 247
Far East 4, 118, 135, 142, 143, 147,
    150, 199, 208, 212, 229, 235, 246,
    252, 253, 312, 317, 329, 334, 346
"Fast Move" operations 230
Federal Aviation Administrator 299
Federal procurement cycle 51
"ferret" equipment 3, 348
ferret flights 131
FICON 27
Field Activities, Deputy for 203
5412 Committee 197, 237
fighter 4, 5, 6, 12, 27, 28, 31, 73, 78,
    81, 83, 101, 116, 133, 136, 143,
    150, 152, 180, 185, 190, 211,
    226, 292, 311, 325, 331, 341, 343

fighter conversion 27
Fili airframe plant 113
fillets 286, 298
film 1, 37, 38, 56, 58–60, 62, 108, 116,
    123–129, 151, 158, 187, 221,
    222, 228, 230, 233, 237, 240, 248,
    249, 257, 258–260, 263, 264, 266,
    290–292, 316, 318, 323, 324, 329
film processing 67, 128, 257
film-transport system 62
Firewel Company 70
First Weather Reconnaissance
    Squadron, Provisional
    (WRSP-1) 100
Fischer, C. W. 321
FISH 259, 279, 280, 325
FISH HAWK 259–260
Flickinger, Donald D. 70
FLIPTOP 209
"Flit" 69
Florida 209
flying boat 280
focal-length cameras 15
focal-length lenses 58
Follow-On Group (FOG) 84
Ford Foundation 19
Foreign Intelligence Advisory Board
    45, 202
Formosa 240 (*See also* Taiwan)
Fort Worth, Texas 57
40 Committee 197, 267
forward processing center 226
Foster, John 354
Franco-Prussian War 1
Frankfurt, Germany 3
Free Europe Committee 95
French atomic test area 259
French Indochina 234
French nuclear developments 258
French Polynesia 258
Frogman Incident 101

Fujisawa, Japan 230
Fukien Province 238, 240

G
G-forces 86
G2A aircraft 272
Galbraith, John Kenneth 243, 244
Gardner, Trevor N. 13, 16, 17, 18,
    31, 32, 38, 43, 44, 47, 73, 88,
    106, 340, 342, 344
Gates, Thomas 172
Gaza Strip 123
Geary, Leo P. 68, 73, 78, 80, 85, 157,
    194, 195, 207, 298, 342
General Dynamics 325
General Electric J73/GE-3 12
General Tire and Rubber Company 342
GENETRIX 91–95, 102, 121
Geneva, Switzerland 103, 153, 165
Geneva Conference on Surprise
    Attack 165
Geneva summit conference 103
geological survey 264, 265
German Luftwaffe 26
German scientists 3
Gettysburg, Pennsylvania 128
Gibbs, Jack A. 68, 269
Giebelstadt Airbase, West Germany
    102, 133, 148
Gilpatric, Roswell 218–220
Glennan, Keith 190
gliders 12
Glienecke Bridge 192
Goddard, George 344
Goering, Hermann 72
Goldmark, Peter C 22
golf balls 57
Goodpaster, Andrew J. 97, 104, 107,
    113, 117, 128, 135, 138, 150,
    152, 173, 179, 196, 342
Grace, Frank G. 87

GRAND SLAM 177–185
Granger Company 349
GRC-127 216
Great Britain 4, 6, 8, 25, 27–29, 100,
    101, 123, 125–127, 129, 159–162,
    170, 173, 189, 196, 223, 315, 333
    Air Ministry 101, 160
    counterintelligence operative 101
Greyhound bus 299
Groom Lake 63, 73, 142
Groton 19
ground resolution 259, 290, 291
Guatemala 163
"guided democracy" 224
Gulf Coast 264
Gulf of Tonkin Resolution 242
gust control 55
GUSTO 285

H
H camera 255, 257, 262, 266, 291
Hagerstown, Maryland 10
Haiphong Harbor 257
Halaby, Najeeb E. 299
Hall, William 126, 127, 149
Haller-Raymond-Brown (HRB) 348
"handing off" 95
"hangar queen" 182
Harvard University 21, 26, 35, 57,
    58, 139
Harvard College Observatory 26
Hawk-750 glider kit 353
haze filters 113
HBJARGON 183
HBJGO 183
heavy water 24
Helms, Richard M. 263, 266, 317,
    321, 322
HEN HOUSE 174
HEN ROOST installations 174
Herter, Christian 137, 168

"hiding in the open" 62
high-acuity cameras 25, 57, 340
high-altitude air sampling (HASP) 232
high-altitude aircraft 6, 9, 20, 29, 66,
    154, 155, 316
high-altitude balloon program 27
high-altitude photography 2, 62, 92
high-altitude photoreconnaissance 8
high-altitude reconnaissance 1–20,
    23, 27, 28, 30, 39, 41, 46, 56,
    59, 61, 263, 272, 302, 325, 343
high-altitude weather plane 186
high-impact plastics 327
high-resolution cameras 6
high-speed buffet 83
high-speed reconnaissance aircraft
    270, 273, 281
HIGH WIRE 170
Hilsman, Roger 221
Hitchcock, Alfred 34
Hokkaido, Japan 5
Holcomb, William 295
Hollywood, California 34
Hong Kong 230
Hoover, Herbert, Jr. 132
horizontal stabilizers 55
Horner, Richard 76
Hornig, Donald F. 321
HOT SHOP 168
Houston, Lawrence R. 52
HR-333 camera 262
HRB-Singer Corporation 349
HTAUTOMAT 91, 124, 344
HTNAMABLE 119
human intelligence sources 2
Hungarian uprising 131
Hungary 109, 131, 132
Hurricane Baseline Survey 264
Hycon Manufacturing Company 16,
    57, 262
hydraulic fluid 288, 289

hydraulic pump 289
hydrogen bomb 24, 107
hydrogen weapons 170
hydrogen-powered aircraft 272
hydrologists 264

I
IBM CPC (card-programmed
    calculator) 59
IDEALIST 191, 222, 246, 247, 315
IDEALIST U-2 315
Igarka, Soviet Union 4
ileitis 102
imagery 187, 262, 265, 292, 309,
    315, 323
impeller 301
"in-and-out" operations 212
in-flight refueling 210, 250, 314
Incirlik Airbase, Turkey 122, 189
India 140, 141, 155, 243–245, 250,
    257, 285, 333, 334
Indian Parliament 244
Indian Springs, Nevada 140, 141
Indonesia 223–227, 334
Indonesian Air Force 224
inertial guidance systems 326
inflatable aircraft 272
infrared camera 292
infrared jammer 349
inland waterways 90
instant-film camera 343
intelligence, collection of 19, 39, 89,
    152, 158, 168, 177, 190, 198,
    223, 255, 262, 263, 266, 291,
    311, 323, 328, 334, 352
Intelligence and Research,
    Bureau of 221
intelligence community 3, 25, 39, 45,
    89, 146, 158, 166, 170, 172, 177,
    178, 200, 207, 244, 246, 264,
    309, 314, 315, 316, 336, 352

Intelligence Coordination, Office of 89
intelligence requirements 30, 130,
    198, 245
Intelligence Requirements Officer 89
Intelligence Star 194
Intelligence Systems Panel (ISP)
    25–27, 28, 29–31, 35–39, 42, 340
intercept 2, 94, 95, 116, 133, 135,
    136, 154, 168, 177, 180, 184,
    185, 268, 295, 331, 348
interceptor aircraft 99, 118, 132, 154,
    155, 184
intercontinental ballistic missile
    (ICBM) 143, 146, 164–168,
    172, 179, 207, 330, 332
Interior, Department of the 264
international date line 143
International Geophysical Year 93
international law 119
interrogation 3, 191
intruder 118
"invisible" dirigible 22
ion cloud 311
ionosphere 183
Iran 132, 141, 199
Iraq 141, 158
Iron Curtain 2, 21, 99, 101, 102, 119,
    135, 152
ISINGLASS 325
Isle of Pines 216
Itek Corporation 259, 344
IX spaceflights 264

J
J-3 (Operations) 199
J75 power plant 157
jamming devices 311
Jammu and Kashmir 243
Japanese airspace 5
jet stream 100, 151
jet-propelled glider 13, 30

Johnson, Clarence L. (Kelly) 12, 13,
    15, 16, 17, 20, 30, 31, 35, 36,
    37, 41, 43, 44, 51, 52, 53, 54,
    55, 56, 57, 61, 63, 65, 66, 71,
    73, 74, 75, 76, 77, 83, 117, 140,
    141, 156, 187, 193, 206, 257,
    258, 260, 270, 272, 278, 282,
    285, 286, 287, 289, 290, 294,
    298, 299, 307, 308, 335, 343
Johnson, Lyndon B. 205, 249, 250,
    303–306, 313, 316, 317, 322, 324
Joint Chiefs of Staff (JCS) 130, 132,
    135, 167, 196, 197, 199, 235,
    246, 313
Joint Intelligence Committee 159
Joint Priorities Committee 159
Joint Reconnaissance Center (JRC) 199
Jones, Edwin K. 146
JP-7 fuel 69

K
K-21 framing cameras 56
K-38 camera 58
Kadena Airbase, Okinawa, Japan 312
Kaliningrad missile plant 113
Kamchatka Peninsula 137, 143
Kandalaksha, Soviet Union 184
Kapustin Yar, Soviet Union 20,
    27–29, 118, 147, 172
Kazakh language 144
Kazakhstan 144
Kazan', Soviet Union 173
KC-135 tankers 78, 210
KEDLOCK 295
"Kelly's Angel" 73
KEMPSTER 311
Kennedy, John F. 194, 201, 202, 205,
    206, 209, 219, 222, 236, 241,
    244, 247, 302, 303, 308, 309, 343
Kennedy, Joseph W. 35
Kennedy, Robert 227

Kennedy administration 201,
    206, 236
kerosene fuel 69
Khimki rocket-engine plant 113
Khrushchev, Nikita 101, 103, 107,
    108, 153, 165, 169, 170, 174,
    187, 188, 310
Kiangsu Province 240
KICK OFF 209
Kickapoo Joy Juice 53
Kiefer, Eugene P. 8, 11, 13,
    270, 343
Killian, James R. 32, 34, 36, 39, 42,
    97, 107, 201, 202, 273, 302,
    343, 344
KINGFISH 281, 282, 284
Kirkpatrick, Lyman B. 200
Kirov, Soviet Union 179, 184
Kirtland AFB 85
Kissinger, Henry 265, 266
Kistiakowsky, George 178
Klein, Burton 13
Klyuchi, Soviet Union 143, 149
KNIFE EDGE 173
Kohler, Foy D. 121
Koko Nor 246
Kola Peninsula 190
Kollman Instrument Company 66
Koon, Ralph E. 85
Korea, demilitarized zone (DMZ)
    318 (See also North Korea)
Kotlas, Soviet Union 178, 179
Krag, Jens Otto 310
Kratt, Jacob 72, 86
Kremlin 131
K'unming, China 238
Kuybyshev, Soviet Union 170
KWCORK 122
KWEXTRA-00 66
KWGLITTER-00 66
Kyshtym, Soviet Union 183

L

L'il Abner 53

L-pills 73, 133, 134

Lakenheath AFB, England 100–101

Land, Edwin H. (Din) 22, 25, 34, 35,
36, 37, 38, 39, 40, 41, 43, 88, 97,
107, 201, 202, 270, 272, 273,
280, 282, 302, 343, 344, 345, 347

Land Panel 45

Langley, Virginia 50, 202, 318

Langley AFB, Virginia 28

Laos 229, 232–234, 242, 245, 246

Las Vegas, Nevada 293

Latham, Allen, Jr. 35

Latvia 315

Laughlin AFB, Texas 209, 210

Ledford, Jack C. 218, 219, 297, 308

Leghorn, Richard S. 5–9, 22, 28,
119, 344

LeMay, Curtis E. 13, 17, 67

"Lemon-Drop Kid" 133

Lend-Lease 8

Leningrad, Soviet Union 112, 113,
114, 117, 309, 315

lens 1, 22, 26, 36, 56, 57, 58, 59, 60,
61, 62, 99, 116, 257, 259, 262,
290, 291, 335, 340

lens curvatures 59

lens designs 26, 58, 59, 62

LeVier, Tony 63, 75, 76, 77, 82

LF-1A fuel 69

Libya 129

lightweight film 38

LINCOLN 21

Lindsey Air Force Base, Wiesbaden,
West Germany 87

liquid-fueled missiles 166, 330

lithium deuteride 24

Lithuania 315

Little, Arthur D. Inc. 35

Little Quemoy 228

Lloyd, Selwyn 99, 100

Lockheed Aircraft Corporation 11,
29, 343

Lockheed Day Fighter 17

Lockheed mechanics 73, 140, 236

London School of Economics 19

LONG GREEN 209

long-range bombers 24, 25, 89, 105,
106, 120, 330

LONG SHAFT 255

Los Angeles, California 195, 264

Lovelace, W. Randolph, III 70, 82

Lovelace Foundation for Medical
Education and Research 82

low-level photography 222

low-vapor-pressure fuel 289

Luke AFB, Arizona 80

Luna 2 rocket 169

Lundahl, Arthur C. 4, 90, 123, 124,
127, 128, 144, 159, 201, 221, 344

M

M Building 91

M-12 aircraft 301

M-195 aircraft 10

MacArthur, John 173

Macdonald, Duncan E. 26

Macmillan, Harold 161, 162, 170,
173, 196

Malaya Sazanka, Soviet Union 150

Malinovsky, Rodion 165–166

Manchuria 240, 246, 251

Mandrake 154, 155

Manhattan Project 342

Manila, Philippines 324

manned space program 69

March AFB, California 82

Mark-30 349

Marquardt ramjets 279

Marr, William H. 78

Mars 86

Marshall Plan 19, 340
Martin, Glenn L., Aircraft
    Corporation 7, 9–11, 29, 280
Massachusetts Institute of
    Technology (MIT) 5, 19, 21, 22,
    32, 36, 119, 139, 140, 343, 344,
    346, 347
Matomic Building 50, 112
MATS (Military Air Transport
    Service) 78
Ma-tsu Islands 240
May Day 25, 184, 201, 205
MC-2 and MC-3 partial-pressure
    suits 70
McConaughy, Walter P. 267
McCone, John A. 192–194, 202, 205,
    206, 208, 211, 212, 218, 219,
    244–246, 249, 250, 302, 303,
    304, 306, 309, 312, 341, 344
McCoy, Frederick 101
McCullough Corporation 353
McDonnell Aircraft 325
McElroy, Neil 152, 166–168
McFadden, William 60
McMahon, John N. 194
McNamara, Robert 240, 246, 250,
    263, 295, 302, 303, 309, 312
mechanical fuel totalizer/counters 74
Mediterranean Sea 123, 128, 148,
    149, 158
medium-range ballistic missiles 149,
    211, 217
Melpar, Incorporated 353
Menderes, Adnan 121, 189
mercenary pilots 226, 227
metal fatigue 252
meteorologists 50, 94
MI-6 99, 159, 160
Michigan, University of, School of
    Aeronautics 343
microwave reconnaissance 23

Middle East overflights 123, 125
MiG aircraft 349
MiG-15 116, 154
MiG-17 6, 116, 154
MiG-19 154
MiG-21 154, 155, 211, 250, 253, 254
Military Adviser to the President 197
Military Air Transport Service
    (MATS) 78
MILL TOWN 229
Miller, Stewart E. 22, 25
"million-dollar" photography 120
miniaturization 352
mirrors 60, 61
"missile gap" 163–167, 172, 173,
    177, 330
missiles 2, 20, 27, 28, 89, 105, 106,
    107, 113, 137, 143, 144, 146–148,
    155, 162, 164–170, 172–175, 178,
    180, 184, 185, 211, 212, 216, 217,
    221, 222, 237, 240, 246, 247, 249,
    253, 266, 295, 309, 310, 312–319,
    329, 330, 332
Mississippi River 85, 323
MKNAOMI 73
monthly Activities Book 199
moon 169
Morotai 226
Moscow, Soviet Union 4, 24, 25, 93,
    101, 108, 112, 113, 114, 117,
    133, 149, 152, 165, 173, 185,
    188, 332
MUDLARK 186
multiengine aircraft 15, 29, 30
multiple sensors 27
Mururoa Atoll 258
Myasishchev-4 (*See* Bison bomber)

N
Nagy, Imre 131
Nanking, China 238

Narcotics, Bureau of 264
Nasser, Gamal Abdel 121, 158
National Advisory Committee on
    Aeronautics (NACA) 96, 100
National Aeronautics and Space
    Agency (NASA) 186, 188,
    190, 264
National Air & Space Museum 71
National Intelligence Estimates 23, 248
national intelligence objectives 89
National Security Agency (NSA) 89,
    124, 143, 193, 341
National Security Council (NSC) 34,
    167, 174, 196, 197, 200, 209,
    223, 224, 237, 266, 304
National Security Council Intelligence
    Directive (NSCID) 200
Nationalist China 228, 236, 237,
    240, 241, 249, 333
Nationalist Chinese 212, 216, 234,
    236, 237, 249, 251, 252, 256, 267
  Air Force 235, 236
  insignia 236
  pilots 235, 238, 241, 242, 247, 248,
    250, 254, 256, 263, 265, 333
  U-2 216, 234, 235, 241, 247,
    256, 265
Navajo missile 27
Naval Air Station at Atsugi, Japan 142
naval quarantine 222
Nehru, Jawaharlal 243–245
Nelson, Norman 75
Nevada 62, 63, 122, 140, 142, 156,
    191, 285, 293, 296, 300, 305,
    307, 314, 315, 324
Nevada Proving Ground 63, 285
New Delhi, India 244
Ngo Dinh Diem 242
NICE GIRL 323
Nile River 127
NIMBUS 210

1973 Middle East war 266, 334
9th Tactical Air Force 344
nitrogen 71
Nixon, Richard M. 255, 256, 265,
    267, 346
Nobel Prize 345
North American Air Defense
    Command (NORAD) 299
North Atlantic Treaty Organization
    (NATO) 29, 94, 155, 179, 342
radars 94
North Island Naval Base,
    California 258
North Korea 5, 245, 251, 252, 320, 334
North Vietnam 199, 232–234, 242,
    245, 246, 252, 253, 256–257,
    312, 317, 318, 319, 324, 349, 354
North-East Frontier Agency
    (NEFA) 243
Northrop Aviation 269
Norton, Garrison 16, 17, 18, 37, 77,
    270, 344, 345
Norwalk, Connecticut 57
Notre Dame University 8
Novaya Zemlya 178
Novokuznetsk, Soviet Union 146
nuclear energy 89, 237
Nuclear Energy Division 47
nuclear resonance 345
nuclear strike 302
nuclear testing moratorium 331
nuclear tests 142, 146, 153, 174, 191,
    232, 250, 260, 264, 331
nuclear weapons 2, 24, 106, 153,
    238, 251, 252, 331

O

OARFISH 52
O'Donnell, Emmett (Rosy) 81
oblique photography 144, 198, 255
Offshore Islands Crisis 228–229

OILSTONE 67, 68, 82
Old Executive Office Building 34
OLIVE HARVEST 266
Omaha, Nebraska 67
112A camera 258
112B camera 259, 262
"Open-Skies" 103
optical distortion 291
Optical Research Laboratory 26
optical systems 59
order-of-battle 90, 143, 337
"Oscar-Sierra" unit 247
Overhage, Carl F. P. 21, 25, 345
overhead photography 91, 94, 178, 250
overhead reconnaissance missions 197
Overstreet, Carl K. 108
OXCART 68, 79, 163, 201, 249,
    262, 263, 268–327, 334–337,
    340, 341, 343–346, 349, 352
oxygenation 69

P
P-38 fighter 12, 343
P-40 fighter 341
P-51 Mustang 226, 227
P-80 fighter 12
P-80 Shooting Star 53
P2V7 234
P3A 234
Pacific Ocean 258
Padang, West Sumatra 224
Pakistan 137, 143–147, 155, 169,
    173, 174, 175, 177, 179, 180,
    186, 199, 257, 329, 333
Paksane, Laos 242
Palmdale, California 324, 325
panoramic-type framing camera 60
Paradise Ranch 65, 73
PARAMOUNT Committee
    123–125, 128
Parangosky, John 285, 298, 307,
    321, 345

"parasite" aircraft 273, 279, 280
Paris Summit 179, 190
Pasadena, California 16, 57, 262
Pathet Lao 233
PB-4Y aircraft 234
Pearl Harbor 337
Pearson, Drew 310
Peenemunde rocket project 3
Peiping, China 240
Pellegrini, Joseph J. 7
Pennsylvania State Police 233
Pentagon 7, 11, 13, 16, 17, 46, 47,
    85, 86, 224
People's Liberation Army (PLA) 228
People's Republic of China (PRC)
    92, 144, 212, 228, 234, 241, 243,
    245, 252, 254, 255, 263, 292,
    312, 333, 352 (See also China)
    nuclear weapons establishment 238
    radars 253, 256
    Shuangchengzi missile-test
        range 247
    troop movements 228
periscope 62, 84
Perkin, Richard S. 22, 37, 57, 58,
    59, 345
Perkin-Elmer (P-E) Company 22, 37,
    57, 58, 290, 292
Perkin-Elmer tracking camera 59
Perkins, Courtland D. 270
Peshawar, Pakistan 143, 169, 170,
    173, 174, 179, 180, 182, 183
Photo-Intelligence Division (PID) 90,
    91, 108, 124, 158, 201, 226, 344
photographic chemicals 129
Photographic Evaluation of
    Information on Cuba 21
photographic resolution 290
photointerpreters 91, 116, 120, 124,
    125, 128, 144, 146, 158, 178,
    200, 209, 221, 222, 229, 233,
    249, 259, 315, 320, 344

photomapping 2, 245
photoreconnaissance 1, 5–9, 26
photosatellite 163, 265, 281, 309,
    326, 337, 340, 343, 344, 352
Phouma, Souvanna 232
PID's Special Projects Branch 124
"pioneer" photography 94
pitot -static tube 306
Pittsburgh-Corning Glass Company 61
Plans, Deputy Director for 163, 201,
    202, 340, 346
Plans, Directorate of 72, 80, 89, 163,
    208, 223, 297
Plesetsk, Soviet Union 184
Poland 107, 108, 109, 112, 118, 131,
    151, 315
polarizing filters 34
Polaroid Corporation 22, 25, 39
POLECAT 233
Polish Ambassador to the US 118
Polyarny Ural 178
polygraph examination 193
Pope, Allen L. 227
poppy fields 264
Port Said, Egypt 127
Portsmouth Harbor 101
potassium cyanide 72, 123
powered glider 17, 30, 353
Powers, Francis Gary 96, 126, 132,
    180, 185, 186, 189, 190–195,
    200, 201, 205, 208, 212, 232,
    235, 261, 329, 345, 349
Poznan, Poland 112
PR3 aircraft 6
Pratt, Perry W. 37
Pratt & Whitney 15, 37, 43, 47, 56,
    73, 77, 78, 156, 230, 261, 279,
    280, 294, 295, 296, 300
Pratt & Whitney J58 power plant 280
Pratt & Whitney J75-P13 jet
    engine 156

Pratt & Whitney J75/19W
    engines 294
Pralt and Whitney J57 15, 47
President's Board of Consultants on
    Foreign Intelligence Activities
    45, 137, 172, 177, 200, 202
President's Foreign Intelligence
    Advisory Board (PFIAB) 45, 202
President's Intelligence Checklist 211
President's Science Advisory
    Committee 45
pressure suits 70, 71, 77, 256
pressurized "spacesuit" 70
Prettyman, E. Barrett 192, 193
Prettyman Board 193
Princeton University 35
processing and interpretation
    centers 125
Project Director 68, 89, 342
Project Officer, AFCIG-5 68
Project Staff 47, 49, 50, 51, 62, 141,
    163, 177, 201, 310
Project Three 34–41, 340
propaganda 95, 165, 168, 191, 195, 330
Pryor, Frederick 192
psychological warfare 195, 234
Pueblo 252, 320, 334
Puerto Rico 218, 223
Pulse-Position Indicator display 277
Purcell, Edward M. 21, 35, 119, 139,
    270, 273, 282, 285, 345, 346
Putt, Donald L. 13, 42, 43, 47
PVO (Soviet Air Defense) 180
Pyroceram 279, 282

Q

Quarles, Donald 88, 137, 151, 273, 277
Quarters Eye 50
quartz glass window 292
Que Building 91, 120
Quemoy 228, 240

QUICK KICK 230
quick-reaction capability 313

R
Raborn, William F., Jr. 312, 313, 346
radar 3, 4, 8, 9, 18, 23, 28, 90, 94, 95,
    101, 104, 109, 113, 114, 119, 131,
    138–141, 143, 147, 150, 154, 155,
    174, 182, 184, 185, 208, 223, 227,
    241, 247–251, 253, 256, 266, 268,
    269, 272, 273, 277–280, 282, 284,
    285–287, 304, 305, 311, 315–319,
    323, 324, 331
radar camouflage 138
radar cross section 18, 119, 269,
    272, 277, 278, 279, 280, 282,
    284–287, 311, 345, 354
radar deception 139, 140, 141, 143
radar defense systems 208
radar image 268, 346
radar pulses 94, 119, 139, 182, 278,
    279, 285, 286, 349
radar signature 354
radar technology 8–9
radar-absorbing 119, 269
radar-deflecting 269
radar-homing unit 354
Radford, Arthur W. 130–132, 135
Radhakrishnan, Savepalli 244
Radiation Laboratories 343
RADINT 198
radio 2, 8, 23, 82, 85, 94, 183, 195,
    279, 299, 345
RAINBOW 119, 139, 140, 268, 269
Ramenskoye, Soviet Union 24, 113
Ramey AFB, Puerto Rico 223
ramjet-powered 272, 273, 279, 301
Ramo-Wooldridge firm 348
RAND Corporation 24, 32, 92
Randolph AFB, Texas 80
Randsburg Wash 353

Ray, Walter 314
"ray-tracing" programs 59
RB-29 aircraft 4, 5
RB-47 aircraft 3, 4, 27, 190, 194
RB-52 aircraft 27
RB-57 aircraft 31, 42, 47, 142, 235
RB-57D aircraft 7, 74, 134, 135, 168
RB-58 aircraft 27
Reber, James 89, 123, 124, 159, 346
reconnaissance 1–11, 15–17, 21–30,
    34, 36–42, 50, 167, 301, 305, 312
reconnaissance aircraft competition 11
reconnaissance drones 312
reconnaissance satellite project 167
"reconnaissance strike" 301, 305
Reconnaissance Systems Branch 6
records, altitude 335
records, speed 335
RED DOT 263
reflecting cube 290
reflective system 61
refueling 123, 210, 243, 250, 314,
    315, 318, 320
refugees 229
Republic RF-84F Thunderflash 27
Research, Directorate of 203, 297
Research and Development,
    Director of 73
Research and Reports (ORR), Office
    of 89, 259
Returnee Exploitation Group
    (REG) 3
Revolutionary Council 224
Ridenour, Louis N. 22
Ridenour Associates, Inc. 22
Ritland, Osmond 62, 68, 76, 85
ROBIN 28
ROBIN HOOD 224
Robinson, Robert 170
rocket planes 66
rocket-powered aircraft 272, 325

Rodgers, Franklin A. 139, 277, 278, 285, 346
Rodgers' Effect 277
Rolls-Royce Avon-109
engines 7, 28
Romania 109
Root, L. Eugene 11, 30
Rose, Wilburn S. 47, 87
RS-71 305
Ruseckas, Joseph 70
Rusk, Dean 192, 212, 221, 303, 316, 320
Russell, Richard B, 96

S
S-band radar 94
sailplane 12, 30, 31, 54, 55
Sakhalin Island 212
Saltonstall, Leverett 96
SAM site 180, 185, 211, 216, 217, 241, 254, 257, 319
San Cristobal, Cuba 218, 219, 221
San Diego, California 258
Santa Barbara Channel 264
Santa Clara Airfield, Cuba 211
Saratov Engels Airfield, Soviet Union 170
Saryshagan, Soviet Union 147, 174, 244, 349
satellite imagery 309
satellite photography 94, 206, 207, 238, 245, 250
satellites 27, 94, 107, 109, 118, 163, 164, 167, 198, 200, 206, 207, 208, 222, 223, 238, 245, 250, 259, 262, 265, 309, 314, 325, 334, 337, 342, 345
Saville, Gordon P. 21
Schalk, Louis 298
Schlesinger, James R. 267, 346
Schoech, William A. 296

Schriever, Bernard A. 8, 13
Schultze, Charles L. 321, 322
Science and Technology, Directorate of 203, 297, 342
Science and Technology, Special Assistant to the President for 45
Scientific Advisory Board (SAB) 21, 28
Scientific Advisory Committee 21, 97, 345
Scientific Engineering Institute (SEI) 119, 139, 269, 277, 285
Scientific Intelligence (OSI), Office of 17, 26, 47, 89, 104
SCOPE COTTON 322
SCOPE LOGIC 315
SCOPE SAINT 265
SCOPE SAINT-I 265
SCOPE SAINT-II 265
SCOPE SHIELD 256–257
Scott, Roderick M. 58, 60, 290, 346
Scoville, Herbert 219, 297, 346
SCR-270 radar 8
Scranton-Wilkes-Barre Airport, Pennsylvania 233
Sea of Japan 4
Seaberg, John 9, 10, 15, 42, 43, 346
SEAFOAM 232
sealant 296–298
secrecy agreements 305
security 2, 47, 49, 51, 62, 65–67, 88, 100, 134, 136, 148, 231, 233, 284, 293, 332
Security, Office of 121
Semipalatinsk, Soviet Union 137, 146, 153, 174
SENSINT-Sensitive Intelligence 4
sensors 12, 27, 302, 323
Seventh Air Division 96
Severodvinsk, Soviet Union 179, 184

Shanghai, China 234, 238
sheep-dipping 81
Shell Oil Company 69, 341
shellfish toxin 134
Shelton, William 134, 183
shock wave 300
short-range reconnaissance vehicle 353
show trial 191
Shuangchengzi, China 238, 240, 247
shutter assemblies 60
Siberia 4
Sichuan, China 241
Sieker, Robert 140
Sierra snowfield 264
SIGINT Committee 346
Signals Intelligence (SIGINT) 234
"single-pass" mission 318
Sino-Indian border 243–245
Sino-Soviet border 349
"Skonk Works" 53
Skunk Works 53, 77, 141, 260, 272,
    284, 285
SKYLARK 311
Smithsonian Institution 62
"snap-up" 155
Snark missiles 27
Snider, Sammy V. C. 146
snowmelt 264
SOFT TOUCH 144, 147, 149
software algorithms 59
solid-fueled missiles 166, 330
sound barrier 299
SOUTH GATE 299
South Vietnam 242, 253, 312
Southeast Asia 200, 210, 229, 233,
    312, 313, 323
Sovetskaya Gavan', Soviet Union 150
Soviet Bloc 2, 5, 19, 21–24, 94,
    99–164, 205, 208, 223, 344
Soviet Communist Party Congress 165
Soviet Far East 143, 150

Soviet Union 2, 5, 8, 9, 12, 18, 20,
    23, 25, 28, 30, 46–106, 109,
    116, 131, 136, 139, 143, 149,
    150, 156, 158, 168–170, 173–
    175, 180, 184, 208, 211, 230,
    251, 268, 328, 330, 331, 334,
    349–352
  activity in Cuba 211
  air defense system 2, 116, 175,
    208, 331
  air power of the 25
  air show 105
  atomic energy program 330, 331
  bomber 25, 120, 173, 330
  borders 131, 136, 149, 158, 168,
    169, 180, 349
  diplomatic protests 328
  electronic defenses 331
  lighters 30, 156, 230
  G-class ballistic-missile
    submarine 251
  guided missile and nuclear
    programs 143, 170
  guided missile research 106
  guided missiles 89, 106
  guided-missile test range 20
  intentions 5, 331
  intercept attempts 114, 136, 150
  interception of U-2 12, 46–104,
    109, 116, 334, 350, 351
  medium-range ballistic missiles
    149, 211, 217
  missile program 137, 167, 168,
    169, 172
  missile test range 20, 28
  overflight operation 119
  propaganda campaign 330
  Protest Note 117–119
  radar coverage 114
  radars 3, 8, 9, 18, 104, 139, 143,
    174, 184, 268, 352

rail network 173, 330
strategic capabilities 2, 23
Supreme Soviet 187
surface-to-air missile (SAM) 184,
185, 211, 246, 266, 309, 312,
315, 316, 318
surprise attack 23–25, 32, 97, 153,
165, 243, 342, 343
Soviet-Finnish border 315
Soviet-Iranian border 132, 168,
169, 174
Special Activities, Director of 203
Special Activities (OSA), Office of
50, 203, 218, 247, 248, 257, 262,
267, 307, 308, 310, 315, 325
Special Assistant for National
Security Affairs 197
Special Assistant to the DCI 46–47
"special" missions 126
Special Operations Division 202
Spica, Incorporated 58
spotting camera 291
Sputnik 164
SQUARE DEAL 174, 175, 177
SR-71 266, 305, 306, 314, 321, 322,
323, 324, 325, 335
SS-4 (SHYSTER) MRBM 218
SS-6 ICBM 165, 172
stainless steel 281, 286, 289
Stassen, Harold 344
State Department 89, 101, 108,
153, 159, 169, 188, 195, 207,
208, 224, 236, 237, 241,
253, 259
"stealth" research 327
stereo camera 262, 290
stereoscopic lenses 259
Steuart Building 91, 120, 124
Stever, Guyford H. 270, 347
Stockman, Hervey 72, 112
STPOLLY 234, 236, 252

Strategic Air Command (SAC) 13,
21, 100, 222
meteorologists 50
strategic bombing 56
"strategic hamlet" 242
strategic intelligence 90, 124, 157,
314, 317, 326, 328, 333, 334, 337
strategic reconnaissance 129, 242,
306, 308, 309, 327, 334,
337, 343
Strauss, Lewis 63
Strong, Philip G. 17–20, 26, 29, 30,
35, 345, 347
subsonic 10, 17, 269, 272
Suez Canal 121, 123, 126, 127, 265
Suez Canal, Israeli-British-French
attack on 125
Suez Canal Company 123
Suez Crisis 121, 123, 124, 128, 157,
161, 334
suicide pill 72
Sukarno, Achmed 224, 227
Sulawesi (Celebes) 224
Sullivan, Dennis 319
Sumatra 224, 227
SUN SPOT 178
Super Snooper 140
supersonic designs 269
supersonic interceptor 295
supersonic technology 303
Support, Directorate of 49, 91
surface-to-air missile (SA-2) sites
180, 185, 211, 216, 217, 241,
254, 257, 319
surface-to-air missiles 184, 185, 246,
266, 309, 312, 315, 316, 318
surface-to-surface missiles 217, 221,
317, 318
Sverdlovsk, Soviet Union 179,
183–185, 187, 193
Symington, Stuart 103, 166, 167

synthetic lubricants 289
Syria 123, 127, 128, 141, 158
System-I 348
System-II 348
System-III 348, 349
System-IV 348
System-V 135, 227, 348
System-VI 182, 348
System-VII 348, 349
System-VIII 349
System-IX 349
System-IXB device 182
System-X 266
System-XII units 247, 248, 250, 251
System-XIII 247, 249, 250, 251
System-XVI 349
System-XVII 349
System-XX 349
System-XXI 349
System-XXII 349
System-XXIV 266

T
Taber, John 96
tactical intelligence 121–129, 157,
    201, 326, 334
tactical reconnaissance 30, 124, 158
TAGBOARD 301
Tahiti 259
tailless subsonic aircraft , 272
Taiwan 228, 229, 234–242, 245, 249,
    250, 253, 256, 260
Taiwan Strait 240
Ta Khli, AFB, Thailand 230, 231,
    242–245, 250
Talbott, Harold E. 16, 43
TALL KING 304
Tallinn, Estonia 314, 352
Tashkent, Soviet Union 184
TASS 146
Tatar Strait 150

Taylor, Maxwell 197
TCP 34
Technical Services Division (TSD) 134
Technicolor 345
Technological Capabilities Panel
    32–36, 42, 45, 69, 88,
    340–343, 345
Technology, Deputy for 203
television reconnaissance
    package 354
Tennessee 85
test ban 153
Tet offensive 253
Texas Instruments Corporation 292
Third World 223
three-camera trimetrogon unit 59
three-dimensional movies 34
30001 camera 346
303 Committee 197, 253, 267, 313,
    314, 316, 320
Thule, Greenland 178
Tibet 163, 229–231, 244
Time 106
TIME STEP 178–180
Titan ICBM 165
titanium alloy 282
Titanium Metals Corporation 289
TOKEN 94
Tomsk, Soviet Union 146
TOPPER 231
TOUCHDOWN 169
tracker camera 247
tracking 3, 8, 59, 95, 104, 113, 114,
    138, 139, 150, 177, 184, 185,
    247, 268, 273, 278, 299, 315, 319
tracking radars 8, 278
Trans-Siberian Railroad 150
transport aircraft 31, 54
traveling-wave tube (TWT) 249
trimetrogon K-17 mapping-camera
    system 56

Tripartite Declaration 1950 126
tropopause 156
Truman administration 21
TRW Corporation 348
Tuamotu Archipelago 258
"Tuesday lunch" 317
Tukey, John W. 35
turbojet engine 9, 12
Tuslog Detachment 122
Twining, Nathan 67, 102, 108, 137, 172
Type-I camera 290, 316, 323
Type-II camera 291
Type-IV camera 291
Typhoon Winnie 228
Tyuratam, Soviet Union 144, 146,
    165, 169, 172–174, 178, 179, 183

U
U-l 73
U-2
    accomplishments 332
    assembly 53, 54, 73, 82, 170, 289,
        294, 300
    bailout experiments 71
    bases 99
    bicycle-type landing gear 55
    blue-black color 156
    brakes 75
    canopy 88, 156, 184
    cockpit 12, 70, 71, 86, 134, 292,
        302, 307
    cost 52, 65, 156, 245, 260, 261, 273
    cover story 96–97, 187, 190, 218,
        219, 235
    coverage 210–223
    deadstick landing 86
    deployment 81, 84, 85, 95, 96, 99,
        101, 257–258, 266, 312
    design 53–56
    destruction device 185
    detachable pogos 55

ejection seat 71, 184, 314
emergency landing 85, 197,
    233, 326
film exploitation 124
flameout 77, 85, 86, 102, 140,
    209, 240
flight plans 90, 185, 186, 230
flights approval process 196–197,
    253, 313
foreign pilots 80–81, 336
fuel 54, 55, 68, 74, 83, 141, 210,
    230, 231, 243, 248, 256, 292,
    293, 326
fuel consumption 74, 231
fuel gauge 74, 231, 314
fuselage 12, 55, 139, 258, 261
inspection procedures 308
landing gear 55, 76, 96, 231, 258
low-speed stall 83
maiden flight 73, 298
mission 1104 123
mission 1105 123
mission 1314 126
mission 2003 108
mission 2009 109
mission 2010 109
mission 2013 112
mission 2014 113
mission 2020 114
mission 2021 114
mission 2023 116
mission 2029 133
mission 3086 211
mission 3088 211
mission 3089 211
mission 3091 216
mission 3093 216
mission 3095 216
mission 3098 217
mission 3100 217
mission 4016 132

U-2 (*Continued...*)
  mission 4018 133
  mission 4019 135
  mission 4030 141
  mission 4154 182
  mission 4155 174
  mission 6011 150
  mission length 210
  mission plotting 67
  mission programmers 85
  missions 90–91
  Nationalist Chinese crews 234
  oleostrut 55, 75
  operational altitude 83, 86, 116, 156
  Operational Objective system 322
  Operational Readiness Inspection
      84–85
  outrigger wheels 87
  overflights 107–109, 129–138,
      149–154, 164–204, 252–254,
      328–333, 350–351
  paint penalty 156
  payload 12, 58, 61, 94, 157
  peripheral missions 198, 208, 217,
      254–256
  phaseout 267, 322
  pilot fatigue 210
  pilot hypoxia 87
  pilot life-support system 327
  pilot selection 67, 292
  pilot-survival gear 70
  pilot training program 82
  pilot urination 71
  pilots 80–82, 83, 86, 191, 242
  pilots dessicated 72
  pitch-control servo device 306
  pogos 55, 87, 117
  prebreathing 71, 133
  projects 124, 141, 163, 175, 187,
      189, 201, 202, 226, 246, 352
  rocking mount 58, 59
  stall envelope 77

  stalls 87
  tail section 55, 83
  taxi trials 75–76
  training 310–311
  vertical stabilizers 286
  vulnerability study 104
U-2B 102
U-2Cs 157, 207, 219, 222, 230–231
U-2F 210
U-2G 258, 259, 262, 265
U-2R 261–263
U-3 73
Ukraine 114
Under Secretary of State 197, 237
Unidentified Flying Objects
    (UFOs) 78
United Arab Republic 158
United Kingdom (*See* Great Britain)
United Kingdom Requirements
    Committee 159
United Nations 24
United Press International (UPI) 244
United States 3–5, 8, 9, 19, 24, 25,
    32, 67, 80, 84, 85, 93, 97, 103,
    105, 106, 108, 116–119, 121,
    126, 129, 132, 149, 153, 155,
    158–161, 164–166, 169, 170,
    187–192, 212, 228, 232–234,
    236, 237, 241, 243, 244, 255–
    257, 263–265, 295, 304, 309
unmanned reconnaissance aircraft
    301, 316
UPWIND 315
Urals 26, 169
uranium gaseous-diffusion plant 146
uranium-processing facility 146
US Air Attache in Moscow 185
US Air Force, Secretary of the 13,
    38, 85, 88, 340–342
US Air Force
    Air Weather Service 96, 100
    Chief of Air Staff 85

EC-130 152
Inspector General 68
oxygen mask 70
RB-57D Canberra 168
Third Air Force 96
US deterrent force 331
US Geological Survey 264
US House of Representatives
    Appropriations Committee 96
US Marine Corps 49, 257, 341
US Marine Corps Reserve 17
US Military Academy at West
    Point 342
US Navy
    Chief of Naval Materiel 295
    Neptune bomber 4
    Privateer patrol aircraft 4
    Naval Ordnance Test Station 353
U.S. News and World Report 106
US nuclear test monitoring system 146
US nuclear tests 153
US Senate, Armed Services
    Committee 96, 106, 193
US Senate, Foreign Relations
    Committee 193, 194
US 6th Fleet 158
US 7th Fleet 228
US Intelligence Board (USIB) 197,
    199, 208, 339, 346
USS Kitty Hawk 257
USS Ranger 259
utility aircraft 73

V
Vance, Cyrus 312, 321, 323
Venezuela 223
vernier adjustment 83
very-high-acuity lenses 57
Viet Cong 242, 252
Vietnam 199, 229, 232–234, 242,
    245–247, 252, 253, 256–257,
    312, 313, 317–320, 324, 349, 354

Vito, Carmine 87, 112, 133, 134, 226
Vladimirovka, Soviet Union 178
Vladivostok, Soviet Union 4, 134
Vogt, Richard 9
Voigt, Woldemar 9
Volga River 26
von Fritsche, Werner 1

W
WADC's Bombardment Branch 9
Wake Island 317
Walker, Christopher H. 160
wallpaper 139
Walter Reed Hospital 102
Warsaw Pact 94, 95, 131
Washington University, St. Louis 35
Watertown Strip 65
Watton RAF Base, England 162
"weather plane" cover story 188
weather research 93, 96, 97, 141, 190
Weatherwise 229
Wendover, Utah 306
West Potomac Park 50
Western Europe 24, 92, 148
Western Hemisphere 223
"wet-wing" design 74
WHALE TALE 257, 258, 260
Wheelon, Albert (Bud) 297, 347
Wheelus AFB 129
White House 39, 44, 45, 50, 104,
    117, 120, 128, 130, 137, 138,
    179, 195, 198
Wienberg, Charles F. (Bud) 8, 13
Wiesbaden, Germany 87, 101–102,
    112, 113, 116, 123, 124, 128
Wiesner, Jerome B. 45
Williams, John J. 194
Williamsport, Pennsylvania 233
Wilson, Charles 135
wind currents 94
wind tunnels 279, 286
wing teeth 286

wings 7, 9, 12, 28, 29, 31, 53, 55,
    73, 74, 79, 83, 87, 96, 102, 139,
    155, 210, 252, 258, 261, 282,
    286, 296, 326
wiretaps 2
Wonsan Harbor 320
Worcester, Massachusetts 70
world press 93
World War I 1
World War II 1–3, 5, 8, 9, 15, 19, 21,
    26, 50, 56, 63, 70, 94, 102, 104,
    132, 144, 226, 234, 244, 331,
    337, 340–344
Wright Air Development Command
    6, 9, 10, 15, 17, 22, 42, 79
Wright-Patterson 79
WRINGER 3
WS-461L 151
Wu-ch'ang, China 238

X
XF-104 (*See* Lockheed Day Fighter)
X-16 10, 16, 18, 31, 42–43
X-band radar pulses 349
X-rays 301

Y
YAK-25RM (*See* Mandrake)
YAK-26 (*See* Mandrake)
Yakovlev 155
Yakovlev-25 154
Yale University 19
Yancey, William F. 82, 83, 85
YC-97 Boeing Stratocruiser 15
Yerevan, Soviet Union 132
YF-12A 295, 301, 305, 321
Yokota AFB, Japan 142
Yur'ya, Soviet Union 184
Yutzy, Henry 37